3
EDITION

Transforming Nurses' Stress and Anger

Steps Toward Healing

D0725243

Sandra P. Thomas, PhD, RN, FAAN, is Professor and Director of the PhD Program in Nursing at the University of Tennessee, Knoxville. Her initial nursing preparation was at St. Mary's Hospital School of Nursing, and she worked as a hospital staff nurse for 10 years before pursuing new challenges as a nurse educator and researcher. She holds bachelor's, master's, and doctoral degrees in education as well as a master's in nursing, with clinical specialization in mental health. Dr. Thomas has served as editor of *Issues in Mental Health Nursing* since 1997. She is a Fellow of the American Academy of Nursing and the Society of Behavioral Medicine, and serves on the Board of Directors of the International Council on Women's Health Issues. She is a charter member of the Southern Nursing Research Society and also holds memberships in the American Psychological Association, the American Nurses Association, the American Psychiatric Nurses Association, Sigma Theta Tau International, and the International Society of Psychiatric-Mental Health Nurses. Her research has focused on stress, anger, and depression. She has presented her research at numerous national and international conferences and published over 120 journal articles, books, and book chapters. Her previous books include *Women and Anger* (Springer Publishing, 1993); *Use Your Anger: A Woman's Guide to Empowerment*, with coauthor Cheryl Jefferson (1996); and *Listening to Patients: A Phenomenological Approach to Nursing Research and Practice,* with coauthor Howard R. Pollio (2002). *Listening to Patients* received both a Choice Magazine Award as an "Outstanding Academic Title" and an *American Journal of Nursing* "Book of the Year" Award. Previous editions of *Transforming Nurses' Stress and Anger* were published in 1998 and 2004. *Transforming* won AJN "Book of the Year" Awards in two categories.

Transforming Nurses' Stress and Anger

Steps Toward Healing

Sandra P. Thomas, PhD, RN, FAAN

SPRINGER PUBLISHING COMPANY

New York

Springer Publishing Company, LLC
11 West 42nd Street
New York, NY 10036–8002
www.springerpub.com

Acquisitions Editor: Allan Graubard
Project Manager: Cindy Fullerton
Cover Designer: Mimi Flow
Composition: Aptara Inc.

09 10 11 12/ 5 4 3 2 1
Ebook ISBN: 978-08261-25439

Library of Congress Cataloging-in-Publication Data

Thomas, Sandra P.
  Transforming nurses' stress and anger : steps toward healing / Sandra P. Thomas. –
3rd ed.
      p. ; cm.
    Includes bibliographical references and index.
    ISBN 978-0-8261-2542-2 (alk. paper)
  1. Nursing – United States – Psychological aspects. 2. Nurses – United States – Job stress.
  3. Nurses – Mental health – United States. 4. Anger in the workplace. I. Title.
    [DNLM: 1. Nurses – psychology. 2. Adaptation, Psychological. 3. Anger.
    4. Interpersonal Relations. 5. Stress, Psychological – prevention & control.
    WY 87 T4615t 2009]
    RT86.73.T48   2009
    610.7306′99–dc22   2008041345

Printed in Canada by Transcontinental Printing.

Contents

Part I: Uncovering the Layers of Nurses' Stress and Anger

Part II: Connecting With Others

Part III: Healing Ourselves

Part IV: Claiming Our Power and Using It

Preface

I have been to Scutari, to that immense and formidable hospital where Florence Nightingale cared for thousands of British soldiers wounded in the Crimea. Prior to my visit, I had read all about what happened there, but the written accounts of Nightingale's wartime experiences did not adequately prepare me for the emotional impact of being in this place. As I walked through the long dark corridors, the anguished cries of the sick and dying men still rose, reverberating against unfeeling stone. I could see them piled like so many bloody discarded rags, thrashing and moaning. What consternation Nightingale must have felt upon finding 3,000 men crammed into the Selimiye Army Barracks which served as the hospital. Four miles of beds, tightly crushed together, held the mutilated bodies awaiting Miss Nightingale's ministrations. The "hospital" had no kitchens, no laboratory, no operating table, no bed linens. It is hard to imagine the conditions at Scutari.

> There were no basins, no towels, no soap, no brooms, no mops, no trays, no plates. . . . no knives or forks or spoons. The supply of fuel was constantly deficient. The cooking arrangements were preposterously inadequate, and the laundry was a farce. As for purely medical materials, the tale was no better. Stretchers, splints, bandages—all were lacking; and so were the most ordinary drugs. . . . The very building itself was radically defective. Huge sewers underlay it, and cesspools loaded with filth wafted their poison into the upper rooms . . . the walls were thick with dirt; incredible multitudes of vermin swarmed everywhere. (Strachey, 1918/1996, pp. 16–17)

Have any of us in modern nursing ever faced such appalling conditions? So daunting a task? Probably not, unless we have nursed during primitive wartime or disaster conditions. Yet all of us can readily empathize with the enormity of Nightingale's workload. So many patients, so many urgent needs. Compounding the difficulties presented by the sheer volume of work at Scutari was the scathing hostility of the men in authority. The intrusion of Nightingale and her small band of nurses into the all-male military environment was greeted with derision. Obstacle after obstacle was placed before her by the unyielding army bureaucracy. Even today, we can identify with such obstacles. We decry "the system" that prevents us from giving the kind of care we long to give. Nightingale also had to deal with conflict and dissension within her own staff—a destructive phenomenon still common in among nurses. At one point, Florence began to believe that none of her colleagues had the proper dedication to the work. From this place of filth, horror, and death, a discouraged Nightingale wrote in an early letter home: "There should be a sign: 'Abandon Hope, All Ye Who Enter Here'" (Isler, 1970).

But you know the rest of the story. She did not abandon hope. Enshrined in the lore of nursing history are the incredible achievements of Nightingale at Scutari. With energy, vision, and astute management of people and resources, the mortality rate of the soldiers was reduced from 42% to 2% in 6 months. Scutari was transformed to a place of caring, order, and cleanliness. For these remarkable achievements Nightingale was accorded the attributes of near-sainthood. An ideal image of *nurse* entered the psyche of the British people: the gentle "lady with the lamp."

Less well known is the force of Nightingale's *anger*. Late at night in her little room in the Northwest Tower of Selimiye Barracks, she vented that anger in a torrent of letters that document its extent and force. She minced no words as she described the privations of Scutari to the people back home in England: "No sufficient preparations have been made for proper care of the wounded. Not only are there not sufficient surgeons . . . not only are there no dressers and nurses . . . there is not even linen to make bandages . . . the commonest appliances of a workhouse sick-ward are wanting" (Woodham-Smith, 1951, p. 85). Nightingale passionately advocated for better sanitation, nutrition, and medical care for the British soldiers. Her missives were successful in capturing the attention of the public and kindling their rage as well. For Nightingale, anger was a powerful tool: "I do well to be angry," she said (Strachey, 1996, p. 31).

These words could easily be ours, as we look down the corridors of our own Scutari in the 21st century. Again, nurses are facing chaos, vast human need, lack of resources to give proper care, unresponsive bureaucracy, and a highly stressful work environment. Today's nurses feel embattled, assaulted, and *literally* on the firing line. Notes RN Wanda Hooper, "Workplace violence was all but non-existent 25 or more years ago, but it is a very real part of the environment today. It takes many forms, and nurses have been injured, even killed, while practicing" (2003, p. 4). As I was writing this book, nurse Peter Wright was killed, while on duty, at a Georgia hospital, by a man who mistakenly blamed the nurse for his mother's death ("Ex-teacher . . . ," 2008). Wright was shot in the chest and head as he tried to leave the hospital room where the gunman had cornered him. For the 6-year period between 1993 and 1999, there were 429,100 violent crimes against nurses on duty (U.S. Department of Justice, 2001). Nurses experienced workplace crime at a rate 72% higher than medical technicians and at twice the rate of other health care workers. Other safety issues have produced mounting concern. In the course of a day's work, there could be a needlestick injury, a career-ending back injury, or exposure to virulent infectious diseases. Newly licensed RNs studied by Christine Kovner and her team (2007) provided fresh evidence of the hazardous work environment: In their first year of practice, 25% sustained at least one needlestick, 39% at least one sprain or strain, 21% a laceration, 46% a contusion, and 62% verbal abuse on the job (Kovner, Brewer, Fairchild, Poornima, Kim, & Djukic, 2007).

Even if we have escaped threats to life and limb, all too often we leave the workplace bone-tired and soul-weary, trying to shake off the sticky residue of moral distress—that awful realization that we could not give patients the care they deserved. It is not surprising that high scores on burnout were found in a study of more than 43,000 nurses from 700 hospitals in the United States and four other countries (Aiken, Clarke, Sloane, & Sochalski, 2001). In fact, two in ten U.S. nurses told the researchers they planned to quit their jobs within the year. Among nurses younger than 30, one in three said they intended to leave. When they leave, an already critical nursing shortage will intensify, severely impacting the quality of patient care. By 2020, it is estimated that the United States will face a nursing shortage as high as 1.5 million (Bleich et al., 2003). Its timing couldn't be worse, as 78 million aging baby boomers are beginning to escalate demands on the health care system (Jacoby, 2003). And simply producing more graduates is not the answer. Dispirited recent graduates are leaving the profession at rates even faster than their predecessors (Sochalski, 2002). They cite the stressful work environment as the cause.

Thus, we have a disturbing situation that calls for innovative ideas and constructive actions. Nurses' anger about this situation is justifiable. We feel unsafe and unsupported. But our anger is not channeled into constructive actions. It eats away at us inside and takes its toll in fatigue, physical health problems, depression, and substance abuse. It spills over to our own peers, corroding relationships. It even spills over to students (the insidious phenomenon of "eating our young"), as we discuss in Chapter 5.

Like Nightingale, can we do *well* to be angry? Can we transform our anger into something positive? I think we can. Nightingale's words challenge us to "do the thing that is good, whether it is 'suitable for a woman' or not'" (Nightingale, 1859). She decried the societal characterization of nurses as self-sacrificing and subservient: "No *man*, not even a doctor, ever gives any other definition of what a nurse should be than this—'devoted and obedient.' This definition would do just as well for a porter. It might even do for a horse" (Woodham-Smith, 1951). Like the founder of modern nursing, today's practicing nurses—women and men— must speak out passionately about our concerns. Our anger can be a catalyst for personal and professional empowerment. This book charts the course toward a reenergized, powerful, professional workforce. Like Nightingale, we must use sophisticated political strategies to accomplish our goals. Like Nightingale, we must mobilize the power of the pen—and more modern media—to galvanize the support of the public. Our voices have been silent too long (Buresh & Gordon, 2000). Let us heed Nightingale's admonition to carry on her fight: "I am now entirely a prisoner in my room from illness; but none the less I cry out to you 'charge, charge! On, on.'" (Bishop, 1957).

Introduction

A book is always birthed for a reason. This one is born out of the suffering of many of you, my nurse colleagues, all across America. After hearing your stress, fury, and pain in countless workshops and sifting through hundreds of pages of interview transcripts gathered by my research team, I knew that I must write this book. When I wrote the first edition in 1997, I hoped that my suggestions would prove useful. It seems that they were, because the book sold well upon its release in 1998 and upon the publication of its second edition in 2004. While I am honored that the book was well received, it is time to update some of the content. The societal context is different now.

New and very stressful challenges face all of us. Americans were stunned by the events of September 11, 2001, unable to grasp the awful reality that a small band of terrorists had succeeded in penetrating the most visible symbols of our industrial prominence and military power, killing thousands of innocent civilians in the process. My friends at Springer Publishing watched in horror from the roof of their building in New York City as the World Trade Center crumbled before their eyes. Across the country, millions of Americans were glued to television sets, trying to comprehend what we thought must be a "very bad nightmare" or "freak accident" (Thomas, 2003a). We were thrust into an era of unprecedented insecurity and a strange new kind of war with no predictable end point. None of us will ever be the same again (Thomas, 2003a).

Other disturbing trends are dampening Americans' customary optimism. Violent crime has penetrated our children's schools and bloodied university campuses—even a department of nursing, where three nursing instructors were murdered by a failing student. The economy has worsened. Health disparities between the insured and uninsured have widened. Too many children are going to bed hungry, and too many patients with mental illness languish in jails instead receiving the care they need in treatment facilities. Fewer than one-quarter (21.6%) of Americans between the ages of 25 and 74 are considered to be "flourishing"—that is, living enthusiastically and functioning well both psychologically and socially (Keyes, 2003). Confidence in business has eroded with each new revelation of unscrupulous behavior by executives, accountants, and board members. In the morning papers, we read of dishonest journalists, predatory priests, and corrupt politicians. In what—or whom—can we trust? How can we recover a sense of hope for the future?

Given the uncertainty of these times, many people are rediscovering existential philosophy. I have had an affinity for existential philosophy since I was an unhappy 16-year-old reading Sartre's *Being and Nothingness* (1956). I was bedeviled by questions about meaning in life, death, isolation, and freedom—those "givens" of existence that Irvin Yalom (2002) has addressed in much of his writing. What I gained from my study of the existential philosophers was a clear understanding that life is difficult, and we can never be completely free from anxiety. We are often thrown into dreadful circumstances that could sap us of hope. And the future is simply unfathomable. There is no guarantee that we will ever achieve our dreams. But we can choose to go on, one day at a time, imbuing our daily existence with meaning through fulfilling work and relationships.

Work is an integral component of a meaningful life. Yet Americans are finding their jobs more stressful than ever. In the American Psychological Association's 2007 stress survey, 74% of respondents reported work as their number 1 stressor (compared to 59% in 2006) (Anderson, 2008). You and I chose the nursing profession because it promised to meet our need to make a contribution. It still does—in many ways. But a registered nurse today is three to four times as likely to be dissatisfied than the average American worker (Corbett, 2003). Dissatisfaction is especially acute for RNs on the front lines, delivering patient care as hospital staff nurses. Research by Sochalski (2002) found staff nurses to be the least satisfied among all nursing positions. Their dissatisfaction is driven by a host of factors that we examine in this book. One of those factors, sad to say, is conflict with other nurses. Although institutions are undertaking a number of measures to make the work environment more satisfying, *only nurses can bring a halt to our own infighting* (Thomas, 2003b). A transformation must take place in nursing, a transformation in the hearts and minds of individual nurses that ultimately creates peace and harmony in our relationships with one another. If we do not link arms to face today's formidable challenges, nursing's future could be in jeopardy. Nightingale warned us that "No system can endure that does not march." And marchers must be in step with one another.

In this book, I share with you what I know about dealing with stress and anger. Much of what I know is drawn from my research on nurses and their work environment (see Epilogue for detailed information about the research). My studies on nurses were prompted by the discovery that nurses and other human service professionals scored highest among occupational groups on overall anger proneness. I wanted to know what this anger was about and how nurses handled it. Admittedly, I too, have wrestled with virtually all of the anger-provoking situations our study participants described. Much of my learning has been acquired in the crucible of tough life experience. In these pages, bits of my own story are interwoven with fascinating glimpses of the work lives of dozens of other nurses. This book is written to give you hope—and confidence that you can surmount the difficulties you are facing. Bad things are happening, but better things can be done.

In Part I, we uncover the causes and consequences of nurses' stress and anger, then move on to more productive anger styles and empowerment strategies. But emotional healing cannot take place without mending relationships with colleagues, so in Part II we focus on connecting in deeper, more satisfying ways with other nurses and physicians. Forging alliances with patients is also crucial. Part III provides a wealth of suggestions to help you transcend the legacy of a painful or abusive past, in order to achieve healing. Caring for the self receives strong emphasis, because it is the self that nurses so often sacrifice. Part IV is all about claiming our power, solving the profession's problems, and dreaming our future. I will tell you now that I think our future is a bright one, so this is unequivocally a hopeful book.

Just a few more words of introduction, and then we'll get right to our task. First, let me say that this book is useful for you whether you work in a hospital, outpatient setting, or educational institution. Maybe you do home health or telenursing. Maybe you have a private practice. I would not even presume to list all of the diverse settings in which today's nurses have found a niche. But nursing's issues are not confined to any particular work site. Nor are they confined to American nurses. My international travels reveal commonalities among nurses around the globe. What we explore in this book are universal issues.

I also believe that you will find the book valuable whether you are male or female. As I wrote it, I was ever-mindful that not all nurses are women. Too much of nursing's literature has been addressed to the "sisterhood" of women, ignoring the men in the profession. I have tried to avoid feminine pronouns, but do forgive me if I inadvertently slipped once or twice. Next, let me explain my use of the term "patients" for the recipients of nursing services. Although debates continue about the proper term (clients, customers, consumers), I mainly use the term *patients*. By using this term, I am not implying dependency or lack of ability to enter into a relationship of mutuality with caregivers. But think about it: Patients really don't have the freedom of choice that a consumer has. Insurers and physicians often mandate the use of specified hospitals and diagnostic facilities. A hospitalized journalist wondered why patients came to be called "consumers" in the first place: "I can tell you that when you're lying there trying to remember what feeling good feels like, you're not a consumer. You are not shopping. You are spending, mostly expending, more energy than you have on things that you should not have to worry about. The crisis that brought you to the hospital is all that should be on your mind, not being safe, or clean, or ignored" (Abramson, 1996, p. 29).

Although RNs comprise my intended audience, hospital executives will also find this book enlightening. According to a report produced by the Health Research Institute at PricewaterhouseCoopers, hospital executives "are in a state of denial about nurse dissatisfaction" (Nelson, 2007, p. 19). After reading the words of dozens of nurses who vividly describe their dissatisfaction, denial cannot be sustained. Throughout the book, I will be drawing from several studies of nurses and patients in which I served as the principal investigator or as a co-investigator. Unless indicated otherwise, all of the nurses' words are taken verbatim from interviews by my research teams or from stories spontaneously shared with me by nurses at workshops or professional meetings. Since publication of the first edition of the book in 1998, I have made presentations in more than 30 states. I hear stories everywhere I go. Often, these stories continue to tug at my heart as I wait for an airplane to take me somewhere else.

All names appearing in the text are pseudonyms unless individuals gave permission for their real names to appear. I am grateful to a number of noted nursing leaders from the American Academy of Nursing who contributed stories of transforming their own stress, anger, and pain. Contributors from the Academy included Angela Barron McBride, Wanda Mohr, Dan Pesut, Phyllis Stern, Rosalee Yeaworth, Dixie Koldjeski, Jeanne Quint Benoliel, Joellen Hawkins, Barbara Barnum, Sharon Valente, Luther Christman, and Hildegard Peplau. They gave permission for their real names to appear, and I thank them for allowing their wisdom to grace these pages.

Uncovering the Layers of Nurses' Stress and Anger

Telling Our Stories: What Are Nurses Stressed and Angry About?

American nurses are frustrated, stressed, and angry. And they are hurting. Seasoned RNs I talk with at conferences and meetings sound more weary, disheartened, and cynical than ever before. And new graduates become disillusioned very rapidly: Hospital turnover rates range from 35% to 61% for new graduates during their first year (Casey, Fink, Krugman, & Probst, 2004). In survey after survey, high percentages of RNs voice alarm about unsafe staffing and report decreased quality of care at their facilities. For example, 75% of nurses in an American Nurses Association (ANA) survey felt that deteriorating working conditions had impacted patient care; over half of them said they would not recommend the profession to their children or their friends ("Nurses concerned," 2001). In a 2008 ANA survey, involving over 10,000 RNs, 73% reported insufficient staffing on their units, and over half were considering leaving their positions (see www.safestaffingsaveslives.org). Even during the upheavals created by Medicare's DRGs in the 1980s and the misguided nurse layoffs during hospital "reengineering" and "downsizing" in the 1990s, there was not such widespread distress. What is fueling all this stress? Listen to the words of nurses:

> *You've always got at least 100 things going through your mind at one time. The frustration for me is when I know that I'm giving 100%, running 90 [miles per hour], doing everything I can possibly do, and I have not been to the bathroom in 10 hours, haven't even thought about the possibility of a lunch break—that was out of my mind a long time ago—and you're busting your tail end and people are still unhappy.*

> *Patients are not receiving the quality of care that they should receive. We have a lot of patients who are on tube feeding and have diarrhea, sometimes constantly, sometimes around the clock. It takes more than one person to do the cleaning, and I find it really frustrating trying to find other staff who could take a minute or two to help you out. There are no techs to help us do these things, and patients do not get turned as often as they should have, do not get cleaned as often as they should have. It isn't right. It isn't fair to the patient or the patient's family. I could be really sympathetic to the patients and the patient's family because 7 years prior to graduating from nursing school, my mother died from lung cancer after a long battle with it ... When I look at a patient lying there in bed, I see my mother in their eyes, and I expect the care for that patient to be what I would have wanted for my mother, and so often it isn't.*

> *When I first started in nursing 12 years ago, I thought it was a profession, and I don't feel like it is anymore. I think the professionalism is pretty much gone, as in being the patient advocate and taking care of the patient and doing the best you can for the patient. With all the rules and regulations of insurance and Tenncare [the Tennessee version of Medicaid], OSHA, Joint Commission, and the lawsuits and lawyers, it's "Am I following this rule, am I following that rule, am I going to get sued over this or that?" You worry more about people complaining, wanting to file lawsuits or calling and complaining to your manager about their care, even when it was not warranted. I think it has turned tremendously away from the skills of nursing to the paperwork of nursing, and the covering your butt of nursing, and following the rules for so many commissions and agencies and hospitals. It's just a very different environment than it was 12 years ago. When I first started, I had that nurse-itis where you think you can really make such a difference ... now I realize I'm taking care of 5 and 7 people at a time, you do the best you can, you go as fast as you can, as hard as you can, for 12 hours, try to keep within all these guidelines and try to keep everybody happy, not just the patients, but fellow coworkers, management, hospital, patients' family, physicians, and now you have so many sub-areas of the hospital: lab, X-ray, CT, ultrasound. I find it very, very trying to keep all these people in check.*

> *It's gotten too mechanized. Charting nowadays is not what it used to be, we get in a hurry, there's check marks [for the vital signs], there's a lot of times that you don't think of the patient, what he looks like, how he's feeling. You ask a question about pain, check boxes, it has nothing to do with what the patient looks like, what your instinct is telling you. . . . It's not the hands-on feely touchy that nursing really has to be.*

I've been a nurse thirty-some years. I can remember when we actually sat down and taught patients to give their own insulin and things such as that. Now, things seem to be so much more hurried. We have less staff. It's imperative to get patients in and out, and we don't get to sit down and talk to them and really explain things. We don't have time to answer their questions. We used to educate them on every medication: If you give them Lanoxin, you tell them to take their pulse, if it's below 60 don't take it that day. Different things like that. Now, you don't do that. You just hand them their leaflets and they go. And half the time if people come in with a pulse of 40 and they're on dig, you say, "has anyone ever explained to you about this medication?" Most of them say "no."

I don't think nursing has changed but I think the other aspects of health care have changed. . . . Everything's more cost conscious. . . . They have all the new equipment and machines to treat people with but after they find out what's wrong, they just toss 'em to the wind, saying "go away." A lot of these people, especially people who can't read or write or have no family, can't just be tossed to the wind. I get real frustrated because I know that they cannot be compliant, a lot of them do not have anyone to help them at home, and the way the laws are with home health, they won't go in and check on 'em. . . . You try to talk to 'em but you've only got so much time, and then after they leave, you don't have anybody checking on them in the community and [ascertaining] why they don't want to take their medicine or the reason they keep smoking or why they're so anxious or whatever. It seems like nobody cares about that anymore. They've got the big things solved but not the little things. Nobody really cares 'cause it's all into cost containment now. I don't think it's just that way here. I think it's that way everywhere.

The stories of these six nurses are just a few of the ones that I, along with the members of my research teams, have collected from nurses across the country. And there are thousands more RNs who have their own tales of injustice, outrage, and emotional pain. Undoubtedly, you have some stories of your own, whether you are a staff nurse, administrator, or educator. I do too.

Although it's comforting to know that we're not alone in our pain, this book is not about bemoaning our lot and licking our wounds. This book is about managing our stress and doing something *positive* with our anger. But, as we do in clinical practice, we must assess before we take action. We must unpeel the layers of nurses' tangled emotions.

The nurses' stories that we examine in this first chapter illustrate the complexity of RN stress and anger. The intertwining of stress-producing *institutional factors* (such as hierarchy, bureaucracy) and *individual characteristics* (such as RNs' perceived powerlessness) complicates matters tremendously. Nurses know a lot about stress management. After all, we teach our patients relaxation, imagery, and other stress-relieving techniques. I argue, however, that simplistic stress management strategies will not work to address the disheartening work environment that nurses face today. Sorry, but deep breathing and muscle relaxation just won't cut it. System problems will require system solutions, as we discuss in Chapters 10 and 11. Where does anger come into the picture? Anger is the emotional response to stress. For example, our "anger titer" rises when we are stretched too thinly by multiple demands on our energy and time. Nurses' anger is triggered for other reasons too, such as violations of our rights as human beings. Too many nurses are literally inflamed with anger that they cannot manage effectively, and it's burning them out. Let's examine the themes and patterns of nurses' stress and anger that I've observed from Knoxville to Nevada. As you read the compelling words of your RN colleagues, reflect on your own experience. Do you resonate with the themes we discovered through our research?

Themes and Patterns of Nurses' Stress and Anger

- I feel overloaded and overwhelmed.
- I am not treated with respect.
- I am blamed and scapegoated.
- I feel powerless.
- I am not being heard.
- I feel morally sick.
- I am not getting any support.

"I Feel Overloaded and Overwhelmed"

The first theme, not surprisingly, pertains to heavy workload, overwhelming demands, and constant time pressure. A foreshadowing of this theme was apparent in the first quotation used at the beginning of this chapter. Here are the words of other RNs:

> *I had a ridiculous assignment. They were the worst patients on the floor. Some were on one end of the hall and some on the other end. One was totally confused. One was dying, and I had a lady across the hall that was a new stroke. And then I had an elderly lady that was 90 years old that had just had a fractured hip. And I said, "Wait a minute, now I am not an Olympic sprinter here. There's no way I can do all these people." So the secretary said to me, "What are you doing, causing trouble?"*

One nurse in our study recounted feeling like a robot "that somebody just pressed the button and said, 'go' . . . I just felt overwhelmed. I jumped from one room to the next trying to meet these patients' needs. I couldn't do this for this number of patients." Another related: "Everybody expected Supernurses. I wanted to live up to the expectation. I tried hard, but I would go home frustrated. The patient load was so heavy. I don't feel like I did the care they deserved. I would get really angry."

Inability to take time for breaks and meals was a common complaint of our study participants. Even skipping breaks, many nurses weren't able to complete their patient care within the specified hours of their shift. Some spoke of working as many as 3 hours extra after a 12-hour shift and then returning the next day, tired before their new shift even began.

> ***1.1.*** *A sense of utter futility at meeting impossible demands was evident in the words of this RN:*
> *"I think of the fairy tale Rumpelstiltskin, where they would put the person in the room full of straw every night and say 'Produce gold!' That's how I feel. I feel like I'm in that room full of straw and I'm being asked to produce gold."*

Forced "floating" is a frequently mentioned frustration. Like medicine, nursing has become highly specialized, and nurses pride themselves on their clinical expertise and technical proficiency within their own specialty area. RNs are angry about being given responsibilities when they lack the knowledge to assume them. For many years, my specialty area has been psychiatric nursing. I remember my anger when I was pulled from the psychiatric unit one day and assigned a patient who was to have a blood transfusion. Frantically, I thumbed through the unit's procedure books to refresh my rusty knowledge (we don't give blood on the psych unit!). This story has a happy ending: I hovered over that patient, paying scrupulous attention to his vital signs, and he had no adverse reaction to the blood. But I remember thinking, "Why am I here? This is crazy! A nurse is not a nurse is not a nurse." So, I readily empathized with all of you who told me stories about forced "floating" to units outside your specialty areas. Indignantly, one nurse told of being required to rotate among five units. Another sustained a leg fracture while scrambling to hook up a new type of monitor she had never been oriented to use. These accounts are illustrative:

> *I would be floated to orthopedics . . . given a 5-minute in-service on a complex drain, different kinds of medication, two different pumps . . . and left with that patient, plus eight other patients. And that really, really, really angered me.*
>
> *My background was women's health. I'd done intensive care before, but it had been a long time, and the particular respirators they were using were different from the respirators I had used.*

Mandatory overtime is bitterly resented. Employers of RNs began this practice in the late 1990s; by 2002 two-thirds of nurses were being required to work some mandatory or unplanned overtime every month (Foley, 2002). Nurses are told they will be fired if they refuse to do so. This practice not only contributes to nurses' fatigue and job dissatisfaction but also to the possibility of errors in clinical judgment that jeopardize patients. Research by Anne Rogers and her colleagues showed that when nurses work more than 12.5 hours, the likelihood of making an error is more than three times as high (Rogers, Hwang, Scott, Aiken, & Dinges, 2004). New York RN Julie Semente told a journalist: "After a 12-hour shift, you can't see straight. You stand there looking at this medication sheet and then at the patient, and you're saying, 'May God help me. Please don't let me make a mistake with a decimal point'" (Pekkanen, 2003, pp. 88–89).

Unquestionably, stress in the work environment has escalated because of the acute nursing shortage. As shown in the words of our study participants, the nurses remaining on the job must do more and more with less and less. Their job satisfaction soon plummets. Nurses in hospitals with the highest patient workloads are twice as likely to be dissatisfied with their jobs and more than twice as likely to experience burnout, compared with nurses in better-staffed hospitals (Aiken, Clarke, Sloane, Sochalski, & Silber, 2002). As Unruh (2008, p. 64) pointed out: "It's a vicious cycle: inadequate staffing leads to reduced job performance and diminished patient and nurse satisfaction; the resulting burnout and high turnover rates worsen staffing levels."

Nurses in academia are encountering new pressures too. Faculty are expected to pull in research dollars or collect fees for clinical services in addition to their teaching, advising, and publishing. Remember the phrase "publish or perish"? That's not the half of it in today's financially strapped colleges and universities. Many faculty resonate with the it's-so-funny-it-hurts comparison to the Pushmi-Pullu presented in a witty article by Judith Vessey and Susan Gennaro (1992). Borrowing from the menagerie of Dr. Dolittle, they selected this two-headed animal to represent the faculty member who must do two sets of tasks at the same time. The greater the amount of pushing and pulling on the beast, the greater the internal dissension and conflict. The number of Pushmi-Pullus in the halls of academe has increased exponentially in the tight fiscal environment of modern universities, and the species is not likely to become extinct in the near future.

Carol Carter has been a nurse educator for the past 5 years, but she still works part-time in her clinical specialty area in a hospital also. She enjoys caring for the patients but resents the university's failure to give her time to do this work: "They don't give you any time off. Your regular workload is still expected of you. You have to do it on weekends or evening shifts. It makes my evaluation look good, but it makes me angry that we're in a rat race again. Some days, it's like I'm between a rock and a hard place. I have all these student papers to grade and school commitments and family commitments. It's running me down. Some days, some weeks I feel angry."

"I Am Not Treated With Respect"

Uncivil or demeaning treatment provokes much anger within the nursing profession. When my research team conducted interviews with nurses, many narratives of being patronized, chastised, and scolded were elicited. Offenders included physicians, supervisors, faculty, and peers. Some nurses attributed such treatment to their age, race, gender, sexual orientation, or position in the institutional hierarchy. Others remained bewildered, unable to find any rationale for the disrespectful treatment they received. Mike Evans's story is a good example. Mike is an ICU-CCU nurse with 12 years of experience. He told of a physician who "thrashed me verbally in front of my peers. . . . It was a bizarre reaction on his part. I didn't feel deserving of any criticism. His outburst was totally unprofessional and unwarranted. I really had no idea what had set him off." The incident was especially galling because the "thrashing" took place in front of his colleagues.

Bob Hayes's story also took place in the ICU setting, but his attacker was a nursing supervisor, not a physician. Bob's patient had been in an auto accident and had both arms in casts. The physician was examining the casts and the circulation in the patient's fingers, when Bob's supervisor came flying into the unit and started yanking curtains around the patient's bed, berating Bob for violating the patient's right to privacy. Bob relates, "I didn't feel the need [to close the curtains] because the patient was not exposed, there was no procedure. There was nothing going on that would be offensive to anyone. The patient was not bloody or gory. And she [the supervisor] comes in and makes this big fuss. Embarrasses me in front of the doctor, my coworkers, and the family members. She raised her voice and there was no need for that. She could have called me to the side. Raising her voice made me angry. I was feeling embarrassed and humiliated. I just wanted to clock out and head for the house."

This incident was only one of many that occurred soon after Bob graduated. He grappled with feelings of incompetence when his rigid, stern supervisor continued to criticize his performance, and he thought seriously about leaving the profession: "I almost threw in the towel. I almost quit and went back to K-Mart. But I knew I would be wasting 4 years of my life." Much has already been written about the crucial transition from the role of nursing student to new graduate. Plenty of research evidence shows that the graduate experiences "reality shock," (Kramer, 1974), a "crisis of competence" (Cherniss, 1995), and self-doubt about the ability to perform procedures (Casey et al., 2004). But 40% of newly licensed RNs report that "seldom" or "never" did anyone show them how to work successfully in their institutions (Kovner et al., 2007).

Support from more experienced nurses could be vital to the novice in that important first year of practice. Yet, many new RNs in our study reported they had been treated disrespectfully, adding to their stress. For example, Eve Sanders vividly recalled being "picked on" by an older nurse in her first job as a new graduate: "I was still young, 23. And it was a very intimidating experience. She was a bit older, very pushy, bossy, telling me that is not the right way to make a bed... something I had been doing for some time... treating me in an infantile manner."

Age is no guarantee of respectful treatment. Joy Carpenter was more than twice as old as Eve when a similar incident occurred during her master's program in midwifery. Despite her maturity and experience, Joy was treated like a child by her preceptor: "One time, she had assigned me to a patient and told me to manage the labor and everything, and so I did vaginal exams when I thought they were appropriate. She called me aside and reprimanded me and scolded me as if I was a child: 'How dare you do that when I am not in the room?' I've done thousands of vaginal exams in my life, and then all of a sudden, because I'm in the student role I'm not competent to do that anymore."

Although many of the foregoing stories took place in hospitals, disrespectful treatment of nurses takes place in other locales, as well. Irene Martin is a master's prepared nurse practitioner who performs contract services for a physician. She was appalled when he questioned her invoice for her time:

I was very angry because he was not treating me like a professional. He sent me a message through his office manager to tell me that if my invoices were not going to be consistent, then I needed to start to clock in. I can't stand people to question my integrity. I requested to speak to him to discuss the issue, but he didn't want to discuss it with me. When he refused to speak to me, that also made me angry.

Sexist Treatment and Sexual Harassment. Under the broad umbrella theme of disrespect, our analysis revealed a strong subtheme of sexist treatment and sexual harassment—frequently reported by both female and male RNs. Much more has been written about discriminatory treatment of females, because for most of the profession's history, nurses have been female and physicians and hospital administrators male. Florence Nightingale was keenly aware of sexual harassment and noted that "no male hospital administrator or official...would intervene on the side of a woman [against] a higher status male, for example a physician or surgeon" (cited in Mrkwicka, 1994). Bullough (1990) calls sexual harassment a dominant theme in American nursing, noting how frequently incidents of it were reported in the biographies of noted nursing administrators and educators. In *American Nursing: A Biographical Dictionary* (Bullough, Church, & Stein, 1988), there are numerous accounts of female nurses running into trouble with male colleagues and either quitting or being fired. While I was in nursing school many years ago, I remember how frequently my classmates and I experienced physician harassment, including speculation about our sex lives and jokes about our bra size. It was not unusual for doctors to grab our breasts when we were scrubbing for surgery or to make propositions. Once a psychiatrist exposed himself to me in his office at the mental hospital where we did our psychiatric rotation. Most of these incidents were shared only with our classmates, because no one dared to confront a powerful male doctor.

Sexual harassment is illegal now, under Title VII of the Civil Rights Act, but studies document that it continues. More than 70% of the female staff nurses surveyed by Libbus and Bowman (1997) reported sexual harassment. Many episodes involved inappropriate touching, although the number one form of harassment was a sexual remark. Although nurses become angry at such offensive behavior, they still fear humiliation, retaliation, or job loss if they report the harasser. One study of nurses found that the greater the nurse's distress, the *less* likely the incident would be reported (American Nurses Association, 1993). The nurse may fear that it is his or her fault for not setting appropriate limits—or may not understand what those limits are. Complicating matters is the unspoken norm on some units that a little flirting is useful in cajoling irate physicians. In the ICU, Bob Hayes observed a lot of physician–nurse "rubbing and massaging each other...in an inappropriate, nonprofessional way." Similarly, in the labor and delivery department Joy Carpenter related, "I saw other nurses being touched in ways that were just totally inappropriate...physicians feeling that they had a right to do that....Don't ask me how I did it, but I just knew how to maneuver and get away from them." Greg James resented a female colleague trying to use her "womanly wiles" on him: "She does it with doctors all the time, and they eat it up. I don't. She can't control me like that. All that did was make me very angry at her for being so unprofessional. She's a thorn in my side."

A 2003 study substantiates continuing sexual harassment of nurses and nursing students (Bronner, Peretz, & Ehrenfeld, 2003). Participants were queried about seven types of harassment, ranging from minor (dirty sex jokes) to more intrusive (physical touch) to severe (attempts to have sexual relations). Ninety-one percent of the participants experienced at least one type of harassment; 30% experienced at least four types. Seventy-five percent of the perpetrators were men harassing women. But the male nurses in this study (20% of the sample) received more severe types of sexual harassment (being forced to touch someone intimately in a way that is not required by the nursing role, and suggestions to have sex against their will).

Disrespect of Men in Nursing. Men in nursing certainly have ample justification for anger. Historically, they have experienced rampant discrimination, including insinuations of homosexuality, denial of opportunity to practice in some clinical settings, and exclusion from the Army Nurse Corps for nearly half a century. They often face the double whammy of being discriminated against by other men as well as their female nurse colleagues. Although men had been prominent in nursing during the Middle Ages and the Renaissance, the modern image of the "ideal nurse" was feminized as the Nightingale system of training nurses swept the world. When Christian Hospital in St. Louis admitted a male nursing student in 1908, the Missouri State Board "declared that the 'young man' did not fit into the group, and as a result he left the school" (Aldag & Christensen, 1967, p. 375). Despite their chilly welcome, small numbers of men continued to enter the profession, mostly attending all-male schools such as the Mills School of Male Nurses. Even within schools such as these, men encountered discrimination. Legendary nursing leader Luther Christman, speaking of his student days at the School of Nursing for Men of the Pennsylvania Hospital, remembers:

> *It did not take me long to realize that men were a minority in the profession and were viewed with suspicion by female nurses....I was called a pervert for answering a urologist's request to examine a specimen under a cystoscope while in the presence of a fully draped female patient and female nurse. A similar reaction occurred when I requested a maternity experience....I was denied because of my gender. (Christman, 1988, p. 45)*

Males in nursing are often slotted into specialty areas that are seen as "masculine," such as the emergency department or administration, rather than obstetrics or general floor duty. A man interviewed by Williams (1995) had always aspired to working in OB/GYN but was prevented from participating in that rotation in nursing school and assigned tasks that demanded physical strength instead. Donald Bille went on active duty in the Army Nurse Corps in 1966 after completing his BS degree. He requested the Army's school for public health nursing when he finished basic training. But, the first day of the course he was told that the only public health care he could do was changing Foley catheters on the retired Army population, and any care involving women would require a chaperone. He asked for reassignment (Cooper, 1997).

Prominent nurse leader Tim Porter-O'Grady writes of "quiet, unspoken and insidious" reverse discrimination against male RNs (1995, p. 56). He says it is very challenging for men to break into the "old girls club." Males are expected to assume leadership roles, but when they prove successful in these roles, that success is attributed to their maleness: "he is a man and...he is somehow advantaged because he is" (p. 57). Further reproach results from the assumption that he has prevented an equally qualified woman from obtaining that leadership position. Discriminatory treatment has undoubtedly been a factor in the relatively slow increase in the proportion of men in nursing (currently only 5.4%

of RNs) (Spratley, Johnson, Sochalski, Fritz, & Spencer, 2000). Even today, men in nursing hear comments such as, "Surely you're going to pursue your MD!" or "Why nursing?" Data from the National Sample Survey of Registered Nurses showed that men were less satisfied in nursing than women were. Even those in advanced practice roles were less satisfied than women (Sochalski, 2002). This dissatisfaction, if widely communicated, could inhibit the recruitment of men to the profession. Men who participated in a study by our research team expressed anger over female nursing colleagues treating them differently because of their gender, calling on them for their "heave-ho-ness" rather than their knowledge (A. Brooks, Thomas, & Droppleman, 1996). Greg James, manager of a med-surg floor, reported that "if there's anybody heavy to be lifted, even as a manager, I would be called to help lift them because I'm a male, instead of the carriers being called." Some men felt excluded from the "sorority" of female nurses and compared themselves to members of other minority groups who are forced to try harder to validate their worth.

Disrespect of Minorities in Nursing. African American nurses surely identify with the feelings about discriminatory treatment expressed by the men. Many of those in our study talked of feeling excluded by the White majority and having to constantly prove themselves. Georgia Preston's words were typical:

> *I first started out as an LPN. I was the only African American woman in the class. The instructor tried everything to encourage me to drop out. And I recall one OB test that I made 100 on. She just couldn't believe that I made 100. She re-tested me. She said, "I just don't see how you did this." So, she gave me another test. I made 100 on that one. She never really let up. That continued on, through the 13 months. . . . Then, a year after that, I started RN school. I went through with a breeze. I was top in my class. I passed state boards with flying colors. And I've been a nurse now for a long time. And everywhere you go, you have to really prove yourself. If I go to a new hospital, I have to prove myself like this is my first day. . . . People judge you just by your color alone. . . . When I was with [name of hospital], there were two or three black RNs on the floor, and we were taking trays in to the patients. Even the doctors would say, "Oh there come the girls from the kitchen now." You'd have the name tag on, you'd be dressed like all the others, why would you be the girl from the kitchen? Sometimes I get so mad I can see fire.*

Elizabeth Barton, who termed herself, "young, black, and successful," echoed Geraldine's complaint of being mistaken for the kitchen help. On one occasion, although she was the instructor, she was questioned about being the student. She has also been mistaken for a nursing assistant. She feels that her colleagues do not respect her. When working with four White nurses, she is the last to be asked to attempt starting an IV: "They'll say something like, 'Well, so-and-so tried and she's good.' And then I'll go in and get it on the first attempt. And that's when they get a different opinion of my abilities. And it just makes me angry trying to figure out why they didn't ask me in the first place. Was it because I was Black, or was it because I was young, or just what factors did they feel made me less capable of starting an IV? So, most of the time I have to prove myself. It makes me angry that I have to prove myself."

Fannie Williams, now 58 and a clinical director, recounted a number of episodes of humiliation and abuse during 31 years of employment at the same hospital. She sums up the racism she has encountered in her career: "Racism is like rain; if it's not falling in your location, it's gathering force somewhere nearby."

The "rain of racism" falls on other ethnically diverse nurses as well. Asian nurses—recruited to work in the United States by administrators scrambling to avert the crisis of the RN shortage—have experienced discrimination, marginalization, and exploitation (Xu, 2007). A Filipino nurse "sensed" an unwelcoming attitude from her American peers: "They hate our accent. That's why they don't want to work with us. Although they don't say that, you just sense it" (Lopez, 1990, p. 84). A nurse from India sadly reported, "Nobody learned my name for four months when I first came, and when they did . . . they shortened it and pronounced it wrong. I finally stopped correcting them" (DiCicco-Bloom, 2004, p. 26). Drawing together the findings of 14 studies of immigrant Asian RNs, Xu (2007) called attention to "worst" patient assignments, harassment, and bullying inflicted by physicians, peers, supervisors, and even subordinates such as aides. The Asian nurses, mostly women, felt that respect was hard to earn. They felt vulnerable because of their soft voices, short statures, and unfamiliarity with many aspects of Western culture and the English language.

A final note about disrespect: By elaborating on the plight of some minorities in detail, I do not wish to minimize the struggles of other groups within nursing that have received egregious mistreatment. See, for example, the stories of lesbian nurses in Giddings and Smith (2001) and Chinn (2008). *No one deserves to experience the disrespect that we have discussed in this section of the chapter!*

"I Am Blamed and Scapegoated"

The next theme in our data pertained to scapegoating. As if nurses don't have enough to deal with, just keeping up with their own workload, they also catch the blame for the mistakes and omissions of other health care workers. The lab hasn't drawn the blood, dietary just fed the patient who's N.P.O., X-ray didn't come to get the fellow whose films were to be done before surgery—and the nurse gets the flak. We've all been there: it's infuriating! Lisa Thompson, a clinical director with 30 years of experience, noted the tendency of physicians to attribute blame to "that stupid bunch of nurses on the floor." She offered the following explanation: "I think somebody has to relieve the pressure, has to be blamed, and more often it's nursing. They're quick to be scapegoated. It is so easy to blame the nurse. And that's especially true in acute care and labor situations. The physician says he's not responsible: 'The nurse didn't call me,' but the nurse reported to him when the first little flicker happened on the fetal monitor. I've seen that quite a bit when the physician was not available. They're quick to let the nurses take the responsibility and take the blame. I think nurses are getting smarter in the way they document and notify, trying to stay out of a bad situation, but there's still a lot of them who do get caught up in a bad situation."

Joy Carpenter questioned why a doctor couldn't own up to his role in an incident that upset a patient's family: "Why did he have to make *us* a scapegoat? I had done everything I was supposed to do and followed the rules. It's like you never know when you're going to get the rug pulled out from under you."

> *1.2. Mike Evans was devastated by a physician's accusation of advancing a Swan-Ganz catheter, which he had not done, although he had no way to prove that he hadn't done it. The situation was especially traumatic for Mike because the physician's accusation replicated a childhood experience of being unfairly blamed:*
>
> *"I can still remember a situation when I was barely 6 years old and my [grandmother] found a pair of pants in the living room and went off to my mom raising a big ruckus about how I just stepped out of my pants and left them there. And I hadn't done it. I had no idea how they got there."*

Eve Sanders described being belittled by physicians and yelled at in the hall. When asked what provoked the physician ire, she related, "Well, I lay it on the line for the patients. I've had physicians be angry with me for telling a patient more than the physician wanted them to know at a particular time. I've borne the brunt of the physician's anger, 'Why did you tell her duh duh duh duh duh?' 'Because she wanted to know.' I have to put myself in the patient's place. I wish I had more guts to confront the physician. To say, 'Now look, what you did really hacked me off. You have no right to talk to me that way.'"

"I Feel Powerless"

Feelings of powerlessness were pervasive throughout the data we have obtained from nurse interviews. Nurses wanted someone or something to change, but they did not know how to make that happen. They spoke of their powerlessness in many different situations. RNs were angry about not being involved in the redesign of their units, not having a place at the table when decisions were being made, and not having sufficient resources to do their jobs. Some decried the repercussions when they tried to speak out, consistent with descriptions elsewhere in the literature. For example, Iowa RN Colleen Donlin repeatedly reported an electric bed that was shocking staff members. She was told that the hospital did not have the money for repairs in its budget, and a written reprimand was placed in her personnel file because of the way she spoke to her supervisor, which was allegedly "threatening" (Kittle, 2007). Psychiatric nurses in a large public hospital described a similarly intimidating atmosphere that constrained their attempts to change the way their unit was run. After observing negative consequences for speaking out, one RN admitted, "I keep my head low. Anybody that has complained or gone up and spoke their mind . . . Well, they got burnt" (Shattell, Andes, & Thomas, in press).

Many nurses in our studies seemed to feel that the work environment simply could not be controlled. For example, Eve Sanders spoke about her lack of control when ancillary personnel were pulled from her unit by the supervisor: "Basically, my protest was a meek thing, a meek protest. I could not say to the supervisor, 'No, you cannot take my aide.' You know, they did not call to *ask,* they called to *demand.*" Likewise, another study participant perceived that there was no choice when her manager mandated her to assume a heavier assignment:

In ICU, your capacity is two patients at the most, because you have fully lined trach-ventilator patients. I walk in; they say "we don't have anybody. You're going to have to take these other two patients." And I talk to my manager, "This is a very, very dangerous situation. It's my license you're putting on the line." And the only reply I got was, "You do it or you don't have a job."

Carol Carter felt pulled in so many directions, that she could not give good patient care:

I knew the stuff I was taught to do, but I did not have time to do it.... It is like a rat race. We are here to push pills and drugs, but no time to do patient care.... It seems I always fall behind on time and that makes me angry... It is like you are pulled in 20 different directions.... I have no control, no control over the situation.

Joy Carpenter decried the scarcity of resources: "They tell you to do the job, but they don't give you the wherewithal to get it done." Bonnie Hartman made a similar complaint: "We don't always have the supplies we need, and certainly not the quality, because we always get the cheapest—whatever was the lowest bid on the contract."

Lisa Thompson chafed at closed communication lines and political power struggles in the large teaching hospital where she works as a clinical director:

I have a lot of anger at those higher up in our establishment, because I feel like decisions get made without asking the right people. For Pete's sake, we learn from the Japanese that even the person on the line can help with these decisions, but we still are not really doing that. Decisions are made that I am perplexed as to how I can make them work. You have to do it because so-and-so said. Communication lines are often closed that really should be open. And there are still a lot of political power struggles that overshadow what really needs to be done.

1.3. Public health nurse Bonnie Hartman decried the capriciousness of decisions that are made on the basis of politics rather than patients' needs:

I get angry at the system—it's that feeling of powerlessness. So many of the things we do in public health are tied to politics. We have money for whatever a particular administration wants us to have. We get a new program because it is a pet project of the governor or better yet, his wife! We had lots of money for prenatal care during Governor A's administration. It was his wife's project. As soon as the administration changed, the prenatal money was gone. Is this really fair to the people we serve?"

Often, nurses have the knowledge to remedy a problem, but lack the authority to act on it. For example, Ann Smith was well aware that the staffing pattern for her unit was unsafe, but "It took a doctor getting upset to change it and make administration realize that we were functioning unsafely. It's frustrating to me that a doctor has to come and tell [administration] 'The unit's not safe,' when the nurses are trying to tell that already." The testimony of study participants like Ann Smith is consistent with a national study of hospital RNs by Eileen McNeely (1995), in which 85% of the nurses reported "none to very little influence" over decisions about closing a unit to admissions, ordering agency staff, or refusing to float off their floors.

Research shows that nursing jobs with *high demand but low decision authority* produce stress, negative emotions, and emotional exhaustion, and result in reduced nursing performance (Johnston, Jones, McCann, & McKee, 2008; Steen, Firth, & Bond, 1998). The combination of high demand and low control also contributes to poor physical health, as shown in studies of workers conducted in the United States, Canada, and Europe (e.g., Kuper & Marmot, 2003). In a review of health records of workers in 130 occupations, Stringer (1990) found nurses to have a higher than expected rate of stress-related disorders. Not surprisingly, nursing fell into the group of occupations characterized by high job demands and low control. A study of 21,290 female nurses showed that the declines in health associated with high-demand-low-control jobs are as significant as those associated with smoking and sedentary lifestyles (Cheng, Kawachi, Coakley, Schwartz, & Colditz, 2000). A particularly dangerous combination of factors was identified by Duke researcher Redford Williams and his research team (1997). Women in high-demand-low-control jobs often had a pattern of increased negative emotion (anxiety, anger, and depression), along with reduced social support, and a preponderance of negative versus positive feelings in dealing with their coworkers and supervisors. These factors are known to be predictive of an increased risk of cardiovascular disease as well as mortality from other causes (Williams, Barefoot, Blumenthal, Helms, et al., 1997).

"I Am Not Being Heard"

I consider it the epitome of powerlessness when individuals feel that they do not even have a voice. A female nursing faculty member lamented, "In my particular work situation, we women are absolutely in the minority, a significant minority in a very paternalistic system. It's a 'good old boy' system. It's Southern, it's male-dominated, we are referred to as 'the girls.' We don't get the same ear as a unit that's bringing massive grant money. We just don't have a voice." When nurses do try to make their voices heard, too often no one is really listening to them. Geraldine Vincent, an operating room nurse in Hawaii, repeatedly requested that her hospital hire aides to help with moving heavy equipment. Although she has been injured on the job twice in the last 7 years, she cannot get her point across: "There's no acknowledgment that there has been a shift in the type of work we're required to do in the operating room...it now requires heavy lifting and moving" (cited in Helmlinger, 1997). Geraldine's job-related injuries exemplify a national problem—lack of federal legislation—even though nurses incur more strains and sprains than construction workers (Johnson, Martin, & Markle-Elder, 2007).

It was a bit of a surprise to the research team that *men were just as likely as women to feel that they are not being heard.* Mike Evans spoke of feeling helpless because he was dealing with someone who would not listen. Tom Parker was very frustrated and angry about a chronic problem of heavy assignments. His female colleague always took a lighter load. Over time, this inequity rubbed Tom the wrong way: "Sort of like an ill-fitting pair of shoes. You can get by with them for awhile, but after awhile, they're going to rub a sore on your foot, maybe eventually a blister." When he tried to talk with the other nurse, nothing got resolved. She threw up her hands, saying "I don't need this" and walked off. Her failure to listen *really* made him sore. He said, "I don't like to be just blown off. What I say doesn't necessarily have to be agreed with, but I want it to be considered. I can tolerate inequity to a point, if I feel like there's been some kind of communication."

In Linda Harvey's case, it was the charge nurse who failed to listen—to her legitimate concerns about a patient's condition. Linda relates, "I had a patient who had had a stomach stapling, and something happened that she wasn't absorbing the nutrition. So, what they had to do was go back and redo some of that. . . . After the surgery, I was her primary nurse. She got along pretty good, but when she was getting ready to go home, all of a sudden she started having God-awful stomach pain. This woman's not ready to go home. And so I said this to the charge nurse. The charge nurse was a real flippant young girl. She says, 'There's nothing wrong with her, she's always complaining about stuff.' The woman was doubled up with pain, and I was giving her everything I could give her to try to get her some relief. What ended up happening is they discharged her but she was readmitted to another hospital, and she had a bowel obstruction."

Joy Carpenter summed up what it meant not to be listened to: "I am most angry at the lack of being heard, that what I need and want does not matter . . . you are a nonentity. . . . I would like the courtesy of being heard."

"I Feel Morally Sick"

Nurses told many stories of situations in which they observed, or participated in, treatment of patients that was unethical, harmful, and/or dehumanizing. In some situations, the nurses were able to take action, but their actions did not always bring about the desired outcome. When circumstances were beyond nurses' control, and they were unable to intervene, they were left with a terrible anguish that is termed "moral distress" in the literature (Corley, 2002).

The following account vividly depicts this distress:

We had a young patient that died. And I was in the room watching the procedure. No one said anything to the doctor, just "Maybe . . . " or "Have you thought . . . " or "Could we stop?" I was very angry that day. And I broke out in a sweat, nauseated. I've never lost control at work like that in my life, in 14 years, but I did that day. I mean my heart was racing. She [the young patient] said, "That hurts," and she was told "No it doesn't" by the doctor. And that made me angry. I mean this was just a kid, she was my daughter's age. And I wanted so badly to just spit in his face. I just felt like he had treated her in such a non-human manner. . . . And then of course when she coded, oh, it was like there's nothing that could be done, you know."

In the next situation, the patient was not given a proper opportunity to make her own decision and give informed consent regarding impending surgery. Linda Harvey became quite emotional as she recounted this incident that occurred when she was working evening shift on a surgical unit and went to get an elderly patient to sign the permit for a scheduled mastectomy. Finding that the patient was barely literate, Linda read the permit to her and her daughter. But the patient still did not comprehend that removal of her breast was planned; she insisted, "They're going to remove the lump. I don't want my breast removed." Linda called the physician, relating to him, 'She understood that she's having a lumpectomy, and that's the only thing she wants.' The doctor said, 'No, she's going to have a mastectomy. You must have said something to confuse her. Go back and get the permit signed.' Linda refused to do so, and here's the rest of the story:

> When I left that night, I explained to the oncoming shift that the surgery's going to have to be cancelled. Or else they're going to have to make sure they're only removing the lump. The next night, when I came back to work, she had had a mastectomy. The resident had talked to her, and she signed the permit. It was so upsetting. She was a vulnerable person. She was not real educated. It was like, you can dupe them because they don't understand.

Basing care on a patient's socioeconomic status was morally repugnant to the nurse who related this story:

> I remember one particular situation, and this was a diabetic patient who came for prenatal care . . . to a resident clinic which is supposed to be overseen by staff physicians. And that just wasn't done in this case. And this patient was very brittle, eventually lost the baby. She kept getting different residents, and nobody took that assertiveness to step in and manage her care. . . . And this patient needed that badly. That was the most angry that I believe I've ever been. I went to the chairman of the department and laid it out. And he says, "Well, we just can't give that kind of one-on-one care to all patients, you know. This is a patient in the clinic, it's not a patient who's a paying, private patient." I was furious.

In the final example, the nurse still ponders the death of a child after a fierce conflict between two physicians. She is unable to achieve a sense of closure:

> It was a 7-year-old drowning victim, brought in by ambulance . . . We got his heartbeat back but really not good response pupilwise or anything else. It was Dr. S. working on the child, and at the time we did not know it was another physician's child. And the other physician came storming in and wanted us to stop. He saw the pupils were pinpoint and such, and he did not want us to continue. Dr. S. did not realize that the father was a physician; he was on the phone to the children's hospital with Dr. W. asking what else we could do. It was a very uptight time. The father grabbed the child off the table and said, "No, let him go."
>
> I found out later that Dr. S. had almost drowned as a child. Someone had gotten him back, and he was fine. He really did not want to stop. . . . We thought we had done fairly well in getting the child back. We didn't know what the neurological prognosis would be, but felt we should give the child a chance . . . I felt we should have given him a day or two on the respirator to see if he would come back. They wouldn't go ahead and give him a couple of days. That was

the most stressful thing. It was just like you couldn't get the answer why. I've always wondered why they did not do that.

This nurse, like others in a recent study by Gunther and Thomas (2006), was left to wonder, "Could I have done anything else?" Webster and Baylis (2001) assert that unresolved moral distress can result in *moral residue*, which can exhaust one's ability to deal with future situations. Moral distress could prove to be an important contributor to burnout. In one recent study, 25% of nurses left a position because of moral distress (Corley, Minick, Elswick, & Jacobs, 2005).

"I Am Not Getting Any Support"

Lack of support was one of the most poignant aspects of the nurses' anger stories collected by my research teams. Joy remembered the sarcastic retort of her night supervisor when she called to ask for help: "I needed help desperately in Labor and Delivery. The night supervisor said, 'Well, where do you think I'm going to get these nurses, cut out paper dolls?'" Linda, speaking of nurse administrators, asserted that "I have never seen where they will be your advocate. They sell you down the tubes. They have totally lost sight of the nursing side. And you shouldn't be at sides or at war." Many nurses spoke in the language of war as they talked about their work. They used an incredible number of military metaphors and similes: "It's like being on the firing line," "We feel sabotaged," "It's like an armed camp," "We really don't know how to fight back," "I don't know if I'll ever muster all that it takes." It became clear to the research team that nurses yearned for some *allies* in their daily battles. They especially wanted affirmation from managers. But affirmation is not what they got.

Nurses were angry because they were always being told what they were doing wrong. No one mentioned what they were doing right. A woman in one of my anger workshops described her first evaluation conference on a new job. Her supervisor told her only negative things. "Much to my embarrassment, I cried," she told me. "I felt bad with no positive affirmations." Bob Hayes provided a graphic description of his autocratic nurse manager who walked through the unit "like a stick stirring up rattlesnakes," getting all of the nurses "in an uproar and tense... pointing out these small things.... She would only let you know when something was wrong. And that was quite frequently in her opinion." Sue Green believes she is doing some good things but "nobody will remember it."

Lack of support from management has been a consistent theme in studies by other researchers, too. Fewer than half the nurses in Linda Aiken's massive five-country study felt that management listened to their concerns, acknowledged their contributions to patient care, and provided opportunities for them to participate in decisions (Aiken et al., 2001). Other evidence of dissatisfaction with management support appeared in the report of the *NurseWeek*/AONE National Survey of Registered Nurses, which involved more than 4,000 randomly selected American RNs (Brown, 2003). In a Pennsylvania survey, nurses thought their managers cared more about pleasing upper administration than about their needs—or the needs of patients (Trossman, 2005).

Nurses want support from *colleagues* as well as managers. In the following excerpt from our interview data, the nurse had a powerful spiritual experience with a patient and wanted to share it with her colleagues. She was hurt and disappointed by their response:

> I had a little guy, and we were doing neuro checks every 4 hours. I did one at 4:00, which was normal, and then at 8:00 he was completely unresponsive. He wouldn't track, pupils were very sluggish, BP dropped significantly. I had to call the neurologist, who sent him for a stat MRI of his head. He came back from this MRI and was still basically unresponsive. He was out of it for over an hour–and then it was like he just snapped out of it! He just totally came out of it. I called him by name, "Mr. —, you really scared us there. What happened?" He pulled my hand, and pulled me nose to nose with him and said, "I've been to see Jesus," and I said, "Yeah," because I believe that kind of thing can happen, but this was the first and only time I've ever had this happen to me. I said, "Do you remember me talking to you?" and he said, "No, I've been to see Jesus, and I have a message for you." That kind of scared me, but I listened. I remember it being a very peaceful thing. It was just the two of us in the room because his family had stepped out in the hall to talk to the neurologist. He says, "God is gonna richly bless you." And within the next couple weeks, I found out I was pregnant. That may be coincidence, but it touched me.

> I saw the change in that patient myself. I was kind of excited about it. This just doesn't happen all the time, that somebody has an experience like this. I went out there and told some of the other nurses. They laughed and acted like he was crazy and confused, and that really hurt my feelings. I feel like there is an afterlife. I feel like there is a heaven and there is a God. He was talking about the light and how it looked. And of course when they laughed and acted like he was crazy and confused, that was really disappointing.

Throughout our studies of nurses' stress and anger, the longing for support has been expressed by nurses at all educational levels—from AD to PhD—and at many diverse practice sites. Although a few nurses described a coworker who could be counted on for an encouraging word or a hug, many did not seem to have a workplace support person. Sue Green ruefully acknowledged, "One of the biggest voids in my life is peer support." Many RNs were reluctant to ask for support from others, even from those they trusted. It was not unusual for a nurse to be going through a life-changing event of major proportions—such as a divorce—without sharing the news. This reluctance to ask for collegial support is common in the helping professions, because the usual (and more comfortable) role is to be a giver of help, not a receiver of it. Asking for support is somehow equated with inadequacy or weakness. Nurses say they do not want to *burden* others. Carol Carter explains: "I was brought up that you don't burden other people with your problems. I'll be there for someone else, but it's like I don't feel like I have the right to burden other people with my problems."

I contend that it's time for us to lay down some of our burdens. Most of us, as shown in the stories throughout this chapter, are carrying too heavy a load of stress and anger.

The rest of this book is devoted to the unpacking and transformation of that stress and anger. Some of the work we must do alone, because only we know exactly how we got all that stuff packed in the bag. But we cannot do all of the work alone. We need to enlist some helpers. In some cases, they may be friends, family, or therapists—but remember that your nurse colleagues will have the best grasp of the unique frustrations and anger provocations in this profession of ours. Don't leave them out. As you do the assignments in this book, watch for "Steps Toward Healing" in every chapter. Find a partner or a support group to go on the healing journey with you. The bag won't be nearly so heavy if its load is divvied up.

A Last Word

In my view, we cannot give the care that society needs us to give to hurting people unless we:

- care for *ourselves*, which includes acknowledging and acting on our real feelings,
- and care for *each other*, which includes making a daily effort to be supportive to our colleagues.

As Lynda Carpenito phrased it: "When you go out in the nursing world, hold hands before crossing the street and stick together."

Exposing the Consequences of Mismanaged Anger

"We are often blind to the psychological causes and correlates of our health problems... If we are aware of the conflicts influencing our bodies, we can act to overcome these conflicts."

—James Pennebaker in *Opening Up: The Healing Power of Expressing Emotions*

In this chapter, we take a hard look at the ways mismanaged anger takes its toll:

- Burnout
- Depression
- Physical symptoms
- Hypertension and coronary heart disease
- Addictions
- Cancer

The good news is that nurses can circumvent or attenuate these deleterious consequences of anger. Each of us can begin to take the Steps Toward Healing that appear throughout the chapter—a potpourri of strategies that you can adapt to your own lifestyle and preferences.

23

As shown by the powerful testimony of nurses in Chapter 1, much of the anger felt by RNs is understandable. It is kindled in situations that are incongruent with our values and rights as human beings and professionals. Nurses *value* their unique opportunity to be present with the injured, the sick, and the dying, providing empathy and comfort. It is their *right* to have a reasonable patient assignment, so that they can give their best to each one. Clearly, the values and rights of nurses were trampled in the examples we reviewed in Chapter 1. Anger can be a healthy self-protective response in such situations, and it can fuel advocacy for patients as well.

However, I see a lot of destructive nurse anger. Whether or not it is justifiable, it's too frequent, too intense, too prolonged, and too punishing to ourselves as well as others. In this chapter, we will look at some of the manifestations and consequences of all this anger. You will learn how to self-assess and diagnose unhealthy anger management methods, substitute healthier ones, and move toward emotional healing.

Nurses don't feel good about the ways they handle their anger. Although some RNs told our research team that they screamed or discharged anger in motor activity—by throwing charts, hitting doors with fists, or stalking off from an offender—they seldom felt relief from such actions. Instead, they were ashamed of losing control. Much more often, they kept their distressful emotion hidden. Angry feelings were stifled or somatized, held inside the body until the nurse had a splitting headache or an upset stomach. *Mismanaged anger can make you sick!* Think of the last time you "swallowed" your anger at work, and it sat there all day like a greasy doughnut, heavy in your stomach. The anger might have caused you to have *heartburn:* Anger does "hurt around the heart," as one of our research subjects told us (Thomas, Smucker, & Droppleman, 1998). And, if anger becomes chronic, it might propel you along the path to *burnout,* that unhappy state when you feel like saying "Take this job and shove it!"

The Anger–Burnout Link

What is burnout? How do nurses get that way? Could this happen to you? Burnout is a familiar term, but most of us have not stopped to consider what it really means. It involves stress, but it is not synonymous with stress. Nursing has always been a stressful occupation, but not all of us burn out. Research shows that the type of nursing unit doesn't matter. Whether we work in intensive care, medicine, surgery, or psychiatry units, some of us burn out, but others do not (Duquette, Kerouac, Sandhu, & Beaudet, 1994). Nor is the burnout syndrome equivalent to depression; it is more like emotional exhaustion (Jones, 1982; Schaufeli, Bakker, Hoogduin, Schaap, & Kladler, 2001). Maslach (1982) described three phases of burnout: in the first, individuals begin to experience emotional exhaustion. They just feel drained. Next, they develop negative ideas about their patients, coworkers, and themselves. Finally, there is the phase of reduced capacity to perform. A burned-out nurse could become physically or mentally ill if the condition persists over time (Duquette et al., 1994). For example, research shows that burnout increases workers' risk of cardiovascular disease as much as lipid levels, smoking, and excess weight; it also ups the risk of type II diabetes, sleep disorders, and even male infertility (Melamed, Shirom,

Toker, Berliner, & Shapira, 2006). In the ICD-10 disease classification system, burnout is classified as a mental illness. As shown in a new Swedish study, the condition can result in long-term sick leave (Eriksson, Starrin, & Janson, 2008).

Eriksson and colleagues interviewed burned-out individuals, including nurses, and delineated the progression of stressors that culminated in their exit from the workplace. In addition to the increased job demands and lack of support documented by our own studies, the Swedish participants complained about "sitting in front of the computer all the time and not having time for the patients" and not being able to provide care that was "fit for humans" (Eriksson et al., 2008, pp. 625–626). Eventually, these men and women reached a phase of "collapse," described by one man as follows: "[It was] a beautiful autumn day ... [I looked out of the window, and said,] 'No, I'm not going back again, ever again,' so I just sat down; it was all empty, everything was empty ... all the energy flowed out of me" (Eriksson et al., 2008, p. 628). Participants in this study had been on sick leave between 1 and 35 months; some doubted that they could ever return to work.

Obviously, burnout is a serious concern, not only because of its health consequences, but also because it may mean the tragic loss of a highly skilled nurse. I recall the fantastic group of nurses who cared for my stepdaughter during her treatment for Hodgkin disease in 1999. Emma had every complication of treatment that you can imagine, including massive infections and septic shock. She almost died. Fortunately, she had superb nursing care. Daily, I watched David, Karen, Wilma, and all the others as they worked their 12-hour shifts, shouldering enormous responsibility with grace and humor. I watched them as they helped Emma don her prom dress and wig. With their own money, they had bought accessories for her to wear to the prom. They shared our family's joy that Emma could leave the hospital to attend the prom (albeit with a perforated bowel, undiagnosed at the time!). They were with us through all the ups and downs of that terrifying time. I have never been so proud of my professional colleagues. I shudder at the thought that nurses like David, Karen, and Wilma may be lost to burnout someday.

What starts the process of burning out? I have a colleague who believes that burnout is *not* likely to occur in those nurses who have *never* been "on fire," and I think the literature proves her right. The syndrome tends to afflict highly idealistic professionals who begin their careers "on fire" with the desire to provide compassionate help to others. These individuals become overly involved in their work and overly burdened by the needs of their patients. Eventually, they begin to doubt their competence, because they can't keep up with the demands. The metaphor of being "engulfed like fire" is alluded to by one nurse who is burning out: "I hate coming to work because I feel once I'm here it engulfs me like fire" (Larson, 1987). It makes sense that nurses who feel this way might begin to emotionally distance themselves from patients as a survival tactic. Unfortunately, they feel even worse for doing so, blaming themselves for not being able to enact their idealized image of the "good nurse" (Larson, 1987).

Cary Cherniss (1995) conducted a valuable study of teachers, lawyers, therapists, and public health nurses, documenting their loss of idealism in the first year of practice. All had approached their work with unrealistic expectations of themselves and their clients. When confronted with uninterested students and noncompliant clients, they felt ineffective and blamed themselves for failure to accomplish what they had set out to do. For example, public health nurse Sarah Prentiss was distressed when an older woman told her, "I don't know why you're bothering with me. I just want to die" (Cherniss, 1995, p. 19). Sarah took this client's statement personally, asking herself, "Gee, what's wrong with me? . . . I might have done something wrong. Maybe I just turned her off. Maybe it was just a personality conflict. But I didn't see it, and that's the thing that bothered me—that I didn't have enough insight to see the problem" (Cherniss, 1995, pp. 19–20). Sarah did not consider that her client was weary of illness and poverty. Nor did she acknowledge that even the most seasoned, highly skilled professionals are unable to motivate some clients to change their attitudes and behaviors. Sarah eventually left public health nursing.

Sarah is one of those nurses who show up in turnover statistics. Leaving is the most commonly selected solution: leaving the problems, leaving the agency, or leaving the profession. But some who burn out do not leave. You can find them in every health care workplace, disillusioned and disengaged, but sticking around because they see no alternative. Some don't know where else to go, or whether they can handle the stress of job-hunting or going back to school. The barriers to leaving are undeniable for many: They and their families cannot do without the income, and even a temporary disruption in salary would be disastrous to their financial status. For public health nurse Jessica Andrews, staying in her job was mainly a matter of economics:

Unfortunately, my divorce was final in June. That's another reason I'm staying at the health department and doing what I'm doing. . . . I need the insurance, I need the pay. . . . I don't want to go through the risks of setting up my own business right now. I want Blue Cross, and I want orthodontic care and eyeglass care and all that. And you can't do that privately. (Cherniss, 1995, p. 60)

Where does anger come into the burnout picture? Correlational studies show that burnout is linked to conflict and anger, but cannot tell us if anger leads to burnout or is a by-product of it. In a study of 297 hospital nurses, researchers found that those with high burnout scores reported the greatest amount of conflict with other nurses and supervisors (Hillhouse & Adler, 1997). Another study showed that anger directed at the *self* was more strongly correlated with burnout than anger directed outward toward others (Firth, McKeown, McIntee, & Britton, 1987). Both outwardly and inwardly directed anger were common in the Swedish participants interviewed by Eriksson and colleagues (2008). For example, one man recalled losing his temper and insulting people. Several women seemed consumed by rage, as exemplified by this woman's words: "I came to work and then went home; was angry and slept; ate, slept, and shouted; was angry and wept—all the time" (p. 627).

I suspect that frequent job-related anger *predisposes* an individual to burnout. Take the case of the perfectionist. Fran Erwin, one of our study participants, is a good example. Fran told us, "Performance equals approval, performance equals worth." It makes sense that if a nurse like Fran approaches her work with a high degree of perfectionism, a lot of anger is going to be generated—at others for making errors and at oneself for failure to achieve perfection. If the anger often erupts in confrontational interactions with others, it can drive away that nurse's potential sources of support. Even if it is not verbally expressed, sitting on a lot of anger certainly has the potential to sour one's attitude toward the job.

Burned-out RNs do the bare minimum. Understandably, higher burnout in nurses is linked to lower patient satisfaction (Leiter, Harvie, & Frizzell, 1998). During this era of declining satisfaction with the quality of nursing care (see Chapter 6), it behooves the profession to devote greater attention to burnout prevention. Astute managers should counsel employees when early signs of decreased performance and/or escalating sick days are observed. And all of us should reflect, from time to time, about the level of enthusiasm we feel for our work.

Self-Assessment

Are you on the path to burnout? Before you deflagrate, take a few minutes and respond to these questions:

1. Do you feel discouraged about work and often think about quitting?
2. Do you feel irritable and angry on the job?
3. Have you noticed more difficulty getting along with your coworkers?
4. Have you lost interest in the patients? (If you teach, substitute "students.")
5. Have you felt fatigued during the workday?
6. Have you missed work lately due to colds, flu, dyspepsia, or other minor illnesses?

If you answered "yes," to several of these questions, you probably do need to rekindle your flame. Read on for some burnout remedies.

Steps Toward Healing

- *Relinquish perfectionism.* In Cherniss's (1995) study, those professionals who were least likely to recover from burnout were those who set unrealistic goals for themselves. Adjust your expectations for yourself—and for the others you work with. We all have limitations and vulnerabilities. We all make errors: They are excellent learning experiences.
- *Take action to address problems in the work environment* instead of leaving your unit for greener pastures. Research shows that workers who take action report less burnout than workers who respond passively (Maslach & Leiter, 1999). Nurses need to know how to negotiate and "work the system." However, few of us learned how to do this in nursing school. Negotiating skills can be learned in continuing education courses and practiced in workshops. Recruit some colleagues to join you, make a plan, then act. Use the American Nurses Association's (ANA) *Bill of Rights for Registered Nurses* and the *Code of Ethics for Nurses* (available from www.nursingworld.org) to bolster your case that you have the right to a work environment that is conducive to providing quality care.
- *Make a change*, either in type of job assignment or type of nursing. If your work is unsatisfying, and there is no hope of negotiating to bring

about a more satisfactory state of affairs, do consider a change. Research shows that chronic job stress brings people to a *turning point* (Wethington, 2003). The outcome of such a turning point can be positive or negative—it's up to you. Research also shows that a change in job assignments every 5 years or so is a good way to keep enthusiasm for work fresh (Pelz & Andrews, 1966). Nurse practitioner Brenda Thomas felt emotionally and physically burned out after working for years in a doctor's office. She made a big switch. Now employed in a women's prison, she finds great satisfaction in her work and intends to remain in correctional nursing until retirement ("Caring for Criminals," 2008).

■ *Take a sick leave.* If your emotional exhaustion is too severe to consider changing jobs, take a sick leave to avail yourself of treatment. You do not want to reach the state of collapse depicted earlier in the study by Eriksson and colleagues (2008). And nursing cannot afford to lose you!

■ *Focus on the intrinsic rewards of nursing again.* Think back to your motivation for entering nursing. What was it that led you to pursue such a difficult course of study? What was it that you really loved to do? How could you recapture that initial excitement?

Our energy tends to become fully available for anything to which we are highly committed, and we often feel more energetic for having done it. We tend to find little energy for anything to which we are not highly committed, and doing these things leaves us feeling 'spent,' drained, and exhausted." (Marks, 1979, p. 31)

The Anger–Depression Link

Burned out, angry nurses are not so hard to identify. Most know how they feel and readily verbalize their disillusionment with their work. But depressed nurses are not always aware that they have become depressed. Alfred Adler (1956) called depression the "silent temper tantrum." Its onset is insidious; it can sneak up on you. That is exactly what happened to a friend of mine. She didn't know she had depression. She had no idea what was wrong. Although she had always loved people, it seemed to require too much effort to get out and see them. She was intelligent and well-educated, but concentration was difficult, and she kept forgetting things. She didn't have the energy for her usual physical activities: Her swimsuit hadn't been wet in months, and her Nordic-Trac had gathered dust. One day I told her I thought she was depressed. After a thorough examination, her doctor came to the same conclusion and prescribed antidepressant medication. She's much better now.

My friend's experience is typical of many women. She learned early in life that her own needs were not important, that she was destined to give care to others. Her first thought in any situation is how to tend to the needs of those around her. When others are not happy, she assumes excessive responsibility for their unhappiness and intensifies her efforts to make things right. She takes on others' stress and worries, doing their worrying for them. Even when she is tired and would like to rest, she finds it very difficult to tell someone "no." She would feel guilty if her "no" caused disappointment. And she takes the blame for the failure of her marriage, although her former husband was a self-centered man whose unhappiness could not have been assuaged, no matter what she did to love and please him. After their divorce, she was down on herself rather than angry at him.

Not surprisingly, my friend selected a profession in which she nurtures, and also chose to specialize in maternal–child care. She has always "given at the office" and given at home, too. Not surprisingly, her role socialization, both as a woman and as a nurse, to be a selfless, ever-nurturing, mother figure placed her at greater risk for stress and depression. Some researchers speak of depressive symptoms as the "cost of caring" for women (Turner & Avison, 1989). Statistics consistently show that women's risk for depression exceeds that of men by two to one. Although female gender role socialization plays a part in increasing that risk, no single theory or set of predisposing factors provides a complete explanation of the 2:1 ratio. Depression involves biochemical change, but no one knows if the chemical changes in the brain *cause* depression or *result* from depression. Psychologist Marty Seligman (1998) says the evidence is actually stronger for cognitive causation (i.e., a style of thinking called *pessimistic explanatory style*) than for biochemical causation. Suffice it to say that the etiology of depression is complex, with genetic, environmental, and psychological factors continuing to vie for scientists' attention. We do know from research that demographic characteristics make little difference in the likelihood of becoming depressed. Depression afflicts women of all income and educational levels, and claims as its victims White, Black, and Hispanic women. Depression can occur whether a woman is married or unmarried, employed or unemployed (McGrath, Keita, Strickland, & Russo, 1990).

The Connection Between Depression and Anger

The connection between depression and anger has been probed by researchers for a long time. Commonly, it is believed that holding anger in leads to depression. You probably remember the depression-is-anger-turned-inward hypothesis from nursing school. One example of a study that supports this hypothesis was done by Bromberger and Matthews (1996). The researchers followed 460 middle-aged women for 3 years and found that introspective, passive, women who held their anger in were indeed more prone to bouts of depression. Why is this so? Here is my explanation: When anger is not expressed, injustice cannot be remedied and interpersonal conflicts cannot be resolved. The person ruminates about the issues that made her angry in the first place, prolonging and increasing the bad feelings. When a person ruminates, she is like a cow chewing a cud—chewing over and over "Why did he do that? Why didn't I say something to him? Who does he think he is?"

Women are more likely to ruminate after negative events than are men, whereas men tend to distract themselves by doing something physical, such as playing a sport (Nolen-Hoeksema, 1987).

The anger-turned-inward view of depression has been challenged. Carol Tavris, who sparked much debate with her book *Anger: The Misunderstood Emotion,* contended that, "If anything, anger is depression turned outward. Follow the trail of anger inward, and there you find the small, still voice of pain" (1989, p. 14). A woman who participated in one of our own studies told us: "Through counseling, I've learned that I handle depression through being angry. . . . I would lash out at everything and really didn't know why. . . . I had all this anger to work through and to understand."

What can be concluded from all of this? Whether depression is anger turned inward or anger is depression turned outward, *the bottom line is that anger and depression are significantly correlated.* In the Women's Anger Study, which involved more than 500 women aged 25 to 66, my research team found that depressed women definitely have higher levels of anger than women who are not depressed. And, they manage anger arousal in *both* of the unhealthy ways we have talked about so far: turning it inward and venting it outward in harsh attacks on others (Droppleman & Wilt, 1993). Research by Sperberg and Stabb (1998) corroborated the link between depression and these two nonproductive anger management styles in their sample of women aged 18 to 54. Our studies of anger in RNs suggest that nurses are *at risk* for depression because they have high levels of anger and tend to use the same two unhealthy anger management styles.

Incidence of Depression in Nurses

A new study found a sizeable 35% of female RNs to be depressed (Welsh, in press). This figure is higher than the 20% to 25% incidence of depression in community samples (McGrath et al., 1990). Correlates of depression in Welsh's sample of med-surg nurses were job-related stressors, such as inadequate staffing; stressful life events, such as taking out a loan or coping with a death in the family; and somatic symptoms, including fatigue, trouble sleeping, headaches, and musculoskeletal pain. What about depression in male RNs? I located only one study comparing levels of depressive symptomatology in female and male nurses. Its conclusion was unexpected: *Male* nurses had higher levels of depression than did females (Firth, et al., 1987). Thirty-seven percent of the men in this study were mildly or moderately depressed, as compared to 28% of the women. The incidence of depression in male nurses was significantly higher than the incidence in males in the general population, which was only 10%. This British study needs to be replicated in the United States.

Self-Assessment

Despite the knowledge you acquired about depression in nursing school, you may not be aware that you, or perhaps your colleague, have symptoms and need treatment. Depression can occur in mild, moderate, or severe forms. Although severe symptoms, such as psychomotor retardation, are likely to be noticed by family members and coworkers, more subtle manifestations, such as appetite change, may escape their notice. You yourself may not attribute your weariness and loss of interest in things to depressive illness. A simple self-assessment will help you determine if you have symptoms of clinical depression.

Have you experienced five or more of the following symptoms during the past 2 weeks?

Depressed mood most of the day
Diminished interest or pleasure in activities
Weight loss or weight gain
Insomnia or hypersomnia
Psychomotor agitation or retardation
Fatigue or loss of energy
Feelings of worthlessness or guilt
Diminished ability to think or concentrate
Thoughts of death or suicide

If you have five or more of these symptoms (at least one of which is *either* depressed mood or loss of pleasure), and you do not have hypothyroidism or other medical conditions, you may have a *major depression* (American Psychiatric Association [APA], 1994). Note that other symptoms will be evident in a person with bipolar disorder (manic-depression) or psychotic depression; these conditions will not be dealt with here.

After answering the listed questions, perhaps you were relieved to find that you do not have a *major* depression. But there is another disorder that we need to mention. Some individuals have a more chronic kind of depression: *dysthymic disorder*. The symptoms are similar to those listed above for major depression, but less severe. In fact, the symptoms are so much a part of the affected person's day-to-day experience that they usually go unreported to health care providers. People with dysthymic disorder often say, "This is just how I am," meaning that it is "normal" for them to be self-critical and unhappy. The most common symptoms of dysthymic disorder are feelings of inadequacy, generalized loss of interest or pleasure, social withdrawal, feelings of guilt about the past, irritability or anger, and decreased activity or productivity. Have you experienced depressed mood for most of the day, for more days than not, for at least 2 years? And, along with the depressed mood, have you noted symptoms such as these? If so, then you may have dysthymic disorder (APA, 1994).

While mental health professionals continue to debate the "cutoff" separating subclinical and clinical levels of depression, I believe that *even subclinical depression deserves prompt attention*. "Moderately depressed" persons may have significant problems keeping up at work (Nolen-Hoeksema, 1990), and if they manage to get through the workday, they fall into bed, exhausted, when they get home. I have, in fact, known a number of nurses who worked their shift, ate, slept, and returned to work, engaging in *no* recreation or social interaction. The quality of their lives was greatly diminished. They were depressed but did not realize it.

New research showing that depression may contribute to heart disease, stroke, and osteoporosis heightens my concern for depressed nurses who are not seeking treatment. If you are depressed, you need to see your health care provider. A visit is urgent if you are preoccupied with thoughts of death or suicide. Be aware that both medication and psychotherapy have proven effectiveness. However, I recommend psychotherapy along with the antidepressants because of the high risk of relapse—as much as 60%—with medication alone

(Antonuccio, Danton, & DeNelsky, 1995). You will feel better about yourself when you learn the principles that will help insulate you from later episodes of depression (Yapko, 1997).

Depression *can* serve an important adaptive purpose, permitting resolution of a deadlock in functioning and leading to learning and growth (Gut, 1989). Out of depression, you can emerge more psychologically whole.

Steps Toward Healing

You can begin to use a number of self-management techniques to combat depression:

- *Stop blaming and criticizing yourself* when you have not met every patient's or student's need. Instead, focus on the people you *have* helped and the things you have done *well* each day. Aaron Beck (1976) has pointed out that the failures of those who are depressed are no more severe than the failures of nondepressed individuals: It is how they interpret their failures that differs. As you review your day, make sure you affirm yourself for at least *one good thing.* I try to do this while driving home from work. For example, I might say to myself, "If I hadn't been there today, that student wouldn't have had a shoulder to cry on."

When psychiatric nurse researcher Ann Peden studied recovery from depression, her study participants emphasized the importance of positive affirmations:

"I try to put a positive thought in when I start having negative ones, and I use writing affirmations and keep a lot of scrap paper. . . . I just write over and over again."

"I had some positive affirmations that I had memorized. I've got them written on index cards. I had them pasted up around the house." (Peden, 1996, p. 293)

- *Learn to tolerate ambiguity.* Psychologist Michael Yapko (1997) claims this is the most important skill for warding off depression. According to Yapko, it is in response to ambiguity that many individuals make negative interpretations that can lead to depression. In most life situations, there is no single correct answer but a variety of possibilities. As Yapko puts it, "Life is inherently ambiguous; an experiential Rorschach" (1997, p. 75).
- *Find an activity to distract yourself from rumination.* Physical activities work best because they lead to the release of endorphins that lift your mood. Walk, swim, or garden. Make yourself get off the couch and go outside. And, make yourself call a friend to join you. You need to be with people. I know it's hard, but you'll be glad you made the effort.
- *Mourn losses.* If you have experienced the loss of a valued relationship through death or divorce, you do need to mourn the loss. Your depression

is the result of mourning that was never completed. Give yourself permission to cry or rage. Let the guilt go. There is a wonderful little book that I have recommended to countless friends and clients: *How to Survive the Loss of a Love,* by Colgrove, Bloomfield, and McWilliams (1991). Buy yourself a copy. You *can* survive this loss, and you *can* have other relationships.

■ *Use your good times.* Even while depressed, there are always some times of day when you feel better. Use those times to engage in activities that you used to enjoy before you got depressed. How long has it been since you treated yourself to a luxurious bubble bath? Or bought yourself a totally frivolous gift? Build more pleasure into your life. This is a time to care for yourself with the same loving devotion you give to so many others.

■ *Use the stress and anger management strategies presented throughout this book.* For stress management, pay particular attention to Chapter 9. For anger management, see Chapter 4.

■ *Keep a journal to track your progress of recovery from depression.* Writing itself is therapeutic. Anne Frank's words are a compelling testimonial: "I can shake off everything if I write; my sorrows disappear, my courage is reborn."

Anger's Link to Physical Symptoms

Now let's turn our attention to the physical effects of angry emotion. As nurses, you already know that anger produces a powerful physiological arousal. To briefly review, the cerebral cortex signals both the adrenal medulla, which secretes adrenaline and noradrenaline, and the adrenal cortex, which secretes cortisol. The heart pounds harder and faster, blood pressure rises, respirations increase, and fat cells release fat into the bloodstream (which is converted to cholesterol unless burned up in intense exercise). The arteries carrying blood to the skin, kidneys, and intestines constrict, and the arteries to the muscles dilate. The body is primed to take action. Stevick (1971) aptly described it as a "wanting-to-burst-forth body" (p. 144). When this strong arousal is not dissipated in action of some kind, a variety of bodily discomforts can result: tense muscles, headaches, GI upsets, and just plain fatigue—that bone-tired, wiped-out feeling when you are not sure you can put one foot in front of the other to walk your tired body out to the parking lot at the end of a day's work.

Not only tension headaches, but also migraines, are connected with anger. Georgia Witkin, a psychiatry professor, presented case material of a patient who feared her own angry impulses and suppressed them: "Rosemary knew that her migraine attacks always followed situations in which she was enraged, but felt that she couldn't express her anger. She claimed that she had had years of 'nonassertiveness training,' and feared that showing her anger would destroy her image as the patient wife and mother" (Witkin, 1991, p. 57). Research supports Dr. Witkin's clinical material. In an interesting study comparing the reactions of female migraine patients and women without migraines in an anger-provoking situation, researchers found that the migraine patients tended to suppress their anger. Expressive behaviors, such as facial expressions, pounding the table, and verbal expressions, occurred more often in the women without migraines (Grothgar & Scholz, 1987).

Research in the field of psychoneuroimmunology (PNI) shows that anger even affects the functioning of the immune system (Kiecolt-Glaser et al., 1993; Larson, Ader, & Moynihan, 2001). Scientists studying PNI have identified 60 to 100 biochemical messengers (neurotransmitters, neuropeptides, growth factors, and lymphokines) that link emotional states with the immune system. The autonomic nervous system directly talks to lymphocytes and macrophages. Neuropeptide receptors are found throughout the body. Therefore, emotions are not contained in the mind or brain, but are "out there" throughout the body as well (Pert, 2002). Researchers are examining anger's connection to natural killer cell activity, T lymphocytes, and cytokines that elicit antibody activity (e.g., Larson et al., 2001; Miller, Dop, Myers, Stevens, & Fahey, 1999). One study documented significant inhibition of salivary IgA (the first line of defense against pathogens in the upper respiratory tract, GI system, and urinary tract) for 5 hours after experiencing anger (Rein, Atkinson, & McCraty, 1995). Another study found that the common cold was linked to increased anger and tension during a 4-day period prior to the onset of symptoms (Evans & Edgerton, 1991). It appears that the subjects' emotional state lowered their resistance to the cold virus.

Somatic Metaphor

Inhibiting angry feelings is hard work (as we shall discuss further in Chapter 4). Holding in such feelings places stress on the body (Pennebaker, 1992). Some of our study participants understood the connection between suppressed anger and their physical symptoms. In fact, the particular symptom often aptly *expressed* their feelings. In the literature, this is referred to as *somatic metaphor* (Broom, 2002). One's body is saying something about the events being experienced. A nurse who told us she "had the experience as a nurse of being voiceless, of having no voice" realized that she often developed a sore throat when she became very angry about work-related matters over which she felt she had no control. Another woman (not a nurse) displayed remarkable insight in the following narrative:

> I very much believe in the mind/body connection. . . . I can think of specific examples . . . when something was happening that I just couldn't stand and then that's the way I'd express it—I had lower back pain and I couldn't stand up straight. Then there was another time when I wanted to tell someone something that bothered me, and I just couldn't bring myself to do it. I got laryngitis and couldn't talk. Then . . . there was some project [my husband] wanted to just bulldoze through. I like to do projects, but I'm kind of meticulous. I take my time and do it slowly. . . . He was pushing us through . . . and my neck started hurting. It's a "pain in the neck," you know.

Self-Assessment

Tuning in to your own bodily sensations of anger is important. In times of stress and anger, most of us have a particular organ or system that seems to get the brunt of it. Take a few minutes to think about your most common somatic symptoms. Do you get a severe headache? Do you get a knotted feeling in the stomach? Do you become constipated? Do your neck and shoulders tighten? What incidents or interactions trigger these symptoms?

Muscle tension is an excellent indicator that your stress level is escalating. Holistic nurse Leslie Kolkmeier recommends a simple technique called *body scanning* that you can use to assess muscle tension:

> *It has been estimated that we spend 40 minutes a day, or at least 2 years of our lives, waiting. We can choose to spend this time simply waiting (and probably growing impatient, thus adding to our tension burden), or we can use it to scan our bodies for muscle tension. Body scanning is taking a moment to inventory all parts of the body mentally and identify areas that are full of tension. (Kolkmeier, 1995, p. 584)*

Once the tense areas are identified, a relaxation procedure can be used. You can do this during the workday when the person at the other end of the telephone line has placed you "on hold" (surely one of life's most annoying delays for a busy professional person!), when you are standing at the elevator waiting (why is the one *you're* standing by always the slowest in the building?), and anytime you have a free minute or two. When this practice becomes part of your daily routine, the buildup of extreme tension can be avoided.

Steps Toward Healing

- *Value the feedback your body is giving you.* The wisdom of the body was greatly respected by our ancestors, who listened more closely to its cues. We tend to consider bodily aches and pains as mere annoyances that must be banished with chemicals—instantly, if possible. But symptoms have a communicative function. Listen to what they are saying to you.
- *After a careful analysis, take action on the body's message.* Tailor the remedy to the particular symptom. If possible, choose a nonpharmacological approach. Here is a great example:

> *2.1. Several years ago, I realized that I had developed a pattern of splitting headaches in conflict situations in which no kind of resolution occurred. These situations most often happened at work. A favorite expression became: "I am so mad I could spit." After one such expostulation, my husband said, "Why don't you? Maybe you will feel better!" Suddenly, I realized that I probably needed to spit out (express) my anger in more productive ways. My strategy for handling anger was a form of self-punishment. I muttered, I simmered, I fumed, and took no purposive action. I eventually faced up to the fact that a psychophysiological response to anger was a very human response—even for a psychiatric/mental health nurse—and had to be dealt with through some kind of intervention. My preference was to use an intervention that was nonpharmacological. My quest took me on a number of discovery experiences until I found one that is effective for me. It has two phases.*

Phase 1. Redirecting Feelings

The first phase is to make myself recognize my anger. This consists of using verbal and body cues that an interaction has aroused anger. At this point, I suggest that those of us involved in the interaction take responsibility for what is happening. Acknowledgment of feelings at this point can open the door to identifying what is preventing movement toward some kind of resolution. I state my position as tactfully as possible and listen to that of others. If communication can be established that acknowledges feelings and areas of conflict, there is a good possibility that interactions will have a successful conclusion. For me, this Phase 1 intervention has been successful in reducing my anger-provoked headaches and making conflictual interactions more collegial and resolvable. But when my Phase 1 intervention does not work, I go to Phase 2.

Phase 2. Mind and Body Engagement

I think of Phase 2 as "using my head for something besides a headache." But before I describe my intervention, I need to digress a moment to explain a situation that was quite significant in helping me to develop it. Bear with me please.

Our home is on a tidal inlet that connects to the ocean. Oysters, clams, and scallops (mollusks) are plentiful, and I have sat many hours watching them survive through the cycles of tides. Mollusks have powerful muscles for attachment, protection, and feeding purposes. Only for an hour before and after the tide changes—ebb tide—can they relax their muscles to move around without being at the mercy of the tidal pulls. The message to me was that I needed to create a situation when I had a headache that would allow me to relax and free myself from the pulls of interactions and demands made by others.

This is what I do.

When my Phase I intervention is not working—when it becomes apparent that there is no intent by participants to reach a resolution—I accept that . . . temporarily. Next, I find a solitary place. I lie down, put on a Mozart sonata at very low volume, and begin the process of freeing my mind of the persons and circumstances involved in the anger-producing situation. I relax my body and my mind to become like a mollusk—free to give up old ways of doing and thinking and to explore. In my mind, this freeing-up process is analogous to their being free from the tidal forces that push them hither, thither, and yon, giving them the freedom to move themselves, find a new attachment, or find new food sources. So, I visualize myself as a mollusk to get this state of nirvana, becoming freer and freer of concerns. As I do this, I usually drift into a light slumber for 10 to 15 minutes. When I suddenly awake, I find myself feeling different, free from burden, my headache gone. Now I can think at a lower level of emotionality about the anger-producing situation and consider some new ways of handling it. I go on to identify what to do next and do it!

Well, my strategy works for me. I rarely get headaches any more. And unlike mollusks, which become easy prey to harvesters at ebb tide, I haven't been caught and ended up in a stew—yet!"

—*Contributed for this book by Dixie Koldjeski, RN, FAAN*

Anger's Link to Hypertension and Coronary Heart Disease

We turn now to the cardiovascular sequelae of anger. Although space doesn't permit an exhaustive review of the research, I will provide a glimpse of the linkages that have been demonstrated between anger and various cardiovascular consequences. We'll begin with blood pressure. Anger causes the largest blood pressure increase of any other emotion or mood state, even more than fear (G. Schwartz, Weinberger, & Singer, 1981; J. Schwartz, Warren, & Pickering, 1994). Now that researchers have the capability of using ambulatory blood pressure monitoring, a number of studies have examined workplace anger. Both systolic and diastolic blood pressures are strongly related to angry thoughts and behaviors at work (Durel, et al., 1989). Given nurses' reports that their workplaces are rife with hostilities (A. Brooks, et al., 1996; Smith, Droppleman, & Thomas., 1996), it is likely that their blood pressures become elevated many times during a shift. Some nurses we interviewed were acutely aware of this. Greg James, when describing an angry incident to our research team, reported, "My blood pressure went to 200. I could feel my hands shaking. I could feel my heart speeding up and my face getting red."

Blood pressure increases are particularly notable during interpersonal conflicts. In one study, blood pressure rose considerably during a discussion of marital problems, attaining a mean of 160/100 mm Hg (Ewart, Taylor, Kraemer, & Agras, 1991). After an angry interaction, it takes quite a while for the pressure to return to normal—as long as 25 minutes in one study (Engebretson, Matthews, & Scheier, 1989). Logically, if you suppress the anger, the physiological arousal will last longer than if you take some action to discharge it. What do most of us do when we get angry at work? We suppress it. Over and over, day after day. Eventually, we could develop hypertension. Prospective studies (e.g., Perini, Muller, & Buhler, 1991) show that suppressed anger accelerates early development of hypertension, although other factors (such as family history of hypertension) are involved as well. This is a good time to point out that no claim is being made here that anger is the *sole* etiologic agent of the diseases we are focusing on. However, growing recognition suggests that all disease is *multifactorial* in origin, resulting from a combination of genetic, environmental, and behavioral–emotional factors.

Some of the factors involved in development of high blood pressure (such as hereditary predisposition) cannot be modified, but angry thoughts and behaviors *can* be! One of the basic premises of this book is that emotional habits are *learned*, and therefore they can be *changed*.

Steps Toward Healing

▪ *Make an assertive response to anger provocation.* In a study done by Kathleen Lawler, blood pressures were monitored while the subjects recalled and described an angry incident. Study participants who made assertive responses significantly decreased their diastolic blood pressure (Anderson & Lawler, 1994). See Chapter 10 for tips on assertiveness.

■ *If you can't make an assertive response, find a confidante and get those angry feelings off your chest.* Choose wisely, however. You want someone who will simply listen, *not* offer you advice or fuel more anger by making inflammatory comments (such as "How dare him!" or "I can't believe the audacity!"). Regularly discussing your anger in this way (rather than suppressing it) is associated with lower blood pressure and better health (Thomas, 1997a; 1997b).

■ *Physically discharge your anger.* If you can't do either of the first two, at least discharge the anger through physical activity. Run, jog, hit a tennis ball. You can combine imagery with any of these. For example, as you run, imagine yourself out-running the anger, leaving it far behind. As you play tennis, envision a good swat at the person who provoked your anger each time you smash that tennis ball across the net. It's very therapeutic! You can even use household chores to dissipate the anger that built up all day at work. As you empty the garbage, empty your psyche of the workday garbage as well. As you floss your teeth, engage in mental flossing. Regardless of what happened on the job, it won't do you any good to hold onto that anger all evening. And you need some R&R before you go back to the salt mines tomorrow!

■ *Learn a calming technique that you can regularly employ to let the anger go.* See Chapter 4 for specific instructions for the Relaxation Response (Benson, 1993), deep abdominal breathing, and progressive muscle relaxation. See Chapter 9 for instructions regarding meditation.

Coronary Heart Disease

Now let's take a look at coronary heart disease. The biological mechanisms by which anger may increase the risk of coronary heart disease (CHD) include discharge of catecholamines, increased myocardial oxygen demand, coronary artery vasospasm, and increased platelet aggregability. Pioneering cardiologists Friedman and Rosenman (1974) observed how easily their cardiac patients were provoked to anger. Subsequently, research evidence of a link between anger and CHD was provided by longitudinal studies, in which initially healthy individuals were enrolled and then followed over a number of years, so that researchers could ascertain which predictors proved to be significant in the development of heart disease. The research findings with regard to anger are somewhat different for men and women. We'll start with men.

The Western Collaborative Group Study was the first big study of coronary-prone behavior—dubbed the "type A personality" by Friedman and Rosenman. The all-male sample included more than 3,000 subjects. After 8.5 years, type A men were twice as likely to have symptoms of heart disease as type B men. Furthermore, the angry, competitive type A pattern of behavior increased cardiac risk *independently* of other known risk factors, such as elevated cholesterol, smoking, and high blood pressure. Of the men who died of CHD during the longitudinal study, 88% were type A (Rosenman, et al., 1975). A rash of media publicity followed the publication of these findings. Everyone was talking about type A for awhile. But you may not have kept up with the subsequent research literature (unless you're a specialist in cardiac care). Over the years, this line of research has taken some interesting twists and turns. To make a long story short, some of the original components of the type A pattern turned out to be unrelated to heart disease. *But anger and hostility proved to be key elements.*

Hostility is not the same thing as anger; it's a cynical, distrustful mind-set with which hostile individuals approach the world. In popular parlance, we might speak of a perpetual "chip on the shoulder." How does hostility relate to anger? Hostile people are highly reactive to events that would not threaten or rile the ordinary person, frequently exploding in outbursts of anger. For example, a hostile person goes ballistic when another driver butts ahead in traffic or a coworker is inefficient or clumsy. Although these things are annoying to most of us, the reaction of a hostile person is extreme. During the course of a typical day, hostile individuals have more tense, angry, and confrontational interactions with other people than nonhostile individuals do (Brondolo, Rieppi, Erickson, Sloan, & Bagiella, 2002). In hostile men, anger causes dangerous increases not only in blood pressure but also in stress hormones and testosterone. Hostile behavior is a consistent predictor of CHD in men, above and beyond traditional risk factors such as smoking, alcohol consumption, and visceral obesity (Bunde & Suls, 2006; Hecker, Chesney, Black, & Frautschi, 1989; Niaura et al., 2002). And for these men, expressing the anger *outwardly* in a volatile manner is more strongly associated with cardiovascular hyperresponsivity than having the angry feelings but holding them inside (Suarez & Williams, 1989; Suarez & Williams, 1990; Suarez, Williams, Kuhn, & Schanberg, 1990). In the Normative Aging Study, individuals who had CHD at 7-year follow-up were those who had admitted back in 1986 that they were hot-headed and sometimes felt like swearing, fighting, or smashing things (Kawachi, Sparrow, Spiro, Vokonas, & Weiss, 1996). In contrast, another longitudinal study showed that men with *moderate* anger expression were *less* likely to have had a myocardial infarction (MI) or stroke at 10-year follow-up (Eng, Fitzmaurice, Kubzansky, Rimm, & Kawachi, 2003).

Both hostility and the tendency to have volatile anger outbursts are correlated with atherosclerosis. When we are angry, adrenaline stimulates fat cells, which empty into the bloodstream. If the fat isn't burned, the liver converts it into more cholesterol, which collects in the blood vessels. Over time, the cholesterol forms plaque. Research shows that people with high levels of hostility have more severe blockages of their coronary and carotid arteries due to atherosclerotic plaque and more CHD (Pollitt, Daniel, Kaufmann, Lynch, Salonen, & Kaplan, 2005; Williams, Haney, Lee, Blumenthal, & Whalen, 1980). Hostility is also associated with coronary artery calcification, which is a marker of subclinical atherosclerosis. The CARDIA study, a longitudinal study begun in the mid-1980s, indicates that high levels of hostility in 18- to 30-year-olds more than double the risk of calcification in the coronary arteries 10 years later (Iribarren, et al., 2000).

Overt anger expression (e.g., yelling, tantrums) was the critical determinant of coronary artery stenosis severity in a study by Siegman, Dembroski, and Ringel (1987). In cardiac patients whose arteries are already narrowed by plaque, anger causes the vessels to constrict (Boltwood, Taylor, Burke, Grogin, & Giacomini, 1993), reducing left ventricular ejection fraction (Ironson, et al., 1992) and producing myocardial ischemia in daily life (Gabbay et al., 1996) and even acute MI (Mittleman, et al., 1995). And the story's not over: Hostility even undermines the benefits of angioplasty, as shown in a study in Baltimore. The risk of restenosis was more than doubled in those patients who scored high on hostility (Goodman, Quigley, Moran, Meilman, & Sherman, 1996).

Although there *are* hostile women who are at risk for heart disease just like their male counterparts, studies consistently show that hostile, aggressive behavior is more prevalent in men (e.g., Vella, Kamarck, & Shiffman, 2008). This gender difference makes sense to me, because the disease-prone behavior we've been talking about is merely a more extreme version of the competitive macho response style that is inculcated in many males from a very early age. Which brings us to the socially approved behavior for the female gender: being "nice" and keeping a lid on anger. Some women have learned "niceness" so well that they deny ever having angry feelings!

Suppressing and denying anger have deleterious consequences, however. One interesting line of research looks at cardiovascular reactivity when individuals are placed in anger-producing situations. Reactivity is important because it is considered a predictor of CHD risk. Cardiovascular reactivity experiments commonly employ criticism of the subjects' performance on challenging laboratory tasks. The experimenter may say things like "You're still too slow" or "You're obviously not good at doing this, try harder." In one such study of women, the resultant anger was measured, as well as *denial* of the anger. Subjects scoring high on denial of anger were *highly reactive*, as indicated by their blood pressures and heart rates (Emerson & Harrison, 1990).

In the well-known Framingham Heart Study, a prospective study of heart disease risk factors, not showing or discussing anger predicted increased incidence of CHD (Haynes, Feinleib, & Kannel, 1980). I'm sure it doesn't surprise you that the Framingham data also showed that women in the human service professions stifle a lot of their anger. Nurses, teachers, and librarians were less likely to show overt anger than housewives or men (Haynes & Feinleib, 1980). Another study, which enrolled initially healthy women in Sweden, found that suppression of anger predicted MI at 12-year follow-up (Hallstrom, Lapidum, Bengtsson, et al., 1986). In the Tecumseh study, an American study spanning 17 years, women who suppressed their anger were twice as likely to die of cardiovascular disease (and other causes) (Harburg, Julius, Kaciroti, Gleiberman, & Schork, 2003). In another study, researcher Lynda Powell tracked a group of women who had already had one heart attack for 8 to 10 years to ascertain predictors of subsequent death. The strongest predictor was suppression of emotion (Powell, et al., 1993). Unfortunately, research on heart disease in women is much less abundant than that involving men. See Merjonen, Pulkki-Raback, and Keltikangas-Jarvinen (2007) for further information about studies of anger and cardiovascular health.

To summarize the scientific information in this section of the chapter: Neither scathing attacks nor silent seething promotes healthy hearts. And, going around with a negative, hostile outlook or perpetual chip on the shoulder is particularly risky!

Steps Toward Healing

Coronary-prone behavior *can* be modified, as shown by the success of intervention programs such as the San Francisco Life-Style Heart Trial (Scherwitz

& Rugulies, 1992) and the Recurrent Coronary Prevention Project (Powell & Thoreson, 1987). Compared to those receiving standard medical care, post-MI patients receiving hostility control training achieve significant reductions in both hospital days and medical costs in the months following the training (Davidson, 2000). But don't wait until you have an MI to start curbing hostility and bad anger habits. Here are some pointers:

- *Work toward greater tolerance, empathy, and compassion* for other people, if you have tendencies toward cynical or hostile thoughts. Most of the people in this world are simply doing the best they can, given their particular life circumstances and coping abilities. Why get bent out of shape when others do not conform to *your* ideas of efficiency or perfection? Why assume that you know better than they how they should work, vote, drive, dress, and manage their finances? What would it be like to walk a mile in their moccasins?

- *Learn not to "bite at every hook,"* if you have a tendency to become easily aroused to anger from diverse provocations. Participants in the Recurrent Coronary Prevention Project were taught to imagine themselves as fish (Powell & Thoreson, 1987). Try this imagery yourself: As you swim along each day, numerous "hooks" appear. There are always going to be rude salesclerks and inconsiderate drivers. In the work world of nurses, there are always going to be irascible and demanding patients. But you have a choice of whether or not to "bite" at these daily "hooks."

- *Turn down the volume when you express anger verbally.* Researcher Aron Siegman and his colleagues conducted experiments in which the subjects talked about anger-arousing events in three different ways: "fast and loud," "slow and soft," or "normally." The researchers found that the highest heart rate and blood pressures occurred when subjects spoke "fast and loud" (Siegman, Anderson, & Berger, 1990). Bolstering my case that new anger habits can be learned, Siegman trained people to talk slowly and softly when angry (Siegman & Boyle, 1992). The results were quite positive: There was a reduction in the anger itself, and in all of the elevated cardiovascular measurements.

- *Try the Freeze-Frame technique* used at the Institute of HeartMath in California to disengage from strong emotional reactions to a situation. The five-step self-management technique involves recognizing your feeling and then shifting the focus away from the disturbed emotion to the physical area around your heart. Then recall a positive emotion such as love or appreciation for someone or something. Feel this feeling. Then, using your intuition, ask your heart what a better response to the situation would be and listen to what your heart says in answer to the question. Research shows that individuals trained in this technique can use it in real-life stressful situations in the workplace. A transition occurs in heart rate variability waveforms from a noisy wave of large amplitude to a harmonic wave of similar amplitude and then to a smaller-amplitude wave (Tiller, McCraty, & Atkinson, 1996).

- *Meditate.* A 58-year-old heart patient decided to follow cardiologist Dean Ornish's rigorous low-fat diet and exercise regimen, which actually reverses arterial clogging (Ornish, 1990). However, he could not make such radical changes in his lifestyle in one fell swoop. So, he called Ornish and asked him to recommend the single most important component in the treatment regimen. Dr. Ornish's reply? "Meditate." Give it a try (see Chapter 9 for details).

Anger's Link to Addictions

My colleagues who work in substance abuse treatment are well aware of anger's link to addictions. There is even an acronym—HALT—used by Alcoholics Anonymous to remind its members that they are especially vulnerable to craving a drink when they are *H*ungry, *A*ngry, *L*onely, or *T*ired. Many of us can identify with this acronym because we, too, want something to make such feelings go away. Every one of us chooses something to numb our discomfort—perhaps mindless TV watching, compulsive eating, or a shopping spree; the addict chooses chemicals. Schaub and Schaub (1997) point out that the early stage of addiction is marked by acceptance of chemicals as a way to change "unsafe feelings." The type of chemical chosen has something to do with the specific feelings the person is trying to assuage. Obviously, sedatives appeal more so to the person who is anxious or rageful, whereas stimulants are attractive to someone who is depressed or shy. In opiate addicts, the most striking emotional pattern is their lifelong difficulty handling anger and rage; with opiates, they finally feel normal and relaxed (Khantzian, cited in Goleman, 1995). In a study of female marijuana users, smoking increased on days when the women experienced anger (Babor, Lex, Mendelson, & Mello, 1984). A nurse in our study who turned to alcohol to numb her rage and anger related: "I can remember as a new grad coming home, and I needed a couple of stiff drinks every night. You kill yourself all day, and then you numb out at night. I could not allow myself to look at the rage and look at the anger."

How Nurses Become Addicted

Although an occasional use of a chemical remedy to soothe your emotional pain is not problematic, habitual reliance on a drink or a pill becomes cause for concern. When nurse researcher Sally Hutchinson studied the process through which nurses became dependent on drugs and/or alcohol, the nurses described both physical and psychological pain. Living itself was painful for them, and they sought to obliterate their pain with chemicals. They used a variety of drugs until they found their drug of choice, the one that "made those horrible feelings go away" or provided "temporary amnesia" (Hutchinson, 1986, p. 198). They justified use of the drug or alcohol to alleviate the pain and help them survive the day. Hutchinson's research documents a tragic trajectory toward self-annihilation. As drug use increased, the nurses withdrew from family and friends. Later on, physical addiction became dominant, and normal life became impossible. The nurses took patient medication for their own use, even using while they were on duty. Suicidal ideation and attempts were extremely common. Hutchinson comments: "Ironically, the nurses' attempts at self-care backfired, ultimately bringing more pain than ever" (p. 200).

> Nurses are an at-risk group for chemical dependency because they have such easy access to powerful mood-altering drugs, and they are accustomed to thinking of drugs to relieve pain.

The facts and figures about the drug problem in our profession are quite disturbing. The incidence of chemical dependency is 50% higher in nurses than in the general population (Kabb, 1984). According to the American Nurses Association (ANA), 8% to 10% of nurses have serious problems with drugs or alcohol, and the number may be even higher than that. In fact, Trinkoff and Storr's (1998) national survey of more than 4,000 nurses showed that almost one-third of nurses reported smoking, binge-drinking, using illicit drugs, or using prescription drugs nonmedically (i.e., on their own) within the last year. Nurses in one recent study defended their use of substances to deal with the stress of their work (Lillibridge, Cox, & Cross, 2002). They also said they needed substances to feel good about themselves. Some initially set limits on themselves, such as never taking injectable drugs, although they ended up addicted anyway. There was a frightening lack of acknowledgment that drug use on duty could harm patients, as shown in the following excerpt from the study data: "so I did go to work both stoned and usually hung over or stoned, in a bad way, but you know it didn't particularly affect my work, I don't think. I didn't feel like anybody ever suffered" (Lillibridge et al., 2002, p. 223).

Reading this study, I was struck by the nurses' assertion that *their coworkers did not notice or comment on their substance misuse.* Many of the study participants said they would have sought help sooner if a colleague had confronted them. They felt that their colleagues did not care. It is not a kindness to overlook a nurse who exhibits symptoms of addiction. Nor should nursing faculty overlook signs of drug use or problem drinking in students. Given several studies about binge drinking and the dangerous "drinking games" of college students, Durkin (2008) has urged faculty to become more vigilant. It is truly sobering that one-third of nursing students were found to be at risk for drinking problems in a study by Marion, Fuller, Johnson, Michels, and Diniz (1996). Studies show that nurse addicts often grew up in chaotic families, where they experienced victimization (Mynatt, 1996). Many had parents who were alcoholic or depressed (Mason, 1995). The rate of family alcoholism is higher for nurses than for other health care providers (Kenna & Wood, 2005). A drinking parent may have modeled drinking as a way to cope with anxiety, anger, or unpleasantness. Nurses are more likely to use substances when workplace access is greater, when their social networks contain more drug users, and when they have lower religiosity (Trinkoff, Zhou, Storr, & Soeken, 2000).

In Trinkoff and Storr's (1998) study, alcohol was the drug of choice for nurses. But other research shows that patterns of nurse drug use often vary according to age and gender. Older nurses tend to use more alcohol and prescription drugs, whereas younger nurses are more likely to use marijuana and cocaine (Tirrell, 1994). Male nurses are more likely than females to be dependent on narcotics (Mason, 1995). There are differences among nursing specialties, with oncology nurses and administrators more likely to engage in binge drinking, whereas critical care and emergency nurses are more likely to use marijuana and cocaine

(Trinkoff & Storr, 1998). Consistent with research on the general population showing that heavy use of one substance is highly correlated with the use of others (Lex, 1991), polydependence is also characteristic of many nurses (Tirrell, 1994). The chemical use of nurses tends to be solitary rather than social (Mason, 1995).

> *2.2. The story of Chuck Mann illustrates many of the dry facts and figures about RN drug use. Chuck's drug use was so secret that neither his colleagues nor his wife knew about it. He had been working double shifts for months, trying to support his wife and four kids. Says Chuck, "I was the guy you could always call at the last minute and get to come in to work the 11–7 on Saturday night." Sometimes he skimped on a patient's dose of narcotics to obtain a little relief for himself. He'd been sure that, as a nurse, he could control his drug use. But at the time he was fired from his job in a burn unit, his habit was up to about 130 to 140 mg of morphine plus six to eight oxycodone (Percodan) tablets a day (Sandroff, 1982).*

Gender Differences in Substance Misuse

Alcohol is a dangerous remedy for the emotional pain of nurses, whether male or female. But gender differences are evident. Across the globe, men are more likely than women to drink alcohol and to drink more heavily (Holmila & Raitasolo, 2005). Women progress more rapidly from the onset of drinking to problem drinking and the stages of alcoholism (Orford & Keddie, 1985). The enzyme responsible for the metabolism of alcohol in the stomach does a less thorough job in women (Frezza, et al., 1990). A shorter period of drinking produces anemia, ulcers, malnutrition, high blood pressure, and other health consequences for women, as compared to men (Ashley, et al., 1977). Women are also more vulnerable to alcohol-induced liver diseases such as cirrhosis (Kilbey & Sobeck, 1988). Another reason for special concern about female nurses is the stigma that society attaches to women's drinking, which can be a barrier to getting professional help.

It is interesting—and problematic—that no such stigma is attached to pill use by women. Women may have to hide their whiskey bottles, but they do not have to hide their tranquilizers, sedatives, and analgesics, especially when the drugs have been medically legitimated by a physician's prescription. Women are more willing than men to report psychological distress to their doctors, and many doctors expect women to need mood-altering medications. Drugs may be offered without a careful assessment of a woman's emotional state or an exploration of alternative approaches. For as long as I can remember, statistics have consistently shown that twice as many women are given prescriptions for psychotropic medications (e.g., Cafferata, Kasper, & Bernstein, 1983). Data from a National Institute on Drug Abuse survey about drug use over the life span revealed that 99% of women age 35 and over who had used tranquilizers, sedatives, or analgesics had been given prescriptions for them (Horton, 1992). And, once women receive prescriptions for psychotropic drugs, they tend to continue using them for an extended period (Cooperstock, 1978). Women are more likely than men to misuse and become addicted to prescription drugs

(Horton, 1992). Obtaining a prescription is even easier for RNs than for the general population, because a nurse can simply ask a physician with whom she works. Nurses in Hutchinson's (1986) study said that getting medication from physicians was "a piece of cake." Even if physicians begin to take a stronger stance against pharmacological remedies for women's psychological pain, many women will still *self-medicate* with one of the 500,000 over-the-counter (OTC) preparations that require no doctor's order. In a study of our own, mid-life women with higher anger symptomatology were high users of both OTCs and alcohol (Grover & Thomas, 1993). Women have a much higher probability of using OTC tranquilizers than do men (Bell, 1984). The most frequent user of OTC drugs is a White, middle-class woman (Schuckit, 1989). And of course the "average" nurse, in terms of a statistical profile, is a White, middle-class woman.

If you, or a colleague you care about, are using chemicals to "unwind" after work or "make it through a stressful time," bear in mind that you can become physically addicted *accidentally*.

It's easy to come up with excuses for substance abuse. Perhaps you tell yourself that you just need the chemicals to get through a rough time. One of the best nurses I ever knew—the epitome of the competent clinician—became an alcoholic after intensifying her drinking during a divorce. What a loss to the profession! Don't let this happen to you. Despite the denial evident in the statement of the nurse we quoted earlier, drug use *can* interfere with your delivery of safe nursing care and eventually lead to loss of your nursing license. The havoc drugs can wreak in your personal life is immeasurable. The night Chuck Mann was summarily fired by his supervisor, he walked the darkened streets of Birmingham trying to figure out the easiest way to commit suicide. He did not know how he could go home and tell his wife he'd lost his job. Finally, he dialed the number of a 24-hour crisis hotline and was convinced by the counselor to delay taking his life until morning, when he could be seen at a mental health center. Says Chuck, "Getting off drugs is the hardest thing I ever had to do" (cited in Sandroff, 1982, p. 46). But he was surprised at the support he got when he told his parents, in-laws, neighbors, and friends that he was a recovering addict. And now he counsels other nurse addicts, offering them friendship and hope. If you have a problem with chemicals, there is reason for hope for you, too. Current research demonstrates that the biochemical abnormalities associated with addiction can be reversed through *learning*. Cognitive therapy and other psychosocial interventions can and do help. But the earlier the intervention, the better the prognosis.

Self-Assessment

Do you have a problem with alcohol or drugs? You have a problem if your answer is "yes" to two or more of the following questions (taken from Fleming & Barry, 1992):

Have you felt you ought to cut down on your drinking (or drug use)?
Have people annoyed you by criticizing your drinking (or drug use)?
Have you felt bad or guilty about your drinking (or drug use)?
Have you ever had a drink (or used drugs) first thing in the morning to steady
   your nerves or get rid of a hangover (or to get the day started)?

Perhaps you are saying to yourself: "I don't have a problem, I can still say
'no' to these questions." Perhaps you may be saying, "I only drink a six-pack
daily." Did you know that this is a higher level of consumption than 85% of
all Americans? You may be headed down the road to a more serious problem.
Developing *psychological* dependency is certainly cause for concern. Here are
the early signs of psychological dependency:

Keeping a supply of the substance on hand
Becoming restless and dissatisfied when the substance is unavailable
Planning activities around use of the substance

If you recognize that you are exhibiting these symptoms of psychological
dependency, why wait until you are physically addicted to get help? As shown
in Hutchinson's research, there's no way to go but *down*.

> *2.3. A drugged existence is a pseudo-life, a living death. You are not fully alive*
> *when your emotions are deadened by chemicals. One of our study participants*
> *phrased it like this:*
>
> > *Drugs are a way of padding the cell, for not meeting it [your anger] head*
> > *on. And what I mean by padding it, they make you go to sleep, and you're*
> > *not thinking when you're asleep with drugs.*

Steps Toward Healing

▨ *Admit you have a problem and become involved in treatment.* A good place
   to begin looking for a facility may be your institution's Employee Assistance Program (EAP). No stigma is attached to seeking help from an EAP,
   and confidentiality is maintained. Detoxification will be essential, as well
   as commitment to remaining in treatment for an adequate amount to time.
   Although alternative modalities such as Outward Bound experiences, art
   therapy, and meditation are being incorporated into addiction treatment,
   most professionals still recommend involvement in a 12-step program. In
   my own clinical experience with chemically dependent patients, I have
   observed the enormous healing power of Alcoholics Anonymous (AA)
   and Narcotics Anonymous (NA). I believe the power of these programs
   is derived from their emphasis on spirituality. You must stand humbly
   before God (however you understand God) and take a personal inventory. As you complete the "first step," you will be asked to give examples
   of feelings and emotions you have tried to alter with the use of alcohol or
   other drugs. Later, you will learn how to achieve "natural highs" without
   substances.

■ *Allow others to support you.* In AA or NA you will find a community of persons who are trying to "walk their talk" just like you are. Accept the fellowship that is offered you. See if there is a Caduceus group (a group open only to health care workers) in your area. And let your nurse colleagues to support you, too. Most states now have organized programs (Peer Assistance or Impaired Nurse programs) that provide confidential, compassionate help. Canada has a program called Project Turnabout (Gaskin, 1986). Contact your state board of nursing or nurses' association for more information. Nurses' AA groups are active in many locales, and if none exists in your area, you may want to start one. Nurses in the 2002 study by Lillibridge and colleagues felt they could not relate well to generic treatment programs that focused on street drugs; they wanted to be in programs with other nurses like themselves.

■ *Do all that you can to prevent relapse.* Avoid people and places that will heighten the temptation to indulge. Find a beverage, such as club soda, that you can sip on during social events when everyone will have a glass in hand. Appropriate recognition and expression of anger and hurt will help prevent relapse. Danger signs are out-of-proportion anger, blaming, and self-pity. If you do have a relapse, forgive yourself. Realize that you have a chronic disease and, therefore, relapses are to be expected.

Recovery is a process. Take heart that thousands of recovering RNs are back on the job. For example, Florida's peer assistance program reports that 80% of their nurse clients returned to practice; less than 15% relapsed (Griffith, 1999). When you have a relapse, climb back on the wagon again. What is important is marshaling *courage* to renew your commitment to a drug-free life.

The Other Addiction: Nicotine

Let me tell you a little story about student nurses and smoking that still saddens me. I had been invited to another university to give a speech. Although I had been given clear directions regarding how to get to the university, I was not sure exactly where the nursing department was located. I drove around the pleasant, tree-lined campus, reading the names of the buildings. As I rounded a bend, I saw a crowd of young people smoking on the steps outside one particular building. In a flash it occurred to me, "This must be the nursing building!" And so it was. While some individuals already smoke prior to entering nursing school, Elkind (1988) found a trend toward increased consumption during the first year. Interestingly, the students who smoked did not experience greater stress than the nonsmokers, but they felt more anger. In a 2001 study, 24% of nursing students smoked, and half the smokers reported that they began, or resumed, smoking in the nursing program (Gorin, 2001). How sad to think of a new generation of nurses becoming hooked on cigarettes. Many of my generation were hooked (me included). Shift report often took place in a room thick with smoke. In psychiatric settings, everybody smoked—staff and patients alike. Now, clinical agencies are becoming smoke-free, but many nurses still go outside for smoke breaks when they can.

Across the globe, plenty of nurses are still puffing away: A review of 73 studies on nurses' smoking in 21 countries showed that smoking is still prevalent among both female and male nurses and, in many countries, the percentage of nurses who smoke remains higher than that for the general population (Adriaanse, Van Reek, Zandbelt, & Evers, 1991). In U.S. studies, male RNs are more likely to smoke than females, and RNs who specialize in psychiatry, gerontology, or emergency nursing have higher rates than those in other specialties (Trinkoff & Storr, 1998). Female hospital nurses are more likely to smoke than females in similar occupations, such as teaching (Ferguson & Small, 1985). Smoking is especially prevalent among hospital nurses who work rotating shifts: In one study, 43.5% of a sample of rotating shift workers smoked (Barak, et al., 1996). In the Women's Anger Study, smoking was more prevalent in unmarried women and in women who admitted to more depressive symptoms (Seabrook, 1993).

Perhaps you have never thought of smoking in connection with anger. But there is a fair amount of research showing that many people acquire the smoking habit in situations of conflict and anger (Theorell & Lind, 1973), use nicotine to regulate their moods (Hughes, 1985), and have difficulty controlling anger and tension when they try to quit smoking. A British researcher found that student nurses who experienced difficulties with staff in their early ward placements were more likely to start smoking (Spencer, 1982). Nurses interviewed by University of California Los Angeles (UCLA) nurse researcher Linda Sarna and colleagues (2005, p. 85) believed that their cigarettes were "stress-relieving devices"; one said, "It's either cigarettes or Valium, and I went for the cigarettes." Also important was the special bond among nurse smokers, who enjoyed the camaraderie of breaks outside the building with their "smoking buddies."

> *2.4. Once an individual has come to rely on nicotine to regulate moods, it's almost like an automatic reflex to reach for a cigarette when upset. A student of mine described this reflex action:*
>
>> *This has not been a good day. In the process of paying bills, I discovered that my spouse had spent $325 on car speakers. He had not discussed this with me, and this sort of expenditure is not within our budget. I was very upset and, as soon as I got off the phone with him, I immediately picked up the cigarettes. I didn't even think about it. A cigarette was my sense of solace in my time of being hurt and angry. I hate that smoking has become such an involuntary action when I'm stressed or upset.*

I became aware of smoking as a coping mechanism during my clinical practice as a psychiatric nurse. I often observed that, just as strong emotion was coming to the surface, a client would light up a cigarette. As the client vigorously puffed, she quite effectively created a "smoke screen" that camouflaged the emotion from view. And the nicotine gradually produced the relaxation that might have been achieved by talking through the angry feelings with the therapist.

Nicotine is one of the most toxic and addictive drugs known (Ray & Ksir, 1987). It causes dependence, increased tolerance, and withdrawal symptoms on cessation of use. Some people become severely depressed when they stop smoking, as noted by Christen and Cooper (1979): "At one of our clinics, a woman was overheard to say that she mourned more when she quit smoking than she did when her husband died." Clearly, quitting smoking is not an easy proposition.

Studies show that women are more resistant to quitting than men (Stoto, 1986), perhaps because they, more so than men, rely on cigarettes to deal with negative emotion (Biener, 1987). Smoking relapse is associated with anger and loneliness (Macnee, 1991), just as drinking is.

The consequences of smoking are grim. Lung cancer has now surpassed breast cancer as the leading cancer killer of women. And researchers have conclusively linked smoking to excess mortality of nurses from many other conditions besides cancer. Using data from the well-known Nurses' Health Study, which began in 1976 with 121,700 female RNs age 30 to 55, researchers compared number of deaths among never-smokers, past smokers, and current smokers, as of 2004. Smokers were more likely to have died over the years of the study, and 64% of deaths in current smokers and 27% of deaths in past smokers were attributable to smoking (Kenfield, Stampfer, Rosner, & Colditz, 2008). Despite knowing the hazards of smoking, many nurses have been unable to quit. Knowledge alone is never enough to bring about behavior change, especially when we are speaking of a physiological and psychological addiction. The good news is that it *is* possible to quit. Millions have done so successfully. I kicked the habit when I was 27 and caring for two female patients in their forties—one a nurse, the other a teacher—who were dying of lung cancer. One of them smoked until the end. It made a profound impression on me to see her remove her oxygen, sneak to the bathroom to smoke, and return to bed, gasping for breath, with ghastly cyanosis. I finished my last package of cigarettes and never bought another.

Steps Toward Healing

- *There is no "right way" to quit smoking.* You do not have to quit "cold turkey." Nor do you have to participate in an organized smoking cessation program. More than 90% of successful quitters do so on their own (Fiore et al., 1990). Explore the various approaches and choose the one that is right for you.
- *Once you have made the decision to quit, get rid of all smoking materials.* Remove ashtrays, lighters, and other smoking paraphernalia from your home. Freshen your environment by cleaning the draperies and carpets and changing furnace filters. Be aware that places where you typically smoked (e.g., the living room sofa) may induce craving even after you have thrown your smoking paraphernalia away, so you may need to devise alterations in the environment or your daily routines (Stambor, 2006).
- *Make a public commitment to your family and colleagues and ask for their support.* Perhaps you can persuade your spouse, or a friend, to quit smoking with you. Warn your support persons that you will probably be irritable and unpleasant during nicotine withdrawal.
- *If you fear weight gain, be aware that the average weight gain after smoking cessation is only 5 pounds* (U.S. Dept. of Health and Human Services, 1990a).
- *Find a substitute activity* (crunching ice, chewing gum, eating fruit, sipping fluids). When I quit smoking, I missed cigarettes the most after meals. My substitute was a cup of coffee. Treat yourself to a cup of vanilla- or hazelnut-flavored coffee (if you need to avoid caffeine, make it decaf).

■ *Don't try to quit smoking until you've learned effective ways of managing your anger and other negative emotions* (see Chapters 4 and 9). Relaxation and imagery are helpful to many people. And research shows that physical activity during smoking cessation not only improves mood but also increases the likelihood of staying smoke-free (Prochaska et al., 2008).

■ *Try alternative nicotine delivery systems.* Many people have found a nicotine patch or gum helpful in quitting smoking, although some researchers have concluded that smokers who are angry, tense, and/or depressed may need psychotherapy in addition to these products (Brody, 1994). My practitioner colleagues who prescribe medications are enthusiastic about a new medication, varenicline, that reduces nicotine craving; dosing begins a week before the selected quit date and continues for 3 months (see Tobin, 2007, for additional information).

■ *As you are probably aware, smoking and drinking often go together.* As you improve your health by kicking the smoking habit, you may want to reevaluate your alcohol consumption as well. Drinking is said to influence smoking more than smoking influences drinking. If you are at a social gathering, having a drink, you may be vulnerable when someone offers you a cigarette. Eat a piece of cheese or a cracker instead.

■ *Avail yourself of the smoking cessation resources provided by Tobacco Free Nurses*, available on the Internet at www.TobaccoFreeNurses.org. On the web site, you can even obtain the counseling and social support of Nurses QuitNet, including nurse-only chat rooms.

■ *Be heartened by the fact that quitting reduces the excess mortality rate* found by Kenfield and colleagues (2008) in the Nurses' Health Study. By quitting, you are literally adding years to your life!

Medicating Emotional Pain With Food

Although some nurses would not think of smoking or drinking, they do indulge in another kind of drug to medicate emotional pain: food. Nurses are not unique in choosing food to soothe; almost everyone does this from time to time. In fact, some say that in our stressed-out modern world, the fight-or-flight response has become "stew and chew." There is a reason why we obtain stress relief from eating. A pain-killing peptide, cholecystokinin (CCK), is released in the gut after a meal, creating a feeling of well-being (S. Hall, 1989).

2.5. Some of our study participants were keenly aware that they used food as a drug:

> *"Food is such a wonderful drug. It's so easily accessible. Nobody's ever gonna bust me for havin' a burger and fries in the car."*
> *"When I'm angry, I want to eat. Some people's stomachs close up. Mine says 'feed me, feed me.'"*
> *"Fat is really my drug of choice...I have eaten cheese, particularly, a lot...escapades with mayonnaise...when used as a drug it's just to numb my feelings."*

As with an occasional beer or margarita, an occasional food "fix" for anger or stress may not be a problem. But 100 extra calories a day results in 10 extra pounds a year, and most "mood foods" have far more than 100 calories. Once you've started munching, it is very difficult to stop. Weight can become a very "weighty" problem. Obesity in American adults increased 74% between 1991 and 2001; presently, one in three Americans is overweight (Flegal, Carroll, Ogden, & Johnson, 2002; Mokdad, Ford, Bowman, et al., 2003).

For the next few paragraphs, I want to address female nurses specifically, because women eat more in response to mood states than men do (Forster & Jefferey, 1986). And, across all age groups, women are more obese than men. I found no studies on obesity in male nurses, but a study that compared female nurses to women in the general population found a higher percentage of the nurses to be overweight (Pratt, Overfield, & Hilton, 1994).

Obese women are stigmatized in our society because they do not conform to the culturally approved lean and leggy look. Thus, the longing to be slimmer sends millions of us to weight loss programs, where we outnumber men nine to one (Bennett, 1991). And many of us become angry at ourselves for food excesses and inability to shed the pounds, which leads us back to anger again (yes, it's a vicious cycle, as shown in the research conducted by my colleagues Sheryl Russell and Barbara Shirk in 1993).

We know from the scientific literature that obesity is partly the result of genetics, but there are many other contributing factors, among them anger and hostility. Susie Orbach (1978) was one of the first authors to take a feminist stance, alleging that women's subordinate role to fathers, husbands, or bosses forced them to stuff their anger—and literally stuff their mouths full of food— rather than express anger or disagreement. Kim Chernin (1985) and Judi Hollis (1994) advanced the notion that women's need to sedate their anger with food can be traced back to the troubled relationship between mothers and daughters. Hollis, founder of the nation's first eating disorders hospital unit, explicitly linked overweight and anger in the title of her book *Fat and Furious: Women and Food Obsession."*

Whether you are female or male, you can attest from your own experience that certain fattening foods do soothe negative moods. Women tend to prefer fat–sugar combinations like chocolate, ice cream, and cake for their mood foods, whereas men like fat–protein or fat–salt mixtures such as steak, pizza, and french fries (Levey, 1994). The idea of food being used to deal with painful emotions precedes Susie Orbach by centuries. In fact, there are references in the Talmud to the connection between negative mood states and weight (Siegman, 1994). As I reviewed the literature, I came across a fascinating 1893 story of a nursing teacher at Johns Hopkins who advocated a "cure" for melancholia (depressive illness) called "stuffing"—which meant giving the patient as much food as she could eat (Steingarten, 1994)!

Research documents a link between hostility and anger with overeating and/or obesity. One study found that highly hostile individuals (whether Black or White, male or female) consumed a significantly greater number of calories per day than persons who were not very hostile. Highly hostile Black men ingested 628 more calories and Black women 490 more calories than their less hostile counterparts; hostile White men ingested 594 more calories and hostile White women 295 more calories per day (Scherwitz & Rugulies, 1992). In a study of college students, covert hostility was strongly related to compulsive eating (Kagan & Squires, 1984). In the Women's Anger Study, we found higher obesity in women who reported greater use of anger-suppression *or* anger-ventilation, which was done in an attacking, blaming way (Russell & Shirk, 1993). By now, you are quite familiar with these extremes of unhealthy anger management. Research also shows that anger contributes to relapses from diets (Grilo, Shiffman, & Wing, 1989). In the words of one of our study participants, it is easy to "fall off the wagon" and resort to food for solace when upset: "What the hell, I might as well eat. They don't like me, I didn't get the job, whatever."

Food binges are described with remarkable similarity to episodes of heavy drinking or drug use:

> *I can eat anything to excess. I can binge on carrots, I really can. If I were to eliminate all the foods that I can use for medicating myself, I guess I'd be left with garlic and leaf of rhubarb or something, mango chutney maybe.*
>
> *One dose of sugar could lead to another and another and another. It's an addiction. Maybe someday I can sit down and have a piece of chocolate and say "wasn't that good?" and that's enough, but now I'd eat it and want more.*

Do these quotes from our data sound like things that you might say? If so, it's time to consider alternatives to eating when emotionally upset. In focus groups conducted by members of our research team (Russell & Shirk, 1993), some excellent ideas were shared. Amanda shared that she has learned not to isolate herself when she is angry or hurt:

> *I have certain things I do now that I wouldn't have done before. Before I would have isolated myself. I might not have even told anybody I was upset, or what was wrong. Now I make myself tell somebody what's going on: "I'm really mad about this" or "I was so hurt when somebody said this." Just not isolate, not keep the feelings inside, let 'em out, get 'em out, just telling someone helps me, calling up a friend. . . . It's getting out of myself, not keeping feelings inside and then eating them, eating my feelings*

Here are some other recommendations to help you break the anger-food chain:

Steps Toward Healing

- *Keep a journal to document emotionally induced eating.* Analyze each anger incident and make a plan to either resolve the issue or react differently to it in the future.
- *Begin to explore ways to reduce anger arousal without resorting to food.* For example, use imagery to transport yourself to a peaceful scene where nothing can bother you. Or follow Amanda's advice to ventilate feelings to a friend.
- *Engage in a physical activity to discharge anger*: exercise, gardening, perhaps painting, pottery or other crafts—something you enjoy that is completely incompatible with eating (for example, you can't jog and eat at the same time).
- *If you must do something "oral," try crunching on raw carrots or cauliflower or sip a cool caffeine-free beverage.* Make fish your new mood food—no kidding! Research shows the positive effects of fish intake on mood (Tan-

skanen et al., 2001). And the essential fatty acids in fish have other benefits as well.

- *Become involved in a group weight loss program* in your church, workplace, or community. In addition to programs such as Weight Watchers that charge fees, many communities form competitive weight loss teams, such as Lighten Up Iowa or Lighten up Wisconsin (Norman & Mills, 2004). Camaraderie and competition lessen the feeling that your battle is a solitary one. Also, check out Internet resources that provide support and information, such as the Lean Plate Club of the *Washington Post* (www.WashingtonPost.com/leanplateclub). A useful site with tools to calculate calories in food and number of calories burned in various activities is www.CaloriesPerHour.com. The Center for Mindful Eating has downloadable newsletters and educational materials (www.tcme.org).

- *Don't try a "fad" or "miracle" weight loss plan.* Take a sensible approach. Frequent small meals work better for many dieters because you never reach a state of voracious hunger. Increase your intake of fiber, which is filling and reduces the need to eat excessive amounts of food to have that feeling of satiation.

- *Don't be dissuaded by the noisy anti-dieting movement in this country,* which proclaims that all diets fail. Certainly, the harmful effects of yo-yo dieting are well-known. But if you take a good look at emotionally motivated eating and develop healthy alternatives, some weight loss may follow, even if you have not been "on a diet." Benefits soon become apparent. Just a modest weight loss (of 15 to 30 pounds) produces beneficial changes in blood sugar, insulin, triglycerides, and HDL cholesterol (Dattilo & Kris-Etherton, 1992; Goldstein, 1991; Wing, et al., 1987).

Anger's Link to Cancer

Finally, we consider anger's link to cancer. Like so many other diseases, cancer is caused by a combination of factors, including genetic predisposition, chemical carcinogens, and human behaviors such as smoking. The emotion of anger is only one of these many factors, and we do not want to overemphasize its importance. As noted by White and colleagues (2007), some cancer types are more responsive to the endocrine and/or immune systems than are others. But empirical evidence is worthy of mention. One of the earliest prospective studies was conducted by Caroline Thomas and her associates at Johns Hopkins. In 1946, she set out to find an answer to this question: Are specific psychological patterns in youth predictive of future disease and death? Thomas gave medical students at Johns Hopkins various questionnaires and tests, such as the Rorschach (ink blot) test and, over the years when the study participants became ill or died, Thomas and her coworkers categorized the deaths. Striking psychological similarities were found among individuals with the same disease. The outstanding characteristics of the cancer group included low scores on closeness to parents, nervous tension, depression, anxiety, and anger. When compared to groups who had hypertension, heart attack, mental illness, or suicide, the cancer group had the *lowest scores of all groups* on anger, anxiety, and depression (C.B. Thomas, 1988). The meaning of these findings will become clearer as we consider other research and delve more deeply into what some researchers call the "anti-emotionality" of the cancer-prone personality.

Another prospective study, conducted in Yugoslavia, involved initial assessment of anger, depression, anxiety, and a number of other aspects of emotionality. At 10-year follow-up, the researchers had a 78% success rate in prediction of cancer incidence based on characteristics such as anti-emotionality and need for harmony. The incidence of cancer was 40 times greater among individuals who behaved in a rational, unemotional way (Grossarth-Maticek, Bastiaans, & Kanazir, 1985).

Perhaps the best known of the contemporary researchers is Lydia Temoshok, who uses the term "type C behavior pattern" to describe a set of emotional and behavioral characteristics very similar to those identified in the previous studies. She considers the core factor of the cancer-prone pattern to be nonexpression of emotion. How did she come to this conclusion? From 1978 to 1988, she studied patients with melanoma. The physicians in the melanoma clinic at the University of California, San Francisco, had asked for her help to study a syndrome of "flat" emotionality that they were observing in the melanoma patients who had the thickest tumors. She spent hours talking to these patients before she designed her formal studies, noting that these patients were incredibly nice, and focused not on their own problems but on pleasing their spouses, parents, and others in their network of relationships. They never expressed anger and only on rare occasions did they express fear or sadness (Temoshok, 1985; Temoshok & Dreher, 1992; Temoshok & Dreher, 1993).

Steven Greer and his colleagues in London conducted several studies of women with breast cancer. In Greer's first study, the only attribute that successfully distinguished between benign and malignant breast disease was the way in which women handled their emotions, particularly anger. Both "extreme suppressors" (those who had not openly shown anger more than once or twice in their lives) and "extreme expressors" (those who had frequent temper outbursts) had higher rates of diagnosed breast cancer than women with more moderate or "normal" emotional behavior. Among the cancer patients, there were more anger suppressors than exploders (Greer & Morris, 1975; Morris, Greer, Pettingale, & Watson, 1981). In a later study by Greer's team, breast cancer patients and disease-free women watched stressful videotapes while their physiological reactions were continuously monitored. Despite their public façade of emotional control, the cancer patients had greater physiological arousal than the control group of disease-free women (Watson, Pettingale, & Greer, 1984).

Research on the association of emotion repression and cancer continues, using diverse questionnaires and focusing on different cancers. Findings, understandably, are not always consistent. Whereas Fox, Harper, Hyner, and Lyle's (1994) research supported the link between emotion repression and breast cancer, new research by White and colleagues (2007) did not. However, White and colleagues reported a weak positive association between anger control and prostate cancer in men, the first study to find this association. Here is one final piece of research, looking at a different type of cancer: colorectal. Suppressed anger was identified as a characteristic of patients with colorectal cancer in a study comparing over 6,000 confirmed cancer cases with cancer-free individuals of the same age and sex. The colorectal cancer patients were found to have experienced significant childhood loss and unhappiness, and their adult personalities were consistent with the type C profile of the "nice" person who seeks to avoid conflict and keep negative emotions inside (Kune, Kune, Watson, & Bahnson, 1991).

The childhood loss and unhappiness uncovered in this study brings us to another very important point: Many persons with cancer-prone characteristics developed their tendency to keep feelings under wraps as a defense mechanism during earlier life experiences of loss, stress, and trauma. Some had abusive or alcoholic parents. So, they learned at an early age: "Don't tell anyone how you feel." What served them well as a survival strategy during childhood pain became dysfunctional—even life-threatening—in adulthood. A woman with lymphoma told of the green shoes her mother had given her, a gift symbolizing the psychological entrapment that she felt contributed to her cancer:

> *I had very few clothes as a child, usually just hand-me-downs [from my older brothers and sisters]. My mother would go off on extravagant shopping excursions, but only for herself. Then one day, she came home with something for me! It was a wonderful-looking pair of green suede shoes, with laces and everything. Unfortunately, they were the wrong size, way too small. Still, I never said a word, because I knew [that] if I told her she would just yell at me, or else take them back and not get me any others. So I wore the green shoes, even though every step felt like it was killing me. (Barasch, 1994, p. 311)*

Metaphorically, this woman had worn her green shoes until the day she got cancer. She had continually squeezed herself into emotionally cramped adult relationships, and thwarted her most creative impulses. Walking in the ill-fitting green shoes was indeed killing her. But neither this woman nor any other cancer victim should be *blamed* for bringing their disease upon themselves. According to one study, 41% of breast cancer patients did, in fact, blame themselves for developing cancer, which is unfortunate (cited in Trafford, 1997). Cancer-prone persons do not consciously choose to be the way they are, and much research remains to be done on the link between cancer and emotion. The biological explanation for the connection of emotional suppression and cancer has not been definitively established. Keith Block, medical director of a cancer institute in Chicago, proposes that habitual suppression of negative emotions such as anger results in oversecretion of opioid peptides. The brain is trying to relieve the emotional pain in the same way that it would combat physical pain. Subsequently, the excess of opioid peptides suppresses the tumor-fighting activity of natural killer cells. This immunosuppression can result in tumor development (Block, 1997).

Self-Assessment

Do you have a type C personality? Assess yourself on the following characteristics identified by Lydia Temoshok:

    Inability to express emotions like anger
    Focus on pleasing others
    Avoidance of conflict
    Appeasing, unassertive manner

Steps Toward Healing

- Embark on a journey of self-discovery through counseling, if you have characteristics of the cancer-prone personality. Take heart that even patients with diagnosed lesions have successfully changed type C behavior. Author Alice Epstein, diagnosed with inoperable cancer but currently alive and whole, has written a book about "reversing" her cancer-prone personality. All of her life, she had inhibited anger and sacrificed her own needs to please others. She once got the highest score possible on a test of nonexpression of hostility! Through therapy, she vented all the pent-up emotion: "I was able to rid myself of feelings that I had experienced over a lifetime in a matter of months and sometimes weeks" (Epstein, 1989, p. 201).

  Although Epstein's personal testimony is compelling, you may be wondering about empirical evidence. Here, we can look to the success of psychiatrist David Spiegel's group therapy, which has received national media attention (Spiegel, Bloom, Kraemer, & Gottheil, 1989). When Spiegel began his therapy group for patients with metastatic breast cancer, his main impetus was to minimize their suffering and enhance the quality of their lives. He quickly found that most of the group time was spent discussing strong negative emotions such as fear and anger that needed to be expressed. The group provided support and encouragement for the candid expression of these feelings. Expressing negative emotions liberated positive ones as well; the patients reported better mood (Spiegel & Cordova, 2001). At 10-year follow-up, Spiegel found that the women in therapy lived almost *twice* as long as those who had been assigned to a control group receiving routine medical care. Survival rates improved in direct proportion to the number of group sessions the women attended (Spiegel, et al., 1989).

- *Anger can be an antidote to feelings of helplessness and a spark plug to the immune system* if you are presently battling cancer, research shows. A study by Derogatis and his colleagues (1979) showed that women who openly expressed anger about having cancer had higher rates of survival than those who expressed little or no anger. Lydia Temoshok found that cancer patients who were able to express anger and other emotions had more cancer-killing lymphocytes at their tumor sites. Physician Steven Greer encouraged his breast cancer patients to mobilize their "fighting spirit," and at 15-year follow-up, those with fighting spirit were more likely to be alive (Greer, Morris, Pettingale, & Haybittle, 1990). Nurses who have survived cancer reported that it stimulated personal reflection and changes in their priorities (DeMarco, Picard, & Agretelis, 2004). Low, Bower, Kwan, and Seldon (2008) pointed out that cancer could be a catalyst for the development of active coping resources, which could then be mobilized for response to other stressful life events and for pursuing new paths and priorities.

A Last Word

We have only touched on *some* of the many health conditions in which mismanaged anger is implicated. If I were writing an exhaustive review of the literature,

I would go on to tell you about the research evidence that links anger to chronic pain, rheumatoid arthritis, and many other conditions. But my purpose in writing this book is not to cover the waterfront with regard to *all* the factual information out there. In fact, the literature is burgeoning so rapidly that I can hardly keep up with it. Each new study reinforces my conviction that we must learn—and teach our patients—better ways to manage anger. I hope I have heightened your awareness that what you do with your anger can have important consequences for your health. In the following chapters, you will find many additional strategies for curbing the anger that is making you sick and undermining your *joie de vivre*.

3

Differentiating Between Rational and Irrational Anger

The mind is its own place, and in itself can make a heaven of Hell, a Hell of heaven.

—John Milton, *Paradise Lost*

In this chapter, we differentiate between anger that is *rational* and anger that is *irrational*.

Rational anger is a gift that provides momentum for action:

- To advocate for patients
- To free yourself from unhealthy relationships or jobs
- To work for social justice and enlightened public policy

Irrational anger is:

- Negative and nonproductive
- Fueled by faulty thinking
- Defused by cognitive restructuring techniques

Much of nurses' anger is quite rational. Their emotional response to disrespectful treatment, blaming, and scapegoating is understandable. As you were reading the stories in Chapter 1, I'm sure you could feel your own anger rising in empathic resonance with your colleagues. But not all of nurses' anger is rational. As we interviewed RNs, we heard a lot of "oughts" and "shoulds" indicating unrealistic expectations of patients, management, and themselves. Before you can manage anger effectively, you must learn to differentiate between that which is rational and that which is irrational. To borrow a portion of the Serenity Prayer, you need "the wisdom to know the difference." Imagine taking a *triage approach* to anger (Thomas, 2000). Nurses are good at sorting out the patients who need priority attention. Likewise, they must become more skilled at sorting out anger issues, taking effective action where possible, and discharging the rest of their negative emotion harmlessly. Let's begin this discussion by examining my definition of anger:

> *Anger is a strong uncomfortable emotional response to a provocation that is unwanted and incongruent with one's values, rights, or beliefs.*

Notice that the first major element of the definition is that the angry person is responding to something that he did not *want* to happen. For example, my ire can be aroused when I receive *unwanted* advice or an *unwanted* work assignment. I can stew about the unwanted advice, or conclude that it's not worth stewing about. I can view the work assignment as tolerable, even if it is not what I would prefer. Unfortunately, humans have a tendency to escalate their wants and desires into dogmatic *musts* about the self, others, and world/life conditions (Dryden, 1990). This tendency leads to irrational conclusions and negative behavioral consequences. We'll have more to say about this tendency a bit later in the chapter.

The next element of my anger definition emphasizes that the anger-producing situation or incident was *incongruent with values, rights, or beliefs.* In the pages of this book, you have already seen many examples of nurses' anger in response to provocations that offend their *values.* A lot of what is happening in the health care delivery system offends our values, because we value patients more so than the obscene profits some health care organizations are making.

My definition of anger also emphasizes violation of our *rights* as human beings. Applying this to nursing, I assert that the nurse has *rights* to a reasonable workload, respectful treatment from other members of the health care team, and a clearly specified mechanism for resolution of grievances. Instead, RNs in our study (and studies by others) too often speak of impossible assignments, verbal abuse, and powerlessness to affect change. Their rights are violated, and they are angry.

Our data also show that nurses become angry when *patients' rights* are violated. *Empathic anger on behalf of patients* was generated when RNs saw patients suffering because of dehumanizing or discriminatory treatment. Only recently has empathic anger received much attention in the scientific literature (Hoffman, 1989; Vitaglione & Barnett, 2003), because the traditional focus of scholars is on anger produced by affronts to the self. Empathic anger on behalf of patients is rational and a spark plug for advocacy measures.

The Gift of Anger

When nurses become angry because situations and events are incongruent with their values, beliefs, and rights, I believe that their anger is *rational and justifiable*. Something is wrong and needs to be corrected. In such cases, the emotion of anger should be considered a *gift*. The gift of anger should be claimed—and used wisely. It provides strong momentum for activism. As you feel the anger building in your mind and body, realize that you can use its energy in any way you wish. Feel its power. Imagine it propelling you forward to act. Perhaps you must confront someone who is taking advantage of you or failing to do their share of the work. Perhaps you must challenge workplace discrimination or ill-conceived policies. Anger can empower you to do this. Philosopher Robert Solomon says that anger helps us to "change the world and change ourselves... to ask 'what will I do now?'"

> **3.1.** *For physician Rachel Naomi Remen, the force of her anger proved to be life-affirming. She became ill at the age of 15 with Crohn's disease. Anger has played different roles during her 35 years with this disease, but she is convinced that it is far healthier than apathy, hopelessness, and resignation:*
>
> > *Anger was my way of refusing to accept invalidhood... When I was 15 and I first became ill, I felt an anger that seemed bottomless and lasted for 4 or 5 years. I actually hated well people because I felt hopelessly separated from them. I can remember the very moment that I changed. I was walking on a beach thinking how exhausted I was and how I could not go on, and suddenly I had the experience of being filled with a familiar rage. But this time I experienced the **vitality** of my anger: the life energy that had somehow become caught in the form of anger. At that point, I recognized it for what it really was. It was my will to live and to resist distortion, and I no longer needed to be angry to experience it. (Remen, 1996, p. 25)*

Advocacy for Patients

The gift of anger can enable nurses to risk advocacy for patients, lessening the moral distress that we discussed in Chapter 1. Labor and delivery nurse Ann Smith's anger energizes her to stand up to physicians on behalf of her patients. She tells of a doctor who came in and began fussing at Ann's laboring patient because "she wasn't trying hard enough." Ann relates:

> I told the doctor he couldn't talk to her that way... I took action. I wrote him up, and then I went to his partner and let his partner know what happened.... The doctor that I had the confrontation with has been very nice to me. I've not had any more problems with him. He's been very good to my patients. I feel sure something was said to him.

On another occasion, Ann was caring for a young girl who was a Medicaid patient, and a doctor told her that "Medicaid patients can't get an epidural." Ann asked him repeatedly about the epidural, but he continued to say no. Thoroughly incensed, Ann again acted on behalf of her patient. Whether or not you approve of the tactic she chose, she got results:

> *I took him outside the door, and I said "Okay, I want you to stand right there. Now, you've got a teenage daughter at home. And I want you to imagine that that's your daughter in that bed. And every time we hear my patient scream when she hurts, I'm going to kick you in the shin. And I want you to pretend that's your daughter. And me kicking you in the shin is going to be your heart hurting because it's your daughter that the doctor won't give the epidural to." My patient got the epidural, and I've never had to deal with it again with that particular doctor.*

In the following vignette, the nurse could not save her patient, but she took steps to make sure that future patients would not meet the same fate:

> *I was in a very small hospital. I had a 19-year-old come in with a lacerated liver, and we had one surgeon and he would not come to the hospital. I stood there with pressure on this young man's liver until he died. That was very traumatic, and it made me very angry that I couldn't do anything about it. I couldn't make him come. And so I raised a great deal of trouble with the hospital board, the medical staff, and so forth. Because I thought, you know, that just shouldn't happen.*

Personal Liberation

From an evolutionary perspective, emotions evolved for their adaptive value in dealing with fundamental life tasks and predicaments—even survival itself (Ekman, 1994; Gross, 2006). Emotions are important sources of information about self-identity and personal needs, and the actions that are necessary to fulfill those needs (Dafter, 1996). The word *emotion* comes from the Latin *exmovere*, meaning *to move out, to have the experience of being moved*. When deeply moved by feelings, we have an altered perspective, and we behave differently as well. Anger jolts us out of passivity and stimulates us to become "movers and shakers." One woman we interviewed spoke of the "buzz" that anger gave her, enabling her to assert herself more emphatically: "I felt a real buzz. I felt, you know, like 'I'm not going to be treated this way.' I felt strong. I felt like someone was listening to me . . . I felt in control." Another woman valued her anger for two reasons: it alerted her, and it energized her to take action on her behalf: "My anger makes me find solutions. Whenever I feel anger I try to say, 'Okay, this is an emotion that's alerting me that there is a problem here.' My anger lets me know it's time to take care of something." Similarly, a nurse saw her anger as "a red flag": "I see it as a red flag that says, 'Something just happened here—you were violated.' If I acknowledge my anger instead of trying to stuff it, I can identify solutions."

I like the symbolism of the red flag. It's a symbol with universal meaning: STOP. There is danger. Do not continue on this road. Find an alternate route. Mobilizing anger can be the first step in personal *liberation* when your course is fraught with danger. There are times in each person's life when a new direction must be taken, a new future constructed, or else the self is in danger of extinction. Perhaps you are in a relationship in which you are smothered. Therapist Harriet Lerner reminds us that perpetual anger at someone is an extremely useful clue: "If we are chronically angry or bitter in a particular relationship, that may be a message to clarify and strengthen the 'I' a bit more" (1985, p. 31). *No relationship is healthy if one self swamps the other.* Anger can be the impetus for breaking free from such a relationship—or from a joyless work role that offers no opportunity for continued growth and advancement. Let me tell you a story. There was an elephant that was staked to the ground with a chain. As a baby, no matter how hard she struggled, she couldn't break free. Now, as an adult, the elephant is big enough and strong enough to gain her freedom. But she doesn't bother to try. Many people in miserable situations are like the elephant. They view their conditions as inevitable: "This is the way things are." Have you, like the elephant, stopped trying? Anger can give you the power to break that chain.

Not long ago, I was admiring a huge, vibrant, painting of a single flower in the National Museum of Women in the Arts. No one can paint flowers like Georgia O'Keeffe! Posted beside her glorious painting were some words the artist uttered in 1923: "One day 7 years ago, I found myself saying to myself: 'I can't live where I want to, I can't go where I want to, I can't do what I want to do, I can't even say what I want to'. . . . I decided I was a very stupid fool not to at least PAINT as I wanted to." And so she boldly began to paint differently from the other artists of the time. The world had never *seen* anyone paint like she painted. Critics snarled. But she continued to paint as she wanted to. Anger had unleashed her unique and formidable talent, for which all of us can be grateful.

Moral or Righteous Anger

Anger can also unleash moral or *righteous anger*. It was righteous anger that motivated letters written by whistle-blowing employees of Enron and the FBI. The ripple effect of those angry letters was stunning. Sherron Watkins at Enron wrote a "cold, sharp letter to Kenneth Lay, puncturing the dishonest fantasies of the people around her" (D. Brooks, 2002, p. 30). Coleen Rowley, an FBI agent, wrote a "slashing letter to the Bureau's director that was filled with rage at the passive incompetence of her superiors" (D. Brooks, 2002, p. 30). Watkins and Rowley embody the courage to act alone. Others are propelled to join movements or organizations to marshal the power of the collective.

Righteous anger mobilizes individuals to band together in social justice projects. It is when we get "good and angry" that we join with others in efforts to save the wilderness, build homes for the homeless, or fight crime in our neighborhoods.

I often think about a particular organization, Mothers Against Drunk Driving (MADD). Many of the members of this organization have lost a child to a drunken driver. As a mother, I can think of nothing that would produce more grief and rage. These women could choose to remain, like their acronym, MADD—but instead, their anger is used constructively to work for better legislation and educate drivers. Similarly, RNs form coalitions to lobby for more enlightened public policy. Development of the document, "Nursing's Agenda for Health Care Reform" is an excellent example. Irate at the large number of Americans with no access to health care and the inadequate, patchwork approaches to health care reform, more than 60 nursing organizations united to write this stirring call—as yet unheeded—for a basic core of health services for all citizens.

Perhaps you have never thought of anger as a gift. Because of its pejorative connotations in our society, many people view anger as pathological or bad, in fact a sin. One of the members of our research team was told from the pulpit that "anger is only a *d* away from *danger*." Her minister may have confused anger with aggression. There is considerable confusion about the terms *anger*, *hostility*, *aggression*, and *violence*. Bear with me for a minute while I define these terms. In the previous chapter, you learned about *hostility*, that mental attitude of antagonism toward the world and the other people in it. *Aggression* involves an actual or impending physical or verbal attack on someone, and *violence* is a unjust, forceful assault that inflicts injury. But *ordinary anger is not hostile, aggressive, or violent, and it is not a sin*. The research of James Averill (1983) showed that physical aggression during anger is relatively rare in a normal, nonclinical population, occurring in only 10% of angry episodes. What most of us experience in everyday life is *anger*, a natural and healthy human response to a provocation. Anger pertains to events of greater significance than minor irritations or mere annoyances, but it is less enduring and mean-spirited than hostility, and less destructive than aggression or violence (Thomas, 1995).

I am indebted to Carroll Saussy (1995), a professor of pastoral care and counseling, for her insightful "theology of anger." Her exploration refutes the old notion that displaying anger is un-Christian. She carefully examines the Bible's teaching on anger, pointing out that a lot of anger occurs in both the Old and New Testaments. Although there are warnings about anger in some passages ("He that is slow to anger is better than the mighty," "Anger resteth in the bosom of fools"), God gets angry, Jesus gets angry, and anger is an important component of the human lives that are presented in these texts. Anger can be *holy*, according to Saussy: " . . . holy anger [is] a response to the experience of being ignored, injured, trivialized, or rejected, as well as an empathic response aroused by witnessing someone else being ignored, injured, trivialized, or rejected" (1995, p. 115).

Sinful Anger

There *is* sinful anger, defined by Saussy as "a vengeful, hostile, sometimes explosive reaction [that] aims to injure persons or institutions and tears at the fabric of society by destroying relationships" (1995, p. 115). *Sinful anger—* which should really be called aggression or violence rather than anger—is attributed to "broken-hearted" persons who have not been respected or loved sufficiently. The etiology of their broken hearts can be dysfunctional family backgrounds, abuse, and/or poverty. Their violent acts are attempts to overcome their perceived worthlessness and helplessness (Rothenberg, 1973). Nurses see the horrifying consequences in the bruises of battered women, the broken limbs of children, the gunshots and knife wounds that are routine Saturday night fare in the emergency departments of every metropolitan hospital. Often, the destructive anger is taken out on the next generation, perpetuating the broken-heartedness.

I will never forget a boy of about 11 or 12 whom I cared for in the ICU. His father had literally stomped him with heavy boots, along with delivering many blows with his fists. The boot prints, still visible days after his admission, went deep into his flesh. One day his father, a slight figure in baggy overalls, came into the ICU during the visiting period. I asked him what the boy had done to provoke his anger. It seems the boy had not done his chores properly! I was stunned and sickened by the father's disproportionate reaction. I wonder if that boy, now grown into a man, is beating his own children.

Although it is beyond the scope of this book to delve more deeply into the topic of violence, a complex and multifaceted problem that deserves a book of its own, I do believe that all of us must begin to work toward solutions. Violence in America is an ever-growing social problem. Each new set of statistics is more alarming, particularly with regard to the propensity of our young people to set-tle their disputes with fists and guns. A survey of more than 15,000 teenagers showed that 75% of boys and over 60% of girls had hit someone in the past year when they were angry (Josephson Institute on Ethics, 2001). National data from the Centers for Disease Control and Prevention (CDC) showed that more than one in 13 students were threatened or injured with a weapon (such as a gun, knife, or club) on school property in the past year (CDC, 1999). Although the problem of societal violence may seem so immense that no individual action can make a dent in it, learning to manage our own anger is a place to start. After we nurses have acquired anger management skills, we need to teach them in both inpatient and outpatient settings, to children and adolescents, as well as adults (Thomas, 2001a).

One of my pet soapbox topics is the glamorized violence on television. The National Television Violence Study revealed that 58% of TV programs contained violence, and three-fourths of violent scenes on TV contained *no remorse, criticism, or penalties* for violence (Seppa, 1997). I have particular concern for impressionable children, who have difficulty distinguishing between fantasy and reality. Forty percent of violent incidents on television are initiated by characters that are attractive role models for children (Seppa, 1997). Although some argue that violent television—or movies—provide harmless entertainment, I believe otherwise. A study that tracked children from ages six to nine into their 20s has provided some strong evidence that a steady diet of TV violence in childhood is associated with aggressive behavior in adulthood (Huesmann, Moise-Titus, Podolski, & Eron, 2003). The association persisted even when the effects of socioeconomic status, intellectual ability, and parents' childrearing practices were controlled.

Of the men who were heavy viewers of TV violence as children, 42% had pushed, grabbed, or shoved their spouses at least once in the last year (compared to 22% who did not watch violence as children). Of the women who were heavy viewers of TV violence as children, 40% reported throwing something at their spouses (compared to 17% who did not watch violence). Obviously, this study did not include the effects of exposure to today's violence-saturated Internet content, video games, and song lyrics. Video games not only actively involve players in violence but reward them for it (Winerman, 2006). Research shows that violent song lyrics increase hostile and aggressive emotions and thoughts

(Anderson, cited in Palmer, 2003). Parents need to be informed of these research findings, so that they can set limits on their children's consumption of violent media. Nurses could conduct parent education programs at PTA meetings, churches, and community centers (see Thomas, 2003c) to alert families to this danger.

Combating Aggression and Violence

Before they will halt their aggressive actions, violent individuals must begin to encounter *penalties* for their behavior. As we all know, behavior is repeated when it is rewarded. The person who bullies another and gets away with it is surely likely to remain a bully. A disturbing study of juvenile offenders shows that the negative *consequences* of a violent solution never cross their mind (Slaby & Guerra, 1988). They held beliefs such as "It's okay to hit someone if you just go crazy from anger" and "People who get beaten up badly don't really suffer that much."

Certainly, many of the aggressive individuals whom Saussy calls "brokenhearted" need far more than acquisition of skills like talking about their feelings or penalties for aggressive behavior. Some have such severe psychopathology, dating back to abandonment, unmet needs, and abuse in infancy, that intensive treatment will be necessary. They have no trust in other people, little or no impulse control, and no empathy for the suffering of those whom they hit and maim in the heat of anger. Much work with a trusted therapist will be needed before they learn not only what they missed, but also learn more normal patterns of response to replace their dysfunctional ones. There is some basis for hope. Therapists who conduct anger management groups in Veterans Administration facilities across the country are finding that traumatized adults can learn to control aggression (Gerlock, 1994; Novaco, 1996). Without such control, veterans—and you and I—cannot successfully live and work in harmony with others.

> *3.2. April Gerlock (1994), a nurse therapist, led a series of six different 8-week classes with groups of six to twelve veterans, most of whom were Vietnam veterans with a diagnosis of posttraumatic stress disorder (PTSD) from their deeply disturbing war experiences. These men had high levels of out-of-control anger and rage upon entry into Gerlock's classes. Goals of the treatment were to reduce the level of anger, as well as promote constructive management of it. Participants were encouraged to take responsibility for their anger behaviors, rather than externalizing blame. As the weeks of treatment went on, Gerlock learned that a large number of the men had been victims of childhood trauma—sexual exploitation, physical violence, witnessing domestic violence—prior to the trauma of their military service in a war zone. Despite all of the severe trauma that these men had endured, they responded positively to the anger management intervention. A statistically significant decrease was noted in their scores on a widely used anger measure that was given at the first and last anger classes. One Vietnam combat veteran summed up his learning from treatment as follows: "I thought I had control because people were afraid of me... people feared what I might do. That was a delusion... with the anger, I didn't really have control over myself" (Young, 1996, p. 57).*

Developing Emotional Intelligence

Control of emotions is one aspect of *emotional intelligence* (EI), a concept that attracted widespread attention after publication of Daniel Goleman's book in 1995. Drawing on the scholarly work of Peter Salovey and John Mayer, Goleman contends that EI—the regulation of emotion in a way that enhances living—may be more crucial to personal and professional success than IQ, academic achievement, or acquisition of specific job skills. The cornerstone of EI is *awareness* of your own feelings, because with awareness, you can learn to exercise self-control and select appropriate coping mechanisms. Goleman recommends, as I have in the previous chapter, tuning in to somatic markers of emotion, our "gut feelings." Basic skills include identifying and labeling feelings correctly and knowing the difference between feelings and actions. EI also involves skills in interpreting social cues, understanding the perspectives of other people, and managing your moods effectively. (For further information about EI, including books and materials, see www.eiconsortium.org.)

Most of us had no classes in school to help us develop emotional competence; all of our schooling was focused on acquiring information and technical skills. Now, emotional literacy programs, such as New Haven's Social Competence Program and New York City's Resolving Conflict Creatively Program, are under way in some schools. Many of these programs include special classes for parents as well. Students learn to harness emotions productively, so that classroom disruption, fighting, suspensions, and expulsions decrease, while self-control, assertiveness, problem-solving, and cooperation increase. Teaching nonviolent conflict resolution skills must become a part of every school curriculum. In the national priorities outlined in *Healthy People 2010* (U.S. Department of Health and Human Services, 2000), specific objectives pertain to adolescent fighting and weapon-carrying to school. Unfortunately, many teachers and parents are unaware that programs to promote emotional competence exist. And our world is still populated with far too many emotionally illiterate individuals. In fact, a worldwide trend shows the present generation of children to be more troubled emotionally than the last: more depressed, nervous, angry, and aggressive (Goleman, 1995).

I see my book as one tiny square of the quilt that is being pieced together by psychologists, teachers, social workers, nurses, and other helping professionals to address emotional health. Although many of Goleman's recommendations pertain to preventive programs for children, I write for you, my colleagues, who are depressed, nervous, and angry during this turbulent time. I like to think of this quilt pulled around the shoulders of those who are crying, warming those whose emotions are cold and numb because it hurts too much to feel anymore. I hope that by the time you finish this book, your emotional reactions to events will be less distressing. I want to give you hope.

In contrast to old ideas that everything important is set in concrete in early childhood, we now know that emotional development continues in adulthood. Adult emotional development involves both the acquisition of new emotional habits and the abandonment, or diminished use, of old ones.

It is never too late to change and grow. Researcher June Tangney and colleagues (1996) examined constructive versus destructive responses to anger across the life span with samples of 307 children, 434 adolescents, 214 college students, and 195 adults. The researchers assessed anger arousal, intentions, cognitive and behavioral responses, and long-term consequences. Across the life span, there was a clear increase in constructive intentions and adaptive behaviors and a decrease in malevolent intentions and aggressive behaviors.

Cognitive Processing

Today's scientists and therapists are also paying more attention to *cognitive processing* of emotions. The term *cognitive processing* refers to thoughts we have before an event—our *expectations*—and thoughts after the event—our *appraisal* of what happened. Both expectations and appraisals can generate quite a lot of emotion. Let's take a situation in which a nurse named Alice is angry because she is left to "pick up the pieces" when others did not complete their work properly. Although we can certainly view such a situation sympathetically, Alice's cognitive processing makes matters worse. For starters, her *expectation* is that "These idiots can't do anything right." With this expectation, she is primed for anger from the very beginning. Alice's internal dialogue runs like this: "I'll bet I am going to have to clean up their mess again. It isn't fair. I do my work, why do I have to do more than my share?" Sure enough, her prophecy is confirmed. Now *appraisal* comes into play. Alice makes a judgment that her coworkers are lazy or careless, thereby stoking the anger fire so that it burns even more brightly. In this example, it's easy to see that both the expectation and the appraisal fuel excess anger. There's a lot of pejorative labeling: The other workers are thought of as incompetent "idiots," and their behavior is construed as "lazy" or "careless." Not only does Alice have to pick up the pieces today, she "*always*" has to do so. The other characters in the story have no redeeming features, while the nurse herself is virtuous: "*I do my work*." Furthermore, she rates herself favorably with regard to the quantity of work (she does *more* than her "share"), and she makes an invidious comparison about the *quality* of the work, because the others "can't do anything right."

In contrast to earlier depictions of anger as a primitive force that may seize us, or a knee-jerk response to a stimulus, cognitive theorists say we become angry only after our brains have processed a situation sufficiently to label it an offense. Novaco (1985) explains that "there is no direct relationship between external events and anger. The arousal of anger is a cognitively mediated process" (p. 210).

> *3.3.* Beliefs *regarding the* meaning *of an event are crucial determinants of emotional experience. This anecdote from psychologist Carol Tavris is a delightful example:*
>
> > *One afternoon, as I was leaving the subway at rush hour, trudging tiredly up the stairs, I felt a hand brush my rear. It was an ambiguous gesture, considering the size of the crowd, so I did nothing, but my heart began to pound and my face flushed. I felt a mixture of excitement ("My first New York pervert! Wait'll I tell the gang!" and fury ("How dare this creep molest me!"). The hand struck again, this time unmistakably*

a pinch. I spun around, umbrella poised to strike a blow for womanhood and self-respect... and stared face-to-face at my husband. (Tavris, 1982, pp. 87–88).

Our beliefs about the meaning of a situation can make it worse because they are not always *rational,* which brings us to the work of Albert Ellis, founder of Rational-Emotive Therapy (later called Rational-Emotive-Behavior Therapy). Perhaps more than any other individual, Ellis (1973) confronted us with the irrationality of much of our thinking. While I disagree with his oft-stated premise that anger is *always negative* and *always stems from irrational beliefs,* I credit him for his enormous influence on psychology and psychiatric nursing. Because of Ellis, we understand that people do not *get upset* but instead *upset themselves.*

External events do not *cause* people's responses. Unlike laboratory rats, humans think about and *interpret* stimuli and make their responses accordingly. One way of defusing anger is to challenge the irrational beliefs that trigger it.

Irrational Beliefs and Anger Arousal

A belief is irrational if it is demanding, rigid, inaccurate, and unhelpful in assisting people to achieve their goals (Walen, DiGiuseppe, & Wessler, 1980). Let's examine some beliefs that are irrational and do not serve us well. Psychologist Melvin Lerner (1980) says that many of us have a need to believe in a Just World in which the good people are rewarded and the bad people are punished. When events challenge that belief, we search for an explanation that somehow preserves it. For example, if a coworker is fired, we tell ourselves he must have deserved it. Or, we might console ourselves by deciding that he will grow and become a better person through this negative experience. Our need to believe in a Just World is so great that we will blame ourselves for an event rather than relinquish the belief. For example, parents of terminally ill children may berate themselves—"If we had only done this..." or "We shouldn't have done that"—because it is unthinkable that a child should suffer in a Just World. But the world is *not* just. To expect it to be is ultimately an untenable expectation.

The Limits of Personal Control

Another widely held belief—at least, in Western cultures—is that each of us has a tremendous amount of personal *control* over stressors, mental and physical health, social situations, and so forth. Several decades of research on "internal locus of control" (a construct invented by researchers to describe belief in the personal controllability of outcomes) convinced many of us that control is quite a good thing. The literature generally portrayed "internals" as more competent, effective persons who take responsibility for their actions and take steps to change aversive situations. Training programs were established to teach people how to be "internals," as opposed to being "externals," who believed that events in their lives occurred due to fate, luck, or chance. But then scientists began to reconsider the concept of control (Shapiro, Schwartz, & Astin, 1996). Seeking and having control has its negative aspects. And personal control has its limits. Research shows that many people *overestimate* the amount of control they have in a situation (Seligman, 1991) and *underestimate* the risks associated with their behavior (Weinstein, 1984). Strong belief in personal control can result in excessive self-blame for mistakes. It can be particularly detrimental to have a high desire for control in an environment that will not permit it. Anger can be fueled by futile attempts to control events that are uncontrollable.

People are notoriously uncontrollable too! Enormous energy is wasted when we try to control the behavior of our coworkers and significant others. It is irrational to believe that other people should act in accordance with *our* standards of behavior. When someone acts in a way that violates our belief system, we often find ourselves making judgments such as "Nobody has a right to act that way" or "He should have done such and such." To counter this tendency, Deffenbacher (1995 a) reminds us of the "paradox of freedom:" If *we* have the right to make choices (even dumb ones), so too do our coworkers, friends, and family members (even if dumb and dumber). We are abridging others' freedom if we insist that everything should be done our way.

And let's don't forget patients in this discussion of control. Nursing scholar Myra Levine wrote an insightful paper back in 1970 on the intransigent patient—that is, the patient we cannot control, who is unwilling to follow "explicitly and faithfully, every instruction given him for 'his own good'" (1970, p. 2106). Some of the factors involved in our poor tolerance for the intransigent patient are moral indignation, personal anxiety, and guilt. An unrealistic premise exists that patients can be *taught* unquestioning obedience. But the patient is a captive student who may not want to learn what we have to teach—or do what *we* think he should do. He may not want to learn about an unappetizing low-salt, low-fat, high-fiber diet even if we think he *should* care about his heart health. Levine urged nurses to adopt more realistic expectations. She deplored the "arrogance that pervades all of nursing practice": that the patient does not know what is good for him. We need to drop the "shoulds" and "oughts" from our vocabulary regarding patients.

"Shoulds" and "oughts" are also quite frequent in our self-talk. Many of these imperatives pertain to unrealistic standards for our own performance. We believe that our self-worth is contingent on our performance. I have graduate students every semester who castigate themselves if they do not make an A on every paper. They show up in my office to plead that a B+ or A– be changed to an A, despite my assurance that a B+ or A– grade indicates that they have done fine work. I try to point out that it is an irrational expectation that every paper should be evaluated as excellent in a rigorous nursing graduate program. But, we faculty are self-critical too. As we drive home from work, reviewing our own actions, we often harshly criticize, telling ourselves, "I should have. . . . " Some of us find themselves heavily "should-on," as one humorist puts it.

Nurses Waiting for Rescue or Change

An irrational belief that we identified in our study of female nurses was their notion—or fantasy—that *someone should rescue them* from their difficulties

(Smith, et al., 1996). Nurses said things like "I kind of wish the system would change" or "We don't seem to have the leadership." Some expected to be rescued by management, even though they had not made their needs known! And they became angry when help was not forthcoming. For example, Fran Erwin related, "We were short-staffed, we were not getting any support, nobody really cared...I had not come out and said to the supervisor, 'We need some help,' but she was aware of the census and what was going on. I blew up." A bit later in the interview, Fran contrasted this "uncaring" supervisor—who had failed to come to the rescue—with her "lifesaver" who had been out of town: "My lifesaver, resource person [the nurse manager] was not in town that week...she'd have found some help."

Although we can sympathize with Fran for having to work short-staffed, at no point in her narrative is there any evidence that she considered taking action herself. Fran may have been operating under another irrational assumption: that nothing could be done. What could she have done? Well, at the very least, she could have made a direct request to the supervisor for some assistance, rather than assuming that the supervisor must have been aware of her need. It was illogical to merely wait for someone in authority to come to the rescue. In a clever article about games nurses play, Roberts (1986) called this the "Pass to a Higher Authority" game. Players in this game speak of "they," not "I" or "we." They refer every issue to someone in a position of higher authority. Interestingly, the male nurses we studied don't seem to be involved in this game.

Although there were many commonalities between female and male nurses in our studies, this irrational belief was typical only of females. Socialization to the feminine gender role inculcates the belief that if one waits patiently, a handsome prince or fairy godmother will magically appear and make things right. My friends, it's time we shelve the fairy tales.

Ineffective Complaining

Shelving ineffective complaining should be next on our "to do" list. Another irrational belief held by many nurses is that *complaining gets results.* Although direct and clear anger expression is rare, complaining is rampant in nursing. Gripe sessions occupy most of our lunch and coffee breaks, and all too often pervade our after-hours socializing, when we should be putting work out of our minds. Complaining actually preserves the status quo, because as long as we just complain to each other, nothing changes. Maya Angelou's grandmother taught her a valuable lesson about complaining: "What you're supposed to do when you don't like a thing is change it. If you can't change it, change the way you think about it. Don't complain" (Angelou, 1993). *Changing our thinking can defuse a lot of nonproductive anger.*

Irrational Beliefs of Nurses

All of the following are irrational beliefs held by many nurses, and I'm sure you won't have any trouble adding to my list:

1. Good nurses work until they drop—and do overtime or double shifts PRN.
2. Good nurses don't make errors.

3. Other nurses should do their work the way it "ought" to be done—i.e., the way that I would do it.
4. Patients should be cooperative and grateful for our ministrations.
5. Patients should be interested in what we want to teach them about self-care.
6. Patients' families should be attentive to their loved one, but stay out of our way.

How do these irrational beliefs connect to anger? In the ABC framework of Ellis's (1973) rational emotive therapy, "A" is the activating event (for example, a patient complains about the nurse's care), "B" is the belief ("patients should be grateful, I'm working my tail off here"), and "C" is the consequence ("I'm really furious at this ungrateful patient"). In this example, holding the belief that patients should be grateful is clearly a problem. Instead of exploring the patient's complaint in an empathic way, which might reveal his fears about helplessness or abandonment, this nurse responds angrily. What is important here is to understand that "A" does not *cause* "C," because the disturbed angry feelings are primarily generated by "B," the irrational belief.

Research Linking Faulty Thinking and Anger

Research evidence (Hazaleus & Deffenbacher, 1985) supports the association between faulty thinking and anger arousal. Statistically significant correlations have been found between anger arousal and all of these irrational beliefs:

1. I must have love and approval from others.
2. I must be perfect—and consider myself worthless if a mistake is made.
3. People should be blamed and punished when they do wrong.
4. It is a catastrophe when things are not as one would like them to be.
5. Unhappiness is caused by external circumstances that are beyond one's control.
6. Possible negative events should be worried over constantly.
7. The influence of past events can never be changed or removed.
8. For every problem, a perfect solution always exists and must be found.

If you groaned a bit in self-recognition as I reviewed these irrational beliefs, it's not too late to alter your mind-set! Psychologist and philosopher William James observed, "The greatest revolution in our generation is the discovery that human beings, by changing their *inner* attitudes of their minds, can change the *outer* aspects of their lives."

3.4. Well-known nursing author and leader Barbara Barnum has some excellent advice on altering your mind-set, so that you are no longer aroused to anger by irrational expectations:

The anger response is certainly addictive. It probably resides in some conceptualization that the world, our employers, our friends "owe" us something or some particular way of behaving. Life works better, I believe, if most of one's expectations are for oneself, not for others. Yes, I am one of those "we create our own worlds" people. In essence, my philosophy is to avoid an anger response, which is helped by seeing life as a school in which things are designed for character formation, not for ease of passage. I've recently recovered from an excruciating rupture of a disk, C6–C7, and I was profoundly grateful to escape surgery. The first two people I met on returning to work asked, wasn't I mad to have had such a bad injury? It's all in the mind, isn't it?

Steps Toward Healing

- *Try cognitive restructuring techniques* when your anger is generated by irrational thoughts. RN Diana Taylor calls this "giving your mind a makeover." Begin with self-monitoring to identify biases or distortions. Write down the thoughts you have during anger episodes for a week. Look for absolute terms in your thought patterns: *always, never, must,* etc. Dispute these thoughts. Then, develop and rehearse new cognitions that decrease the anger. A more rational cognitive appraisal can mediate the effect that an event has on your behavior. Many situations can be reinterpreted in a more positive light. At the minimum, you can relabel a situation in neutral terms. As you catch yourself thinking irrationally, correct yourself (Hazaleus & Deffenbacher, 1986; Moon & Eisler, 1983; Novaco, 1975). How, exactly, is this "mind-set makeover" accomplished? Here are some specific tips:
  - If you tend to catastrophize ("This is the worst thing that's ever happened"), substitute more realistic thoughts such as these:
    - *"I'll do what I can. If it works, great. If not, well I did the best I can."*
    - *"Getting all bent out of shape doesn't help."*
    - *"It's not the end of the world."*
  - If you tend to demand that others behave in a certain way ("They should have done that"), substitute the following:
    - *"This is not what I would prefer, but I can't always expect people to act the way I want them to."*
    - *"I don't really know why he/she did that. Maybe I need to ask."*
  - If you blow things out of proportion ("I'm never going to get over this"), try to stay with a more realistic appraisal:
    - *"This is negative, but it's not that big a deal. No need to make myself all upset about this."*
    - *"All things considered, this is pretty small."*
  - If you engage in one-track thinking ("They are doing that deliberately to get to me"), try to consider other explanations:
    - *"Maybe they didn't know."*
    - *"I may not have all the facts."*
  - If you tend to apply derogatory labels ("bitch," "jerk," "idiot"), realize that humans are too complex to be given a single global rating. Even if behavior in a particular incident is clearly reprehensible and deserves condemnation, most people are not rotten to the core. Try to substitute a more nuanced evaluation of the other person:
    - *"Maybe he's having a bad day."*
    - *"I better not make a global judgment about him on the basis of one incident.*

A final tip: Some people find it helpful to write rational self-statements such as these on 3 × 5 cards for quick review until they have been committed to memory (Dryden, 1990). You will need to practice thinking differently in real-world situations of interpersonal conflict and criticism.

- *Stop it.* If you are troubled by a particular obsessive thought that you cannot banish, try *thought stopping.* This procedure was developed by Cautela in 1969. The principle behind the procedure is that if the thought is consistently interrupted whenever it occurs, its occurrence will eventually be eliminated. There are two steps:
  1. Sit in a comfortable position, close your eyes, and deliberately think the unwanted thought ("I'll never pass that certification exam. I've heard it's a killer")
  2. As you begin to think the specific thought, shout "Stop!" Do this 10 to 20 times per day for 2 or 3 days. Then move to a modification of the procedure, in which you say "stop" to yourself, rather than aloud, every other time you practice. Then say "stop" to yourself every single time. After a few days of practice, you should be able to halt the unwanted thought whenever it begins.
  3. In a variation of this procedure, Diana Taylor suggests using a kitchen timer or alarm clock, set for 3 minutes, shouting "Stop!" when the alarm rings. When in public, you could unobtrusively snap a rubber band on your wrist to stop the obsessive thought.
- *Make a greater effort to understand the other person's point of view or motives.* In a very interesting study, participants in a conflict were asked to provide narratives about their anger experience. Angry people nearly always insisted that the other person's behavior was *wrong,* while their own was *justified.* They described the offenders' actions as unreasonable, arbitrary, selfish, even malicious. The offenders did not see their actions in this way at all, and offered coherent and reasonable explanations of their motivation and behavior. Descriptions of the incidents were entirely different. The individuals who had been angered described the incidents in long-term contexts, with few extenuating circumstances, and lasting adverse consequences. The offenders held a much more benign view of things. Although acknowledging that they had done wrong, the offenders minimized the severity of the incidents. In their view, the angry incidents were time-limited, with mitigating circumstances and happy endings. The researchers concluded that anger is characterized by "a gap in interpersonal understanding" (Baumeister, Stillwell, & Wotman, 1990). I would say that's putting it mildly!

I am reminded of a conflict between two students who were working together on a project. One of them had come to me on several occasions to express her resentment at the perceived lack of interest on the part of the other student. In her view, the other student had little intrinsic investment in the project and was contributing in a minimal, perfunctory manner. In due time, the "accused" showed up to tell me her side of the story. The words rapidly tumbled out as she recounted her extreme frustration, especially with the "do-it-at-the-last-minute" style of the other student. I soon gained an appreciation of the conflict from her perspective, which was quite different from the impression I had initially formed. Each student made some very valid points. There was no clear "right" or "wrong," just two very different personalities and styles of getting work done (Thomas, 2003d).

A Last Word

In this chapter, we addressed—and challenged—thinking patterns that produce nonproductive anger. Relinquishing an "I'm-right-and-they're-wrong" stance is critical to improved emotional health. I have learned that behavior that ticks me off can often be explained—at least in part—by differences in tempo (turtles versus racehorses), need for order in the environment (neatniks versus slobs), or ways of thinking (left-brain versus right-brain). I give my students the Myers-Briggs Type Inventory to fill out, so that they will have a better understanding of personality. This test could be useful in your workplace, too. Much potential for conflict exists within a work group because different personality types are bewildered by one another. For example, introverts can't imagine why extroverts have to talk all the time. Extroverts can't fathom why introverts need time alone to recharge their batteries. Logical analysts are puzzled by the deeply emotional—and so forth. With a better understanding of personality, we are more likely to appreciate and value our opposites. I have learned a tremendous amount from two of my friends. Because I am very logical and goal-directed, I plunge ahead with my eye on the goal, taking the most efficient way to get there. I am not looking at the flowers as I go, much less taking time to smell them. Time is important to me: being on time and using time wisely. My friends are almost always late to our meetings, blissfully unaware of time passing. They are looking at the scenery, chatting with passersby, and appreciating things that I miss completely in my rush to get to my destination. Rather than getting angry at their lateness, I have learned from their relaxed orientation toward time and their esthetic sensitivities—and they have learned to tolerate my impatience to move on. Sometimes, it is an uneasy truce, because we are very different, but our friendship is important. What helps is that we are able to talk freely with one another. If you work with someone who infuriates you, consider what his view of your conflict might be. It is unlikely that this person is *deliberately* trying to make your life miserable. Wouldn't it be interesting to explore their interpretation of the conflict? Give it a try.

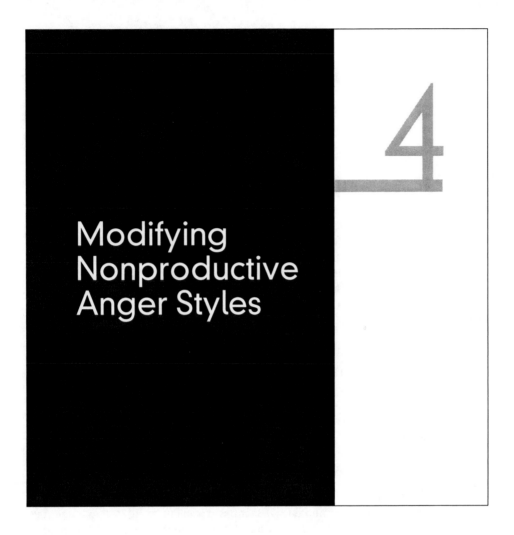

Modifying Nonproductive Anger Styles

Anyone can become angry. That is easy. But to be angry with the right person, to the right degree, at the right time, for the right purpose and in the right way—that is not easy.

—Aristotle

In this chapter, we examine anger styles. You will find out if you are mainly an "onion person" or a "garlic person." You will also learn about healthier anger management styles and the ABCs of effective action.

Managing Anger

What do nurses do when they are stressed out and angered on the job?

> "I was screaming at my nurse manager. I got frustrated and angry and screamed at her."
> "I go to the medicine room and cuss."
> "I kind of back off."

"I really blow up, and I start crying, and I feel better it's out, but I wish I had
  handled it a little better."
"I stood there and took it. It's kind of like kicking a dog, and the dog never
  runs off."

None of these nurses felt good about how they handled their anger. In fact,
most nurses I've talked to about work-related anger incidents echo that last
statement: They wish they had handled their anger a little better. Learning
to modify a nonproductive anger style can be one of the most important self-
management projects you will ever undertake. Both your career and your health
will benefit. And the profession itself will benefit. Some nurses are harboring
their anger until, like a malignant growth, it chokes the love of nursing out of
them. Feeling powerless to effect change and giving up the hope of being rescued, they leave—either physically, by changing employers or professions, or
mentally, by remaining on the job but merely going through the motions. These
are the dispirited walking wounded in every health care setting.

Nursing leader Beverly Malone has this to say: "Nurses have a legitimate right to be angry, but along with that right come consequences and
challenges. The goal is not to eliminate anger but to acknowledge it and
channel it into positive, life-supporting interventions. Acknowledging
the anger will remind nurses of how far they have to go; programmat-
ically channeling the anger will remind nurses of how far they have
already come." (Malone, 1985, p. 45)

Why change your anger behavior? Because if you continue to do what you've
always done, you'll get what you've always gotten. And you must have some dissatisfaction with the status quo, or you wouldn't be reading this book. I like Bev
Malone's emphasis on "positive, life-supporting interventions." That is my emphasis throughout this book. Anger *can* be controlled and channeled into constructive actions that improve your work life and your relationships. But most
people simply don't know how. The research of Dianne Tice (1990) is informa-
tive. In a free-format response questionnaire, more than 400 men and women
were asked about their strategies for controlling—and altering—negative emotional states such as sadness, fear, anxiety, and anger. For each emotional state,
the study participants were asked if they had tried to change it while experiencing it, and if so, how. People had *fewer strategies* for controlling anger than
for the other emotions, and they viewed their strategies as *less successful* than
the strategies they used to control other emotions. Tice's findings should not
really surprise us, given the difficulties we see with anger management in our
society. All around us, we see outbursts of road rage, air rage, and desk rage. A
pervasive notion in American culture insists that anger is involuntary—that it is
not controllable.

How did we get such an idea? It is derived from influences of Darwinian
evolutionary theory, Freudian theory, and research on aggression in animals.
Anger is considered a powerful instinctive drive. Therefore, holding it back or

bottling it up is deemed unhealthy, because it will eventually erupt in some form. According to Weiner (1991), the metaphor of *machine* is applicable to this view. A machine has a fixed amount of energy; if energy is spent performing one function, it will be unavailable for others. The language of hydraulics is evident in Freud's terms cathexis (filling) and catharsis (release). Although Freud himself never recommended the full-blown overt expression of anger for catharsis, others within the psychodynamic tradition began to do so. Irate individuals were urged to "get in touch with those feelings," or "let it all hang out." So-called catharsis was allegedly achieved by ventilation. In the heyday of this "ventilationist" era, in the 1970s, a number of people became involved in encounter groups and other therapies that encouraged expression of their pent-up feelings. I remember patients on psychiatric units being told by staff to pound pillows, rip up telephone books, and throw bean bags to "get the anger out." In a 1974 book called *Creative Aggression*, readers were actually advised to insult, scold, and scream at other people. The authors also recommended the formation of "insult clubs" and "family aggression festivals" (Bach & Goldberg, 1974). During this period, primal scream therapy was the latest rage—literally!

But virtually no empirical testing was performed to judge the efficacy of these ways of managing anger. In fact, until the era of behavioral and cognitive-behavioral therapies, there was a dearth of research on anger interventions of any kind. Research failed to support the idea that ventilation is therapeutic. Psychotherapy clients who demonstrate the most catharsis don't necessarily demonstrate the greatest change (Safran & Greenberg, 1991). As Gendlin (1973) has pointed out, "If you are living in an intolerable situation, no amount of catharting will exhaust your anger; it will arise anew every time you are in, or put yourself into, the situation" (p. 385). Explosive venting of anger actually makes a person *angrier,* rather than having a cathartic effect.

> *4.1. Try this experiment the next time you're furious: Yell at the top of your lungs and note your physiological arousal. Take your blood pressure and pulse. Keep yelling. Are you getting the anger off your chest, or fueling more of it? I think you'll find that anger fuels more anger. You can also conduct this experiment when someone is yelling at you. Yell back. Turn the volume up. Chances are, the other person will also turn up the volume. Infuriating, isn't it? As the conflict escalates, are you feeling better or worse?*

It is a cultural myth that you'll feel better if you respond to other people's anger with a vociferous blast—"giving back as good as you got," as the saying goes. An interesting study was done of men and women who give traffic tickets in New York City. You can imagine how unpopular these workers are, and how often they are bombarded by angry motorists who just got a ticket. The study showed that the workers who responded angrily to confrontation were *more* upset afterward. In contrast, those who used a calm conflict-management style felt better about the way they handled the confrontation (Brondolo, Bendetto, Storrs, Baruch, & Contrada, 1993).

A new view of anger stands in stark contrast to the shout-it-out ventilation-ist school of thought: I call this one the stuff-it-in stoic approach (in scientific writing, I call it the suppressive/ruminative anger coping style [Thomas, 2007]). This suppressive approach has gained prominence because of the compelling research on the overtly angry, coronary-prone personality. It is clear that unrestrained ventilation could be dangerous, even fatal. Thus, anger has been labeled by some as a toxic emotion, in fact "suicidal." One book was given the sensational title *Anger Kills* (Williams & Williams, 1993). Its authors claim that getting angry is like "taking a small dose of some slow-acting poison—arsenic, for example" (p. xiii), and they recommend that anger be "cut off" (p. xvi). And so the pendulum has swung to the other extreme: This lethal poison must be controlled.

The stuff-it-in stoic view is not really new. The Stoic philosophers thought emotions just caused misery and therefore must be harnessed. Typical of their advice are these words from Seneca (a Roman philosopher born in 4 B.C.): "Hesitation is the best cure for anger." Similarly, an old Chinese proverb advocates patience: "If you are patient in one moment of anger, you will escape a hundred days of sorrow" (cited in Seldes, 1985). Once again, hesitation and patience are in vogue. Not only are the old maxims like "Count to 10" being revived, but the new line of advice to the public is "Just don't get angry." In my opinion, this advice is simplistic. *Our goal should not be the eradication of anger.* In the Women's Anger Study (Thomas, 1993a), anger occurred mainly in encounters with intimates (spouses, children, friends, or coworkers) who had behaved disrespectfully or irresponsibly. It seems unrealistic that anger within these close interpersonal relationships could ever be eradicated. And suppressing it practically guarantees that it will take a devious course, ultimately causing relationship damage because the anger-provoking issue has never been worked through. As I emphasize throughout this book, anger has useful functions in self-protection and correction of injustices.

> *4.2. Here is another little experiment that I recommend to you. The next time something makes you angry, try to abort the emotion. Stuff it, squelch it, try to make it go away. What happens? Not only is the physiological arousal prolonged, but also the rumination about the grievance that provoked the anger. So, it doesn't go away. There is a nagging unrest because you have not acted on your true feelings. And suppression of anger, as we have seen in Chapter 2, is linked to higher blood pressure and a number of other physical problems. Avoidance of painful emotion is considered the core of many mental health problems as well (Perls, Hefferline, & Goodman, 1951). Peter Whybrow (1997) explains: "Emotion is an instrument of self correction—when we are happy or sad, it has meaning. Seeking ways to blot out variation in mood is equivalent to an airline pilot ignoring his navigational devices" (p. 72).*

Reviewing the conflicting, confusing advice that abounds in the literature, many of us are left wondering what we are supposed to *do* with our anger. Neither shouting it out nor stuffing it contributes to improved relationships with coworkers or family members, and neither is good for our own health. Nor should we turn anger on *ourselves,* making self-deprecating comments like "What a fool I was for trusting her" or "I'm furious with myself for accepting that assignment in the first place." Isn't there a rational alternative? That is what we are going to talk about now.

Anger Discussion

You *can* handle anger in an adaptive and health-promoting way, although it has received much less scrutiny by scientists. Consistent with everything else in medical and behavioral science, the focus is pathology rather than health. Thus, researchers have mainly studied the two extreme modes of expression you've just read about: "Anger-in" and "Anger-out." The earliest mention in the research literature of a healthier way of expressing anger was in 1978, in a study by Harburg, Blakelock, and Roeper. These researchers described a reflective anger coping style that was used to handle an angry boss. The style involved inhibiting impulsive reactions, waiting until the heat of the anger had cooled, and then having a rational discussion. Individuals who used this method had lower blood pressures compared with those who held anger inside or expressed anger outwardly. Interestingly, females were more likely to choose this approach than were males. In the same year as the Harburg paper, the first reports of the Framingham Heart Study were hitting the scene (Haynes, Levine, Scotch, Feinleib, & Kannel, 1978; Haynes, Feinleib, Levine, Scotch, & Kannel, 1978). Along with "Anger-in" and "Anger-out," the investigative team had measured a rational alternative: *"Anger-discuss,"* which involved getting anger off one's chest through discussion of the incident with a friend or relative. Subsequently, I used the Framingham Anger Scales for a number of my own studies, because I wanted my study participants to have the opportunity to say whether they used this adaptive anger management style. Coming from a nursing perspective, I wanted to know what behavior would be *health-promoting,* rather than focusing exclusively on what is health-damaging.

Through the years, I have found that "Anger-discuss" is the only anger expression style to correlate *positively* to general physical health (Thomas & Williams, 1991). Anger discussion is also correlated positively with self-esteem (Saylor & Denham, 1993), and it is *inversely* correlated with stress (Thomas & Donnellan, 1993) and depression (Droppleman & Wilt, 1993). In other words, you feel better about yourself and experience less stress and depression when you get anger off your chest by talking to someone. Other research findings are encouraging, too. One of my doctoral students found that anger discussion is correlated with a stronger sense of self-efficacy and optimism (Ausbrooks, Thomas, & Williams, 1995). In a study of mine, involving over 400 men and women, ages 18 to 77, I compared Anger Discussers (those who say they usually discuss their anger) with Non-Discussers (those who do not usually discuss anger). Discussers had lower systolic and diastolic blood pressures and lower body mass index (an obesity indicator). Additionally, Discussers were more likely than Non-Discussers to value their health highly, perceive better current health status, and engage in regular aerobic exercise (Thomas, 1997a). The findings of these studies are consistent with James Pennebaker's (1992) research on the beneficial health effects of sharing feelings about troubling events. Whether they disclosed to a human listener or to a tape recorder, study participants who verbalized emotion had better immune system function and fewer visits to health care providers.

In addition to the "Anger-discuss" scale, researchers developed some other tools to measure adaptive anger. Spielberger (1988) introduced a scale measuring Anger Control that includes tendencies to be patient and calm when angry, lessening one's cognitive and emotional arousal. A Reciprocal Communication scale was developed by Deffenbacher (1995b) to assess expressing one's thoughts and opinions clearly and tactfully, asking others for their opinions (and listening to them), and working toward compromise solutions. A scale called the Constructive Anger Behavior—Verbal Style Scale was developed by Davidson and colleagues to measure the tendency to deal directly with the person with whom you're angry, in order to find resolution to the situation (Davidson, Mac-Gregor, Stuhr, Dixon, & MacLean, 2000). Studies using these newer scales show that when people use these constructive modes of anger management, they are less likely to suffer a variety of adverse consequences. For example, Anger Control and Reciprocal Communication are negatively correlated with depression and anxiety, alcohol use, property damage, and damaged friendships (Deffenbacher, Oetting, Lynch, & Morris, 1996). Constructive anger verbal behavior has a significant beneficial effect on blood pressure, even when the researchers take into account the effects of standard hypertension risk factors, such as age, sex, body mass index, physical activity, education, parental history, and use of cigarettes and alcohol (Davidson, et al., 2000). As you can see, the findings of these researchers are consistent with my own.

If we apply the findings of these studies, we can learn how to behave more effectively when provoked to anger. The work situation may be bad, but we will be in a better position to cope with it. Simply put, what the research suggests to the angry individual is *talking*, in a normal tone, about the grievance. Ideally, direct discussion takes place with the other party in the dispute. The goals of the discussion are resolving the grievance and maintaining—not damaging—the relationship. I realize, however, that this direct discussion is not always possible due to situational constraints. When we are at work, we often need to remain calm and pleasant to patients and persons in authority over us, even if we are boiling inside. We are like flight attendants in this regard, a group that must suppress their anger at demanding and obnoxious passengers. Hochschild (1979) studied this group, finding that the flight attendants experienced considerable emotional problems. Some reported that they felt emotionally "numb" because of the continual suppression of annoyance, irritation, and anger. The researcher speculated that any individual in an occupation with strong rules inhibiting anger will experience difficulties similar to flight attendants.

Finding a Confidante

The research shows that we cannot afford to remain silent in our emotional discomfort. Therefore, when discussion cannot take place with the provocateur, we need to find a confidante, such as a good friend, and unburden ourselves. This gets the anger out harmlessly. There are a number of other benefits of discussing anger as well. Discussion is:

- a healthy way to review what happened
- an effective method for obtaining empathy and feedback
- a good means of formulating ideas to solve problems.

However, there is a caution. As you talk about the incident with your confidante, you do not want to prolong or escalate your anger. So, avoid raising your voice, pounding your fist, and using profanity. And choose someone who will listen attentively but *not* fuel additional anger by making inflammatory comments. As I mentioned in an earlier chapter, it is not helpful if the other person injects her own views (as in "Why didn't you just give him a piece of your mind?") Select a confidante who was not involved in the anger-producing episode and has no built-in bias or prejudice about any aspect of it. For example, if your anger is directed at a doctor, you would not want to tell your story to a person who is known to detest that doctor. Your goal is to get the anger off your chest and let it go.

Confronting the Provocateur

Although getting anger off your chest to a confidante can be very therapeutic, you may be wondering how this approach can lead to resolution of the original issue. You're right: it can't.

The poet William Blake sums it up far better than I:

> *I was angry with my friend:*
> *I told my wrath, my wrath did end.*
> *I was angry with my foe:*
> *I told it not, my wrath did grow.*
> (cited in Seldes, *The Great*
> *Thoughts*, 1985, p. 44)

At some point, you have to bite the bullet and take your anger to the "foe" for a one-to-one discussion that can lead to resolution of the problem. For example, if you have been treated unfairly by a supervisor, first cool down and reflect, then discuss your feelings about the unfair treatment with the supervisor. Your goal is to clearly and tactfully express your anger to the other person in a nonblaming way. Listen to the response, and move into a bargaining mode, prepared to negotiate and compromise. Few problems are entirely one-sided.

If you are sitting here reading all of this and saying to yourself, "There's not a snowball's chance in Hades that I would be able to go to my supervisor and do *that*," keep on reading. Because now we turn to *very specific techniques to change your anger behavior.* And I can assure you that I have seen amazing transformations in people's emotional habits. I strongly believe that all of us are moving forward toward wholeness throughout life, and being able to master a wide repertoire of emotional behaviors is an important aspect of being whole persons.

> *4.3.* The first step in changing anger behavior was spelled out by one of nursing's greatest scholars, teachers, and leaders, Hildegard Peplau:
>
> > It is important to gain an understanding of what occurred in situations in which anger is evoked. This requires a review and analysis of interaction data, including one's own participation in the event. Control of anger, as a response in situations, flows from recognizing the anger and understanding what evoked it. (contributed for this book)

Self-Assessment

1. As Peplau recommends, I ask you to engage in some careful introspection. I realize that focusing on oneself takes courage. It's more comfortable to find the other person at fault. But research shows that this step is a crucial one in any self-change endeavor (Williams, Pettibone, & Thomas, 1991). Anger is a confusing emotion for most of us. In the heat of an argument, we often lose track of the original provocation. Later on, with a cooler head, reflection produces some insight. I recommend keeping an *anger diary* or *log* for a month or so, recording accounts of conflictual interactions at work. If you really hate writing, an alternative way of keeping a diary of your anger episodes is tape-recording. Whether you write or make audiotapes, try to include all pertinent details about the interaction. What I am asking you to do is somewhat like the process recordings that you did as a student in psychiatric nursing or the field notes that you took during a research project. Just as a researcher does, you are going to analyze the data after collecting it:

   Who provokes your anger at work? What situations or circumstances usually set you off? Do you understand why? What thoughts are going through your mind? Do other people usually know when you are angry or do you keep it inside? What themes or patterns can you find in your anger diary entries? For example, do situations of powerlessness or injustice occur over and over? Are there issues of unmet expectations or betrayal of trust? Does criticism infuriate you? Do you become angered because of events that are outside of your control?

   Are your diary entries peppered with "shoulds"? If you are getting angry at *yourself*, what messages are you giving yourself? Are there differences in the frequency or intensity of your anger lately? How long does a typical day-to-day anger episode usually last for you?

   As you review your log or diary, pay particular attention to the *recurrent* anger themes and patterns. And watch for signs that your anger is *out of control*. It is cause for concern if the anger is too frequent, too intense, or out of proportion to the transgression. It is cause for major concern if your anger has become chronic or spills over onto your patients. And look carefully at the after-effects of episodes. Are you ruminating for a long time, unable to let go of your angry thoughts and feelings?

2. Next, assess your anger expression style. While none of us behaves exactly the same way in all situations, there is usually some consistency in our behavior. If your style is mainly discussing your anger in an effective, rational way, you may not need to read the rest of this chapter. The focus of this section is *nonproductive anger expression styles*. In my work, I have found that two nonproductive styles predominate. They are pretty consistent with the shout-it-out ventilationist and stuff-it-in stoic approaches that I have been talking about. As noted earlier, researchers call these styles "Anger-out" and "Anger-in." But when I am making presentations to the public, I usually refer to the "garlic people" and the "onion people." I'm not sure where I first heard about this little typology, but I have used it in workshops ever since. The "onion people" swallow most of their anger, and just as individuals who eat onions suffer inner distress afterward, so do these anger suppressors.

There's an aftertaste, and the anger just keeps trying to come back up. In contrast, the "garlic people," who freely spread overt anger all around, cause *others* to suffer—often for a prolonged time. But the garlic eater himself is no longer aware of the smell. He's just fine. Which are you?

Assessing Your Anger Style. You are an anger suppressor—an "onion"—if several of the following statements describe your behavior, *at least on some occasions*:

- I become anxious when my anger is aroused.
- When angry, I try to act as though nothing happened.
- I keep my anger to myself.
- I boil inside, but do not show it.
- I am angrier than I am willing to admit.
- I ruminate, pout, or sulk.
- I harbor grudges.
- I withdraw from people.
- I convey anger through an icy stare, frown, or "a look that could kill."
- I convey anger by rolling my eyes or raising my eyebrows.
- I convey anger through body language (folding arms, putting hands on hips, etc.).
- I convey anger through the "silent treatment."

You are a "garlic person" if several of the following statements describe your behavior, *at least on some occasions:*

- I become argumentative.
- I fly off the handle.
- I throw things.
- I strike out at whatever infuriates me.
- I slam doors.
- I raise my voice, scream, or yell.
- I tell people off.
- I say nasty things.
- I lose my temper.
- I hit or break things.
- I call the other person names.
- I stomp around.

Steps Toward Healing. For those who direct anger **inward**:

- *Get in tune.* If you assessed yourself to be an "onion person," you may be so accustomed to denying or disavowing your anger that you are not even sure when you're angry. You need to become more closely attuned to your bodily signals of distress or the defense mechanisms that automatically shunt your anger elsewhere as soon as it's generated. Defenses such as repression, denial, projection, isolation, or intellectualization may have served you well for a long time. It may take a while to give them up. You may have learned that anger is a sin, a notion that I disputed in Chapter 3. Some anger suppressors do not like the word *anger*, preferring to minimize their emotional arousal by using weaker terms. For example, they may say they are "a little irritated" or "kinda upset." Does this ring true for you? If so, your first assignment is to "own" the emotion of anger and add the word *anger* to your vocabulary. Recognizing, naming, and honoring your *legitimate anger* is important. Set incremental goals for yourself. For example, begin by changing your self-talk: "It's all right to be angry." Then work on saying—out loud—"I am angry" instead of "I'm kinda upset."

▨ *Learn to experience and express anger*. Give yourself permission to do so. You are not a truly free human being until you are unafraid to feel each emotion, including anger. When anger is inhibited, it just rolls up into a big ball, as one of our study participants described: "It's like you build up so much anger inside... without really sitting down and talking about the problem... it just rolls up into a big ball and you're not even sure what it's really about." This woman's metaphor conjures up an image of a multicolored ball of yarn, a tangled skein of grievances that have accumulated for a long time. If you've been rolling all your anger and aggravation into a big ball like this, it may be frightening to contemplate unraveling it. Be assured that you don't have to do it all at once. Nor am I urging you to begin using anger to confront *all* of your problems! I have seen women go from marshmallow to Medusa after a few sessions of assertiveness training. That's *not* what we're about. What you *will* need to learn is to express anger at the time of its provocation, rather than hiding it, ruminating about the grievance, and connecting it to a host of past grievances, so that another big ball of anger begins to accumulate.

In the words of George Schrader: "Anger is better disposed of as it arises in the commonplace situations of everyday life. What we need is to be free for our anger rather than to be free from it" (1973, p. 349).

▨ *Realize that anger is not catastrophic.* Women who participated in our qualitative study of anger (Thomas et al., 1998) feared they would alienate others if they expressed their feelings. Anger was viewed as something that "breaks the circle" of the relationship, as one woman phrased it. Another study participant said, "I guess I'm afraid that if I express anger, I will be rejected because I'm expressing myself and my needs, and I feel like if I do express needs at all... I'll be rejected." In our studies of nurses, males as well as females reported withdrawal from coworkers for fear of catastrophic consequences (A. Brooks, et al., 1996; Smith, et al., 1996). However, research by James Averill (1983) showed that *relationships are strengthened, not weakened, by honest expression of anger*. Targets of anger often gained rather than lost respect for the angry person. I like the metaphor of a *short circuit* to describe an angry encounter between persons. Wires pop and sparks fly, but the connection *can* be restored (Schrader, 1973). In contrast, withdrawal when you are angry *severs* the connection and leaves the other person in the dark about what ticked you off.

■ *Work through guilt about being angry.* Harriet Lerner sagely noted: "Anger and guilt are just about incompatible. . . .Nothing, but nothing, will block the awareness of anger so effectively as guilt. . . .Nor is it easy to gain the courage to stop feeling guilty and begin to use our anger to question and define what is right and appropriate for our own lives" (1985, pp. 6–7). Research shows that women experience more guilt about anger than men do, and our guilt has been attributed to empathy for the victim (Campbell, 1993). How do we get rid of this guilt? By expressing anger in the right way, at the right time, *assertively*. Assertive anger expression does not hurt the other person. There is no need for guilt when anger is being used to call attention to issues that are vitally important to us because of our values, beliefs, and rights as human beings.

■ *Learn to tolerate the inhibiting responses of others* when you try out new assertive behaviors. If you have been Doris (or Don) Doormat, your colleagues may want you to stay that way. Why wouldn't they? They could always count on you to work a double shift or take an extra patient. Likewise, your family didn't mind a bit that you were the one loading the dishwasher at midnight or going around picking up all the dirty towels off the bathroom floor. When you start requesting them to shoulder more of the workload, their response is predictably unenthusiastic: "What's gotten into you?" Lerner (1985) calls it the "Change back!" reaction. You may be accused of coldness or selfishness. The old guilt-button will get pushed.

Don't be discouraged if you get this kind of resistance to the "new you." Expect it. Remind yourself that what you are doing is good for you, and ultimately good for the other people who have used you as a doormat. Suppressing or turning anger inward does *not* prevent negative consequences. Research by Deffenbacher and his colleagues (1996) showed that Anger-in was significantly correlated with a variety of negative consequences, including damaged friendships and feeling physically ill and depressed. Moreover, holding anger in was highly correlated with feeling ashamed, dumb, embarrassed, and bad about oneself. Many of our study participants who suppressed their anger eventually erupted in volcanic outbursts that also left them ashamed and embarrassed (Thomas, et al., 1998). Here is an example from our data. A woman had simmered and stewed about her 16-year-old son wrecking the car, but said nothing. Several nights later, she was roaming the house, sleepless, ruminating about the accident—and becoming angrier at her son. At 2 A.M. she awakened him and blasted him: "It was like a volcano: once it erupts, it all came out, little by little by little. I thought, 'I have just lost control, I'm a crazy woman.'"

Clearly, suppressing the anger had only postponed the inevitable confrontation with her son, and her outburst was much more ineffective than a forthright discussion at the time of the accident would have been. You can imagine what a fearful sight she was to her sleepy teenager!

■ *Give yourself a mental flossing.* If you tend to pout, sulk, or ruminate about stressful and angry interactions for a prolonged period, try *mental flossing*. As you floss your teeth at night, you remove the food particles that will be a breeding ground for bacteria in your mouth. In the same way that flossing teeth leaves your mouth cleaner and less prone to gum infection or caries, mental flossing gets rid of troublesome thoughts that can "infect" your mental health. It does no good to keep thinking about what happened over and over again. In fact, you may be revving up your blood pressure as you rehash what happened. Research shows that rumination can rekindle the physiological responses (such as elevated blood pressure) that you experienced at the time of the original provocation (Glynn, Ebbeson, Christenfeld, & Gerin, 1998). This research adds impetus to cleanse your mind and heart at bedtime.

■ *Speak up.* If you tend to express a lot of anger through somatic symptoms (headaches, gastric distress), you need to learn to use *words* instead. Play detective for a few weeks, tracking the connections between getting angry at particular people or situations and the onset of these physical symptoms. How much time elapses between the feelings of irritation, tension, or fury and the headache or churning stomach? What strategy could you adopt to discharge the anger more constructively? With whom could you talk honestly about how you feel? There are many reasons why you may have difficulty in finding words for your feelings, such as early life experiences with your mother or growing up in a family that restricted emotional expression. In addition to the self-help strategies in this book, you may need the assistance of a counselor. Verbalization can be practiced in individual counseling or group therapy. You can learn to use body scanning (see Chapter 2) to identify early cues, like tense neck muscles, that anger is escalating. If you are extremely *anxious* about verbalizing anger, gaining control of your anxiety will be crucial. Ferreting out the source of the anxiety will probably lead back to your relationship with your parents. During the course of development, anger is felt most consistently toward parents. If they recoiled or responded harshly to your childish anger outbursts, it is understandable that anxiety accompanies anger arousal in later life. Techniques such as deep breathing and progressive muscle relaxation (see the next section for details) may be helpful in managing the anxiety that seems to go hand-in-hand with anger.

Steps Toward Healing. For those who direct anger **outward**:

■ *Be less reactive.* If you assessed yourself to be a "garlic person," your first assignment is to become less reactive. Chances are that you are getting bent out of shape too frequently and/or too intensely. You have a "short fuse," and your goal will be to achieve a longer fuse and a more moderate response style. Many daily provocations are relatively trivial and should simply be ignored. They are not worth getting angry about. If you cannot ignore what is happening, distract yourself. Imagery can be useful in shifting your mental focus. For example, visualize an idyllic scene in the mountains, high above the petty irritations that plague you so. From this lofty vantage point, you can see the molehills for what they really are.

■ *See the funny side.* Another tactic to dispel excess anger is to find a bit of humor in a frustrating situation. Humor creates a subjective state that is incompatible with anger. Some folks already know this: participants in Dianne Tice's (1990) study said they were more likely to use humor to control anger than to control other negative moods such as sadness. I have learned how to do this from my husband. He is good at discovering something to laugh at when circumstances are maddening. For example, when trapped in a colossal tie-up on the interstate, he began to watch the other motorists. He would call my attention to their faces, which portrayed the gamut of furious reactions to the traffic jam. People were screwing their faces into the most hideous expressions, snarling and spitting angry words into their cellular telephones. It became quite comical. We laughed, time passed, and we moved on when the accident was cleared away. It was a good lesson to me.

■ *Learn calming techniques.* You must reduce your physiological arousal before you can think clearly and take appropriate action on anger provocations. Here are four excellent, simple, calming procedures.

1. *The Relaxation Response* was developed by Herbert Benson, a professor at Harvard Medical School. According to Benson (1993), many studies have shown that anger and hostility decrease in people who regularly elicit the Relaxation Response. Here are his instructions:

   First, make arrangements so that you will not be interrupted.
   Pick a focus word or short phrase consistent with your belief system.
   Sit quietly in a comfortable position.
   Close your eyes.
   Relax your muscles.
   Breathe slowly and naturally, repeating your focus word as you exhale.

   If other thoughts come to mind, gently return to the repetition of the focus word.

   Continue for 10–20 minutes. You may open your eyes to check the time, but do not use an alarm. When you finish, sit quietly for a minute or so. Do not stand for 1–2 minutes.

2. Deep abdominal breathing (belly breathing) can also help dispel anger or stress. Most babies breathe this way, but adults tend to take shallow chest breaths. You will notice how different abdominal breathing is when you do this exercise. Begin by lying down and placing a book on your abdomen. Inhale and exhale deeply, watching the book rise and fall. Then sit up and place your right hand on your abdomen and your left hand on your chest. As you continue to breathe, strive to keep your right hand rising and falling while your left hand remains still. Try to breathe in slowly, filling your abdomen for 5 seconds. Then breathe out slowly for 5 seconds. You may want to have a watch or clock with a second hand in view while you do this exercise.

3. Another good way of cooling down a hot temper is *progressive muscle relaxation* (PMR). Familiar to most nurses, this technique involves first tensing and then relaxing the muscles, most often from head to toe. You will need to sit in a comfortable chair or lie on a carpeted floor.

Loosen tight clothing. If the technique is new to you, I recommend the purchase of an audiotape to guide you through the steps for the first few times. When finished with the procedure, you should feel deep calm and peace.

4. Still another approach is taking a *time-out* from the situation in which your anger is building. Taking time-out does not mean stalking off in a huff. It means making a sensible choice to postpone a confrontation until you can present your concerns more effectively. If possible, leave for 1 hour. Do not get in your automobile! We do not need any more angry drivers on the road! Instead, engage in something physical, like walking briskly. Do not return to the situation until you feel more solidly in control.

■ *Assess the real source of your anger.* A reason exists for your overreaction, although it may not be immediately evident. Your anger diary or some dream work can be helpful here. You may be surprised at what you discover. Author Gail Godwin describes her "angry year" in which she "seethed from morning till night with a hot, unspecific anger" (Godwin, 1983, p. 241). Everybody infuriated her, but she did understand why. At last she identified "the Culprit." She was really angry at *herself.* She relates that the Culprit's "favorite trick is posing as other people whom I hate until I realize I'm hating myself" (Godwin, 1983, p. 258).

■ *Plan ahead to avoid negative outcomes of angry behavior.* In the psychotherapy literature this is called "thinking-ahead training." First, identify the negative outcomes of your anger in a contingency statement: "If I lose my temper, then I will have an upset stomach." Then, when you walk into the workplace and run smack into the very individual who drives you up the wall, remind yourself of the negative consequences and substitute alternative behavior (Feindler & Ecton, 1986).

■ *Decrease ventilation.* Although spouting off may temporarily be satisfying, providing you with some release of tension, it decreases your personal and professional effectiveness. When you ventilate frequently, other people are likely to say, "Oh, there she goes again!" People begin to tune you out or avoid being around you. Decide whether an issue is really important enough to respond to, and then respond in a less extreme way.

■ *Be assertive, not aggressive.* If you prize your aggressiveness and fear that you will become a pushover or wimp without it, try reframing the aggression as weak and cowardly, while being able to stay cool and calm in negotiations as strong and powerful (Deffenbacher, 1992). You are probably accustomed to some benefits of aggressive behavior—such as getting others to comply with your demands—but keep in mind that these benefits are ultimately offset by damage to interpersonal relationships. Other people are left feeling coerced and resentful. Deffenbacher (1995a) suggests thinking about how you would want your coworkers to describe you at your retirement party. I believe that you can get much of what you want with assertiveness, with a lot less fallout. See Chapter 10 for specifics about assertive behavior.

■ *Consider systematic desensitization treatment.* Developed by Wolpe in 1958, this treatment involves collaborative development by the counselor and the client of a hierarchy of anger-arousing situations. Listed in the hierarchy are typical scenarios in which you experience strong reactions, ranging from the least anger-provoking to the most anger-provoking. After you learn a relaxation technique, such as PMR, you use imagery to generate the anger you would customarily feel in the first scenario on the hierarchy. Then, while aroused to anger, you counteract it with relaxation. Once you have mastered anger control in the first scenario, you move on to others of progressively more difficulty in the hierarchy.

Steps Toward Healing. For **everyone**:

Some anger management principles apply to everyone, regardless of your expression style. And, I'm aware that some of you alternate back and forth between shouting it and stuffing it. The "onion" and "garlic" types are, of course, extremes of the anger continuum. So, read on for other helpful steps toward healing. Thousands of nurses can attest to their usefulness!

- *Take constructive action on the precipitants of your anger whenever you can.* My ABC's of effective action are: *A*ssertiveness, *B*argaining, and *C*oalition-forming (Thomas & Droppleman, 1997). Be aware that emotionally loaded topics impair your ability to communicate clearly; that is why you should not approach the other party (such as a supervisor) in the heat of anger. Instead, make a plan, such as asking for an appointment with your supervisor on Monday. Then rehearse what you are going to say. Translate your anger into an *assertive* request (clearly stated as "I need _____"). *Bargain* for better conditions. Get other nurses to join with you in a *coalition* to tackle a common problem. We will have more to say about taking collective action in Part IV, Chapters 10 and 11.
- *Let it out.* If constructive action is not possible, find a spot where you will not be interrupted—the bathroom if all else fails. Then do this short anger-releasing exercise: close your eyes, breathe deeply, and focus your attention on repeating the word "peace." Exhale your anger. Let it out. Breathe out anger, breathe in peace. Barbara Dossey (1995) suggests the establishment of a Healing Room in your worksite, a place for staff to go for 10 or 20 minutes to nourish themselves. In the room are comfortable chairs or pillows on a carpeted floor, beautiful pictures, and a library of music, relaxation, and imagery tapes. This idea, called Sanctuary for Healing, has been implemented on many units in hospitals in Indianapolis (see Kerfoot and Ivy, 2004, for additional information).
- *Cry if you want to.* If you tend to cry when angry, do not be ashamed or apologetic about your tears. And do not leave the interaction. Crying simply indicates that you have strong feelings, and you can say this to the other person: "I'm crying because I feel so strongly about this issue." I read once that three kinds of saltwater heal: sweat, tears, and the ocean. Women cry out of anger more frequently than men, their tears emerging from the frustration that what they are saying is not being heard—or is being rejected out of hand. Ultimately, the solution to this frustration

is to master the techniques in this book that will allow you to deliver verbal messages with more confidence and oomph. Hang in there because there's lots more to cover.

4.4. *Tears on the job are not at all unusual. Plas and Hoover-Dempsey (1988) found that 80% of women and 50% of men have cried at least once during their working lives. Although some episodes of crying resulted from sadness, the tears were an expression of anger for many people.*

- *Don't displace work-related anger on the folks at home.* Both "garlic" and "onion" types do this, sometimes unknowingly. The garlic person may be slamming pots and pans or snapping at the kids, while the onion person's anger may be disguised in unresponsiveness or inertia: "I'm just too tired. You go to the movies without me." Family members may be hurt and bewildered by such behavior. I recommend a decompression time during the drive home from work, to mentally "finish" with the emotional upheaval of the workday and prepare to greet your family in better spirits. As you reflect on your workday, try to think of *one good thing* that you accomplished and recite the following affirmation: "Because I was there today (that upset student found a listening ear, that patient had a period of restful sleep)." Even if a work situation is infuriating, or you have been treated unjustly, perpetuating an angry mood serves no good purpose. Displacing your anger onto the wrong targets cannot produce satisfaction. "Lighten up" before you walk in the front door to greet your significant others.
- *Remember that stress fuels anger.* Know your limits, and once you're close to the breaking point, institute stress management strategies. If you're highly stressed at work, cut yourself some slack at home (and vice versa). Cry, laugh, exercise, play, pray. Use commuting time to listen to beautiful taped music or an audiobook. At the end of a "shift from hell," slip into a darkened movie theater and transport yourself to another place and time. Take a mini-vacation by getting out postcards or souvenirs from your favorite vacation place and flying off to that place—in your imagination—for a few minutes. Turn off all instant messaging systems, and let your answering machine screen your telephone calls. Converse only with callers who will uplift your mood or make you laugh. Avoid "stress carriers," those gloomy people who consistently drag us down with their pessimism. (See Chapter 9 for other stress-relief tips.)
- *Avoid useless, no-win arguments.* If possible, simply exit gracefully. Why let yourself get involved in heated discussions of abortion, politics, religion, or other value-laden topics? If you are ultimately drawn into the argument, try to find some areas of agreement to emphasize: "There are good points on both sides of this issue," "We're both right," or "We both want the same thing." Avoid the impulse to try to win. You can't.
- *Walk away.* Avoid environmental stimuli and interpersonal situations that you know from past experience will "push your button." If it drives you up the wall to listen to Joann's nonstop monologue at lunch, go to lunch with Karen instead. If you fume every time you walk past Adrian's messy office, go down the other corridor, so that you won't have to look at it.

If every board meeting of an organization is spent in fruitless bickering, resign from the board and lend your talents to other groups.

■ *Work on anger issues left over from your family of origin, your divorce, or other past events.* Chronic, festering anger can be devastating to your physical and mental health. Find a counselor who will help you let go of old anger (and see Chapter 8 for plenty of good self-help strategies).

4.5. *Psychologist Jack Kornfield (1993) tells of a man who visualized his anger as enormous—like a bomb, a nuclear explosion. When instructed to let his anger open as much as needed, the man imagined that it burned up the whole universe. Kornfield relates,*

> The whole universe became dark and dead and full of ashes. A great fear arose in him. He felt that for a long time much of his life had been dead; now the deadness felt stronger, as if his life would be that way forever. I suggested that he let the deadness and ashes fill the universe forever and see what would happen. . . Then, to his amazement, there came a green light far off in the distance. . . It was a new planet being born, with oceans, green plants, and young children. Seeing this, he realized that even the greatness of his own pain had an end. The anger and frustration that had been there so long began to lose its power over him and an inevitable renewal began to take place. (Kornfield, 1993, pp. 115–116)

■ *Reward yourself for trying new anger behaviors.* Rewards are essential in learning and maintaining any new skills. Buy a new CD, browse in a bookstore, or go to the beach. Spend time with people who support the changes you are making. Their affirmation can be immensely valuable to the success of your behavior change project.

■ *Consider taking an anger management class.* It is helpful to learn new anger behaviors in a group, so that you can receive feedback from others regarding your tone of voice and nonverbal communication. Behavioral practice in the safety of the group gives you greater confidence that you can enact new behaviors in real-world situations. Contact your local mental health center or university to find anger management or assertiveness groups. I regularly conduct groups in my community, using an anger management manual I developed (Thomas, 2001b). The support that I see the group members giving to each other is at least as valuable as my cheerleading for their efforts—maybe more valuable.

■ *Deliberately generate positive emotions* by tallying the positive events that occurred in your day. In laboratory experiments, positive emotions (such as joy) actually down-regulated the undesirable cardiovascular after effects of negative emotions (Fredrickson, Mancuso, Branigan, & Tugade, 2000). In an intervention with cancer and AIDS patients, beneficial outcomes resulted from tallying positive events at the end of the day, describing these positive events to others, and identifying how the events were meaningful. The patients felt less stressed and more able to cope with their conditions. They also reported positive states of mind and personal growth (Chesney, Darbes, Hoerster, Taylor, Chambers, & Anderson, 2005). Sounds like a good daily practice for everyone, doesn't it?

A Last Word

In this chapter, we presented some of the most important anger management concepts and tactics of the entire book. This is a chapter that you may need to refer to again and again. Particularly crucial to success in changing nonproductive anger patterns are: (1) keeping an anger journal or log, (2) taking steps to transcend "onion" or "garlic" behaviors, and (3) rewarding yourself for trying new strategies. Practice is essential. You are acquiring a new skill set, in the same way that you customarily acquire new nursing skills. Try out your new skills in the workplace, and watch for improved relations with coworkers!

Connecting
With Others

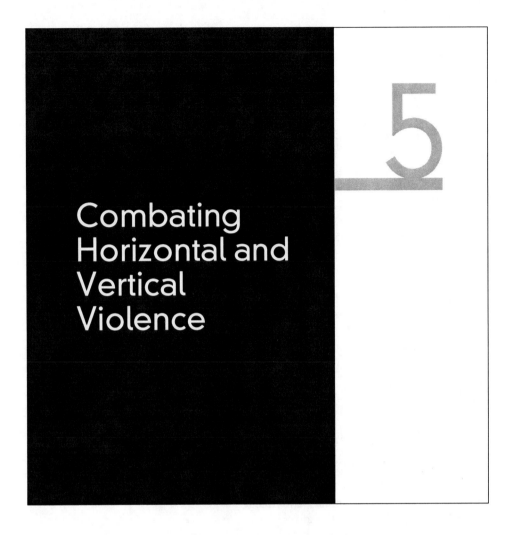

Combating Horizontal and Vertical Violence

Man is but a network of relationships, and these alone matter to him
—A. de Saint-Exupery

The healing we need in our profession cannot be accomplished by each of us working on our anger management tactics in isolation. *Healing takes place in relationships*, and this chapter focuses on our relationships with colleagues— other nurses, supervisors, and physicians. Disharmony exists in all of our collegial relationships, as so vividly shown in the nurses' words in Chapter 1. We will address both horizontal and vertical violence, and provide concrete recommendations for eradicating these destructive phenomena. Whether you are a manager or a staff nurse, you will find helpful guidance for achieving improved relationships.

Wounding One Another: Horizontal Violence

5.1. "I was the child with a lifetime dream of being a nurse and caring for the sick. . . . I am totally fulfilled as a nurse caring for children, but so often it is the

> hostility nurses show toward each other that frustrates me most and makes me want to leave this profession."
>
> —e-mail from an RN with 22 years of experience

One of the most disturbing aspects of our research data on nurses' anger is the *vehemence of their anger at each other.* This nurse-to-nurse anger is not healthy anger. Words taken right from our interview transcripts include *faultfinding, bickering, backbiting, needling, snapping,* and *cutting.* When I was in California recently doing workshops, I heard that the nurses were constantly writing each other up. I heard a lot about nasty notes on locker doors, too. These hurtful behaviors are manifestations of a phenomenon called *horizontal violence* or *lateral violence* in the literature. I have known about this destructive phenomenon—and experienced it, of course—throughout my nursing career. Its existence has been documented in a variety of institutional settings for at least 75 years (Stevens, 2002). It can include covert tactics (such as spreading unkind gossip) or overt behaviors (such as critical remarks). Today, hostile messages from coworkers can be transmitted even faster in workplaces with networked computers—in those snippy e-mails with a little zinger at the end.

Have You Experienced Horizontal (Lateral) Violence From Your RN Colleagues?

Here is a list of common manifestations:

- Subtle nonverbal behaviors, such as rolling eyes, raising eyebrows, giving a cold shoulder
- Sarcasm, snide remarks, rudeness
- Undermining or sabotaging
- Withholding needed information or assistance
- Passive-aggressive (behind the back) actions
- Spreading rumors and destructive gossip
- False accusations, scapegoating, blaming

What causes nurses to engage in horizontal violence? Scholars such as Roberts (1983) say that the behavior is characteristic of oppressed groups who fight others at the same level of a hierarchical system because they cannot safely vent anger upward to their superiors. Roberts (1983, 2000) pointed out similarities among oppressed groups, such as colonized Africans, Jews, and African Americans. Throughout the history of modern nursing, physicians, supervisors, and hospital administrators have held the power over nurses. Today, despite many notable advances in the profession, the majority of nurses still work in hospitals or other facilities where a hierarchical system exists, with one or more levels of personnel above them. And they still express their hostility horizontally— toward their own peers. Rowe and Sherlock (2005) found that 75% of nurses at an urban teaching hospital had been verbally abused by other nurses. In another recent study of hospital nurses and ancillary staff, 65% reported frequently observing lateral violence among coworkers (Stanley, Martin, Nemeth, Michel, & Welton, 2007).

When the hostility is overt, as in a verbal blast or sarcastic put-down by a colleague, it may be easier to deal with than when it is an ambush or covert sniper fire. It's harder to identify a hidden sniper who is carrying tales to management or spreading malicious gossip. It's also hard to defend yourself when you don't know exactly what is being said—or you don't have a clue that you have apparently offended someone. I was certainly caught off guard a few years ago when colleagues of mine went behind my back to the director of the educational institution where I taught at the time. I was serving on a committee that was spinning its wheels. I grew weary of unproductive debate and suggested that a small task force or subcommittee be appointed to delve into the matter and bring recommendations back to the larger group. No one voiced an objection to this suggestion, and the meeting was adjourned shortly thereafter. To my astonishment, the next day I was summoned to the office of the director. I was informed that the other committee members thought that I was "rude," and that I had hurt their feelings. My action was perceived as cutting off debate prematurely. Rather than forthrightly saying to me, "No, appointing a task force is not the way to go," members of the committee had gone to the director to complain. The director warned me to be more careful in the future.

Examples of the more subtle forms of horizontal hostility abounded in our research data:

"I tend to draw back from her and give her a lot of the cold shoulder."

"I am a female Southerner, trained from birth to be passive-aggressive. You can cut them, but don't let them know they're bleeding until they look down and see it."

5.2. Helen Campbell spoke to the research team of experiencing coworkers "hugging you and stabbing you at the same time." She had experienced no hostility from these coworkers when she was an LPN, but when she returned to the same ICU to work as a charge nurse, their attitude was different. She isn't sure whether their behavior should be attributed to racism or gender:

I've worked at this institution for 17 years. I was tolerated as long as I was an LPN. I wasn't a threat, because I was on a lower level. Now I'm an RN like everybody else, and I'm the only Black in the ICU with eight White nurses. I've always had the ability, but now I've got the license to go with it. And now they all resent me. I didn't ask for a charge position, it was offered to me. There were plots. They would do deceitful things. I found out females do that anyway.

Helen Campbell's experience (see 5.2) begs the question: Does horizontal violence occur in our profession because nurses are predominantly women, "trained from birth to be passive-aggressive" as one of our study participants described? In a 2001 book, author Phyllis Chesler spent 551 pages documenting women's inhumanity to women. Included in her weighty tome were abundant examples of undermining, manipulation, and cruel abuses perpetrated by women on women. After reading Chesler, one might conclude that the gender composition of our profession is the culprit in the phenomenon of horizontal hostility. Chesler derives her explanation of the phenomenon from psychodynamic theory, but she acknowledges the influence of patriarchy as well. In a patriarchal culture, women are viewed as subordinate and inferior to men, and they internalize the culture's view of them. Nursing has been viewed as "women's work," and certainly "women's work"—nurturing and caring for others—has been devalued in our society, just as women themselves have been. Thus, it is difficult for women to view other women as valuable.

You may find gender a plausible explanation of horizontal hostility in nursing. Researchers do find chilly silence, cattiness, snide memos, and other passive-aggressive behaviors pervasive in female-dominated professional groups. In one survey, more than 75% of the female nurse respondents said they had been undermined by another woman (Briles, 1994). But I argue that gender cannot be a sufficient explanation. It was clear from our study of male nurses that *horizontal hostility is not confined to females.* We saw many instances of it in our sample of male RNs. They too made disparaging remarks about colleagues. They too experienced frequent verbal attacks from coworkers. One male nurse spoke of being "wounded with words." Another said, "She purposely attacked me, embarrassing me in front of others, humiliating me, trying to make me look incompetent. I should have been more assertive. But I wasn't at that time." The devastating phenomenon of horizontal hostility does not occur just because most nurses are women. *It occurs because all of us in the profession—male and female alike—have been oppressed.*

Bullying

Especially in the British and Australian nursing literature, authors often use the term "bullying" to describe the same behaviors that we call lateral violence in the United States (e.g., Quine, 1999; Stevens, 2002; Turnbull, 1995). However, the term "bullying" actually should be reserved for behavior that is deliberate and repeated by the perpetrator for at least 6 months or more. Bullying produces serious psychological consequences for the victim, such as anxiety, shame, and even posttraumatic stress disorder (PTSD) (Felblinger, 2008; Namie, 2003). According to the report on abusive workplaces of the World Bullying Institute, victims endure their maltreatment for an average of 23 months if they are unable to mount an effective response (Namie, 2003).

Devaluing One Another

Other forms of nurse-to-nurse hostility include *name-calling* and *disparaging the competence of one's colleagues.* For example, Sue Green refers to some of her colleagues in advanced practice as "dizzy Lizzies" and "bad apples": "There are some of us that really throw piles of shit on that image because they are so incompetent or you know, dizzy Lizzy, and I think that is a situation where one bad apple can spoil a bushel."

Carol Carter calls her charge nurse a "dingbat" and asserts that the woman is unqualified and lazy: "She was getting paid for charge nurse. They had a body to fill the slot. They didn't care if they had a *qualified* body.... She was getting paid, but yet she didn't do anything. Here I'm working my behind off as a staff nurse and my other coworkers working their behinds off and yet we had another body getting paid more salary, doing nothing."

Ron Murray related an acrimonious exchange with a "haughty" coworker who questioned his nursing knowledge: "She got loud, sort of haughty, and I said, 'You just better stop 'cause I'm not taking this crap off of you. I don't give you crap and you're not going to give me crap. It's disrespectful.'"

Not only do nurses devalue each other, they also devalue themselves. It was distressing to the members of my research team to hear so many nurses—smart and capable professionals—devaluing their own work. For example, Eve Sanders, a master's prepared nurse practitioner, referred to her work as "scut work" and "taking care of the petty things." Every nurse whom we interviewed used the word "hierarchy" and had a definite perception of where they and others belonged in the hierarchy of health care providers. Doctors held superior rank in the echelon, and a hierarchical ordering even existed within nursing itself, with critical care nursing accorded higher status than psychiatric or maternal–child nursing. Sadly, nurses who provide magnificent direct patient care every day, a vital service to humanity, put themselves down by saying "I'm just a staff nurse" or "I was never able to go back to school to get my BS degree."

Identifying With the Oppressor

Some of us deal with the oppression in nursing by *identifying with the oppressor*. Here is an example, drawn from letters to the editor of my local newspaper. A woman who had a satisfying birth experience in the care of a nurse-midwife wrote a very positive letter. Other letter writers joined in the ensuing dialogue, expressing largely favorable opinions. There was only one dissenting voice: that of an obstetric nurse. In her belligerent letter, she claimed that a woman would choose a nurse-midwife only if "there is no higher skilled person available or because they (women) have been misinformed as to the merits of nurse-midwifery." The obstetric nurse's hostility toward her colleagues became even more painfully evident as she continued: "I would like to make a point of saying that over the history of legitimate obstetrical care, it has not been the nurse-midwife who has made the advances in prenatal care possible for pregnant women. It has been the physicians and the vast bodies of research and development available to them." By glorifying physicians and denigrating the work of those in her own profession, what this letter writer is doing is identifying with the oppressor. It is a way of dealing with her feelings of inferiority. The obstetric nurse believes she will gain greater respect and approval by aligning herself with physicians. It is physicians, not nurse-midwives, who give "legitimate obstetrical care." She cannot even acknowledge that research is done by, or available, to nurses.

When the role of physician assistant was new, a number of nurses felt very special in being chosen by a particular physician to receive additional preparation and then work with him. After their transformation into what they thought was a more prestigious position, they would come to the units wearing lab coats, not uniforms, seeing the physician's patients and writing orders—signing their names with PA after it, instead of RN. Leaving off the RN credential was a clear repudiation of their former "inferior" status as a nurse. Identification with the oppressor is also seen in nurses who align themselves with hospital associations and other groups to fight against changes in legislation being proposed by their own colleagues in the state nurses' association or board of nursing. Many have internalized the views of their hospital administrators, and they believe that "the hospital knows what's best for us." I have observed numerous examples of this over the years.

Vertical Violence: It Starts in Nursing School

The oppression starts in nursing school for many of us. Just as nurse educator Judith Meissner (1986) proposed in her classic article, nurses *do* eat our young. Nurse educators are the first offenders. Rather than encouraging students to develop and use their personal power, too many teachers are "drill sergeants" commanding obedience. In the clinical area, more emphasis is placed on *judging* students than on assisting and supporting them. And the classroom is a place of humiliation for many new nursing students. Accustomed to making good grades in high school or prenursing college courses, they are devastated by grades of C—or worse—in nursing courses. According to Meissner, "We assign unrealistic study loads and written assignments that may seem little related to their clinical activities. . . . But it's in testing and grading that we become the great gobblers of our young. We write minutiae-filled examinations that make it nearly impossible for students with excellent grades in general courses to attain similar grades in work that matters to them most—their major. Is it any wonder that many students who entered nursing with great expectations fail to thrive?" (Meissner, 1986, p. 52).

While Meissner called the phenomenon *insidious cannibalism,* Jarratt (1981) proposed that faculty behavior is analogous to child abuse: "The 'we' who were being mistreated or misunderstood then, are the 'they' of today" (p. 10). I prefer the term *vertical violence.* Regardless of what you label it, it is clear that inhumane treatment of nursing students has been going on for a long time.

> *5.3. Distinguished nursing scholar Jeanne Quint Benoliel was a student nurse in a diploma program from 1938 to 1941. She was 500 miles away from home, living by a strict code of rules in a dormitory next to the hospital. Even after all these years, she vividly remembers how she felt when accused of stealing from a patient:*
>
>> *Fear of negligence was inculcated in us by the attitudes and actions of the faculty, who seemed to equate making mistakes with committing mortal sins. . . . I was assigned to obstetrics. I had not been there very long and had little experience or knowledge about the prepartum events to expect. I was assigned to stay with a woman of Italian background who came in on the evening shift with her husband and her mother. She had started labor while they were having dinner, and while in the hospital, she started vomiting. I think that part of what I did was to complete the admission process, but I mainly remember being in the room with the three of them and not knowing what to do to help this woman feel better. She was not easy to be with because she expressed her discomfort vocally and loudly.*

> *At some point, I was relieved by someone else, and I went to the dorm to get some sleep. In the early morning hours, I was awakened to take a phone call from the night supervisor, who wanted to know what I had done with the woman's valuables. The tone of her voice was accusatory. I could not remember. So I got dressed and went to the woman's room to see if I could remember anything. I looked in the bedside drawer—and lo and behold, there were her things! I reported the information to the night supervisor and then went back to my room, where I cried and cried. I was angry at being treated as though I were a criminal, but I assumed that I had to "take it" because that was the pattern of superior-subordinate relationships. . . . I remember the incident as another of those "put-down" experiences by a senior nurse.*

"Put-down" experiences, such as that described by Jeanne Benoliel, are still reported by our novice nurses. Students in Clark's (2008) study described faculty behaving in demeaning and belittling ways, treating them unfairly, and pressuring them to adhere to unreasonable demands. Faculty power and rank prevented the students from speaking out in response. Negative interaction with instructors was identified as the most anxiety-producing aspect of clinical experience in a study of baccalaureate students conducted by Kleehammer, Hart, and Keck (1990). In a study that I conducted with colleagues Johnie Mozingo and Ellie Brooks, baccalaureate students reported that they were "intimidated" by faculty and "drilled in front of doctors and nurses" (Mozingo, Thomas, & Brooks, 1995). These statements were typical:

> "Few instructors give encouragement and tell you when you have done a good job—you always hear the negative."
> "It seemed as if instructors constantly looked for wrong things."
> "Instructors give it to us good when we mess up."

Practicing nurses interviewed by my research team provided additional evidence. One nurse recalled an instructor who obviously delighted in pouncing upon a student's inadequacies: "You could hear her out at the nurses' station and somebody would say to her, 'How's everything going?' and she'd say, 'Oh, I'm just sitting here giving that student just enough rope to hang themselves.'" Another nurse told us: "Faculty sometimes can see a student with a lot of potential and will cut a student down just to put them in their place." Anne Ricketts, in a letter to the *American Journal of Nursing* about her nursing school experience, said, "The instructors' motto was 'Those who can be discouraged, should be.' I made it through, but not without scars" ("On Mentorship," 2001, p. 65).

Out of the Frying Pan and Into the Fire

Hospital staff nurses often carry on the "trial by fire" where the faculty leave off. For several years, I have collected anger narratives written by junior students in a BSN program. The vertical violence perpetrated by hospital staff RNs is a recurrent theme. I will share just a few of the student stories here (see Thomas & Burk (in press) for a full report of the research). The stories may make you want to cry. Rather than being welcomed into a supportive milieu for learning, students discover that they are unwanted and in the way:

> *I was preplanning for my second day at Hospital A when I overheard one of the young nurses saying, "They better not give me any nursing students tomorrow." Nurse A was no more than 24 years old and had not been out of nursing school long. Her words made me angry because, even though nursing students may make things more difficult, we are just trying to learn. I thought Nurse A should have realized that she was in our position only a few years ago.*

The students often find themselves "easy targets," being unfairly blamed and scapegoated by the floor nurses, as shown in this example:

> *An incident when I became angry was during a clinical experience. Our group had left to go to lunch at our scheduled time around 11:00 A.M. After lunch, I came back and checked on my patient's blood sugar, and it was very low (about 54). My instructor had been in the room with me, and we immediately gave the patient the amount of D50 that was ordered by the physician. We then noticed that his tube feeding had been stopped, and the tube taken out. I went and asked the nurse about it, and she yelled at me saying, "I told you he needs to be on a continuous tube feeding." Needless to say, I was extremely angry, as I had not stopped the tube feeding. I told her that I had not stopped the tube feeding.... She left as if she did not believe me and [implied] that I had purposefully endangered the life of the patient. I held in my anger for awhile because I was so shocked that she had not really listened to what I had said. The nurse later came back to me and informed me that two CNAs had moved the patient to a chair while I had gone to lunch and had stopped his tube feeding.... She did not apologize for yelling at me, and so I remained a little bit upset about the whole incident.*

Being yelled at by an RN was especially upsetting to the students when it occurred in the presence of patients, visitors, or peers:

> *Last semester, I was giving a bath to a disabled boy. His mother inquired whether the seizure medication had been given that morning. I told her that I would check with his nurse. When I found Nurse X, she was irate that I had asked. The mother was making a simple inquiry because she was concerned about her son. Instead of going to the mother and answering her questions, Nurse X yelled at me in the hallway while the mother was listening. It was an embarrassing situation for everyone involved. Afterwards, I avoided that nurse for the rest of my time at Hospital Y because I was afraid she would yell at me again.... I was also more timid and did not like going to ask the floor nurses questions.*

In the following story, staff Nurse R's treatment of both the student and the patient was appalling:

> *I was working with Nurse R one day. We had a 92-year-old stroke victim who was wonderful. Right off, I felt that Nurse R did not like nursing students. She*

was very abrupt with all of us. I made several overtures of friendship toward Nurse R that were all rebuffed. . . . Later in the day I was changing my lady and needed to give her a suppository—which I had never done. I asked Nurse R for help. . . . Nurse R was extremely rude and condescending; she treated my wonderful patient like she was a sack of potatoes. I was so mad at Nurse R that I could barely speak. . . . I did not express my anger to Nurse R. It did not seem right to take her to task in front of an audience, even though she did not treat me with respect, I needed to give her the respect of not trying to humiliate her. After this run-in with Nurse R, I felt let down. I had enjoyed my time at Hospital B until then. She was a fly in the cream of my experience.

Bear in mind that many of the students' stories pertained to incidents within the first days or weeks of their clinical experiences in hospitals. The way they were treated by staff RNs increased their anxiety, decreased their self-confidence, and made some of them question if they really wanted to become nurses.

It Continues When New Grads Hit the Workplace

When new graduates hit the workplace, their idealism may be mocked and their shortcomings magnified (Duchscher & Cowin, 2004a). They are expected to "hit the ground running" (Duchscher & Cowin, p. 291), although this expectation is unrealistic. Their transition from student to graduate is difficult enough without hazing by senior RNs. One particularly disturbing study by New Zealand researchers surveyed new graduates in their first year of practice. A sizable percentage (34%) reported experiences of direct verbal hostility, including unjust criticism and/or behavior that was rude, abusive, and humiliating. The new graduates also reported more subtle types of horizontal hostility, such as having their learning blocked and being treated like a student. One in three respondents had considered leaving nursing because of a particularly distressing "intracollegial incident" (McKenna, Smith, Poole, & Coverdale, 2003).

The words of one of our own study participants echoed the New Zealand participants' reports of the more subtle type of horizontal hostility. The staff simply didn't orient this RN or help her; she felt abandoned as she struggled to adjust to the demands of a busy ICU:

I was fresh out of nursing school, and it was very difficult and stressful and frustrating. I never felt like I got my orientation. . . . Whenever anybody else needed help, my preceptor would run off and abandon me. I had question after question trying to learn these things that were so foreign to me. A lot of the nurses did not want to get up and help other people. I didn't know that I had options. I should have gone to the nurse manager and said, "Hey, I don't feel like I'm getting the education that I need. I'm not comfortable." I was always uncomfortable. Every day I went in there, I was nervous—and a lot of times, I left there in tears out of frustration. I should have gone to the supervisor, but I didn't, and that was naive of me. I should have taken the bull by the horns and said, "Hey, you know, I need help here," but I didn't.

Here is another poignant example from our data:

When I first started working here, we had a new grad who is an excellent nurse. . . . and I think other nurses were jealous of her. She was a baccalaureate nurse, and a lot of the nurses on my floor are not. . . . You could just see the potential in this girl. She was so good with the patients, and she had a lot of energy. . . . But other nurses would never help her. It was almost like [they were] setting her up. . . . to fail. . . . She told me, "I really wonder if I should be a nurse. Maybe I. . . . should do something else." So I encouraged her to get off that unit. I said, "You can't let other people destroy you."

Difference in educational preparation was problematic in the last example. Other differences can create problems between senior and junior nurses. Nurse researcher K. Lynn Wieck points to "generational gaps" between age cohorts: "The older nurses—those over age 50—are from a generation that obtained much of its socialization in the military model, where they were taught to 'do as I say' and not question authority . . . On the other hand, nurses from Generation X and Y have been socialized to ask questions and voice their dissatisfaction" (cited in Trossman, 2007, p. 1). These generational differences can lead to considerable tension and frustration, with each cohort unable to understand and appreciate the strengths of the other.

The Effects of Hazing

Hazing has driven several qualified and valuable nurses from my depart-ment . . . in the past year, eight nurses have come and gone . . . I've seen my fellow graduates leave the profession after having dreamed of becoming nurses since childhood. . . . They were disappointed that their work environments reminded them more of the halls of their junior high schools than of institutions designed to help people. (Anonymous RN, in "On Mentorship," 2001, p. 66)

The exodus of hazing victims is too costly: The cost of replacing an RN is between 75% and 125% of the RN's annual salary (Pine & Tart, 2007). Clearly, we must stop the nurse-to-nurse hostility. It drains vital energy from nurses and undermines institutions' attempts to create satisfying work environments that could stem the exodus (Thomas, 2003b). There is no possible winner in our destructive skirmishes with one another. Furthermore, as Theodore Roosevelt said, "There are enough targets to aim at without firing at each other." In fact, if we stay focused on fighting among ourselves, we will not have energy left for fighting the bigger battles that so urgently need our attention. Nor will we ever feel satisfied with our jobs. *Group cohesion* (a sense of belonging and together-ness) strongly influences nurses' job satisfaction (Lucas, Atwood, & Hagaman, 1993; Shader, Broome, Broome, West, & Nash, 2001). In a study conducted by the *New York Times*, the most important factors in job satisfaction were good re-lationships with other nurses and good schedules ("Demand for nurses," 2002).

If our profession is distinctive because of our caring, as claimed by Jean Watson, Margaret Newman, and Madeleine Leininger, then we must start *caring for each other*. We must substitute caring, support, and empathy for antagonism, sabotage, and mistrust.

The benefits of caring and support are legion. The more a nurse perceives support from colleagues in the workplace, the less he burns out, as shown in eight studies reviewed by Duquette, Kerouac, Sandhu, and Beaudet (1994) and a newer study by Moffett (2002). And the beneficial effect of collegial support in preventing burnout is evident *regardless of the level of job stress* (Ogus, 1990). Support does not lower nurses' stress, but it does aid them in coping with it and it adds positive need-fulfilling elements to their lives. Nurses reporting high support from coworkers also have a stronger sense of personal accomplishment than nurses reporting few sources of support (Ogus, 1990; Moffett, 2002). Clearly, healing the emotional pain in nursing begins by *connecting with one another.*

Steps Toward Eradicating Horizontal Violence

- *Begin to share of yourself.* Sidney Jourard's (1971) groundbreaking research on self-disclosure showed that none of us can attain health and fullest personal development unless we permit our authentic selves to be known. What does this entail? Candidly telling a coworker that you are scared or hurt. Dropping your mask of perfection or imperturbability, your defensive front, and permitting yourself to be vulnerable and real. Schopenhauer compared humans to porcupines that are trying to huddle together on a cold night to get warm. The closer they get to each other for warmth, the more they hurt each other with their sharp quills. Yet, even porcupines have a soft side that is not so well defended against being touched. Thus, they can turn their soft vulnerable undersides toward each other and achieve intimacy.
- *Listen to your colleagues when they disclose their real selves and their honest opinions.* I am talking about listening in a new way, engaging in dialogue that creates a culture of cooperation. Here, I am drawing from the ideas of the late David Bohm (1990) about dialogue. He envisioned diverse people coming together to listen deeply to one another and discover new ways to work (or live) together. In dialogue, individuals give consideration to views that differ substantially from their own. Dialogue proceeds at a slower pace than normal conversation because deeper levels of listening and reflection are required. Dialogue among a team of nurses who work together is always enlightening, because each RN's view of the work situation is only a partial view. When all members of a team disclose their perspectives to one another, awareness is enlarged and creative strategies to cope with problems are developed. Behaviors that support dialogue are (1) listening and speaking with judgment suspended, (2) respecting differences, (3) setting aside individuals' usual roles and statuses, (4) keeping a proper balance between inquiry about

another's perspectives and advocacy of your own ideas, and (5) focusing on learning from one another and expanding your understanding.

5.4. Questions to Ask Yourself

A bit of introspection about barriers to dialogue may be useful. Ask yourself:

- What do I do that shuts others down?
- What do I do that leaves others feeling insignificant...silenced, walled off, unwilling to be open when they are with me?
- What do I do that prompts others to try to convince me of their rightness, of my wrongness...to not speak directly to me, or to ignore my presence or even my very existence? (Roth, 1999).

- *Make a warm, empathic response to a colleague in distress.* Empathy is not a new concept to you, and you have heard many definitions of it. I like this one from Martin Buber:

> *Empathy means, if anything, to glide with one's own feeling into the dynamic structure of...a man (sic), and as it were to trace it from within, understanding the formation and mobility...with the perception of one's own muscles; it means to "transpose" oneself over there and in there... (1965, p. 97)*

There is abundant nursing literature on empathy with patients, but I found little on nurses empathizing with each other. Just as we take note of a patient's heavy sigh, slumped shoulders, or downcast eyes, resonating with his feelings of discouragement, we can likewise be more attentive to these cues about the feelings of our colleagues. We can take a moment to show concern by putting a hand on that slumped shoulder, making contact with the downcast eyes, and offering an encouraging word. It can mean so much to a colleague if you understand that things are not going well.

When working alongside someone, our own feelings can provide useful cues about what the other is feeling. While in a group working on a care plan for a patient, Wailua Brandman (1996) tells of looking across the table at another nurse and suddenly feeling as though he himself were about to cry. Brandman did not understand why he felt this way and said nothing at the time, but after the meeting the other nurse suddenly began to cry, explaining that the meeting had been difficult for her because emotions about her father's death had surfaced. In a powerful moment of empathy between colleagues, Brandman shared his experience of wanting to cry during the meeting. The two were able to talk together about grieving.

Responding with empathy is more difficult when a coworker has just put you down or maligned you. It would be so much easier to respond to horizontal hostility in a hostile fashion, delivering a nasty zinger of your own or plotting a diabolical act of revenge. But take a moment to remind yourself that the person who put you down did so to elevate himself. Temporarily, he (or she) feels bigger and better than you. But he's not bigger and better. Inside, he's insecure. Surprise your coworker by not retaliating. A hostile response will only generate more hostility. RN Kathleen Bartholomew (2006, p. 94) reminds all of us:

"Every day, in every interaction, we either approve of the old script or write a new one."

■ *Make a commitment to supportive colleagueship.* This does not mean that you must like everyone with whom you work. Nor do I suggest that you ignore others' half-done tasks or take them on yourself. But deal with anger issues promptly and honestly, as they arise, and maintain civility. Talk directly to the person you're angry with, not to others. Keep your discussion private. When the dispute is resolved, let bygones be bygones. Eschew destructive gossip. If an angry incident is still festering because you were too infuriated to constructively problem-solve at the time, commit to reconnecting with the other person within 36 hours following the episode (Plas & Hoover-Dempsey, 1988). Heed the advice of professor Randy Pausch, a terminal cancer patient, whose "last lecture" moved millions of people: "Look for the best in everybody" (Pausch, 2008, p. 7). Resolve to notice something positive about another RN each week and pass it on to him or her (Gropper, 1994). Congratulate colleagues who obtain promotions, certifications, and advanced degrees. Write thank-you notes or give small gifts to coworkers who have "gone the extra mile" during tough times. As our research has shown, RNs yearn for the affirmation of their colleagues, but seldom receive much of it.

■ *Refuse to get caught up in workplace negativism.* Emotions, like viruses, are highly contagious when people live or work together in close proximity. This is especially true in the noisy, crowded, hectic, workplaces where health care is delivered. Angry negative coworkers evoke our own anger. Nurses may be particularly prone to "catching" others' emotions because of their training to be empathic with others' suffering. However, the acute sensitivity to feelings that gives us a clinical advantage may become a disadvantage when it comes to dissipating nonproductive anger that is heating up the workplace. Research shows that women from a variety of occupations are more susceptible to emotional contagion than men are (Doherty, Orimoto, Singelis, Hatfield, & Hebb, 1995). So, it may be more important for females than for males to learn how to turn down emotional arousal or leave an angry scene to preserve their equilibrium. Research comparing female and male RNs in this regard has not been conducted, however. The male RNs we studied seemed quite affected by the negativism in their job sites. For example, Ron Murray, an oncology nurse, seemed unable to resist being dragged down by the attitudes of others:

You can't come to work and have a good day because everybody's in a bad mood. You just sort of get in a negative attitude too. And if you're negative, you just do what you have to do to get through the day. When I work with different people, I have a much better day.

Ron needs to develop better resistance to the virus of negativity!

■ *Be vigilant regarding disrespectful treatment or bullying of colleagues.* Although it is not always possible or appropriate to directly intervene during an incident, a supportive word afterward can mean so much. Ann Smith has a colleague who is her "sounding board." In trying moments, the two meet in the locker room. Not only does Ann obtain release by talking, but also by "hug therapy" or massage: "You're tense, you sit down and rub each other's necks, pull your shoes off and let me rub your feet....We do a lot of that...and a lot of hugs." Beyond provision of support, encourage a colleague who is being bullied to document the incidents in writing, report them to management, and use the services of the EAP.

■ *Institute a wellness day for your work group.* Although "mental health days" have long been advocated—and are actually permissible in some job sites—they tend to be days of solitary activities, such as sleeping late and "vegging out." Far better is the approach taken by a home care team in Virginia that is responsible for 1,500 patients. As their caseload increased, the 22-member team noted increases in their stress, anger, and frustration. Two team members had to start taking antihypertensive medication. "Wellness day" was a creative approach to the stress and helped the nurses draw closer to one another (see 5.5).

5.5. A Wellness Day for the Team

On a sunny October morning, the team gathered in a park with a large pavilion and fireplace. They sipped coffee and munched muffins by a roaring fire. Team members with various talents had planned facets of the day. For example, one RN whose first undergraduate degree had been in music planned an activity involving music. Among the activities as the day went on were yoga, storytelling, writing songs, an imagery exercise led by a mental health nurse clinician, and an exercise involving affirmations—along with plenty of healthy food like vegetarian chili—and plenty of laughter. Members of the team had this to say about their wellness day:

> *Weeks after the activity, the effects were apparent.... Team members expressed themselves with greater freedom and trusted their colleagues to support them.... We learned to recognize each other's gifts and strengths as never before. The closeness and mutual respect were reflected in how we worked with and supported each other. (Extended Services Team, 1997, p. 68).*

■ *Build team spirit by socializing outside the workplace.* Business has long recognized the importance of lunches, dinners, golf outings, and birthday and holiday celebrations in team building. There is something very important about humans breaking bread together and playing together. Nurses need to give themselves permission to play more! Perhaps our workaholic ways can be traced back to the days when nurses' residences were located right next to the hospital, so that nurses mainly shuttled back and forth between the two, seldom leaving the grounds for social outings. In essence, it was a monastic existence. Even today, we seem reluctant to build time for play into our lives. Think about the last nursing conference you attended. Typically, sessions start at dawn and continue far into the night, leaving virtually no free time for socializing. A speaker is even scheduled during lunch, so that no time whatsoever is wasted in "idle chit-chat." What other profession so systematically deprives its members of pleasure?

I encourage you to begin connecting with your colleagues on a social basis. Some of my best memories of my staff nurse years are the zany laughter and joyous camaraderie when a group of us would go together after work. I find the same satisfaction in impromptu gatherings of faculty at my university. Socializing need not be expensive: Hikes and picnics cost little. If people in your agency have not mingled socially before, take the first step and invite everyone to a covered-dish brunch or supper at your home. Keep it simple. Just have fun!

- *Become involved in a support group* (if you are a psych clinical specialist or have comparable training in group leadership skills, consider offering your skills to lead a group). It is important that such a group have an experienced leader, so that it does not degenerate into a moan-and-groan session. Here is a good example. A psychiatric nurse specialist was asked to work with RNs in a neurological intensive care unit who were experiencing conflict after a change in unit leadership. Aligned on one side of the rift were the former manager and senior nurses, some with as much as 15 years experience, while on the other side were the new manager and newly hired nurses. The staff voted to have a support group, led by the psych nurse, for six sessions of 1 hour every other week (possibly to be extended after evaluation). Everyone understood that the group was not to be a therapy group, but a support group to facilitate better communication and more harmonious functioning of the unit. As the sessions proceeded, hidden anger and pain were discovered and processed, leading to healing for these nurses. Notably, the animosity between the old and new managers decreased, and the larger group perceived an improved ability to communicate with each other, their patients, and the physicians who admitted patients to their unit (Brandman, 1996).

The gender composition of this group was not described, but I do want to mention some dangers of all-female groups, because in some nursing settings, the workforce remains all female. It is likely that the support group leader will be perceived as a maternal figure, which will activate a host of reactions within the members: fears of being engulfed by the "mother," dependency, neediness, anger, disappointment, envy, competition, and sibling rivalry among the members vying for "mother's" acceptance. Thus, complex transference and countertransference dynamics will need to be examined. It is also likely that group members will have trouble acknowledging their own vulnerability, trusting that support is there, and accepting others' support when it is offered. As women, they have been socialized to meet the needs of others while denying their own, and, having internalized society's low view of their worth, they do not feel deserving of the caring of others (Ewashen, 1997). Despite these mitigating factors, all-female groups can be important vehicles for fostering personal growth and meaningful connections among the members. See Jacobs, Fontana, Kehoe, Matarese, and Chinn (2005) for an excellent example of emancipatory group work that could be replicated in your work setting.

■ *If you are an administrator, assess the organizational climate and take action if you discover bullying and intimidation.* This is costing your institution. For example, a third of bullied nurses in Farrell's (1999) study took more than 50 sick days per year. After one Australian hospital reached a nursing turnover rate of 28.4%, management took action (Stevens, 2002). Assessment of the situation showed that bullying existed at every level: "Staff who were named in confidence to the research team as perpetrators of this behavior themselves cited intimidation from the next level" (Stevens, p. 191). Daylong workshops were held for nursing supervisors. Material on conflict resolution and performance management was presented. Despite some denial and resistance, antibullying policies and practices were instituted. The outcome was a significant decrease in turnover.

Management must take more definitive actions against workplace bullies, including stern warnings, disciplinary actions, and dismissals (MacIntosh, 2006).

Steps Toward Eradicating Vertical Violence Toward Students

■ *If you are a faculty member, do your part to stop the intergenerational transmission of oppression.* Support your students when they encounter staff RNs who belittle them or resent their questions, and lend your support when they express anger on behalf of patients (see 5.6 for an example). Use postconferences for processing abusive incidents that occurred on the units, and help students generate strategies to protect themselves from future incidents of vertical violence.

5.6. An Example of Effective Instructor Support (as told by a junior student):

I became very angry while doing a clinical rotation at Hospital A due to the lack of care and attention being given to patient B, who had testicular cancer. The patient had become bitter and angry at the world . . . [and] most people on the floor tried to avoid him. . . . This particular morning, I went in to give Patient B a bed bath and realized no one on the floor must have given him a bath in days, possibly weeks, due to the amount of bodily secretions built up on his clothes, body, and sheets. . . . After I was finished giving the bath, I went straight to my instructor and reported what had happened. She went to the nurse manager about the problem, and the nurse manager called a meeting with the nurses and nursing assistants on the floor.

■ *Listen.* When a student is angry about a grade or another perceived injustice, take time to listen to the student and make a good-faith effort to understand his point of view (Thomas, 2003d). Convey empathy in your response, "It must be difficult to get a low grade when you have been trying so hard." If the student's expectations are unrealistic, gently encourage a more realistic perspective. Take time to explore the student's life circumstances (perhaps a life crisis has intruded, or taking a part-time job has limited study hours). If it is feasible for you to do something, such as offer an extra-credit assignment or refer the student to a grievance committee, do so. If there is nothing that can be done at this point, at least the student will leave your office knowing that the complaint was heard. (See Thomas, 2003d, for additional suggestions for handling angry students.)

■ *Resolve to establish a warm, caring environment in your classroom* and to convey caring when you do clinical supervision and advising. How will students learn to be caring nurses if they see no models of caring to emulate? A qualitative study of student perceptions of faculty caring (Beck, 1991) showed what students really want and need from their teachers. Forty-seven caring experiences were described by the nursing students; 19 had occurred in an advising session, 12 in a discussion of personal problems, eight in clinical, and eight in the classroom. In caring interactions, the students perceive their teachers to be nonjudgmental and unhurried. Attributes of faculty caring include focusing their complete attention on the students, conveying respect, and sharing of themselves. A faculty member's time is perceived as a valuable gift to a student. After experiencing a caring interaction, the student wishes to reach out to someone else through caring. The enormity of the effect of just one caring interaction is expressed by two students:

"I shall never forget that day in her office. It was truly a moment that could have changed my destiny. Because at that moment I made the decision to tough it out and see if I could make it. That was 1 year ago."

"I get goose pimples every time I think of this beautiful experience although it happened over 2 years ago. Thank God she listened, as all nurses should listen, not to the words or what happened but to the pain that was pouring from the heart. And because she did that, I am a happy, healthy, productive, and worthwhile human today." (Beck, 1991, p. 18)

Steps Toward Easing the Transition of New Graduates

■ *Develop a plan to promote your team's acceptance of new graduates.*
■ *Monitor grads for signs and symptoms of reality shock or alienation.*
■ *Encourage individualism and celebrate differences*, rather than mandating conformity to unit norms.
■ *Provide preceptors, mentors, and buddies* who will share their expertise and provide support.
■ *Encourage graduates to join professional organizations and workplace committees.*

—Adapted from Duchscher & Cowin (2004)

Resolving Conflict With Supervisors

Our next challenge is resolving conflict with supervisory personnel. In our interview data from nurses, anger at their leaders was common. In the following discussion, I often use the generic terms *supervisor* or *manager*, although today's nursing leaders have a plethora of job titles. What made staff nurses angry was leadership behavior that they perceived as authoritarian, faultfinding, and uncaring. Bob Hayes, who left ICU for home health, described humiliating episodes of being castigated by managers who were "rigid" and "militant." His description of one such episode is illustrative:

> *Her body language was that of a smart ass. She was shaking her head, batting her eyes. And she had that smirky look in her face. I don't like that at all. It was just a disrespectful look. And when you do that, you're not going to get positive results. You're not going to get a change. What you're going to get is a counter reaction. I was feeling rage.*

Ann Smith, a labor and delivery nurse, had a manager who listened but did nothing. Ann was both frustrated and hurt by her manager's uncaring behavior. When she went to the manager with concerns about an unsafe staffing pattern, this is what happened:

> *She uses a lot of psychological terms: "I hear where you're coming from. I understand what you're saying." And then I get the feeling that she puts it in her back pocket and goes. . . . It's frustrating to me that the person that's directly over me and directly controls what happens in my surroundings is out of touch with what's going on with me and the people I'm working with. This is a unit-wide complaint. It's not isolated incidents. It's a long-term, day-after-day problem.*

Joy Carpenter, another obstetric nurse, reported feeling a complete lack of support from her supervisor: "The minute I needed something, the supervisor would leave the floor. It was almost like the minute I said, 'I need to see you,' she would leave." Ron Murray, an oncology staff nurse, viewed management as *taking* from him rather than *assisting* him to get what he needs to perform his job according to his standards: "They're always cutting this, cutting that, cutting staff. . . . I feel like I have certain standards that I should be able to keep, and when they cut staff then you're not able to keep those standards."

Linda Harvey, a med-surg nurse, told us of experiences where managers sabotaged her. Clearly, she has begun to view them as the enemy:

> *I have never seen where they will be your advocate. They sell you down the tubes. Nurse administrators are no longer nurses. They have totally lost sight of the nursing side. I don't ever see it where they're really on the side of the nurse. They're loyal to the other side. And you shouldn't be at sides or at war.*

Understandably, hostility builds over time when managers consistently fail to display effective leadership behavior. Social gatherings of nurses who work together are often dominated by sharing fantasies of ways to get rid of their witchy manager: burning her at the stake, or perhaps in hot oil. In an imagery exercise in a workshop I conducted, one nurse fantasized taking the door off the closet and putting her head nurse's desk in there, behind the door. With glee, she imagined the head nurse shrieking, "It's too dark, I can't see!"

Although the grievances of nurses like Bob, Ann, Joy, and Ron appear to be legitimate, another dynamic is at work in some of the animosity that staff nurses feel toward their supervisors. Davies (1995) observed that "nurses have long reserved their most withering contempt for their colleagues who move up the managerial ladder, seemingly leaving real nursing for pay and power, especially when their presence in these elevated posts seems to offer little support and resourcing in the clinical setting" (p. 8). We've all heard scuttlebutt in the cafeteria about those who have "sold out to the enemy," shedding their uniforms for designer duds, and leaving their poor colleagues trapped in the trenches. When the supervisor is female, as is often the case, much of this hostility toward nursing leaders can be attributed to the same devaluing transferences seen in other predominantly female groups (Ewashen, 1997). The leader is expected to be an all-perfect "mother" who will sense their needs and nurture them.

Nurses often look to their leaders for emotional support more so than for decision making. Since the ideal of a perfect, ever-nurturing mother is impossible for leaders to achieve, nurses are often disappointed, denigrating the leaders and colluding to prove that they are incompetent.

In a group culture of discouragement and anger, cliques may form, based on emotional ties of some of the workers to one another. Barritt (1984) used the term "emotional nepotism" to describe these cliques. Being in a clique may result in favored treatment (holidays off, raises, promotions, new computers, office furniture, whatever the distributable "goodies" are), while the outsiders fume at the inequities, file grievances, and take other measures to fight back. During the infighting among the workers, scapegoats may be targeted, energy evaporates in fruitless conflict, and the productivity of the unit declines. Does this sound familiar to you? It certainly does to me. I have experienced this whole destructive scenario in more than one female work group during my career.

Women distrust powerful women. They have dared to stand out from the rest—a situation not looked on kindly within oppressed groups. When I was growing up in Memphis, I heard such individuals referred to as "uppity." From childhood, girls learn that their peers will disapprove if they are too self-confident or aggressive. Many women who have achieved prominence in nursing have endured considerable horizontal hostility from colleagues. Not long ago, I was reading about Loretta Ford, who developed the first program for nurse practitioners. Her colleagues at the university heaped abuse upon her, and some groups even wanted to excommunicate her from membership (Fondiller, 1995). The biography of famed nursing leader Hildegard Peplau reveals numerous painful incidents in which colleagues sought to undermine her, even spreading rumors that she was alcoholic or psychotic; Peplau became "weary of fighting the destructiveness of nurses" (Calloway, 2002, p. 311).

5.7. After 10 years of the women's movement, novelist Margaret Atwood commented,

> *We like to think that some of the old stereotypes are fading, but 10 years is not a very long time in the history of the world, and I can tell you from experience that the old familiar images, the old icons, have merely gone underground, and not far at that. We still think of a powerful man as a born leader and a powerful woman as an anomaly, a potentially dangerous anomaly; there is something subversive about such women, even when they take care to be good role models. They cannot have come by their power naturally, it is felt. They must have got it from somewhere. (Atwood, cited in Eisenstein, 1988).*

Many years after Atwood's observation, it seems that we still do not trust or feel comfortable with women leaders. Conflict with our supervisory personnel contributes to nursing turnover and even to departure from the profession. Public health nurse Sarah Prentiss, whom you met in Chapter 2, burned out after 10 years and left the field. Although her demanding, unsympathetic supervisor was not the only cause of her disillusionment with nursing, Sarah believes that the supervisor's behavior exacerbated her situation. Sarah related, "She didn't understand the frustration. She was in her office, and she just had unrealistic expectations for the staff. She'd say, 'Oh, come on, try this, go back and try this.' And I'd say, 'No, we've tried that.' She just had no idea" (Cherniss, 1995, p. 72).

Unlike Sarah Prentiss, Rebecca Simpson remained in her public health position. But after her relationship with her supervisor soured, she felt that her initiative and creativity declined. When she proposed innovative solutions to a problem, they were not well received. Eventually, her self-esteem was affected: "I started not feeling very good about myself, which I think, probably sometimes came across in my work. . . . I would have liked to have avoided the whole mess because that was not good for me, as far as my confidence goes, and self-image, and everything" (Cherniss, 1995, p. 140).

What Is the Manager's View of All This?

Our interviews with nurse managers and directors made it clear that being in a leadership role is no picnic. From them, we heard another side of the story. Clinical director Lisa Thompson is weary of the competitiveness among her staff and sees her job as "continually in this sandwich of making peace with all." She also arbitrates between the staff nurses and physicians, with the physicians "not willing to give an inch, not an inch, in many, many situations." Although she speaks warmly of most of the staff she supervises, she has difficulty with some of them who see nursing as "a job to make money and go home and pay the bills and cook supper. It's more than that. I guess I'm idealistic, but people need to see it as more than that. I wish they would move on. And it's hard for me not to tell them just exactly that."

Greg James echoed Lisa's frustration about having to supervise nurses who "don't realize that they are burned out and that they need a change. And they won't broaden their horizons." Tom Parker spoke of dealing with a passive-aggressive staff member who was a chronic problem. He recalled a particularly infuriating episode when the nurse did not like his patient assignment and set off a chain reaction on the unit: "He was messing up the assignments of several other people. The others were getting angry and I was getting flak from that. I had tried to be as fair as I could with everyone. I asked everyone to take a turn in helping with this particular area, so that I wasn't putting it off on any one person. His attitude angered me. I had been getting a lot of resistance from this person for a long time."

Kathy Hall, a charge nurse in labor and delivery, spoke of her onerous responsibility as a manager of everyone's emotions: "It's quite challenging and frustrating because you have people coming in [to work] in bad moods and try to get them in a good mood—and some people, you just can't, and you know, 'please take care of the patients well today and don't let them see your emotions.' So, you have to be the leader but then you are stressed inside because you feel responsible for everything."

Sally Jones, a head nurse of surgery, felt that staff nurses do not understand her tremendous management responsibilities: "In their view, when you're sitting behind a desk it's not 'real nursing,' but I'm responsible for interviewing, hiring, firing, payroll, time and attendance, seeing that policies and procedures are carried out, and when physicians have a problem they come to me.... I feel like people use me, I feel like everything's being dumped on my shoulders.... I feel overwhelmed. I guess you don't really know who to talk to."

Greg quit management after a year: "As a manager in a hospital today, it's very difficult. There is no extra money. There are no incentives. There's nothing more you can give your staff. You only have a limited supply of money and positions, and the nurse–patient ratio is getting worse and worse every day. As a manager, you listen to the venting. You get to hear all the problems all day long. If you don't have a person to vent to, you bottle it up. It just finally got to me, and I decided to do something totally different."

As you can see from our interview data, middle managers and executives are frustrated, isolated, and lonely. As Lisa put it, "I will honestly say that I feel pretty much out on a limb most of the time." The work of nurse managers mandates time-consuming meetings with non-nurses who do not understand the problems they are grappling with. Their support network can be pretty thin—or nonexistent. Consequently, few outlets exist for their own anger and fear. They have little opportunity to obtain constructive feedback from peers. It can be hard for a new manager to find a comfortable style. If the manager is female, she may find herself in the damned-if-you-do-damned-if-you-don't double bind that snares women in positions of authority.

Particularly poignant in a 2007 study of nurse managers was their lack of preparation for their management positions, as shown in this excerpt from the data: "It's been really hard...I was a staff nurse for 8 years before I took this job...I was organized. I was excellent...an expert...When I came into this job...I was *so* unprepared...I didn't have any idea about organizational theory or...more technical things like scheduling, staffing, payroll type issues, human resource issues" (Shea-Messler, 2007, p. 34). Other managers felt ill-prepared for disciplining and counseling employees about absenteeism and negativity. They questioned themselves, "Why am I still here?" (Shea-Messler, p. 34).

Dropping "They" and Becoming "We"

You've heard both managers and staff articulate the frustrations of their respective roles, often blaming one another ("if only *they*..."). It's time to move beyond polarized views of "we" versus "they." Let's work toward dropping "they" and just becoming "we." Clearly, a crying need exists in our profession for the development of less antagonistic, more supportive relationships between managers and their staffs. The bottom line is that *nurses are all colleagues*: managers and their staffs, deans of nursing and their faculties, coordinators and those whose work they coordinate. We must learn to get along better. The future of nursing depends on it. Current trends such as flattening of hierarchical levels, decentralization of decision making, and shared governance should help to reduce the polarization.

There *are* workplaces where all employees feel like valued members of a team. Consider "the top hospital in America" (North Shore University Hospital in Manhasset, New York). According to an article by Bargmann (2002, p. 51), this hospital is characterized by "a deep sense of community." In contrast to hospitals with nursing vacancies of 10% to 12%, only 5.7% of its nursing positions are vacant. Nurse Debbie Bothe, featured in the article, credits the supportive atmosphere at North Shore with encouraging her to do good work. In the last line of the article, Debbie says, "This is from my heart. I never want to work anywhere else but here" (p. 78).

What would it be like to work in a place with "a deep sense of community?" How can we make it happen? In the following sections of the chapter, we present strategies for both managers and staff. We begin with managers.

What Managers Can Do to Improve Relationships With Staff

■ *Conveying support to your staff must be the #1 priority.* Research data on the importance of supervisor support has been plentiful for decades (e.g., Blegen, 1993; Constable & Russell, 1986; McNeese-Smith, 1997; Laschinger, Shamian, & Thomson, 2001). Being supportive does not mean that you are going to be an all-nurturing parent—an impossible undertaking. But you can be highly visible, approachable, and encouraging. You have heard the voices of staff, throughout this book, expressing their longing for support from their managers. Try to imagine, from the staff nurse's point of view, how it would feel to get a response to your call for help like that made by the sarcastic supervisor quoted in Chapter 1: "Well, where do you think I'm going to get these nurses, cut out paper dolls?" Even if that supervisor had no one to send, a number of other responses would have indicated support: "I'll see what I can do. If nothing else, I'll come up myself and help you for a little while," or "I know it's rough, but the rest of the house is crazy too. I just don't have a soul, but as soon as I put out these fires down here in the ER, I'll be up."

5.8. An Example of a Supportive Manager

Linda Harvey recalled a situation in which she called her head nurse at home after she had a telephone altercation with a physician:

> *I was real lucky because this happened to be a real supportive head nurse and that is something you do not have very often; it is almost unheard of. In fact out of all the places I've lived and worked, she stands out in my mind. She reamed the doctor out for his behavior towards me. What happened is the patient ended up coding and being intubated. Had the doctor come in, that may have been prevented.*

- *Consider staff mistakes as teachable moments.* Your employee will learn from the error if you convey your support while reviewing what happened. Nursing supervisor Karren Kowalski (1992) has provided a wonderful example. She supported three of her staff after a major mistake in which a patient was harmed. Rather than taking a punitive approach, she decided to consider this incident an opportunity for teaching. The nurses were not fired or castigated, but encouraged to learn from their experience. Each nurse was able to identify three things she would do differently next time. Kowalski's support of these individuals became legendary among the staff of the institution.

- *Realize that you, by virtue of your leadership position, are sometimes going to be the "lightning rod" for staff anger in your facility.* This can be extremely threatening and anxiety-producing. It is understandable that your initial impulse may be to avoid the angry person or group. Feeling inadequate to cope with the anger, you may postpone attending to it. However, as pointed out by Morath, Casey, and Covert (1985), "anger that is not dealt with results in lost opportunities for learning and growth; problems are unidentified and unresolved, staff relations are painful, trust erodes, and eventually patient care deteriorates" (p. 45). It is important that you listen to the angry individual in a setting of privacy and confidentiality, without defensiveness or retaliation. Let the nurse have his say. Ascertain if substantive issues are present that need your attention. Then consider alternative responses. If the nurse's anger is irrational or disproportionate to the situation, try the approach of noted leader Rosalee Yeaworth (see 5.9).

5.9. While I was Dean, a member of my administrative team sent very excoriating memorandums whenever she disagreed with something I did or didn't do. Taken by surprise the first time or two this happened, I became angry that she hadn't come to discuss the concerns face-to-face. I sent a rather heated response, trying to explain and defend my reasoning. She, in turn, sent an even more scathing memorandum, and it was obvious that the written word was escalating the angry feelings. I had my secretary arrange an appointment for us to meet face-to-face, and we were able to discuss matters quite civilly. I was surprised that she didn't seem nearly as angry as the memo seemed to indicate. She admitted that sitting down and writing such a memo served as a catharsis, and made her feel much better. During the 12 or so years that we worked together, she continued periodically to send me very angry memorandums, but after my initial experience, I would read them, take a few deep breaths, and put them under my "to do" pile. I would wait a few days until we both had cooled off, and I perhaps had gathered more information, then arranged for a face-to-face meeting. Despite these periodic episodes, we were able to work together, have some good accomplishments, retain respect for each other's perspectives, and I believe, remain friends.

- *Rein in your own anger.* Managers who react in a volatile fashion add to the stress in the work environment and set a poor example for those under their supervision. Remember that the short-term effects of anger outbursts may seem positive (anger does get people's attention), but staff morale and productivity will decline over the long term. Your anger outbursts can also lead to high turnover of staff. Trust and respect of staff are earned by demonstrations of level-headed, consistent, behavior.
- *Take prompt action if bullying or abuse is reported to you.* Nonaction ensures that the bullying will continue. In Farrell's (2001) study, respondents deplored their manager's failure to act when incidents occurred. Your goal should be a climate of zero tolerance for all forms of horizontal violence. If your institution does not have antibullying policies to guide your actions, create a task force to develop them and then widely publicize them.
- *Enlarge your repertoire of conflict management strategies.* As shown in our research, leaders are required to serve as third-party managers of conflict among staff members, although they dislike having to do so (see guidelines in 5.10). McElhaney (1996) contends that conflict management skill is more important than planning, communication, motivation, and decision making. However, a synthesis of research by Valentine (2001) showed that *avoiding* was the most frequently used conflict management strategy of nurse managers. Avoiding is really not a strategy! The longer that conflict festers among staff, the more resistant it becomes to amelioration.

5.10. Guidelines for Resolution of a Conflict

Set up a meeting in neutral territory. If possible, choose a conference room with a round table or arrange chairs in a circle. Lay out the ground rules at the outset. Each person should be invited to present his view of the problem, while others listen without interruption. Work toward agreement on the essence of the conflict. Keep your goal modest (it isn't realistic that individuals who thoroughly dislike one another will suddenly become good friends, but they can learn to behave with mutual respect). Encourage assertive statements, using "I" language. No accusatory or foul language can be used. Ask the conflicting parties to try linguistic shading (McNamee & Gergen, 1999). For example, we shade anger when we say "there is tension between us." Linguistic shading reduces anger and instills the notion that harmony may be achievable. Take a break if tempers flare. And adhere to a predetermined time limit, so that the meeting doesn't degenerate into rehashing and intensification of animosity. If your mediation is unsuccessful, consult resources in your institution such as Employee Assistance.

- *Be alert to troubled nurses who need help.* Behaviors such as extreme anger, subversive activities, decreased productivity, or increased absenteeism indicate a need for intervention. One angry, negative individual can cause tremendous havoc in a work site. Jane Halsey, a director of nursing services in Washington, has discovered that, in many cases, these nurses are plagued by home or personal problems such as marital strife, financial crisis, illness or death in the nurse's family, or inability to conceive a child. Although the old adage advises "leave your troubles on the doorstep" when you come to work, it is difficult to neatly compartmentalize your life, particularly when strong emotions are involved. See 5.11 for Halsey's suggested guidelines for dealing with a troubled nurse.

5.11. Guidelines for Dealing With a Troubled Nurse

Begin by sitting down with the nurse and having a one-to-one fact-finding session.

> *Present facts about the unacceptable behavior.*
> *Ascertain if there are training needs or work environment problems.*
> *If personal problems surface, do not suggest a solution.*
> *Listen, allow the nurse to express feelings.*
> *Consider alterations in work hours or work unit.*
> *Refer the nurse to a counselor. If the work performance is in need of immediate improvement so that the nurse will not be terminated, the referral can be mandatory, and the counselor can be asked to verify kept appointments.*
> *Make plans for follow-up sessions at specific intervals. Give positive reinforcement for improvements in attitude and work performance (Halsey, 1985).*

- *Model individuation for your staff* despite group pressure to be "one of us" (McWilliams & Stein, 1987, p. 149). If you are a female, break out of the protective mother role. Be a mentor, not a mother. Deal with staff dependency, envy, and competition. In a largely female professional group, the opportunities for female nurses to replay difficulties of separating from mother, individuating, and satisfying dependency needs are endless. But in the replaying, corrective learning experiences can take place: You, as a new kind of mother-authority figure, can mentor younger nurses to grow in self-definition and autonomy (Ruiz, 1988).
- *Foster staff autonomy.* This is important not only for their personal growth but also for you and your institution. Autonomy is related to job contentment, commitment to the organization, and intent to stay on the job (McCloskey, 1990). In this difficult time of nurse shortage, when everyone is wondering how to retain RNs, nurse consultants Kramer and Schmalenberg (2003) urge managers to make greater efforts to empower staff. Their 2003 study of staff nurses in magnet hospitals supported the earlier study

of McCloskey, corroborating the strong relationship between degree of autonomy and job satisfaction. How do you foster staff autonomy? By conveying trust and allowing freedom to take risks. And, you must reward staff for displaying more autonomous behaviors. For example, evaluation forms could include items related to taking initiative.

■ *Learn all you can about transformational leadership.* Take courses, attend continuing education conferences, consider pursuit of graduate preparation in nursing administration. Too often, the goal of nursing managers is to *control.* While managers control an enterprise, leaders know how to bring out the best in people and to respond quickly to change (Naisbett & Aburdene, 1990).

Early views of leadership emphasized motivating workers to do tasks and rewarding them with "carrots" for compliance instead of punishing them with "sticks." But even if the leader uses carrots instead of sticks, the follower will continue to feel like a jackass (Levinson, 1980). Try transformational leadership tactics instead.

Transformational leadership is more effective and satisfying than contingent rewarding. Supporting evidence, in the form of field studies, interviews, case histories, and laboratory investigations, has been gathered all over the world, in every continent except Antarctica (Bass, 1997). Studies specific to the nursing profession show that staff job satisfaction is positively correlated with transformational leadership (Force, 2005; Moss & Rowls, 1997). So, nowadays, the prevailing paradigm is transformational leadership, which motivates followers to go beyond their own self-interests for the good of the group or organization. Transformational leaders inspire their staffs to do more than they originally expected to do (Burns, 1978). They are admired as role models, generating pride and loyalty. See 5.12 for characteristics of a transformational leader.

5.12. A Transformational Leader:

■ *takes stands on difficult issues and displays conviction*
■ *articulates an optimistic, appealing vision of the future*
■ *inspires and challenges followers with high standards*
■ *provides encouragement for what needs to be done*
■ *stimulates in others new perspectives and ways of doing things*
■ *deals with others as individuals, considering their needs and abilities*
■ *listens attentively, advises, teaches, and coaches. (Bass, 1997)*

Florence Nightingale would surely be categorized as a transformational leader. Why has our profession only produced one Nightingale? What are we doing in schools of nursing, employing agencies, and professional organizations to prepare the next generation of leaders? Nurses are hungry for transformational leaders and the organizational climates that they create. We want role models whom we can trust and emulate. Yes, we have some effective leaders and managers in nursing, but we need more. In the meantime, we can't leave all the work of reconciliation to our managers. We must make some efforts to connect more effectively with them, too.

What Staff Can Do to Improve Relationships With Managers

■ *Tell your manager what you want or need.* Contrary to popular assumption, managers cannot read minds. Recall Fran (Chapter 3) who expected her supervisor to come to her rescue, even though she had not asked for help. Fran—and the patients on her unit—would have been much better off if she had made an assertive request for more personnel. When you make a request, be clear and direct. Don't give your manager the impression that you're being critical. Express your appreciation for the opportunity to voice your concerns.

■ *When you have a burning grievance, don't strike while the iron is red hot.* Cool down, strategize, then go to your manager or supervisor. State the issue or problem in very specific terms. For example, "I am angry that I have been changed to night shift for the next month." Only discuss one problem at a time; don't bring up a laundry list of old anger-provoking incidents. Listen carefully to your manager's response. Restate it to make sure you understood exactly what was said, "If I understood correctly, you're saying that you see no alternative but for me to work nights while John is away." Avoid making any inferences or asking accusatory questions (such as "Why wasn't Karen asked to pull graveyard shift? Karen always gets treated with kid gloves"). Brainstorm to come up with alternative solutions. Be willing to accept a compromise. After all, *somebody* has to work nights. Maybe you can take part of the shifts in John's absence, while Karen will be asked to do the rest of them.

■ *Be a team player.* If you are a woman in your thirties or older, you probably didn't have an opportunity to play team sports when you were growing up. Certain concepts, such as loyalty to the team, aren't second nature to you. Men traditionally have had an advantage here. Critique your own behavior, not only your interaction with the "coach," but also with the other members of the team. Are your actions promoting success of the work team or undermining it? Remember that the outcome of leadership rests ultimately with the followers. You will be happier in your job if you feel a part of a well-functioning team. In a study by Kathleen Cox (2003), team performance effectiveness significantly affected nurses' job satisfaction.

■ *Do a little soul-searching* about the conflicts that are occurring within your team. Could some conflict *within you* be influencing your interactions with coworkers? The above-cited study by Cox (2003) examined not only team effectiveness, and conflicts among team members, but *intrapersonal conflict* (that which occurs *within* an individual, because of conflicting values or a mismatch between job responsibilities and expertise or interests). As you might imagine, when a nurse has internal turmoil, trying to reconcile his own conflicting values, there is a greater likelihood of disagreements with others on the team. Some counseling might help you sort things out.

■ *Give your manager some support*. It's a tough job, and it's getting tougher as manager workload increases. In a 2002 AONE survey, first-line managers reported responsibility for as many as 32 to 54 staff members. It would be hard to give enough individual attention to each one's needs! (Andrews & Dziegielewski, 2005). Don't be a crab! Remember the East Coast metaphor of the crab bucket? You do not need to put a lid on a bucket of crabs because when one crab gets to the top, the others will pull it down (Hagberg, 1984). Do you really want to pull your manager down? When you feel critical of your manager, remind yourself that you do not have access to all of the information that he has. Imagine what it would be like if you were the person who must distribute scarce resources. Imagine what it would be like to endure all the crabs pulling at you. When is the last time you told your manager that he is doing a good job? What could you do to make that job a bit easier? Staff RNs at a Florida institution spent two eye-opening days with a nurse administrator, learning more about her struggle to maintain quality care in an atmosphere of budget cutting (Fletcher, 2001). I bet they came away with greater empathy for her.

Resolving Conflict With Physicians

Although their education, training, and traditions differ, physicians and nurses share a common commitment to patient well-being. Because of this commitment, it makes good sense for physicians and nurses to consider themselves colleagues. A more collegial, unified relationship between nurses and physicians will improve patient care.... (Gianakos, 1997)

These words from an article in *Nursing Outlook* were written by a physician. Nurses told my research team that this collegial relationship with physicians is exactly what they want. In too many situations, however, this is an ideal yet to be achieved. As you will recall from Chapter 1, disrespectful treatment by physicians provoked deep anger in nurses. Our study participants described criticism, attacks, tirades, and baseless accusations. They said doctors used them as "scapegoats" and "whipping posts." They experienced being "lambasted," "thrashed," "picked on," "belittled," and "lectured." When witnesses observed these incidents, such as their peers or patients, the humiliation was especially galling to the nurses. The following story, related to our research team by Mike Evans, an ICU/CCU nurse whom you met in Chapter 1, illustrates several common themes, including outrage, helplessness, a sense of betrayal, and ultimately a severed relationship:

There was a cardiac surgeon. I tried to beep him several times during the night to call him some blood gases. He wouldn't return my call. And I ended up having to call his partner. His partner gave me orders not to wean the patient any further until morning. But I knew the first surgeon would be angry about that when he came in and saw that the patient hadn't been weaned. So I went ahead and weaned him . . . to where he could have been extubated shortly after the surgeon saw him in the morning.

The first physician came in the next morning and was extremely angry, not that I had weaned the patient but that I didn't have him already extubated, even though I had orders from his partner not to wean him at all. . . . He just thrashed me verbally in front of my peers. . . . Demanded to see the supervisor and tried to get me fired . . . My supervisor wanted to know why I didn't have him weaned further. I said, "Well, I had orders not to wean him at all."

When asked by the interviewer how he felt, Mike expressed outrage at the physician's behavior: "His outburst was totally unprofessional and unwarranted. . . . What he was angry about was totally, totally ludicrous. . . . I really had no idea what set him off . . . As he was thrashing me, his partner came in and said, 'I told Mike not to wean him further at all.' The second surgeon was supportive of me. . . . I guess it was trying to please the first surgeon that got me in trouble . . . ."

Mike went on to reveal that he had formerly felt pride in his relationship of mutual respect with the cardiac surgeon. He now considers the relationship severed: "He has traditionally liked me taking care of his patients. That's what's really bewildering to me. . . . Because I respected him, I wanted him to respect me. I wanted to have that good relationship. I tried so hard to please him, but there was no pleasing him. I'm sorry our relationship ended the way it did."

Much of the physician behavior described by our study participants can be correctly classified as *verbal abuse*. Make no mistake that verbal abuse is a means of holding power over other people. It is grossly inhumane and unprofessional behavior. And quite a lot of it is occurring: Research reveals a high incidence of abusive behavior by physicians. Ninety percent of a sample of randomly selected staff nurses in Missouri said they had experienced verbal abuse by physicians during the past year (Manderino & Berkey, 1995). Percentages are similar in studies conducted in other states (Carroll, 2003). According to Rosenstein and O'Daniel (2006), surgeons, cardiologists, and neurologists are most likely to exhibit abusive behavior. Emotional reactions reported by verbally abused nurses include anger, frustration, and disgust. Long-term effects include both a negative relationship with the offending doctor and decreased job satisfaction. In some cases, a nurse actually resigns from the facility. Nearly one-third of respondents in a 2002 survey of hospital nurses, doctors, and executives said they knew of nurses who left the hospital as a result of disruptive physician behavior (Rosenstein, 2002). The respondents were also aware that nurses switched shifts or departments to avoid contact with certain physicians.

Some studies document sexual harassment in addition to verbal abuse. Thirty percent of nurses in one study experienced sexual propositions, touches, or insults, with young, White women reporting the highest incidence of sexual abuse (Diaz and McMillin, 1991). In the same study, 64% of the nurses reported verbal abuse from a physician at least once every 2 or 3 months, and 23% of the sample had had at least one experience with a physician in which their physical person was threatened, most often by having an object thrown at them. Most abusive interactions with doctors took place at the nursing station or on the ward; 39% occurred with the patient present. There were adverse consequences for patient care: When doctors acquired a reputation for tantrums, some nurses hesitated to call them about a patient or make suggestions about the patient's care (Diaz & McMillin, 1991).

Some researchers use the term *disruptive behavior* in their studies, defining the term as "any inappropriate behavior, confrontation or conflict, ranging from verbal abuse to physical and sexual harassment" (Rosenstein & O'Daniel, 2005, p. 55). In a 2005 survey by these researchers, 86% of nurses said they had witnessed disruptive physician behaviors. In a 2006 study focusing on the perioperative area, 97% of nurses said attending physicians displayed disruptive behavior (Rosenstein & O'Daniel, 2006). As in the earlier study by Diaz and McMillin, respondents to these surveys reported adverse consequences, such as reduced team collaboration, reduced quality of care, and other negative clinical and psychological outcomes. Particularly chilling are the following verbatim quotes depicting harm to patients:

> "MD became angry when RN reported decline in patient's condition, and did not act on information. Patient required emergency intubation and transferred to ICU. This caused family much unnecessary heartache and disruption in family grieving process."
>
> "RN did not call MD about change in patient condition because he had a history of being abusive when called. Patient suffered because of this."
>
> "Poor communication postoperatively because of disruptive reputation resulted in delayed treatment, aspiration, and eventual demise." (Rosenstein & O'Daniel, 2006, p. 102)

What do nurses do when verbally abused or harassed? At the moment of the abusive treatment, the nurse may feel caught off guard or thrown off balance. The objurgation by the physician may be completely unexpected and incomprehensible, as several RNs in our study related. Bewildered, they struggled to formulate a rational explanation for the abusive attack. They wondered if they could have said or done something differently to escape the attack. It is a mistake to try to analyze abusive behavior because it is *irrational*. How then should we cope with it?

How to Cope With Physician Abuse

Research has shown that factors such as self-esteem and assertiveness contribute most to nurses' ability to cope with verbal abuse (Cox, 1991). Elsewhere in the book are detailed discussions of both of these topics. For now, here are some recommendations about what to do in the moment if you are being verbally abused by a physician (and these are generally applicable to other abusive situations as well):

> ■ *Don't leap to your own defense.* First and foremost, you are not responsible for the abuse and need not defend yourself. No matter what alleged acts of omission or commission provoked the physician, you do not ever deserve to be threatened, yelled at, or insulted.
>
> ■ *Set firm limits on the abusive behavior* by forcefully saying "Stop that" or "Don't talk to me that way!" Make it clear that the behavior is unacceptable, and you will not tolerate it. Stand tall and make direct eye contact.

- *Ask colleagues to support you.* In some institutions, nurses agree to call a special kind of "code" when a colleague is being abused: All nurses on the unit come to stand with the nurse in support.
- *Walk away.* Be aware that you can leave an abusive situation. If the physician is having a tirade, you do not have to remain and endure it. Never allow a physician to verbally abuse you in front of a patient. This is upsetting to the patient and may diminish his respect for both the doctor and you.
- *Report incidents of bullying and abuse to your supervisor* and to the appropriate medical staff committee in your facility. After a reasonable interval, follow up to see what actions have been taken in regard to your complaint. Some institutions suspend or revoke abusive physicians' practice privileges after a certain number of complaints. Find out what your facility's code of conduct entails; if there isn't one, mobilize colleagues to insist that a code be developed (see samples at http://lazoritz.com/samplebehavioralpolicies.html). Unfortunately, in the Rosenstein (2002) study, nearly half the respondents reported *barriers* to reporting physicians' disruptive behavior. Nurses cited fear of retaliation, concerns about future relations, and the belief that nothing would change. They noted that physicians in leadership positions were reluctant to counsel or discipline their peers. Although code-of-conduct policies were in place in most facilities, less than half the study participants thought the policies were effective. This study shows that much work remains.

Understanding Obstacles to Collegiality With Physicians

Not only must physician abuse be eradicated, but we must come to understand the obstacles to more collegial relationships. The nurse–physician relationship has been hierarchical rather than collegial since the time of Nightingale. To inculcate proper subservience, early nursing schools were tightly run institutions, employing harsh discipline. Instructors taught students to stand when a doctor entered the nurse's station, give up their seat if the doctor needed one, and hover nearby throughout the doctor's stay on the unit. The nurse walked behind the doctor as he made rounds, carrying the charts, answering his questions, and jotting down his verbal orders. A good little handmaiden would even serve him coffee PRN. I am deliberately saying "he" as I refer to doctors, because most of them were men, and most nurses were women. From its beginning as a modern profession, medicine systematically excluded women, remaining a male-dominated field until the relatively recent inroads of larger numbers of women. Ashley (1976) described the hospital as a "household," in which nurses were responsible for meeting the needs of all members of the "family," from patients to physicians. Some say nurses looked to male physicians as father-figures, just as we looked to female supervisors as mother-figures.

5.13. Nursing as "women's work," was clearly articulated in literature of the early 1900s: "Women are peculiarly fitted for the onerous task of patiently and skillfully caring for the patient in faithful obedience to the physician's orders. Ability to care for the helpless is women's distinctive nature. Nursing is mothering. Grownup folks when very sick are all babies." (cited by Eisenstein, 1988)

Duplicated in the health care setting was the same gendered world that existed outside, in which males took charge and led, and women respectfully followed. I think that the doctor–nurse relationship was even more autocratic than other male–female relationships because the doctor's self-concept of omnipotence exceeded the average male's estimate of himself. Hans Mauksch once captured the difference between physician education and nursing education in two succinct sentences: "Medicine presents every new fact to its student with a philosophy that goes like this: 'Here's another piece of knowledge that will make you more powerful.' Nursing presents its lore with a different tone: 'Here's another piece of knowledge. Don't you dare forget it, or you may end up hurting someone'" (Mauksch, cited in Barnum, 1989).

The classic study by Erving Goffman (1967) delineated many of the subtle, nonverbal behaviors that maintained the power inequalities of the hospital milieu. For example, doctors frequently called nurses by their first names, whereas nurses were expected to address physicians as "Dr. _____." Doctors had the privilege of swearing, sitting in undignified positions, and initiating joking and bantering with nurses and other underlings, while such behaviors were unacceptable for nurses. You may be thinking, "But Goffman's research is old!" More recent examples of power inequality were observed by journalists Bernice Buresh and Suzanne Gordon (1996). They watched as a nurse who needed to speak to a physician about a patient stood quietly beside him while he talked to another physician. The two doctors continued to talk, never acknowledging the nurse's presence. Eventually, the nurse shrugged and walked away. Later, one of the doctors who had ignored the nurse barged into the nurses' station, firing questions rapidly. The nurses, despite the rudeness of his interruption, immediately stopped their own work and gave him the information he needed. In both instances, the doctors made it clear that their needs took precedence over anything a nurse might want to communicate or do. A nurse's work is interruptible, theirs is not.

Barbara Ehrenreich contends that the history of medicine in the last 100 years could be divided into two phases: "Putting Nurses in Their Place" and "Taking That Place Away" (2002, p. xxxiii). A physician, writing in the *Journal of the American Medical Association* in 1913, argued that "Medicine...has been the habitual critic of [the nurse's] development, and rightly so, because the physician is ultimately the only competent judge of the fitness of the nurse, and the chief sufferer...for her (sic) possible unfitness" (Beard, 1913). Over the years, doctors have sought to maintain their paternalistic dominance over nurses in a number of ways. For example, at the turn of the century nurses were forbidden to read the medical histories of patients, and numbers rather than drug names were placed on drug bottles (Lovell, 1988). Doctors have consistently opposed nurses becoming better educated. The American Medical Association (AMA) opposed federal aid to nursing and successfully blocked bills that would have enabled the profession to upgrade educational levels. In many states, physicians sat on boards of nursing, meddling in the governance of nursing practice.

Traditionally, the doctor's idea of a "good nurse" was one who would precisely carry out his orders. And woe to the nurse who didn't. An angry doctor could march to the supervisor's office and demand that a nurse be fired. Physician wrath could be terrifying. On one occasion, still vivid in my memory, a doctor hurled a bedpan out the window of a patient's room. Doctors were permitted to have temper tantrums—throwing surgical instruments, yelling at nurses, orderlies, and other underlings—but such behavior was unthinkable for nurses. Nurses' anger was expressed only in interactions with each other, through indirect means such as nasty notes in the "communication book" or behind-the-scenes sabotage—the horizontal violence we talked about earlier.

Nurses learned to "handle" doctors to avoid their ire by playing a devious "doctor–nurse game," described in a 1967 article by physician Leonard Stein. The cardinal rule of the game was avoidance of open disagreement, and of course it was the RN's job to make sure that disagreement did not erupt. As in a traditional marriage, where the passive wife "plants" her idea so skillfully that her dominant husband believes he thought of it himself, so nurses were to communicate their recommendations to the doctor without appearing to make them. Making direct suggestions to a doctor would have been insolent and insulting. This "game" stifled nurses' intellect and creativity and probably had an adverse effect on patient care as well. Research shows that the level and quality of physician–nurse interaction significantly affect patient outcomes (Knaus, Draper, Wagner, & Zimmerman, 1986; Rosenstein & O'Daniel, 2005, 2006).

The Beginning of the End of the Doctor–Nurse Game. In the 1970s, as the women's movement and the civil rights movement were shaking up entrenched power imbalances throughout America, some nurses became emboldened. In June, 1975, a nurse at St. Agnes Hospital in Philadelphia refused to give a medication ordered by a doctor because she believed it to be harmful. The doctor–nurse confrontation that followed eventually led to the dismissal of the director of nursing. That part of the story wasn't unique. What followed the unfair firing of the director *was* unique. St. Agnes nurses protested for the director's reinstatement. And 30 courageous RNs resigned their jobs. Their story hit national media and was reported in *Modern Healthcare* (Cleary, 1975). The St. Agnes incident may have been the beginning of the end of the doctor–nurse game, because it showed clearly that nurses weren't as willing to play any more.

The gender composition in medicine is changing; physicians are increasingly likely to be female. Has this transformed the traditional relationship of physicians and nurses? Journalist Suzanne Gordon, who has spent years shadowing nurses as they practice, says "no." The female medical student is still being socialized to believe that her profession is superior. According to Gordon, "Female physicians often measure their success in elite terms—as how far they have moved away from nurses. . . . Some female surgeons complain vociferously because they feel it is demeaning when they are asked to share the same locker rooms as operating room nurses. One sign of their arrival in the higher ranks of medicine seems to be their own female-doctors-only locker room" (1997, p. 81).

Is the doctor–nurse game still being played? In some settings, yes. But when Stein, along with two physician coauthors, wrote a 1990 update, important changes had taken place. Physicians are no longer viewed as omnipotent. Medicine is less mystical and those who practice it are not held in awe. Perhaps of greatest significance is the decreased education gap between physicians and nurses. In 1967, when Stein wrote his article, 90% of working RNs had been educated in hospital programs. By 1990, less than 15% of nurses were being educated in such programs, and the majority of hospital staff RNs had received their education in community colleges or universities. When nursing education moved out of hospital-based schools, students were no longer socialized to relate to doctors obsequiously. According to physician authors Stein, Watts, and Howell (1990), a few contemporary physicians still long wistfully for the return of the hierarchical doctor–nurse relationship, but "the forces of change are inexorable and universal" (p. 548). Stein and his colleagues predict a new, more equal, mutually interdependent relationship between physicians and nurses, a relationship that would be beneficial to both disciplines: "When a subordinate becomes liberated, there is the potential for the dominant one to become liberated too" (Stein, et al., p. 549).

The Continuing Turf Wars. As you were reading the preceding paragraphs, perhaps you were thinking that we should not tar all doctors with the same brush. All of us know doctors who are kind, compassionate, and respectful to other members of the health care team. However, physicians are still our political adversaries on many occasions. Turf wars continue. It is ironic that perhaps the most collegial relationships nowadays are in the joint practices of physicians and nurse practitioners, yet physicians have consistently fought turf wars against NPs for years. They have fought against third-party reimbursement, prescription privileges, and independent functioning. And they are still fighting. As this book goes to press, the AMA—apparently responding to the increasing number of nurses with doctoral degrees—has prepared a resolution to oppose the use of the term "Doctor" by anyone other than a physician. If the resolution passes the House of Delegates, the AMA will seek legislation. Ultimately, nurses holding Doctor of Nursing Practice or other doctoral degrees would be prevented from using the title "Doctor."

The early years of the 21st century have not been rosy for doctors. Medicare, Medicaid, and HMO reimbursements have been falling, and malpractice insurance premiums have been skyrocketing. Many doctors have seen a drastic drop in income. Such tough times bring forth renewed animosity toward "the competition," especially nurses in private practice who could siphon their patients away. Thus, battles over changes in state laws are ongoing in some states. Not long ago, in my state, legislation had been proposed to lift restrictions on NPs. The media campaign conducted by the Tennessee Medical Association (TMA) was downright nasty. On the cover of the TMA political action committee brochure was a large white duck with a stethoscope dangling from its neck. "Don't let reform duck up health care" said the brochure title. Inside the brochure, nonphysician care providers were discredited and referred to in derogatory terms such as "dubious birds" and "daffy ducks." The strong implication was that care provided by anyone other than a physician was "quackery." It was even suggested, in a "Legistat Fax" that TMA sent to its members, that the Board of Nursing would not aggressively pursue violations by NPs. Through intense lobbying, the doctors successfully convinced legislators that the quality of patient care would suffer if nurses were allowed to practice independently, and the legislation was defeated.

Sexism reared its ugly head during the debate. How could female nurses be liberated from male physician control? One legislator made the following blatantly sexist comment: "It's hard not to like the ladies in white dresses with beautiful hats. But if you take the shackles off the nurse practitioners...you're taking a gamble." Use of the word "shackles" clearly brings images of slavery and bondage. I am happy to report that the shackles eventually came off! Furious over the physicians' demeaning, insulting propaganda, Tennessee nurses mounted a grassroots effort to revive and pass the bill. Newspapers across the state were inundated with letters from irate nurses. One year later, a standing-room-only crowd of nurses discovered what their collective anger could accomplish when they heard Representative Gary Odom proclaim: "Free at last, free at last, thank God Almighty, the nurse practitioners are free at last" (Browning, 1994).

> *5.14. Nurses want to have satisfying collaborative relationships with our physician colleagues. In the words of Peggy Chinn (1991, p. 254): "We are seeking a quality in relationships that can exist only when we 'count' as fully qualified, capable individuals.... What we are seeking is not so much freedom (although that certainly is an issue in many cases) as it is a quality of connection with everyone involved in our practice situation that endows us all with abilities to exercise our full human capacities—skill, judgment, and interaction."*

Looking to the Future

Interdisciplinary education for health professionals holds the greatest promise for creating egalitarian physician–nurse relationships. In a few academic health centers, medical and nursing students now take required courses together, in which they learn interviewing skills, history taking, physical assessment, epidemiology, community health, and wellness/illness concepts. Interdisciplinary electives such as ethics, adolescent health, family violence, and AIDS prevention are offered in some locales. Paired clinical assignments of medical and nursing students in rural clinics and other primary care settings have also been used (Larson, 1995). When a larger number of physicians and nurses have studied together or seen patients side by side, hierarchy and territoriality are likely to diminish. These collaborative experiences promote collegiality and mutual respect. The Pew Health Professions Commission (1993) recommended widespread adoption of these innovations, but barriers such as scheduling, cost, and faculty attitudes remain. In the meantime, change is quietly occurring in a number of practice settings. Work environments and roles have changed as a result of managed care. Many doctors and nurses are working well together. Surely, interdependent practice will be the reality of the future because the public will no longer tolerate turf battles among the professional groups.

A Last Word

Conflict is inevitable when human beings interact. The potential for conflicting relationships is even greater when health care providers interact in highly stressful contexts, such as in contemporary acute care hospitals. But transformational leaders and confident, assertive followers can call a halt to the egregious behaviors described in this chapter. It is imperative for nursing to extinguish all forms of horizontal and vertical violence. Will you do your part? Recall the words of Holocaust survivor Elie Wisesel: "I swore never to be silent whenever and wherever human beings endure suffering and humiliation. We must always take sides. Neutrality helps the oppressor, never the victim. Silence encourages the tormentor, never the tormented."

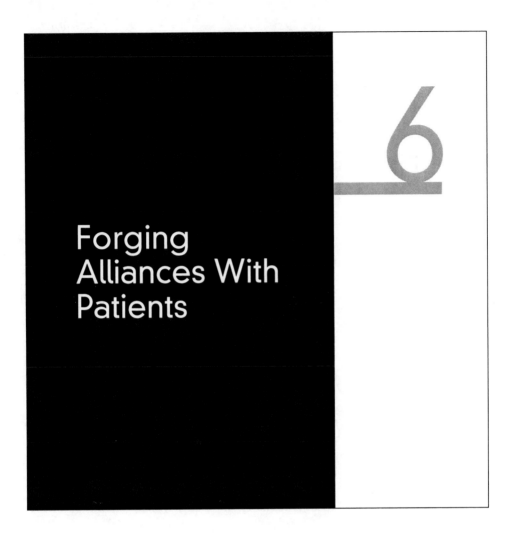

Forging Alliances With Patients

6

There is no "simple" procedure or "minor" hospitalization. . . . The hospital bed reduces all to the lowest common denominator. We have the privilege of connecting with people when they are most exposed and most defenseless. . . . With that privilege of intimacy comes the responsibility to make that connection a healing one.

—Sharon Adkins, MSN, RN

In this chapter, we take a hard look at the patient's point of view, giving special attention to the experience of hospitalization. You will learn how to deal with anger in the nurse–patient relationship. You will also discover new ways to deal with difficult and noncompliant patients. Forging alliances with patients will not only improve patient satisfaction with care but accrue vital support of nursing's legislative and public policy initiatives.

When patients are irritable and nurses are stressed, abundant potential exists for failure to achieve the healing connection to which Adkins refers in the epigraph above. What do patients have to say about being hospitalized? My colleagues and I noticed that the literature contained very few detailed first-person accounts from the recipients of our nursing services. Therefore, our team undertook several phenomenological studies at the University of Tennessee, ultimately compiling a number of them in our book, *Listening to Patients* (Thomas & Pollio, 2002).

Patients' Descriptions of Hospitalization

Research team member Mona Shattell (2002a) interviewed medical-surgical patients with diverse diagnoses, including cancer, atrial fibrillation, stroke, and fractured pelvis. From her investigation, we learned that hospitalized patients view the environment itself as unpleasant, especially if there is no window through which they can continue to participate vicariously in the ongoing stream of life. Time often dragged. The patients expressed intense desire to get out of the hospital. Especially for patients with limited mobility who were largely dependent on nursing staff, the environment was experienced as confined and encased: "You're shut up in here" (Shattell, p. 221). A woman with a radium implant deplored the staff's avoidance of her:

> *Everyone's afraid of you . . . dietary would bring the tray, but then they wouldn't pick it up and here was this food [left in the room] . . . The night nurse acted like she was terrified out of her mind . . . slid my pills around on the tray . . . They didn't clean me . . . you feel nasty."* (p. 225)

The patients' narratives reminded us that the hospital environment is a scary place, lacking aspects of home that help mirror identity and create comfort. For example, the comfort and identity that people derive from familiar food, clothing, and personal objects is missing. Here are typical comments of the patients in the study:

> "They give you a lot of variety of food that I wouldn't eat at home . . . I don't care much about grits . . . I'm not a Southerner."
> "I don't like the [remote] control [for the TV] because I can't go forward or backward, I have to go all the way around . . . Mine at home isn't like that."
> "There was not a shower in the room. I enjoyed my shower at home very much." (Shattell, 2002a, p. 223)

In a concurrent study on the psychiatric unit, time also dragged between the "little games" and "classes." The patients yearned for greater closeness with nurses and other professional staff. The interaction with nurses was limited because the closed nurses' station window was perceived as a barrier. Patients reported, "95% of the time they'll keep their nurses' station window closed unless they're giving out medicine" (Thomas, Shattell, & Martin, 2002, p. 104). The psychiatric patients viewed the small, drab smoking room as "the best place on this floor," because they derived comfort from interacting with other patients there (Thomas et al., 2002).

Many hospitalized patients conclude that they should become "easy patients," so that the nurses will provide them better care. Participants in another study by Shattell (2002b) described deliberate efforts to stay on the "good side of nurses" and "not rock the boat" by complaining. They employed strategies such as remembering their nurses' names, being entertaining, and using flattery:

> With the older [nurses], I would talk about the hospital and what a GREAT hospital it was.... And then the young ones, I'd just ask them why they majored in nursing and with the shortage and that I was encouraging my daughter to do it. Just bullshit, total bullshit. (Shattell, 2002b, p. 29)

Patients believed that these strategies resulted in RNs checking them more frequently and spending more time interacting, as exemplified by the words of this participant:

> If you are grumpy, maybe they [the nurses] won't try to be extra chatty with you... But if you're showing them, "Hey, I'm interested in what you're saying," then maybe they'll be a little more chatty... maybe they WERE checking in a little bit more because they felt like, hey you know, she's a nice person, let's just see how she's doing while I'm walking past her door. (Shattell, 2002b, pp. 30–31)

The patients in all of these studies spoke of the loneliness of hospitalization. It was clear from the data that "being with" a patient is often as significant a role for the nurse as "doing for" a patient (Thomas & Pollio, 2002). The impact of each brief bit of interaction with a nurse or physician is magnified in the perception of a bored and lonely patient. Consequently, routine nursing acts may be extolled in superlative terms—while nurses who are viewed as neglectful or uncaring may be demonized. Both views were evident in Shattell's (2002a) data. For example, one patient reported that "They [the nurses] do everything in the world to make you happy. Those girls are wonderful," while another summarized her nursing care as follows: "They look in on you and they give you a bath every day and they throw a pill down your throat" (2002a, p. 226). These disparate views of nursing care bring to mind Nurse Ratched and other stereotypical images of nurses that we frequently encounter in popular media. Let's take a minute to review them.

Patients' Images of Nurses

Given the unpleasantness of so many invasive things that nurses must do to patients, it is not surprising that negative images of nurses abound in the culture. When nurses are female, as most still are, a plethora of frightening and unpleasant images can be generated: old maids, battle-axes, and torturers (Muff, 1988). A particularly chilling image is the formidable and controlling Nurse Ratched in "One Flew Over the Cuckoo's Nest," who is more concerned with smooth functioning of the organization than the needs of patients (Kesey, 1973). Such an image crystallizes men's fear of powerful women, a fear acted out every day in situations involving male patients and female nurses. Rodgers (1982) points out that nursing, as a predominantly female occupation, conjures up the image of the nursing mother. The breast is the first object of human envy, and by extension, woman is therefore the first person envied. As a consequence, females in the nursing profession are "vulnerable to angry, envious, and destructive, although perhaps largely unconscious, impulses of the many others with whom we deal—patients, as well as physicians and other colleagues" (Rodgers, 1982, p. 347).

Female nurses also evoke sexual fantasies in male patients. Nursing, by its very nature of having to care for patients' bodily needs, violates normal social rules regarding bodily contact. Furthermore, there may be exaggerated expectations based on nurses' warm and caring attitude (Robbins, Bender, & Finnis, 1997). Judging by greeting cards, the stereotypical image of a sexy nurse is a woman with a minuscule brain, luscious lips, and generous breasts. Patients do act on their fantasies by making sexual remarks or touching nurses inappropriately—even if we don't look much like the caricatures of nurses on the greeting cards. Who among us hasn't been asked if we would like to get in a patient's bed? Research (e.g., Libbus & Bowman, 1997) shows that such behavior remains common, despite widespread societal consciousness-raising about sexual harassment in the last few years.

The public's most common stereotype or image of a male nurse is that he must be gay (Williams, 1995). While there are gay men in the profession, it is ludicrous for patients to make an assumption about sexual orientation solely on the basis of nontraditional career choice. Their reasoning is that if a man engages in nurturing human service work, he is effeminate—a "sure sign" of homosexuality. Male nurses experience the gamut of harassment, from outright propositions and cruel taunting to covert snickers and chortles as they go down the hall. To "display" heterosexuality, some male nurses wear wedding bands or deliberately mention their wives and children while giving patient care.

In contrast to these images of nurses as battle-axes, sexpots, or sexual deviants, equally erroneous idealized ones are enshrined in the human psyche: nurse as angel of mercy, handmaiden to the physician, pure and virginal woman in white (Muff, 1988). The strongest of these is probably the saintly Nightingale image of the lady with the lamp, weary but driven by her enormous compassion to continue her rounds far into the night. (We nurses have internalized this one too, driving ourselves like the indefatigable Nightingale to work one more shift, see one more patient, give one more heaping tablespoonful of TLC.)

Not surprisingly, given the irrational expectations that these various images generate in patients, we nurses often fail to do what is expected of us. Angels and saints we are not. And discontent among consumers has been increasing in recent years. Fifty-five percent of nurses in one survey reported an increase in patient and family complaints (Shindul-Rothschild et al., 1996), and a majority of U.S. nurses in Aiken's study indicated that patient and family complaints (and verbal abuse) had occurred regularly during the past year (Aiken et al., 2001). What is it like for you when your patient becomes angry at you?

When the Patient Is Angry at You

Once I was in a patient's room helping another nurse. I do not recall exactly what was said, but the patient became upset and angry. The other nurse told the patient, "I'll go get you something for your nerves." Turning to me, she said, "Will you see if the social worker can come up and talk with her?" I was stunned. Why did we need the Ativan or the social worker?

As shown in this student's report, common responses to angry patients are medicating them or trying to get someone else to handle them. Nurses can find angry patients quite threatening. Nurse behaviors of *disconnecting* (M.E. Smith & Hart, 1994) and *becoming frustrated and angry in return* (Podrasky & Sexton, 1988) are documented in the research literature. Smith and Hart's grounded theory study of med-surg nurses sheds light on the process of managing angry patient situations. Disconnecting from the patient occurred when nurses appraised the anger as a personal attack ("She would call us names...call us 'whores' and other very bad names and I felt very degraded"). Nurses did not understand the patient's reality and reacted with shock and a sense of being off-balance ("It took me totally off guard"). As they struggled to understand, they felt self-blame ("Maybe it was something I overlooked"). Some of the nurses believed that dealing with angry patients was beyond their expertise ("Except for psych nurses, nobody knows and nobody feels able to cope..."). As their own anger arose, they feared its power and sought to hide it. If it escaped, they felt ashamed. After all, they had learned that "good nurses" do not get angry at their patients. Nurses tried strategies such as taking time-outs, transferring blame, seeking peer support, and "returning to smooth," which meant repairing the relationship with the patient. The smoothing did *not* involve talking about the anger incident, but rather acting as though nothing had happened—which I view as a less-than-ideal resolution of the angry episode.

Not all nurses disconnected from angry patients. Three of the study participants were able to remain with the patient, exploring the anger, analyzing its cause (for example, anxiety), and "letting it fly over," rather than taking it personally. The researchers attributed this ability to remain connected during anger to the greater amount of experience these three nurses had (experience of the study participants ranged widely, from 1 to 21 years). Therefore, they concluded their article on a hopeful note that more effective responses to patient anger could be developed by nurses over time. That conclusion certainly fits with my view.

6.1. Stephanie Hart, a Minnesota staff nurse, learned about angry patients from Liz:

> *Initially, she was a difficult patient, her anger and aggressiveness delivered with a swift, biting tongue....She never uttered a "please" or a "thank you"....Why, I wondered, did she refuse important procedures; why wouldn't she conform to my therapeutic regimen?....She angrily rejected my efforts, yet expected me to return to her room on demand....Our relationship slowly evolved with each isolated moment of intimacy, each small revelation about her family life, childhood experiences, and dreams....Only when she was gone did I fully realize what she had come to mean to me....While I thought I was doing all the giving, Liz was giving something back to me: a lesson I didn't learn in nursing school and couldn't gain even from the most comprehensive in-service or the wisest of mentors. In the end, she taught me to recognize the helplessness and fear behind a patient's anger and anxiety and to realize that rejection may be a manifestation of the inability to cope. (S. Hart, 1997, p. 54)*

Joan Carothers discovered that staying the course with her difficult patient produced "amazing" results:

> I was assigned to take care of an orthopedic patient who had been in and out of the hospital many times. She was very difficult to please, according to the other nurses. When I went in to introduce myself to the patient, she was reading a newspaper and didn't even look up. I thought, "well, I'll just try to be nice and try to meet her needs and do whatever I can." She was short in her responses to me, curt and grumpy. I knew she didn't feel well. She had had multiple procedures, a fractured leg and then the incision became infected . . . it was a painful situation . . . we had to do some painful irrigations, so she really had reason to be grumpy. . . . I would sit and spend time with her, and she kind of opened up and seemed to enjoy the interaction. She had never been married, was in her 50s, lived alone. I looked at her chart one night and realized that her birthday was coming up in a few days, so I thought, "what the heck, we'll just get her a cake and some balloons and we'll just have a party." The other nurses didn't want to participate 'cause they had all take care of her, and she had worn out her welcome with them, but finally I talked them into it, and we surprised her with the party. She was just thrilled, real appreciative. It's amazing, and I don't think that I really was the one that turned the corner, but her knee started getting better, and I think she was a little encouraged that maybe there was a light at the end of the tunnel for all of this hospitalization.

Read on for some strategies that may be helpful to you in defusing patient anger.

What to Do When the Patient Is Angry

- *Try to ascertain why the patient is angry.* Chances are, the anger is not about you. Listen to the patient express her feelings and acknowledge their legitimacy. Don't interrupt as the grievance is described. Tell the patient that you understand what she is saying (to make sure, paraphrase what you heard and ask if you are on target). Help the patient articulate what she needs or wants to become more comfortable. Work with her to develop a mutually satisfactory plan to get her needs met. Offering options will help to alleviate the sense of powerlessness that many patients feel when hospitalized.

  Remember that anger may be intermingled with anxiety and fear about scary and uncomfortable procedures. Anger can also be generated by depersonalizing institutional routines. Consider "routine" admission procedure. How often do we really stop to consider what an invasion of privacy it is when we ask those "routine" questions on admission to our facility? It is certainly not "routine" to the person we are questioning to reveal her bowel habits, spiritual beliefs, substance use, and sexual problems (even abuse!) to a perfect stranger with a clipboard. She is already being asked to bare her body and donate its blood and urine, and we are trying to probe her psyche and soul as well. Every blank on the assessment form must be filled. Nothing is sacred now. And it won't be long until somebody else shows up and asks most of those same questions again. Tubes, needles, and other devices of torture are soon to come.

6.2. This story involves a nursing student who persevered with an angry patient despite being told to get out of his room:

> *As I walked into the room for the very first time that morning for assessments and vitals, Patient A was in dismal spirits and requested that I "hurry up." As I finished the assessment and presented educational information, the patient then told me to "get out." I felt upset and angry [but] I returned to the room after breakfast... and discovered the nature of the real problem. The patient was upset about how finances could be managed at home. I then collaborated with Patient A on how the problem could be resolved... Patient A's anger was not toward me.*

■ *When people complain, don't explain.* The patient does not want an explanation, even if it is a very good one. She just wants her needs met. A typical scenario might involve a hospitalized patient who has been waiting a long time for an injection for pain. So she growls into the intercom: "Where in the hell is my shot?" Your *worst response* goes something like this: "There's no need to be hateful. We are really short of help this evening. There are five people ahead of you, and you'll just have to wait." This response *labels* the patient (hateful), *explains* (short of help), and creates *added anxiety* (with five people ahead of her, God knows when her shot will finally come). You have compounded the misery of an individual who is hurting and angry.

So, what's a better approach? Validate the complaint: "I can see why you are upset" or "You're right. This wasn't handled well." Apologize. A genuine apology will go a long way toward extinguishing the patient's anger (see Lazare, 2006, for a thoughtful essay on apology as an emerging clinical skill). Next, focus on what *can* be done rather than what hasn't been done. If possible, assure the patient that you will take care of the complaint *yourself.* She's still not going to be a happy camper if you tell her "I'll try to find your nurse," because a hurting patient already imagines that her nurse has departed for Outer Mongolia. And the delay in receiving the analgesic already seems interminable. I suggest that you say, "I'm really sorry that you've had to wait. I will take care of it right now."

■ *Teach communication.* When the patient is really angry at someone else, such as her physician—and you are just the convenient target on whom it is displaced—teach the patient how to communicate her concerns to the real target. This is basically a matter of teaching assertive communication. For example, your patient's pain is unrelieved by the analgesic ordered by her doctor. Help the patient to speak up for herself: "Mrs. Jones, I think it is very important that you tell the doctor that your new pain medication is not relieving you. Tell him exactly where your pain is and how it feels. He should be coming to the unit to make rounds shortly. I'll make sure he comes to see you first." As the patient develops confidence that she can effectively communicate with her caregivers and have some influence in her plan of care, she is less likely to feel helpless and angry.

▪ *Be alert to transference phenomena.* Is your patient reacting to you the way she reacted to her critical mother or punitive father? Talk with her about important figures in her life and previous experiences with caregivers. The patient may have no conscious awareness that she is transferring strong emotion about a childhood figure to you. As she gets to know you better, and you steadfastly meet her needs for care, she will be able to see you as a unique individual and behave less angrily.

▪ *Set limits.* When you must set limits on a patient's behavior, do it without provoking anger and aggression. The *worst* way to set limits, according to a study by Lancee, Gallop, McCay, and Toner (1995), is making a statement that belittles the patient ("You act like a child, you get treated like a child.") This type of statement by the nurse almost always generates considerable anger. Avoid preachy platitudes like "We practice the Golden Rule here; treat others as you want to be treated."

▪ *Get help.* If you are at your wit's end dealing with an angry, demanding, patient, use the consultants available in your facility, such as a psychiatric liaison nurse, social worker, psychologist, or chaplain. If possible, schedule a team conference to discuss the patient and problem-solve. There are many options to consider: rotating the nurses assigned to the patient, so that no one becomes completely drained, recruiting volunteers to spend time with her, perhaps moving her to a semiprivate room. Make sure everyone on the team is informed of the new approach so that staff behavior toward the patient is consistent.

▪ *Never lose sight of the potential for an angry patient to become violent.* Nurses are the targets of patient violence more often than any other group of health care providers (Arnetz, Arnetz, and Soderman, 1998). Be alert for increased agitation, clenched fists, pacing, and other signs that a patient may become assaultive. Violence is more apt to occur when a patient is under the influence of drugs or alcohol, or has impaired ability to think clearly and behave rationally because of organic brain disease, psychosis, brain trauma, mental retardation, or other disorders affecting the central nervous system. Paranoid individuals may attack you in what they perceive as self-defense against an incipient attack by you. Your goal in dealing with potentially violent patients is safety—of the patient, staff, and yourself. Keep a safe distance from the patient. Don't ever let an agitated, angry patient stand between you and the door. Speak to the patient in a calm, reassuring way. Make sure someone else on the staff knows where you are and is ready to come to your aid if needed. However, in my experience, it can be very frightening to a patient if you panic and call security prematurely. In several situations on our psych unit, just as I was making progress subduing an agitated patient by talking calmly, a technician erred by calling security. When the big, burly, security guards came tromping into the room, the patient completely lost control. I believe that the use of force or restraints should be a last resort. Every health care facility should have a plan for dealing with violent behavior, one that can be mobilized in a crisis situation. This has become increasingly important as violence has escalated in our society. Your facility should provide you with training in assessing angry individuals and preventing violent assaults. Ask administration if your facility is in compliance with the Violence Prevention Guidelines issued by the Occupational Safety and Health Administration.

When You Are Angry at Your Patient

Nurses are human. We become angry at patients for a number of reasons. Some-times the anger is justifiable, as when a patient makes crude sexual overtures. Too often, however, we are displeased because the patient is not being a "good patient" (i.e., she is too demanding and/or not properly grateful). Our beliefs and values about other aspects of patient behavior fuel anger too. Listen to public health nurse Bonnie Hartman:

> I get angry at some of the clients we see, particularly those who are demanding, complain about having to wait, and those who don't even take a bath before they come. They miss appointments or are late because they overslept. Then they demand to be seen when they come. And they don't even have a job—they just overslept. I'd like to oversleep or come and go as I please. But I'm here working as hard as I can to get the clients seen, so they won't complain about the long wait or miss their soap opera!

The tone of moral indignation is clear in this nurse's account of her anger at patients. Notice that Bonnie thinks that the patients should bathe before they come to the health department. Several nurse authors, including Myra Levine, have written about nurses' views regarding *cleanliness*: "'Unclean' has long meant more than merely dirty. But it was the Victorians who married clean-liness to godliness, and with it a moral halo that hovers over many of the deci-sions individuals make for themselves. . . . The poor are castigated if they appear dirty because, as the argument goes, soap is cheap" (Levine, 1970, p. 2108). I'm sure you have heard nurses say things like, "The least these people can do is keep clean."

Although personal hygiene is undoubtedly important, what some nurses mean by "clean" is a particular kind of shiny, well-scrubbed, shaved, and de-odorized ideal that only a tiny minority of the citizens of the world can achieve. Foreign visitors to our home are often astonished that we wasteful Americans take showers every single day—sometimes more than one per day—and wash our clothes after every single wearing. No such stringent standards exist in their cul-tures, nor is there sufficient water. And we don't have to go abroad to gain a dif-ferent perspective. My own views about cleanliness have been badly shaken on more than one occasion when my nursing assignment took me into a patient's home that had no running water, or into a housing project where laundered clothes could not be hung out on the line to dry because the clothespins would immediately be stolen. I wondered how often I would do a big laundry if I had to wash the clothes in the bathtub and hang them on the backs of the chairs to dry.

Bonnie also decries the indolence of her patients who "don't even have a job," unlike she, who arises early and works hard to serve them. Bonnie clearly espouses the Protestant work ethic and makes a judgment that someone who is not working is less virtuous. Although we can surely empathize with Bonnie's sense of unfairness (why must her freedom be constrained when they can come and go as they please?), a note of caution must be sounded. It is easy for care providers of one culture or social class to assume that their own values, norms, and practices are superior to those of other groups. Because the nursing profession in the United States has historically drawn its recruits largely from the white Euro-American middle class, the cultural values of this segment of the population have permeated nursing philosophy, textbooks, and clinical practices. Our way of thinking and doing things seems "normal" and "right," and we make judgments about people who do not conform to our views. We understand neither the idleness of the rich, who fly from one seasonal pleasure spot to another to ski, sail, and sunbathe, nor the idleness of the poor, who "blithely" accept checks from the government and other kinds of assistance from social welfare agencies. We wonder why the poor can't "pull themselves up by their bootstraps." Isn't this the land of equal opportunity?

Consider the following white Euro-American middle-class values that have been well-entrenched: (1) achievement, occupational and financial success, status consciousness; (2) speed, activity, efficiency; (3) youth, beauty, health, self-reliance; (4) science and the use of technology; (5) materialism, consumerism, use of disposable items; (6) conformity to the group simultaneously with rugged individualism; (7) social and geographical mobility; and (8) competitive and aggressive behavior instead of cooperation (Murray & Zentner, 1979). However, many of these ethnocentric values are being questioned now. Individuals of diverse racial, ethnic, and cultural groups are becoming increasingly visible and influential in politics, business, and health care. Today, substantial emphasis is placed on cultural competence within nursing and other professional education programs. All of us must continue to work at leaving ethnocentrism behind.

The Noncompliant Patient

Returning to our discussion of patient characteristics that provoke nurses' wrath, *noncompliance with the treatment regimen* is another frequent anger trigger. When we interviewed female nurses in 1996, (Smith et al.), anger was particularly strong at patients who were self-destructive or "wasting" their time:

> "Addicts, suicidal patients, I could not help but feel a certain amount of anger. You've charcoaled them out because they've overdosed for the third time in a row—OK, fine, do the job next time. Don't call 911 . . . taking up tax dollars and nurse time, it's a waste of resources."
>
> "You have whiners and complainers that are taking your time because they're on the buzzer all the time. . . . Whiners of any kind anger me . . . malingerers . . . 'oh my head hurts, this hurts, that hurts, my big toe, oh please scratch it, you know.' Those [patients] anger me because they're taking

my time away and I only have a certain allotment for a certain amount of patients."

One proposed explanation for nurses' anger toward patients is that "women nurses who have been dominated by others and operate from a male-normed perspective may exact revenge for their own powerlessness in the relationships formed with clients" (Caroline & Bernhard, 1994, p. 85). However, this explanation fails to account for similar behavior we observed when we studied male nurses (A. Brooks, et al., 1996). Here are some examples from our male RN data. Mike Evans was angry at noncompliant patients who refused to change their behaviors (smoking, diet, etc.), resulting in repeated admissions to his unit:

They come in near death and you nurse them back.... Two months down the road you see them again in the same shape.... If they're not a moron, they can listen to instructions and dose their insulin or follow a diet, but they continue all the things that bring them in in horrible shape.... And I have to take care of them. It's disgusting. I wanted to say, "If you're not going to follow any of our advice or do anything to help yourself, then why don't you just stay home and die?"

On one occasion, Mike said he walked out, unable to take care of a patient: "The patient had COPD and then developed laryngeal Ca, had a laryngectomy, had a tracheostomy, and was still smoking. He would smoke through his tracheostomy. And the first time I walked in and saw him smoking, I just had to walk out in disgust. I couldn't take care of him."

Judgment and Abandonment of the "Bad" Patient

Nurses' anger at "bad" patients can be quite virulent—even prompting abandonment, as in the case of Mike, who walked out on the incorrigible smoker. This labor and delivery nurse also walked out on her patient:

It was a very horrible patient. She was just cursing nonstop through labor and just screaming. Most patients will respond to you when you try to get them to breathe and to relax, and she screamed and cursed at everybody in the room. And I just left the room. I couldn't stay in there.

Ron Murray described an anger episode with a patient who had been in restraints because of confusion. After telling the patient that he would undo the restraints "as long as you are good," he caught her out of bed. He attributes this to "acting out," although it is equally likely that the patient was still confused:

She was up walking around the room with the IV cord stretched just as far as it would stretch. And she's real hard to stick.... It was aggravating, and plus the stress of all the other patients that you've got... and here you've got one that's acting out.... I really think she knew what she was doing.

The next example is particularly disturbing because the bad patient was only a baby. The nurse in this situation described herself as "burned out," which seems evident in her account. Notice the faulty attribution that the baby's failure to eat was somehow volitional:

> *A couple of weeks ago, I was feeling really burned out and I had a newborn who wouldn't eat, and when I gavaged him, he spit all the formula back up, and I gritted my teeth and became so angry at the baby. It really scared me because I felt like I could have hit him or something for not eating. I waited about 15 minutes and then tried to feed him again, feeling much better, but I really felt guilty for a long time." (Larson, 1987, p. 23)*

Over the years of our research on RNs, more than a few made a distinction between patients with mental problems and those with physical problems, indicating significantly less tolerance and understanding for individuals with psychiatric conditions or chemical dependency. The words of Lucille Parsons, taken from our 2003 interview data, are illustrative of this attitude:

> *I have to lavage somebody who is fighting back, and it's taking four to five people to lavage, it's taking half your staff to do this one procedure for this one patient. Those patients will be the ones that will ultimately hurt you, hit you, fight with you, threaten to kill you. . . . It can be extremely frustrating because it ultimately can make you think, "why am I spending all this time with this one patient when I've got other patients here with problems?". . . . it's all behavioral . . . it's the behavioral problems that are taking so much time for things that you need to be doing for other patients who have more physical conditions. I have been doing this [ER nursing] for 12 years now, and I think there has been double the amount of people we get in here who have either overdosed or are intoxicated and on narcotics or have been huffing or whatever. I see more behavioral issue patients now than I ever have in my career.*

Tom Parker spoke of a "CD" (chemically dependent patient) who was "whining" and making rapid-fire demands:

> *This person's demeanor, their whole personality just rubbed me the wrong way. The patient had a whining type of attitude, but very persistent, the kind of thing that just pecks and pecks and pecks at you, without a letup. It was the demandingness that really bothered me, it was just rapid fire, demanding attention almost in a hysterical way. He was asking for something that I could not deliver.*

Even students, perhaps influenced by staff RN role models, begin to consider some patients "bad" soon after beginning their clinical experience. We observed this in our study of junior students. The students expressed anger at diabetics who "didn't care about managing the disease," at a patient who "was not doing anything to improve his cellulitis," and a patient with COPD and heart disease whose conditions were "all self-induced." Notice the pejorative adjectives used in this student's description of a patient with history of drug abuse: "She was morbidly obese, lazy, and manipulative." The following negative comment about an alcoholic patient was made on the student's very first clinical day: "Here is someone who is literally self-destructing with their choices and only costing taxpayers more money in his multiple hospital visits, but the problem is never fixed."

The anger at patients in these examples from our research on RNs and students is antithetical to a therapeutic nurse–patient relationship. Many of these nurses have, in fact, rejected their difficult or noncompliant patients and no longer wish to remain in relationship with them. The rationale in many cases? Because the patients "won't try to help themselves." I argue that even when patients refuse to follow our directives, it is unethical to abandon them. Isn't it a bit presumptuous that we always know what is best for them?

Why We Need to Manage Our Anger at Patients

It is important to manage our anger at patients—even intransigent and obnoxious ones—more effectively. The first and foremost reason is to preserve the therapeutic relationship, without which nothing else of any consequence can be accomplished. As Myra Levine put it, "Whether his [the patient's] difficulties are truly self-inflicted or quite beyond his control, no patient is served by moralistic judgments. Nursing care laced with censure is not nursing and not caring. . . . Nursing intervention can provide a transcendent way to a more inclusive humanity for the patient and the nurse. All patients deserve that effort" (Levine, 1970, pp. 2018, 2111). I believe that nurses need more instruction on effective methods of motivating noncompliant patients to change their health-damaging behaviors. One such approach, called *motivational interviewing*, deserves more attention in the nursing literature (see www.motivationalinterview.org for more information).

The second reason why we need to get a handle on our anger is that it is impossible to estimate the ripple effect in that patient's life from one interaction with a nurse. A patient who waits a long time for medication for pain, perceiving the nurse as unsympathetic to his suffering, is going to remember that and form judgments about "nurses who are only in it for the paycheck and don't really care." Patients in our studies related incidents from decades ago when a nurse was snippy or uncaring.

People remember their nurses, because nurses are in their lives during agonizing times of crisis or epiphanies that remain vivid in memory. People also generalize beyond their experience with one nurse to the profession as a whole. In each and every encounter, the potential exists for your patient (and his significant others) to form a lasting impression of nursing.

What to Do When You Are Angry at Your Patient

- *Acknowledge your feelings*. It is understandable that you may have negative feelings toward patients whom you perceive as demanding or obstreperous. What is important is not how you feel but how you behave.

Acknowledge your feelings, and harmlessly discharge them, but continue to give compassionate care to the patient. Remaining in relationship with a difficult or self-destructive patient can be a tremendous learning experience of *oneself*. I recall Hildegard Peplau pointing out that nursing is always a learning experience of oneself as well as of the other individual involved in the interaction. Patients often evoke emotions and memories that their caregivers would rather avoid. But when we shut out a patient because of this, we are closing off access to an important part of ourselves (Stein, cited in L. Dossey, 1984). When a patient evokes strong emotion in you, it should always be a cue to (a) look closely at the defensive maneuvers the patient may be using and (b) carefully analyze your own strong reaction. Is it your own helplessness to control the patient that generates your anger? Is it your own fear and denial of death that makes it so difficult to be with someone who is longing for it?

- *Let it out.* In an atmosphere of collegial trust and support, you can ventilate excess anger and frustration to other nurses in the setting. I found this a necessity in a psychiatric inpatient unit, especially when working with patients who were manipulative and intent on testing limits, splitting staff, and generally creating turmoil. I was fortunate to work for a number of years with a very special group of people who talked freely in staff meetings about their own issues with difficult patients. Together, we found ways to maintain a therapeutic milieu—and our own sanity.

- *Use proven methods.* Specific techniques have been developed for interacting with four types of patients described as "difficult" in a *New England Journal of Medicine* article by Groves (1978) that has become a classic (see box). I don't especially like the labels the author gave these patients, but I can attest that the tactics work.

STRATEGIES FOR DEALING WITH FOUR TYPES OF DIFFICULT PATIENTS

1. Dependent clingers. These are patients who appear to have bottomless needs. In the inpatient setting, they are the ones referred to as "on the buzzer all the time." They may flatter caregivers by saying things like "You're so good to me. What would I do without you?"

Eventually they evoke aversion in their caregivers because their requests escalate from mild ones to repeated cries for affection, explanation, and/or analgesics. The nurse should set limits, give the patient regular appointments at specific intervals (or specify reasonable intervals when you will return to give care, if you are in an inpatient setting), and remind the patient not to call at other times unless it is an emergency. When reassured of regular, consistent attention, these patients will not need to keep escalating their cries for help.

2. Entitled demanders. These individuals use intimidation and guilt induction to obtain care. They may threaten their care providers with litigation. They are unaware of their deep dependency needs and fear of abandonment. The entitlement is an attempt to preserve the integrity of the self during terrifying illness. The nurse's approach should be

supportive of the entitlement because that reassures the patient: "You are entitled to the very best care, and you will get it." Hostile responses will only add to the patient's terror of abandonment.

3. Manipulative help-rejecters. These patients feel that no interventions will help them, and they often report back to you (smugly) that the treatments didn't work. If one symptom is alleviated, they will develop another—because they want to keep the relationship with the caregiver. These individuals evoke feelings of inadequacy and guilt in caregivers. The suggested approach? *Share their pessimism*. In a low-key way, tell them you're not sure this treatment will work. Don't appear invested in the treatment ("Let's give this a try"). Tell the patient that regular check-ups will be necessary (allays fear of abandonment), and be consistent and firm.

4. Self-destructive deniers. These are among the most difficult patients of all, because they are either consciously suicidal or unconsciously self-murderous through behaviors such as heavy drinking despite esophageal varices and hepatic failure. Caregivers may wish that the person would die and get it over with. These individuals are profoundly dependent but have given up hope of ever having their needs met. They seem to glory in their own destruction, and enjoy defeating attempts to preserve their lives. The recommended approach is to fight your impulse to abandon the patient, and after ruling out if a treatable depression exists, then consider the patient as you would any other terminal patient. Continue to preserve life and maintain the nurse–patient relationship as long as possible. (Adapted from Groves, 1978)

Patient Dissatisfaction With Health Care

National surveys of Americans' perceptions of the health care system indicate a crisis of confidence:

- 79% of respondents agreed that "there is something seriously wrong with our health care system."
- More than half (57%) believed that "hospital care is not very good."
- Less than half (44%) said they had "confidence in the health care system to take care of me."
- Eight in ten believed that "quality medical care has become unaffordable for the average American," that "hospitals have cut corners to save money," that "quality care is often compromised by insurance companies to save money," and that "quality of medical care has gone down while costs have increased." ("Survey finds consumer confidence . . ." 1997, p. 5)

Two out of three Americans no longer hold physicians in high regard, and these citizens see health care services as slightly better than automotive repair shops, but less satisfactory than supermarkets and airlines (Aiken, 1992). In other surveys, hospital patients said they were not treated with courtesy and respect by doctors and nurses (Pear, 2008), and outpatients felt they were treated like cattle or like objects on an assembly line (Plaas, 2002). Depersonalizing treatment was also described by inpatients in a new study by Shattell, Andes, and Thomas (in press). For example, patients said they had to rush through their meals ("we have to gobble it up right quick") because it was time for the staff to get off work. Consistent across several studies was the perception that nurses were doing tasks mechanically, with no recognition of patients' individuality. During hospitalization for surgery, I remember how it felt when a nurse came into the room and looked at my IV, then turned and left without ever looking at me. Sidney Jourard (1971, pp. 179–180) called the bedside manner displayed by many nurses "a peculiar kind of inauthentic behavior. . . . Some nurses always smile, others hum, and still others answer all patients' questions about medications with the automatic phrase, 'This will make you feel better.'" Jourard dryly commented that the performance sometimes functions as an emetic. He understood why nurses may armor themselves to maintain professional detachment: "If the 'armor' is effective, it permits the nurse to go about her duties unaffected by any disturbing feelings of pity, anger, inadequacy, or insecurity" (Jourard, 1971, p. 181). The problem, of course, is that the nurse's impersonal bedside manner, whether slightly chilly or falsely jolly, obliterates the individuality of patients.

What Do Patients Really Want?

Like the old song, little things mean a lot. Matt Stolick, hospitalized for knee surgery, shared with me a story that captures the importance of little things:

> The nurse who was assigned to me came in during dinner time, greeted me with a smile, and asked if there was anything she could get me. There was a Coke on the tray, and I told her that I would really like a Pepsi instead. She laughed and apologized, saying that they only had Coke. . . . Early in the morning, I was sitting up in my bed, waiting to see my physician. My nurse came in with her jacket on, ready to leave for home. She had a smile on her face and a Pepsi in her hand. She told me that she had gotten it downstairs and wanted to give it to me before she left. After that, I was much more comfortable in the hospital, in light of this compassionate gesture on the nurse's part.

Like Matt, a patient interviewed by Kralik, Koch, and Wotton (1997, p. 402) fondly recalled the nurse who would "pay special attention to the little things, like drying between your toes. One day when I was sitting out, she said I should put some lipstick on because it would make me feel better. She was right; I put it on every day after that." These stories remind me of the innumerable small acts of kindness Nightingale performed for the soldiers at Scutari. She found time to make nightly rounds in all the wards, stayed with the men during amputations, wrote letters to their families in England, and set up a recreation room for convalescents. The men adored her.

"Little things," but profound ramifications . . . Jean Watson talks about such ramifications when nurse and patient come together:

> Two persons (nurse and other) together with their unique life histories and phenomenal fields in a human care transaction comprise an event. An event,

*such as an actual occasion of human care, is a focal point in space and time
from which experience and perception are taking place, but the actual occasion
of caring has a field of its own that is greater than the occasion itself. As such,
the process can go beyond itself, yet arise from aspects of itself that become
part of the life history of each person, as well as part of some larger, deeper,
complex pattern of life. (Watson, 1988, p. 58)*

I know that you have experienced "the process going beyond," as I have,
when you run across a former patient who thanks you for something you did
that had a profound and lasting influence. You might not have thought much
about what seemed a very simple intervention at the time. One day, a woman
came up to me and said, "I still remember what you taught me about anxiety. I
carry that little card with the stages of anxiety in my wallet to this day. I used
to think I just had 'bad nerves' like everybody in my family. But you showed
me that I can do something when I'm getting too nervous. I stop what I'm doing and start my breathing exercise." I honestly didn't recognize the patient,
or recall that I wrote a little card for her about the stages of anxiety. But she
remembered me.

Forging Alliances With Patients

After the acclaim of Nightingale's patients, the whole world wanted those wonderful Nightingale nurses. Requests poured in for graduates of her training
school to start nursing education programs in other countries. Public demand
may be our saving grace in today's battle to preserve and strengthen professional nursing. I believe that forging alliances with patients should be one
of the most crucial elements in nursing's strategic plan. Heaven knows, consumers are just about fed up with the other players scrambling for their business in today's health care arena. Studies show that *nursing still enjoys highly
positive regard from the public* (P.D. Hart, 1990). Year after year, nurses rank
number 1 among professions for honesty and integrity in national public opinion polls (e.g., CNN/USA Today/Gallup). Through the years, I have been struck
by how interested people are in the work that we do. Casual social conversa-
tions often elicit remarks such as, "Your job must be fascinating," or "I wish I
could have been a nurse." Books such as *Just a Nurse* (Kraegel & Kachoyeanos,
1989) and *Life Support* (Gordon, 1997) capture the interest of laypersons as
well as nurse readers and provide glimpses of the everyday heroism in nursing practice. In consumer surveys, most people say they would like to receive
more health care from nurses. Based on the survey data, the time is ripe for
nurses to undertake new entrepreneurial ventures, and open more clinics, hospices, and other facilities. We are the professional group with years of public
health experience and willingness to go into underserved areas to meet the
needs of the disenfranchised. We are also the professional group best suited
to humanize hospitals and to educate the public about issues such as safe
staffing.

Patients and their families often come forward to support us. Jack Strunk
became a staunch ally of the nursing profession after the death of his wife. Rebecca Strunk died after a routine hysterectomy because she did not have RNs
caring for her. She had developed a massive infection as a result of a nicked

bowel during the surgery. But the unlicensed aides hired to replace RNs did not recognize the symptoms of infection. When the American Nurses Association held a press conference at the National Press Club, Jack Strunk was there, fighting tears, to share his story (Canavan, 1997, p. 12).

As the nation continues to grapple with the worsening nursing shortage, the public will align themselves with us in support of our various legislative and public policy initiatives—if we pitch our story in the right way. Claire Fagin urges us to reframe the shortage as "diminishing access to adequate nursing, which turns the issue from a parochial nursing concern about job availability to an issue of the public's right to nursing care" (Fagin, cited in Diers, 2002). This is excellent advice.

A Last Word

Nursing's "closeness to the customer of health care," as Donna Shalala puts it, is our greatest asset. Nurses must be vocal in policy debates to ensure that all "customers" continue to have access to professional nursing care:

> *Nurses have one foot high in the tower of knowledge, one in the dust and grit of human need. This closeness to the customer of health care is not only a distinctive value and philosophy of nursing, but a strength that can be used to create a vision for health care organizations." (Donna Shalala)*

Healing
Ourselves

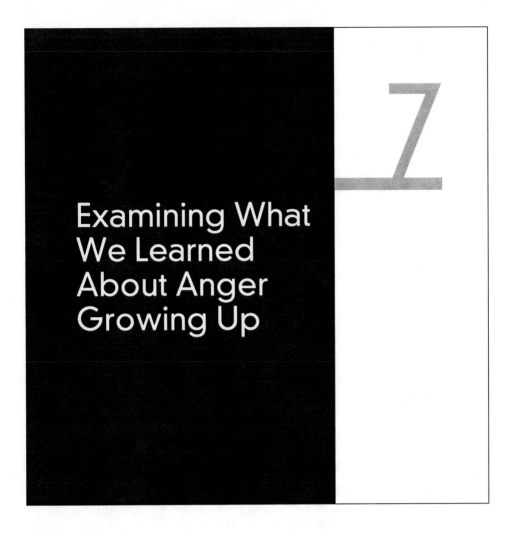

Examining What We Learned About Anger Growing Up

7

Our task, then, is to strengthen our consciousness of ourselves, to find centers of strength within ourselves which will enable us to stand despite the confusion and bewilderment around us.

—Rollo May

Having devoted attention in the last section of the book to connecting with others, in these next three chapters, we move into important material on self-healing. Rollo May has outlined our task quite well. Along with examining new ways of thinking, feeling, and behaving that strengthen us and promote healing, we must reflect on how we got the way we are. Before we were ever nurses, we were learning emotional habits along gendered lines. In this chapter, we focus on gender role socialization and some of the ways it serves us poorly, in both our personal and professional lives.

Gender Splitting

Daniel Levinson (1996) proposed a concept called *gender splitting* that I find more useful than "gender differences," because it more accurately depicts the splitting asunder or rigid division between masculine and feminine in human life. Gender splitting has been pervasive, occurring in virtually every society in the history of the human species. What is sanctioned for masculine and feminine gender roles varies according to historical period, social class, and other factors, but gender splitting always occurs. The splitting operates in institutions, family life, and the individual human psyche.

Growing boys and girls are rapidly inculcated with societal norms about men's work and women's work, men's strength and women's weakness, and other stereotypical polarities. So too, they learn the gendered rules of emotional expression. Lots of forces conspire to produce the traditional "insensitive male" and "overly emotional female." Although emotional habits are modified by later experiences, early childhood learning instills much of what is considered "normal" for masculine and feminine gender roles. What did you learn about anger while growing up? Think about your own experiences as I review some of the literature.

It Starts With Pink and Blue Receiving Blankets

From infancy on, parents apply different contingencies to the behaviors of sons and daughters, showing more acceptance of anger expression by sons (Birnbaum & Croll, 1984). Research shows that mothers emphasize anger more frequently when making up stories for their preschool sons than for their daughters (Greif, Alvarez, & Ulman, 1981). Boys are actually stimulated to aggressive action by their fathers when they are still toddlers (Miller, 1983), although the expression of other emotions, such as fear and sadness, is discouraged. Boys studied by Phillips (2001) described bonding experiences with their fathers while viewing male action and horror movies from ages as young as 3 years. Fathers, by instruction and example, get the message across to their sons that they must not ever be cowardly or weak. By the age of 3 years, boys wrestle, kick, push, shove, and hit far more than girls do (Fagot, Leinbach, & Hagan, 1986). Even throwing or breaking things may be condoned, because "boys will be boys."

In contrast, girls are allowed to be more emotional, as long as they are unaggressive (Block, 1973). With daughters, mothers emphasize that aggressive behavior may hurt people. A girl may be told, "If you can't say anything nice, just don't say anything at all." She watches her mother playing the part of family peacemaker, skillfully placating her father to maintain a harmonious household. She is learning what Jessie Bernard (1981) called the ethos of "women's world" with its prescription that females help, agree, comply, understand, and passively accept. Expressing anger is not consistent with this ethos. The result of this early inculcation of cultural rules for gendered emotional behavior? By preschool age, happiness, sadness, fear, and general emotionality are more evident in girls, whereas anger and aggression are more characteristic of boys (Brody, 1985). Studies of school-age children continue to show that girls suppress anger more so than boys do (e.g., Cox, Stabb, & Hulgus, 2000). On questionnaires administered by researchers, girls endorse statements such as "I hold my anger in," and "I'm afraid to show my anger."

Television, movies, and other powerful socializing influences outside the family take up where parents leave off. Male TV characters show significantly more anger than female characters (Birnbaum & Croll, 1984). History lessons in school portray aggressive men as heroes, while aggressive women are evil queens or wicked witches. Stories that form the foundation of our Western Judeo-Christian tradition identify women as the source of all evil. From Eve, who bit the apple, to Pandora, who foolishly opened the box, these stories teach that when women assert themselves, harm results (Wolf, 1993). The contrast between the stories of Eve and Prometheus is notable. When Prometheus defied Zeus and stole fire for human use, he was declared a hero. But when Eve defied God, she was condemned as evil and evicted from the Garden of Eden (Polster, 1992).

What We Learn Playing Childhood Games

Boys and girls learn many lessons while playing. Competitive games and other rough-and-tumble experiences on the playground teach boys that life is a *contest* in which they need to stay one-up. Meanwhile, the girls, through cooperative activities with other girls who are good friends, learn that *community* is important (Tannen, 1994). When boys and girls play with one another, boys establish dominance early—as early as 33 months. Psychologists Carol Jacklin and Eleanor Maccoby (1978) studied the interaction between pairs of 33-month-olds. Whenever the boys were paired with girls, they clearly dominated play, grabbing, pushing, and ignoring the girls' protests. In fact, the boys were so unresponsive to the girls' protests that the girls usually just gave up, standing on the sidelines and letting the boys monopolize the toys. Sociologist Barrie Thorne (1993) watched an older group of school-age children at play, documenting boys' continued domination and girls' subservience. Boys controlled more space, more often violated girls' activities, and treated girls as "contaminating." Over time, girls learned to tighten and tense their bodies so they will take up less space, to tolerate interruptions of their speech and their activities, to hesitate, apologize, and fall silent. They also smiled more—a facial expression associated with subordinate status.

Much childhood play takes place in same-sex groups. Research shows that there is a "dosage effect," meaning that the more time a child spends in play with same-sex peers, the greater the display of stereotypical gender-typed behavior (Martin & Fabes, 2001). It is an accepted part of boys' games that quarreling will occur. Boys frequently engage in fist fights and other scuffles to settle their disputes, then resume playing the game. Lasting hard feelings are rare. Later on, when they are lawyers or businessmen, they will have no problem going for the jugular and then going for beers afterward (Heim, 1995). In contrast, when quarrels erupt during girls' games, play is most often terminated (Lever, 1976). But stopping the game without resolving the dispute may leave lingering resentments. These feelings may be expressed in a passive-aggressive way, such as two girls whispering together behind another girl's back, or several playmates deciding to shun one particular girl: the scapegoat of the conflict. There are hurt feelings about the ruptured relationships (Simmons, 2002). I watched these dynamics in little girls' play closely when my daughter was younger. In the threesome of Shana, Vanessa, and Whitney, who went all through preschool and the early grades together, Shana and Vanessa would gang up on Whitney, then Vanessa and Whitney would oust Shana, then Whitney and Shana would give the silent treatment to Vanessa, and so on, in ever-shifting triangles that conformed perfectly to Murray Bowen's theory. When it was my daughter Shana in tears over the latest tiff among the girls, I would encourage assertive, direct expression of her anger to her friends. But I was not successful in bringing about healthier resolution of conflict among the three over the long haul. What happened among the three little girls has a name in the child development literature: *relational aggression* (Crick & Grotpeter, 1995). More than 10 popular books have been published on the topic since 2000, as well as a summary of the scientific literature by Geiger, Zimmer-Gembeck, and Crick (2004) that you may find useful.

Anger in Adolescence

During adolescence, studies show that both the *causes* and the *direction* of anger expression are different for boys and girls. Adolescent females become angry because of interpersonal experiences and turn their anger inwardly, whereas males get angry in situations of performance evaluation and direct their anger outwardly (Stapley & Haviland, 1989). In a study of our own (Kollar, Groer, Thomas, & Cunningham, 1991), girls were especially anger-prone when someone tried to take advantage of their friendship. During adolescence, the traditional gender-typed expectations of boys and girls become even more pronounced. Parents, teachers, and peers exert powerful pressures that are difficult to resist. Girls' anger expression is discouraged by a mechanism called *invalidation* (Crawford, Kippax, Onyx, Gault, & Benton, 1990). In other words, their anger is simply trivialized ("You're so cute when you're angry") or labeled as inappropriate ("What's wrong with you? Can't you be a good sport?"). As a consequence, the girl may question her own judgment of the incident or be ashamed of her outburst.

Brown and Gilligan (1992) conducted a 5-year study of the transition from girlhood to adolescence, documenting a kind of "psychological foot-binding" that took place over time. During the study, nearly 100 girls were interviewed yearly. At younger ages, girls could speak about angry feelings. However, under enormous pressure to become "perfect girls" who were quiet, calm, and kind, by adolescence, the girls stopped expressing feelings such as anger. They wanted to be popular and preserve relationships. Many of the girls seemed to be confused about whether anger really exists, and whether they were really feeling angry. Adolescence was a time of repression of the self, and the emotions, to avoid negative repercussions from other people.

Women's Self-Silencing

Although a widespread myth holds such self-sacrifice is an innate female virtue, it is clear that this is learned behavior. What Brown and Gilligan described for us are the devastating effects of learning to be "feminine," that is, to enact the culturally specified gender role: valuing others before themselves, responding to opinions of others, fostering the well-being of others, and silencing one's own voice. The phenomenon of silencing the self to preserve relationships has been widely documented both in the general population of women (e.g., Jack, 1991) and in female nurses (DeMarco, 2002; DeMarco, Roberts, Norris, & McCurry, 2007). RN self-silencing produced alarm when a survey sponsored by the American Association of Critical-Care Nurses showed that 78% of RN respondents found it difficult or impossible to confront colleagues who provided substandard care or took dangerous shortcuts ("New Study Finds..." 2005).

Hazards of Masculinity

Learning to be "masculine" can be just as detrimental for males' subsequent emotional health as self-silencing is for females. The aggressiveness that boys are encouraged to display does not serve them well as adults, when talking about feelings would be more appropriate than punching out walls or other people. Research on adults consistently shows that men are more likely to behave aggressively than women (e.g., Deffenbacher, 1994).

One authority who has studied aggression for many years (Campbell, 1993) contends that aggression feels *good* to men because it confers the reward of power and control over others. For women, aggression does *not* feel good because it means failure of self-control—and guilt about the distress of the person who got the brunt of the attack. When women do become aggressive, their behavior isn't particularly effective in getting them what they want and need. For example, a woman who has an outburst with a spouse or lover may be told to calm down, take a tranquilizer, or get some therapy, continuing the invalidation she experienced in girlhood. She may retreat to more indirect methods of conveying her feelings, such as raising her eyebrows, sighing pointedly, or shaking her head, all of which are more common in women than in men (Deffenbacher, 1995b). Because aggression doesn't work effectively for them, most women just don't employ it very much (Cox, Van Velsor, Hulgus, Weatherman, Smenner, Dickens, & Davis, 2004; Thomas, 2005). And there is another reason why women are less aggressive: such behavior may place them in *danger*. Retaliation in the form of sexual or physical assault is all too common.

Obviously, what we've covered so far is the effect of traditional gender-role socialization. And, it's quite clear that neither men's nor women's culturally assigned emotional behaviors serve them well. To what extent do most adults still conform to what they learned growing up? The results of one massive study, involving data collection in 37 countries across the globe, were entirely consistent with traditional gender-role socialization. Men reported more powerful emotions, such as anger, whereas women reported more of the "powerless emotions": shame, guilt, fear, and sadness (Fischer, Rodriguez Mosquera, van Vianen, & Manstead, 2004). Certainly, there can be "masculine" women and "feminine" men as well as androgynous individuals with some characteristics of both. What we've said about anger behavior applies *to the extent that you behave in accordance with society's gender-specific rules*. Although adult men and women do not differ in the *frequency* of anger arousal (Averill, 1982), high scorers on masculine gender role identity *express* more anger and high scorers on femininity *suppress* more of it, regardless of actual biological sex (Kopper & Epperson, 1991).

Triggers of Anger in Men and Women

My own studies of adult men and women have revealed both commonalities and gender differences (Thomas et al., 1998; Thomas, 2003e). When being interviewed, both men and women told their anger stories with embarrassed hesitance and nervous laughter. Both were aware of constructive uses of anger, but examples of its constructive use were outnumbered by incidents in which anger had caused others pain. Regardless of gender, guilt and self-recrimination were frequently reported. For women, hurt was intermingled with anger too, but men did not use the word "hurt."

Men and women differed in the *triggers* of their anger. For men, anger was generated by an affront to their sense of control and/or their views of right and wrong. Men became angry when they did not have the ability to control or "fix" things, whether the things were inanimate objects (computers, cars, or boats) or work-related problems (demanding customers or incompetent coworkers). As one man emphatically stated, "Whenever I am angry I always want to—*right now—fix it*." Men's anger narratives also pertained to societal issues such as pollution, monopolies, and politics (Thomas, 2003e). Women's anger was provoked mainly within their closest relationships. For women, anger was most often triggered by lack of relationship reciprocity. In other words, women felt that they were giving more than they were getting in their relationships. Many women spoke of being pressed, stretched, and almost pulled apart by the multiple demands of their families. They often spoke of their wish for someone or something to change, but they felt powerless to bring about the needed change. Even when they vented anger in a volcanic outburst, nothing changed (Thomas et al., 1998).

A fascinating difference between men and women was their choice of *metaphors*. Cooking metaphors such as "simmering," "stewing," or "slow boil" were often used by women to describe an undercurrent of unexpressed anger within the body. Men were more likely to view anger as a potentially overwhelming force; they used metaphors like "a runaway horse," "fire," "flood," or "vortex." They had been forced to learn to fight in childhood to defend themselves from schoolyard bullies, and continued to have intense bodily arousal when angry. As adults, however, most men eschewed fighting, reporting that they had not had a fight since their teens or twenties. For some, there had been an acute realization that they had the capability to kill another human with brute force. One man told of this terrible realization as he had his hands around another boy's neck, choking him. As adults, the men did not have any effective mechanisms to discharge the strong physical tension of anger. Throwing hammers and hitting computers provided little relief and left them feeling foolish afterward (Thomas, 2003e).

Is the Social Context Changing?

As Averill (1982) persuasively argued, emotions are socially constituted syndromes that cannot be understood without consideration of the *social context*. It's easy to understand why women's anger has been stifled in patriarchal societies. Angry women threaten the status quo. So, their anger is restricted in all societies in which the military, industry, government, finance, science, technology, and universities are in male hands. A United Nations Human Development Report concluded that there is still no country that treats its women as well as its men (cited in "The War Against Women," 1994). Where women still have lower status, power, and sense of self-worth than men, they must depend on men, and others who are more powerful, for approval. Consequently, they learn to be highly sensitive to nonverbal cues and hide their own emotional reactions to avoid antagonizing those in positions of dominance over them (Bernardez, 1987; Miller, 1983). In the words of Fiske (1993): "The powerless attend to the powerful who control their outcomes" (p. 621).

Women in our own study (Thomas et al., 1998) had learned their early lessons well, as shown in these excerpts from the data:

> "If I got mad I might say something off the wall that would hack everybody off and make a situation worse."
> "It's better to go along with whatever's going on, if something's not immoral, than to push the issue."
> "I try not to say things because I don't want things to escalate."
> "I don't want to be known as a person that's hard to get along with, fussy and that kind of stuff."

Some evidence suggests that societal norms may be changing, which could benefit predominantly female professions such as nursing. Studies show that younger women are more likely to forthrightly express their anger than midlife or older women (Thomas, 1997b; Thomas, 2002). While growing up, younger cohorts observed a different kind of role model than I did, living with an aunt who was the quintessential Southern lady and never used the word "anger" in her life. The women's movement exposed them to fiery activists. Television shows in the 1970s began to feature aggressive heroines such as Wonder Woman and the Bionic Woman. A researcher who had assessed TV viewing habits of young girls between 1977 and 1979, subsequently assessed their aggressive behavior as adults between 1992 and 1995, finding a significant correlation (Huesmann, cited in Seppa, 1996). An even greater number of aggressive role models, such as Buffy the Vampire Slayer, Xena the Warrior Princess, and women wrestlers and boxers, succeeded Wonder Woman in popular media. Aggressive physical activities, such as kickboxing, became popular among young women.

Gendered rules for emotional expression may prove resistant to change, however. Little change is evident in the gender-role stereotypes held by college students (Street, Kimmel, & Krombrey, 1995). Societal prescriptions for women's niceness remain strong (Spence & Buckner, 2000). Brown and Gilligan's (1992) longitudinal study portraying the insidious stifling of developing girls is not encouraging. Female anger is still labeled unfeminine and unattractive. Our language has the word "bitch" to label an angry woman, but no comparable term exists for an angry man. It has been distressing to me to see the kinds of illustrations chosen to illustrate magazine and newspaper articles about my research on women's anger. Over the years, stories have appeared in more than 30 magazines and many newspapers. The photographs or drawings accompanying the articles invariably depict women who look hysterical, crazed, or demonic—even though the text of the stories emphasizes that anger expression can be constructive and healthy.

> **7.1.** *In an experiment by MacGregor & Davidson (1994), videotapes of male and female actors portraying verbal and physical hostility were shown to research subjects. The subjects rated females as more hostile, even though the behaviors of the male actors were identical, indicating that viewers' perceptions are actually distorted when women violate gender role expectations.*

Studies show that young women, just like their older counterparts, often remain hesitant to express their anger with lovers and spouses for fear of relationship loss (Asher & Hilton, 1996; Thomas, 1997b). One of our youngest Women's Anger Study participants, a 21-year-old, had this to say:

> *A lot of women my age are very, very hesitant about, I don't think a lot of us feel worthy of, of being angry, and even when we are angry we're more afraid of, we want peace more than we want to actually express our anger and have somebody have to deal with it. Because then we have to deal with it too. And it's a lot easier just to suppress it and not make anybody unhappy. And not have to deal with a confrontation, which bothers me. Which makes me angry at myself.*

Although some scholars (e.g., Levant, 1995) claim that traditional masculinity has collapsed, boys are still being told that aggression is manly. An essay in *Time* magazine is a case in point. It was a father's advice to his son on the occasion of high school graduation. Its style was reminiscent of the best-selling *Life's Little Instruction Book* (Brown, 2003). The son was being advised to vote, get a dog, do his own laundry, and so forth. But what struck me was the father's advice about fighting: *"If you find yourself in a fight,"*—which I thought was a curious way to begin: how does a young man just *find* himself in a fight?—*"when you hit back, hit hard. Pick your time and place, and nuke 'em. Do not worry about making enemies. The right enemy will be a sign that you're growing up and that God loves you"* (Rosenblatt, 1997, p. 90). As long as fathers are telling their sons to "nuke 'em" and to consider accruing enemies as a badge of manly maturity, we are going to have a violent world.

What we learn growing up, we carry into the workplace with us.

It is time to turn our attention once again to the world of nursing and the emotions flying about us as we do our jobs every day. Similar to the above-cited studies of men and women in diverse occupations, our studies of anger in male and female nurses (A. Brooks, et al., 1996; Smith, et al., 1996) revealed both commonalities and differences. Common to all nurses' narratives was *the hostile work environment*. Whether they were male or female, the nurses' words graphically depicted a virtual war zone, in which they were frequently under assault by managers, peers, physicians, and patients. They spoke of anger as a *weapon* and a *shield* to defend against the assaults. A striking number of military metaphors ("on the firing line") and similes ("it's like an armed camp") appeared in the data:

"I become very fatigued by having to do all these battles."
"I was getting flak."
"I went in with loaded guns."
"You have to fight for what you get."
"I was an easy target."
"We feel sabotaged."
"I see this real resistance and this real territorial stand."
"We really don't know how to fight back."
"There is character assassination."
"You have to work close and not kill each other."
"It's as though if you are the least bit quiet, gentle, nonassertive, you're going to get your head knocked off."

Male Nurses and Anger

As you saw in Chapter 1, both male and female RNs often felt powerless in the hostile work environment, which caused them to be perpetually on the defensive. But our data revealed gender differences in the management of angry emotion on the job. The anger of the men we studied was much more intense and included elements of aggression. They used words such as *rage* and *red fury* that were never used by the women. One man said, "You get so angry, your face turns red, almost as if you are blowing fire out of your nose." Male nurses acknowledged violent impulses—"What I would really like to do is slap somebody, just reach up and slap them real good," "You just want to hit or shake someone," "I wanted to kill her"—although they did not ever act on these impulses. The men thought of violent actions most often when they were being attacked by a physician or supervisor in the presence of other people.

What do male nurses do with their virulent anger? Based on our interview data (A. Brooks et al., 1996), *isolation* was the men's most common response to workplace anger. In the words of Mike Evans, "My way of handling it is to distance myself." Greg James stated, "I shut off everything around me. I turn it inward. I have a sense of being completely alone." Male RNs isolated themselves not only to avoid an episode of uncontrolled anger, but also after expressing their anger or receiving angry attacks from others. Crying was viewed as a loss of control, and when a loss of control seemed imminent, the men chose to remove themselves from the situation. For example, Ron said, "I had to leave after that. I just had to leave."

I find it very understandable that men in nursing would choose to distance themselves after experiencing anger. Generally speaking, men in our society are more likely to internalize their emotional distress, whereas women often seek solace and support from others when they are upset. Men in nursing may be doubly reluctant to reveal emotional distress to their female coworkers because of past experiences of gender discrimination. However, by isolating themselves, men eliminate any possibility of receiving empathy, support, or affirmation from female peers or supervisors. And sadly, the men in our study often told of relationships with colleagues that were completely severed because anger was not ever worked through. For example, Bob Hayes purposely chose to work a different shift after an angry experience with a female nurse. Prior to the anger incident, the two had been good friends who always took their lunch or break together. By changing shifts, he succeeded in avoiding her, but described his shifts as "long and lonely."

Some male nurses described a deliberate controlled form of anger that was not often evident in our female nurse data. This form of anger was called "corrective" or "appropriate," and it was used to gain attention or to be heard. In the words of Tom Parker, "Anger can be a driving force to open up a problem." He went on to explain, "I learned to use anger in a very controlled sense . . . in a way that would make a point . . . drive my point home." This use of anger as a tool is healthy. Women in nursing should marshal it for their use as well.

Female Nurses and Anger

When I, along with my research team, first grappled with the data from female RNs, I was inclined to agree with Germaine Greer (1991), who contended that "Despite the best efforts of feminists to awaken women's anger and to turn their hostility outward so that it becomes a force for social change rather than the procreator of symptoms, we have failed." Although female nurses had no hesitation in pouring out their pent-up feelings to our research team, they had not expressed their ire directly to the persons who provoked them. They were waiting for others to rescue them, take care of them, and make things right. Although overt anger erupted in some situations, more often women's anger was expressed indirectly in passive-aggressive fashion or turned inward on the self. When anger exploded in screaming, the nurse sought to disown her emotion. This account of an anger incident sounded much like a dissociative episode:

> My mind's racing. I'm just coming out of myself, and when I come back I just sometimes look and I can't believe I've done that. Like, that's really not me. I let somebody else provoke me into behaving in a way that I wouldn't normally act, that's not really acceptable.

Nurses' reactions to overt anger expression are consistent with the rules of feminine behavior. When Fran blows up, she feels ineffective, experiences guilt, and views herself as less than professional. Ann refers to herself as a "bitch" when she expresses her anger. Sally says she feels embarrassed. Even the reviewers of the first manuscript we submitted to a journal recoiled in dismay at the "ugliness" of female RN anger. One of the reviewers admitted that she "cringed" at the words used by our study participants and found them "unbecoming for professionals." This reviewer wanted the data sanitized, removing all profanity. I am grateful that the journal editor did not ask us to do this, because it would have been unethical to alter the research data.

The data indicate that female RNs are inhibited in effective use of anger by their gender-role socialization. Maybe it's time for a "killing." Noted author Virginia Woolf found it necessary to "kill off" the nagging internal voice of the ideal feminine homemaker, so that she could go beyond that role and become a writer. As she sat at her writing table to compose a literary critique, she could hear "the Angel in the House" admonishing her that she should flatter the author and never let anyone know that she had a sharp mind of her own. The "Angel" wanted her to be ever-charming, sympathetic, and tender, as she had been socialized in Victorian England to be. But she could not write literary criticism within these rigid confines of gender. And so she killed the "Angel," for "had I not killed her she would have killed me" (Woolf, cited in Levinson, 1996, p. 50).

Female RNs were more likely to verbalize anger to advocate for their patients than to fight for their own rights, just as the Women's Anger Study had shown earlier (i.e., women could assert themselves on behalf of their children—as when a teacher was perceived to be treating a child unfairly—but not to achieve relationship reciprocity with their spouses). Women generally do not have a sense that their anger can be efficacious. Whether they hold anger in or vent it outwardly, they still do not get the desired result and end up feeling that the attempt was futile. For example, a participant in the Women's Anger Study said that her attempts to get members of her family to pick up their strewn belongings were "fruitless. . . . I'll say it and it's just like it goes in one ear and out the other. I'm not stating it right or something. It doesn't work" (Thomas et al., 1998). You can see the same bewilderment and futility in these words of a nurse in one of my anger workshops:

> I work nights. One of the RNs on days is always late. She is a great person. We both graduated from nursing together many years ago. She is slightly crippled, and uses this to get away with always being late. After a 12-hour shift, my crew and I are quite eager to get home. We have teased her, begged her, threatened her, reported her, but nothing has worked. I was angry, I am angry, but it appears that nothing can be done.

These women have not yet learned that when the transgressor does not and will not change, what they need to do is *affirm their anger as justified and move on to problem-solving.* An asset for women is their willingness to confide in a friend or relative when they are upset. Unlike the male RNs who isolate themselves, females do seek a listening ear. As we pointed out in Chapter 4, talking out a problem with a confidante elicits empathy and feedback. Furthermore, as you review the anger incident, you may develop insight into the dynamics of the interaction. Ideas to solve the problem are often generated during the discussion as well. It's the same principle by which psychotherapy works.

A Last Word

It's clear that both female and male nurses have a good bit of work to do. To be an emotionally healthy adult requires transcending the restrictions of masculine and feminine gender roles and developing a diverse repertoire of emotion behaviors. We have all been constrained by what we learned growing up. But it's not too late to chuck the rules. Men in nursing could benefit from allowing themselves to reveal their pain and vulnerability to another nurse, just as women could benefit from learning to use anger as a driving force to open up a problem. Individuals who develop a style that includes behaviors not usually associated with their gender socialization are more creative, flexible, integrative, and spontaneous (Cummings, 1995). Throughout this book, we present new approaches that you can try. However, once you have moved beyond conformity to gender rules, other obstacles to healing and wholeness may remain. One such obstacle, and a very significant one, is painful trauma in your past, which is the topic of our next chapter.

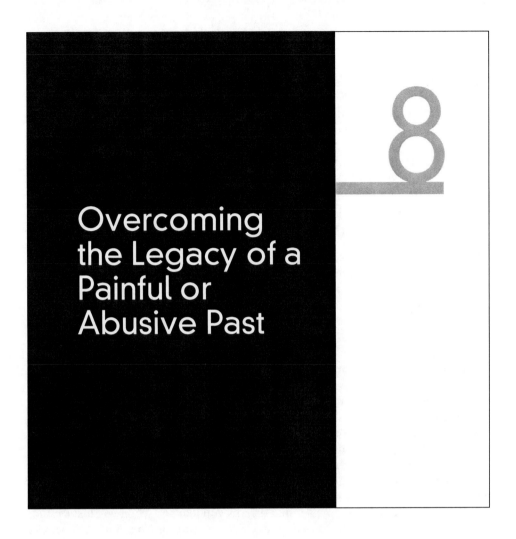

Overcoming the Legacy of a Painful or Abusive Past

8

Anger is healthy, while resentment and hate are detrimental...Anger is fresh, expansive, active, constructive, and varies with changes in the situation. Resentment and hate are past-oriented...They remain and remain, working chiefly on and against oneself.

—Eugene Gendlin

In this chapter, we examine old anger and resentment, and how to let them go. You will learn how to transcend a painful or abusive past, through strategies such as:

- Undertaking psychotherapy
- Keeping a journal
- Strengthening personal boundaries
- Strengthening your self-esteem
- Forgiving and moving on
- Enacting healing rituals
- Taking actions to help others in pain

Many nurses are mired in resentment about the past: pain inflicted by a mother who was critical, a father who was never around, a brother or sister who was the favorite and got more "goodies," a lover who dumped them for someone else, a friend who turned out to be a traitor, a lost educational or work opportunity. Although their anger may be entirely justifiable—at least, initially—it begins to affect their mental health when it's chronic and corrosive. Old angers often mingle with new ones in a multilayered amalgam, hurtful incident piled upon other hurtful incidents, until there is so much bad feeling that there's hardly any room for joy. Remember the woman who talked about her unexpressed anger that rolled up into a big ball? To refresh your memory, here's what she said:

> It's like you build up so much anger inside or resentment towards somebody without really sitting down and talking about the problem that it just rolls up into a big ball, and you're not even sure what it's really about. And then you have to take that ball apart again in little sections, and you've got to ask questions and poke places that are really deep and hurt you sometimes.

This chapter is about unraveling your big ball of anger and taking it apart, bit by bit, so that you can overcome the legacy of a painful or abusive past. Yes, when you poke tender places, there will still be some twinges of pain. For some of you, the event may be the loss of a loved one, and you are still numb because of grief. Perhaps you have lost a parent, a spouse, a stillborn child. The word *bereavement* comes from the Old English "beroafian," which means to rob, to plunder, or to dispose (Sardana, 1997). Death robs us of a loved one, often precipitously. Snatched away is a person who made you feel special, cared about what you were doing, cheered you on to do great things. I first learned what this searing pain is like at the age of 7, when my father left for the office one day and never came home again. Perhaps you learned when you lost a child, and had to bury all the shining dreams you once had for him. For a few weeks after a death, there are calls and cards, and hastily proffered pies and casseroles from people who won't come inside ("gotta run, call me if you need anything"), and then the house is quiet. Very quiet. You are bereft. And healing during bereavement is a long-term process. The anguish seems interminable. In our world of instant coffee, instant communication, and instant relief of discomfort, no one has patience with long-term processes like mourning (Sardana, 1997). So you go back to work and try to act normal even though you feel hollow inside. And, after awhile, no one mentions your loss any more. After all, you should be "all better" by now. It's been 2 years, hasn't it?

Abuse in Childhood

Or, perhaps your hurt and anger are encapsulated, smouldering inside you because of the horror of physical or sexual abuse when you were a child. Perhaps you were abusively disciplined "for your own good." Perhaps your daddy came into your room in the night and did things that you didn't understand. If these things happened to you, you are not alone. The statistics are staggering. According to Holz (1994), 45% of health care providers were victims of abuse during childhood. One in four girls and one in seven boys are sexually abused in some way prior to their eighteenth birthday (Browne & Finkelhor, 1986). One study of undergraduate nursing students at a major university found that 47% of the females and 38% of the males had had one or more unwanted sexual experiences in childhood (Rew & Christian, 1993). Nurses who had experienced childhood sexual abuse revealed its effects on their personal and professional lives in interviews conducted by a Toronto research team (Gallop, McKeever, Toner, Lancee, & Lueck, 1995):

> "I think it definitely has affected... the way I act sexually.... I'm very skeptical that there are really good loving relationships."
>
> "[I have] difficulty trusting [a] male staff physician and one or two co-workers"
>
> "[I] spent many years as a timid, unsure, nonassertive doormat. Afraid of ridicule or being ignored. [I] don't want to be noticed."
>
> "I'm a total wimp.... I can allow myself to be manipulated. I can allow myself to have other people do the choosing and stuff like that."
>
> "I think the abuse contributed to my feeling, kind of... less than worthy."

Abuse From Partners

The nursing profession contains not only survivors of childhood abuse but also many RNs who have experienced partner abuse as adults. One in every three women in the United States experiences abuse from a male partner at least once during her lifetime (Straus & Gelles, 1987). In a survey of obstetrical nurses working in hospitals, private offices, and community health, 31% reported domestic violence involving either self or a close family member (Moore, Parsons, & Zaccaro, 1997). Only recently have researchers devoted attention to abuse of married men, a topic shrouded in secrecy because husbands fear being emasculated if they admit being abused. Findings of Migliaccio's (2002) study of abused husbands revealed strong similarities to previous findings about abused wives (i.e., degrading verbal attacks, steadily increasing violence, broken promises by the abuser to change or attend counseling, and staying in the relationship for the children's sake). Notably lacking for male victims, however, are societal supports such as domestic violence shelters.

Abuse From Patients

Although scant literature exists about it, RNs also receive abuse from patients. The assault rate in health care facilities is increasing (Lanza et al., 1996; Schultz, 2000), and nurses are among the most vulnerable workers because they often work in small numbers or alone (for example, on night shift), and because they have extended contact with patients and families during highly stressful circumstances. Particularly at risk for violence are younger, less-experienced staff and student nurses (Echternacht, 1999; Wright, Dixon, & Tompkins, 2003). One seven-state survey of nurses showed that 30% of them had been victims of workplace violence in the previous year (Carroll & Morin, 1998). Most nurses who were victimized said that patients had assaulted them.

Unfortunately, many nurses do not report assaults—especially those inflicted by patients—and they receive little support from their colleagues and management (Lanza, 1983). Assault on nurses is not even a felony, although assault on bus drivers and umpires (even lifeguards) *is* a felony. Roberts (1991) contends that assault against nurses in the workplace is silenced, just as assault within families is. To shed some light on the experience of abused nurses, Roberts conducted a qualitative study of 12 female nurses who had been assaulted by patients. All of the nurses reported strong emotional responses to the assault (anger being the most common) and long-term consequences for their job performance. They believed that management blamed them for the assault, either explicitly or implicitly. They found themselves labeled as "the nurse who got hit." Their institutions seemed to view violence against staff as "part of the job." Lack of support by the institutions and the police outraged the women. Management seldom supported prosecution of the attacker, and the nurses were reluctant to proceed with legal action on their own. The nurses' coping strategies were mainly avoidant: minimizing, denying, and forgetting about the assault. One nurse intensified her efforts to look like a good, unblemished, and virtuous nurse. She said that in the months following the attack, she bought "the whitest pair of stockings and the whitest pair of shoes," so that she would look like the "quintessential nurse." The traumatic experience of these nurses indicates that much needs to be done to reduce not only the violence itself, but also its damaging sequelae.

Verbal Abuse

There is another kind of abuse, a kind that leaves no visible black eyes or bruises, but deeply scars a person's soul. Verbal abuse can take many forms: ridicule, disparagement, criticism, accusations, threats, name calling, sarcastic "humor" that isn't funny, and the cold silence that conveys rejection. Many nurses have experienced this kind of abuse from a parent or lover. It can take place at the job site too, as shown in our research data (see Chapter 5 regarding verbal abuse by physicians). One of the devastating effects of verbal abuse is an insidious change in the victim's self-concept. She (or he) begins to internalize the criticism and accept its validity: "After all, he knows me better than anyone, and if he thinks I am (unlovable, dumb, unattractive, clumsy, incompetent, you fill in the blank), then it must be true." The abuse is usually kept from friends and relatives because the victim is ashamed, so there is no one to provide a "reality check" and corrective feedback. To complicate matters further, many abusers are socially charming and display their meanness only in private. Thus, there are no witnesses.

The consequences of abuse resemble the posttraumatic stress syndrome (PTSD) common to survivors of disasters and combat: denial, confusion, fear, nightmares, flashbacks, and psychological numbing. But there are some important distinctions: Neither disaster victims nor soldiers were harmed by individuals they loved and trusted. And survivors of disasters and wars do not *blame* themselves for what happened, as abuse victims tend to do. Finally, survivors of disasters and wars can talk about their traumatic experiences without shame.

In contrast, experiences of abuse are often kept secret: I have worked with and taught many victims of abuse who had never told anyone before.

The literature tends to emphasize the devastating sequelae of abuse rather than the potential for healing. Persons who have been abused tend to distrust others, fear those with greater power, and have lower self-esteem. They are at high risk for depression, substance abuse, and other crippling after-effects. They may commit or attempt to commit suicide. But we also know that countless victims of abuse go on to lead satisfying and productive lives (e.g., see Thomas & Hall, 2008, which illustrates healing trajectories of women who had experienced childhood maltreatment). The scars from abuse can, and do, heal. If you have been abused, know that the violence—whether physical, sexual, or verbal—was not your fault. Start on the healing path.

Undertaking Psychotherapy

The word *heal* is defined in the dictionary as "to become well or whole again, to restore ... to health ... to cause painful emotions to be no longer grievous" (*The New Lexicon Webster's Dictionary*, 1989, p. 446). How can we reach a place of peace where painful emotions are no longer "grievous?" There are many paths to peace and emotional healing. Undertaking psychotherapy is one of them. Therapist Carl Rogers used to tell a story about the potatoes stored during the winter in the cellar of his home. Toward the one tiny high window in the cellar, long spindly sprouts would strain to reach light. Rogers saw many of his patients in this way: in a dark cellar of fear, sadness, or self-loathing, yet nevertheless still seeking the light and growing in the process of doing so. I think that all of us are a bit like Carl Rogers' potatoes. Getting to the light—being enlightened, fully aware—takes awhile. A therapist becomes your partner on the journey. Without the assistance of a patient and caring counselor, letting go of a lifetime of angry feelings may seem like a formidable undertaking. The words of this study participant are illustrative:

> How do you get back to point A from point D? Because I've passed B and C, you know. It's like I'm way out here, how do you get yourself back over there? When you've got so much anger built up, how do you get back? How do you get rid of 20 years of your father and your husband and your mother and relationships that you probably shouldn't even care about? How do I get rid of all this? I don't know.

As the words of this woman indicate, our greatest pain is inflicted in intimate relationships. That is why healing also must take place in relationships. It has been my privilege for several years, as part of a multidisciplinary research team, to listen to the narratives of research participants who survived horrific childhood abuse. The relationship with a therapist was a critical element in healing for many of them, as shown in this quote from the data:

> It was the most important relationship I've ever had in my life, and I literally felt like it saved my life, and I'm a different person than I was. (Thomas & Hall, 2008, p. 159)

Throughout life, we work through "unfinished business" from old relationships in new ones. Not only therapists but also lovers, spouses, friends, and teachers help us heal and grow. In addition to letting others help us along the way, we also benefit from introspection. In the next section, we discuss journaling, a mechanism for processing events and gaining self-knowledge.

Looking Within: Journaling

Carl Jung gave the world an enormously helpful, optimistic psychology that emphasized the self-healing psyche: We must look within to discover its wisdom. Many Jungian analysts believe that the healing process can be facilitated by keeping a journal (see 8.1).

> *8.1. Marion Woodman, a Jungian analyst, recommends journaling as a way of facing your "swamp of anguish and aggression":*
>
> *The daily journal is like a mirror. When we first look into it, the blank pages stare back with ominous emptiness. But if we keep looking and trusting in what Rilke calls "the possibility of being," gradually we begin to see the face that is looking back at us. If we stand naked, the mirror reflects things as they are. There is more to the mirror than reflection. The long hours of sitting alone stripping off the self-deceptions, the artificial self-pity, the self-inflicted maiming, build the . . . connection between the conscious and unconscious worlds in a way that connects both. With the mirror, we go through, we take our reality into another world, the world of the unconscious, and find a relationship to our own soul. Journal writing is a way of taking responsibility for finding out who I AM. Facing our dark sides is painful. It is easier to turn away from our own swamp of anguish and aggression and say "It doesn't matter. I've got friends. I'm well adjusted to my job. Everyone likes me." The mirror will not let us off the hook. It says "It does matter. If you're not experiencing life it does matter. Where was your own laughter today? Where are your tears?" (Woodman, 1982, pp. 99, 101)*

There are many ways to journal, from a complex method recommended by Ira Progoff to simple stream-of-consciousness musings jotted down in a notepad. I have kept a journal all my life, and find this activity invaluable. It is especially useful every 5 years or so to pull out some old volumes (my books are all sizes and colors, heaped in a big box in the closet) to see what I was dealing with, and how I understood it, at various times. Working through pain is a lifelong process. My personal growth has been like a spiral, sometimes looping back, then going forward a bit, rather than following a linear trajectory. Throughout my life, I have spiraled back to revisit some of the same painful events, such as the death of both my parents when I was very young. But as I review the journals, I find evidence of progress in my perspective on the events. Each time I let go of a little more resentment, and in so doing, open myself to greater joy. The cruel reality of the events never changes, but my view of them does (see 8.2).

8.2. Old paint on canvas, as it ages, sometimes becomes transparent. When that happens it is possible, in some pictures, to see the original lines: a tree will show through a woman's dress, a child makes way for a dog, a large boat is no longer on an open sea. That is called pentimento because the painter "repented," changed his mind. Perhaps it would be as well to say that the old conception, replaced by a later choice, is a way of seeing and then seeing again. (Lillian Hellman)

If you decide to start keeping a journal, I have only one recommendation: Write it in regularly. Some authorities specify a certain number of pages per day, but I am not so rigidly prescriptive. I do not even insist that you write a journal entry *every* day. But there must be a rhythm of some kind, a process so routinized that thoughts and feelings flow quickly onto the page before they can be censored and "cleaned up" to look respectable. Your journal is for no eyes but yours, so do not sanitize its contents. You can record dreams in your journal too, if you like. Dreams are messages from yourself to yourself, delivered when you are psychologically ready to receive and integrate them. Especially significant are (a) recurring dreams (often dealing with unresolved conflicts); (b) epic dreams (compelling, often life-changing); and (c) nightmares (often related to emotional or physical abuse). When regularly recorded, reflected on, and understood, dreams transmit wisdom from deep in the psyche to your conscious mind. To learn more about working with your dreams, purchase a guidebook. One I like is *Wisdom of the Heart: Working with Women's Dreams* by Karen Signell (1990).

Strengthening Personal Boundaries

Strengthening personal boundaries is a necessary step for many nurses who are trying to overcome the legacy of a painful or abusive past. Boundaries are the demarcation lines that separate me from you. They refer to your physical body and personal space, as well as to your psyche and emotions. If you are overly compliant with others' opinions, fear disagreement, and lack the ability to say "no" or say what you really feel—even when treated badly—you have some boundary problems. Difficulties with boundaries are common in individuals who grew up in families where:

- Parents discounted a child's feelings and needs.
- Independence was thwarted, while dependence or clinging behavior was rewarded.
- Boundaries of the family members were blurred, distorted, nonexistent, or fragmented (for example, in an alcoholic family).
- Boundaries were disrespected or invaded for the sexual gratification of adults.

You will need to work on developing a sense of yourself as strong and separate from others. Boundaries are vitally important to protect yourself from the negative emotions of others and to set limits on others who are mistreating you. Examples of boundary protection include refusing to allow dysfunctional (or abusive) family members to visit your home, refusing to answer intrusive questions from coworkers, and confronting people who try to take advantage of you. Anger, when channeled into clear verbal messages, can be an excellent mechanism for protecting your boundaries: "I am angry that you are bringing up these old issues. I am going to hang up the telephone if you continue." If you have started working with a therapist, she will help you strengthen your boundaries.

Strengthening Self-Esteem

In addition to strengthening your boundaries, it's time to work on strengthening your self-esteem. Although the next few paragraphs may be useful to some male nurses reading this book, I must speak specifically to females for a bit. There's a good reason for doing so: the research consistently shows that *the self-esteem of females is lower than that of males.* This should not be surprising, given the pervasive devaluing of women in our society. Self-esteem is partly a function of the social relations and processes in which individuals are embedded. Women do not have as many sources of external validation as men do. The nurturing work they do—nursing, teaching, child care—is undervalued by society. Mary Catherine Bateson (1990) called attention to the "ingrained and disabling sense of inferiority" characteristic of American women. Although she is an accomplished professional woman, she confesses, "I have slighted my own value so often that it is hard to learn to take it seriously." Even the potent external validation of achieving great fame and influence does not always penetrate a woman's self-perception of her worth. Witness the shocking disclosure of influential feminist activist and writer Gloria Steinem regarding her own low self-esteem in her 1991 book *Revolution from Within: A Book of Self-Esteem.* It goes to show that neither brilliance nor glamour nor renown guarantees a solid sense of personal worth.

And, despite the advances because of the women's movement, in which Steinem played such a leading role, high school girls still have a poorer self-image than their male counterparts. A survey sponsored by the American Association of University Women showed that self-esteem of girls *drops* instead of rising as they mature. Although around 60% of girls were confident and "happy the way I am" while in elementary school, by high school, the percentage had declined to 29% (Freiberg, 1991). It's not a coincidence that the decrease in self-esteem occurs during those years that girls are under enormous pressure to be "perfect girls" and hide their true emotions so that they will be "popular," as documented in the longitudinal study conducted by Brown and Gilligan (1992). The "perfect girls" move into adulthood determined to be perfect wives and mothers—along with their stellar careers. As perfection is an impossible goal, they are setting themselves up for failure and self-recrimination.

What is self-esteem? It's the degree to which we value ourselves, a judgment made largely on the basis of others' appraisals (especially those in our circle of intimates) and to a lesser extent on self-evaluation of our accomplishments. It's a view based in part on the way our parents treated us, but modified by later life experiences. Those with lower self-esteem have often been the victims of physical or verbal abuse. Because they do not have a positive view of themselves, they are at the mercy of others' evaluation, increasing their risk of being taken advantage of in work situations (Gallop et al., 1995).

What is self-esteem's link with anger management? In the Women's Anger Study, our research team found that the lower the self-esteem, the higher a woman's tendency to anger easily (Saylor & Denham, 1993). Women low in self-esteem manage that anger more inappropriately too—stuffing it or lashing out at others. As we have seen in earlier chapters, these ways of managing anger further reinforce low self-esteem, thus perpetuating the cycle. When a woman stuffs her anger instead of telling others her honest feelings, she gets mad at herself for remaining silent. And when she lashes out like a banshee, there's fallout in terms of damaged relationships, remorse, and guilt about the outburst. The woman feels isolated, inadequate, and misunderstood. Obviously, this cycle should be broken—but how?

The good news is that self-esteem is *modifiable* (Crouch & Straub, 1983). But to work on our self-esteem, we first have to develop a different mind-set. Many of us suppose that displaying healthy self-esteem (looking and acting confident, being sure of ourselves, and remaining nonapologetic about making reasonable requests or stating opinions) is unfeminine. We wouldn't want to be viewed as too forward, pushy, mannish, or lacking in proper humility. Sometimes, if we tried to point out our accomplishments, we got negative feedback from our peers—or persons in positions of dominance who preferred a more obsequious employee or lover. As part of our gender-role socialization, we were taught to say "Oh, it was really nothing" when congratulated on successes.

Steps Toward Strengthening Self-Esteem

- *First, engage in some reflection* about the way you developed your view of yourself during childhood. Think back to childhood nicknames, interactions with parents, siblings, and playmates, times of performance evaluation such as bringing home your report card. What tapes are still playing over and over in your mind: "Why can't you be good like your brother?" Look at photo albums, talk to family members. In every family, someone is labeled the "ugly duckling" or "black sheep." Was that you? If so, what were some of the smart and brave things that you did to make it through a childhood that was lonely or traumatic? Begin to give yourself credit for your "smarts."
- *Enlarge your sources of self-esteem.* Some women limit the sources from which they seek validation to just one or two other people—perhaps just their husband or lover—so that the criticisms of these people are inordinately powerful. Find times to be with friends who enjoy your company, appreciate you, and verbally affirm your strengths. Consider a support group in which members validate each other (as we talked about in an earlier chapter).
- *Validate yourself with positive self-talk.* You already know how to give others praise and encouragement. Do the same for yourself. Focus on your strengths instead of your weaknesses. Affirm yourself for trying, making progress, taking risks to do things you never thought you could do. Congratulate yourself for being a member of a noble profession that provides an indispensable service to society. When you succeed at something, give yourself proper credit. Researchers have found that when women succeed, they call it luck; when women fail, they consider

themselves stupid. In contrast, when men succeed, they give themselves credit; when they fail, they blame an outside source (Sanford & Donovan, 1985). Remember that affirmations are always said in the present tense, as if you already have the qualities you desire.

8.3. A participant in one of my anger workshops sought to decrease her outbursts at her ex-husband when he came to pick up their young daughter for his court-designated visitation. As soon as she saw him coming up the walk, she was filled with rage. But she knew that it was not good for her daughter to witness the outbursts. And, she felt badly about herself after flying off the handle. So, she developed an affirmation that she repeated as she walked to the door, "I am calm, confident, and mature. I am calm, confident, and mature." Just saying the words over and over induced calmness. She proudly reported success to the other workshop participants.

▪ *Consult the "wise woman" within.* This is an imagery exercise that I have found very helpful when I work with women. To do the exercise, first become deeply relaxed. Unplug the phone, dim lights, and seat yourself in a comfortable position. Close your eyes. Pay attention to your breathing for a few minutes. Imagine your body as hollow, and allow each breath to fill your hollow body. When you are ready, let yourself become aware that you are not alone. With you is a wise old woman who is concerned with your well-being. You can trust her. Make contact with this woman. Notice the love and wisdom with which you are surrounded. Tell your wise guide anything you wish. Ask her "What do I need to do to feel better about myself?" Listen to the answers that emerge. Maintain an attitude of openness to her advice. After your imagery is finished, reflect quietly. What did she recommend?

Are you aware that the wise old woman is really a part of yourself? Everyone of us has something deep inside that knows our true nature and purpose in life. It has been called the Center. Carl Jung called it the greater Self. Here, we depicted it as the archetypal figure of the wise old woman. You may wish to conceptualize it in congruence with a particular religious orientation (e.g., God within). The important thing is to gain access to your own inner wisdom and benefit from its guidance.

Forgiving and Moving On

But maybe, just maybe, forgiveness exists not to excuse the sinner but to heal those who suffered. This idea seems true and honest to me for this reason: As Mama became less able to forgive my daddy, her anger grew like wildfire and began to burn us all.

(Connie May Fowler, 1996, p. 105)

These words were taken from *Before Women Had Wings*, Connie May Fowler's story of her abusive and impoverished childhood. Her understanding of forgiveness is remarkable, given what she endured: the suicide of her father, dreadful beatings from her alcoholic mother, and even being "jilted by Jesus." I have found exemplars, such as Fowler's, tremendously helpful in my own journey to healing. There is a wealth of wisdom about human suffering, and transcending it, in literature, drama, and film.

I know firsthand that being able to forgive is an essential step in emotional healing. It accomplishes nothing to leave old wounds open so that new salt can inflame them from time to time. What does it mean to forgive? It does not mean excusing the hurtful actions of those who abandoned you or treated you badly. But a lesson that I have learned through my clinical work and research is that the role of victim serves no one well. As long as you define yourself as a victim, you are not free.

Many people hold on to old anger to show the other person that he is wrong, but remember the saying: Resentment is like drinking poison and waiting for the other person to die.

Forgiveness is a way of freeing yourself, so that the person who wronged you no longer has power to define you. It is a way of releasing yourself from the anguish of your past life and moving on. It is a way of caring for the self. It is an important step to acknowledge that you deserved better treatment than you got. The next step is a conscious decision to relinquish the role of wronged victim.

I spent my adolescent years bitter, alienated, acting out, envious of others who had loving families and support. I could not imagine why I had ever been born. I was angry at life, angry at the world, and angry at God—if there was a God. In my distorted view, my misery was unique. I didn't know anyone else who had neither parents nor grandparents. What a life-changing event it was when I went to work at a hospital at the age of 15. My friend Judy, who wanted to be a nurse, had talked me into applying for a job with her at St. Joseph's Hospital. The hospital hired the two of us as nurses' aides on the 3–11 shift; we went to high school 8 A.M. to 2 P.M. and then to the hospital to work. On our floor were young mothers dying of cancer, diabetics losing their legs, and the gamut of gripping tragedy and human suffering. I had never thought about being a nurse, but working with these patients produced a dramatic change in my perspective—and gradually assisted me to begin healing. Even as a nurses' aide with no training, I was able to provide comfort to people who hurt. It was deeply satisfying when I gave my patient a back rub and properly plumped each pillow, then tiptoed out as he softly went to sleep.

Later on, when I became a psychiatric nurse, I moved a bit farther along on the healing path as I listened to my patients describe every kind of abuse and atrocity imaginable. So many of them had endured far more pain and trauma in their early years than I. How could I hold on to my old resentment? When you peer into the hearts and minds of others, you learn that every family is somewhat dysfunctional, and every person is a bit neurotic. Nobody had it easy. Loneliness, failure, shame, loss, betrayal, times of confusion—they're all there, in each and every human psyche.

"The world breaks everyone, and afterward many are strong at the broken places."

(Ernest Hemingway, cited in Viorst, 1986, p. 260)

"Life will send us, not what we want, but what we need in order to grow."

(John Sanford, 1977, p. 20)

Although it is standard advice in many nursing texts to help people "find meaning" in their adversity, I believe that some of the blows from life are never fully comprehensible. We often brood in anger over unfairness: Why me? Why now? What did I do to deserve this? Answers are slow in coming, and we may never find a satisfactory answer. Kierkegaard pointed out that "Life can only be understood backwards; but it must be lived forwards." I don't expect to ever understand everything. Perhaps mental peace is ultimately a matter of becoming reconciled to mystery. And I strongly believe that, for mental peace and healing to occur, we must forgive those who played a part in the pain of the past.

To forgive does not just mean to pardon, it means to let go. . . . If you are tied to a rock that is pulling you down in the water, all you have to do is forgive it . . . and swim toward the light.

(Colgrove et al., 1991, p. 148)

Old anger, bitterness, and sadness can indeed be heavy rocks pulling you down. Why not let go and forgive? How liberating it is to unpack some of the heavy emotional baggage and forgive the parents who neglected you, the friends who let you down, the lovers who betrayed you. Forgiving does not mean that you must reconcile with people who wronged you, nor is it necessary that you have a face-to-face meeting. In fact, those who wronged you may be deceased or far away. *But you can still forgive them, because forgiveness is something that happens within you.*

Steps Toward Forgiving Someone

- *Imagine the person who hurt or injured you.* Look at a photograph, if you have one. Tell the person in the photo how angry you are. Say, "I did not deserve this." When you are ready, say "I forgive you" (adapted from Flanigan, 1992).
- *Write about your traumatic experiences*, perhaps in your journal. Research by James Pennebaker (1997) shows that this can be therapeutic, even if no one else ever reads what you have written. A variant of this would be to make a tape recording.
- *Write a letter to the individual who hurt or abused you.* It is your choice whether to mail the letter. You can write one even if the intended recipient is dead. Novelist Connie May Fowler views her writing as the vehicle for forgiving her deceased parents.
- *Engage in a formal forgiveness meditation.* Jack Kornfield recommends using these words: "There are many ways I have been wounded and hurt, abused and abandoned, by others in thought, word, or deed, knowingly or

unknowingly.... To the extent that I am ready, I offer them forgiveness. I have carried this pain in my heart too long. For this reason, to those who have caused me harm, I offer you my forgiveness. I forgive you" (Kornfield, 1993, p. 286). This meditation is repeated until you can feel a release in your heart.

▪ *Realize that you may need to repeat several of these steps*; forgiving is not a once-and-forever event; it is achieved gradually. You may find additional benefits in the healing rituals presented in the next section.

Enacting Healing Rituals

Many people benefit from healing rituals. For example, you might burn, cut up, or throw away pictures or other items that evoke painful memories. Or, you could make something new. One option is making a piece of pottery, pounding the clay and then firing it in a kiln, symbolically burning away resentment (Thomas, 2003b). There is a painting in the National Museum of Women in the Arts called "Can We Turn Our Rage to Poetry?" by Joan Snyder. Snyder created her painting in response to a heinous hate crime in San Francisco. Snyder explains:

> *"The year was 1978 and Harvey Milk, who was the first openly gay person to have been elected to San Francisco's Board of Supervisors, and the city's Mayor George Moscone were both murdered by former policeman Dan White... In my painting I wanted to move from one mood to another until finally the piece had the possibility of transcendence... [In] the last section, the encompassing field of strong and bright colors is moving towards and turning our rage to poetry... For me, the title of the painting is a directive of sorts. We have to do something with our rage—and at the moment I cannot think of anything better to do. (Snyder, 2001, pp. 14–15)*

The title of Snyder's painting brings to mind wonderful poets such as Marge Piercy, Robert Bly, and Maya Angelou, to name only three. As poets select words to express their emotions, then arrange those evocative words like a string of beads across the page, they dispel some of their inner turmoil. Psychologist Diane Currie (2003) provides a compelling example of venting bitterness through a poem. The poem, "The Song of Divorce," by Joseph Stroud, begins "Bitter the warmth of sunlight, and bitter the taste of apple." The sharp staccato rhythm of the poem engages the reader, taking us into the poet's world of bitterness and anger, a world in which even moonlight is bitter. Anyone who has suffered a loss can resonate with the poet's feelings. When the poem is read aloud, Currie says you can virtually "hear the poet spitting bitter things out of his mouth! Blech...yuck...hock-tuey...splat!" (Currie, p. 138). Currie makes a powerful argument for the healing power of poetry, often finding in it messages of redemption, hope, and transformation.

Although you may not be blessed with the talents of a painter or a poet, there are a number of other ways to creatively release anger and pain. A woman who came to one of my workshops bought different colors of helium balloons to represent different things she wanted to release, then took the balloons to a wide meadow and let them drift slowly out of sight up into the sky. You can even bring a bit of humor to your healing ritual. An acquaintance of mine who was newly divorced threw an "Un-Wedding Party." She served her guests 7-Up (then being touted in ads as the "un-cola"), threw rice at them, and gave them "gifts" of marriage-related memorabilia she no longer wanted in her house. The piece de resistance was a glorious lopsided un-wedding cake of many layers, with globs of cherries cascading down its sides. By announcing her new single status with humor and style, this woman put the heartbreak of a failed marriage behind her. We cheered her ability to forgive her ex-husband and move on with her life.

Taking Action to Help Others in Pain

Taking actions to help others in pain also promotes healing (Montgomery, 1991; Thomas & Hall, 2008). American Academy of Nursing member Wanda Mohr, a passionate advocate for the mentally ill, achieved national prominence because of her courageous exposé of child maltreatment in for-profit psychiatric hospitals in Texas. Soon, she moved on to a crusade against restraining hospitalized children, a practice that is not only cruel but also lethal in some cases. You may have read about her testimony in Congress. But you probably don't know what a long way Wanda has traveled in dealing with her anger (see 8.4 for the story of her odyssey).

> **8.4. Transforming Anger to Become a Force for Social Justice**
>
> *The anger morphed through several stages. I remember as a very little girl that I was more confused than angry. The violence and abuse that characterized those years with my family stripped away my confidence, and I recall being bewildered and perplexed. What had I done to deserve this? I was a good girl, a compliant girl, and I didn't deserve being woken at night from my sleep with one or both of my parents pulling me out of bed to beat me because of some minor transgression, such as soiling a dress or wearing down my shoes faster than they thought I should. When tears came, they were tears of misery and tears of frustration that I just couldn't do the right thing. They were the parents and I was the child. I must have been to blame.*
>
> *They say—those arbiters of conventional wisdom—that no happy child runs away from home. Yet children who run away are punished for giving in to the impulse for a better life, a better place. It seems irrational of me to have run away in one sense, because I had nowhere to go. In another, it made perfect sense. I think this is where I started to feel some anger, anger at the injustice that I saw as my wretched life with parents whom I feared. Of course I was caught and brought back. Even the cynical police were reluctant to take me home, seeing my terror—but their affirmation was something special. It validated that perhaps it was not all my fault. Then the locks, the medications, the psychiatrists, the massive institution where I spent my sixteenth summer seeing people tied down, given shock treatments. It was a nightmare, but curiously I was more content in the hospital than I had ever been at home.*
>
> *After my sixteenth year, I never lived at home again. The anger almost consumed me in the years after that. The drugs to which I became addicted*

took care of it as long as I was wrapped in their gauzy glow. When I was clean, I let myself feel the anger and a very special doctor helped me to understand my anger—but also helped me to see that I can make it work for, rather than against me. It is that same anger turned outward that continues to galvanize my sense of social justice and my life's work. (Wanda Mohr, PhD, RN, FAAN, contributed for this book)

When Rubin (1996) studied individuals who had transcended a difficult past, she found a strong sense of mission in their stories, a commitment to something beyond their personal interests. Like Wanda Mohr, they were determined to use their painful experiences of the past to change the present for others. Individuals who have been abused often choose an occupation like nursing or social work or volunteer their time to work in shelters for the abused. For example, a nurse interviewed by Gallop's research team reported that "I now work in community mental health, do counseling and am very active in the women's movement fighting sexual, physical, and emotional abuse. I have done workshops on violence against women and supervise counselors who do this work" (Gallop et al., 1995, p. 142). This nurse is what Carl Jung called a "wounded healer." In mythology, the wounded healer is represented in Chiron, the centaur-teacher of Asclepius. But we need not dust off our knowledge of Greek mythology, because examples are all around us in health care settings: recovering alcoholics who counsel other alcoholics, cancer survivors who visit patients facing surgery, pediatricians who had been sickly children but now give compassionate care to children. How does working with other wounded individuals assist in healing our own wounds? First, it alters our perspective on our own suffering, redeeming the pain of the past because we can see that healing gifts have resulted from that pain. Second, when we minister to others in a loving way, we are loving ourselves as well, binding our wounds, so to speak. If you have been denying your woundedness, I encourage you to claim it, for you will be a better healer.

Resilience, Coherence, and the River

Thankfully, a new emphasis in the psychiatric/mental health literature is placed on the human capacity for resilience and victory over "handicapping" traumas and tragedies (O'Leary, 1998; O'Leary & Ickovics, 1994; Rubin, 1996; Seligman, 1991; Snyder & Lopez, 2002). Instead of focusing on all that can go wrong when people encounter adversity, researchers are emphasizing what can turn out all right. For example, psychologist Marty Seligman, after years of research on "learned helplessness," now focuses on its opposite: "learned optimism" (1991). Drawing from existential philosophy, Tedeschi, Park, and Calhoun (1998) focus on the human potential for posttraumatic growth (PTG) as opposed to posttraumatic stress disorder (PTSD). A large study of adults, ages 23 to 87, showed that most people who endure divorce, death of a loved one, or other major misfortunes, emerge stronger and better able to cope with subsequent events in their lives (Aldwin, Sutton, & Lachman, 1997). And other important studies debunk the old notions of inevitable emotional scarring or psychopathology from losses, broken homes, poverty, abuse, and the like. We can take heart from the following:

- 75% of the children of alcoholics do *not* become alcoholics (Wolin, cited in Secunda, 1994).
- Despite profound disadvantages of living in poverty and terrible environmental conditions, a number of these children are highly competent and well-adjusted (Garmezy, 1991).
- Women who had childhood stresses, such as divorce or remarriage of their parents or death of a loved one, are *less* likely to become depressed when they face distress-provoking situations in adulthood (Forest, 1991).
- In a study of over 400 famous men and women of the 20th century, researchers found that 75% of them had been highly stressed in childhood by physical handicaps or defects, broken homes, or economic deprivation (Goertzel & Goertzel, 1962).
- 29% of Israeli women who survived the horror of World War II concentration camps, years as displaced persons, and then three wars in the new nation of Israel, were found to be *emotionally healthy* in mid-life (Antonovsky, 1987).

The last-cited study of Holocaust survivors proved to be a dramatic turning point in researcher Aaron Antonovsky's work as a medical sociologist. Even though the percentage of concentration camp survivors in good mental health was not large, Antonovsky was impressed by the resilience and strength they had demonstrated. He wanted to know what distinguished those survivors from others who were overwhelmed by stress and negative emotions. So, he embarked on further studies to find out. What Antonovsky found is something that he calls the "sense of coherence," which is a feeling of confidence that one can manage and find meaning, even in chaos. Holocaust survivors who had a strong sense of coherence said things like:

"You have to take life as it comes."
"When something terrible happens, people look for someone to blame. But I don't, absolutely not."
"I never felt that I was getting a raw deal."
"I decided you just have to overcome, I won't let myself be broken."

In contrast, people with a weak sense of coherence said things like:

"All of life is a constant battle."
"All of life is full of problems, only in dying there are no problems."
"Everyone screwed me."
"They ruined my whole life."
"Things are rough, I don't have any faith left in anyone."
"It's all because my father died when I was a kid, and I kept wandering around" (Antonovsky, 1987, pp. 69–74).

The difference in the two mental attitudes is striking, isn't it? The people who were strong in "sense of coherence" have gotten beyond anger and blame.

They were able to "keep it together" during periods of suffering and darkness in their lives. They are healed. And you too can be healed.

A Last Word

This chapter emphasized relegating your past to the past. Savor the present moment, and resolve to move toward the future with heightened anticipation. It is time to wash away your wounds and bear no scars, as depicted in the river metaphor from David Reynolds' book *Water Bears No Scars:*

> *A rushing stream of water flows around the obstacles that stand in its way. It doesn't stop to dwell on the injuries sustained by a projecting rock or a submerged log. It keeps moving toward its goal, encountering each difficulty as it appears, responding actively, then moving along downstream . . . It washes away its own wounds in its present purposefulness. The water bears no scars.*

9

Managing Stress and Caring for the Self

To allow oneself to be carried away by a multitude of conflicting concerns, to surrender to too many demands, to commit to too many projects, to want to help everyone in everything is in itself to succumb to the violence of our times. Frenzy destroys our inner capacity for peace. It destroys the fruitfulness of our work, because it kills the root of inner wisdom which makes work fruitful.

—Thomas Merton, in "Conjectures of a Guilty Bystander"

As you read the words of Thomas Merton, did you identify with some of those words, such as "carried away," "committed to too many projects," "frenzied?" In this chapter, I talk with you about stepping off the merry-go-round and caring for your self. The hectic pace of the work environment often means postponing breaks, skipped lunches, and the sense of running behind—no matter how fast you are running. But failure to care for the self cannot be blamed solely on the work environment. For too many nurses, it's the tendency to sacrifice the self.

Nurses allow themselves to be engulfed in the needs of others, neglecting their own.

It seems as though self-sacrifice is encoded in our genes, for it has survived intergenerational transmission for more than 100 years. Nurse historians have provided interesting glimpses of the phenomenon in our early days. For example, consider the California debate in the 1900s on hours to be worked by student nurses. In 1911, the state had passed a law that women could not work more than 8 hours per day. However, the law did not cover student nurses, who worked much more than that. In 1912, a bill was introduced to include the students in the law. Doctors vigorously opposed the bill, with a Dr. Young stating that "The element of sacrifice is always present in true service." The superintendent of nurses in one hospital argued that schools of nursing would be hampered in instilling students with the principle of self-sacrifice if they had to adhere to the "self-centered 8-hour law," and she asserted that real nursing could not be timed by the clock. Even the state nurses association passed a resolution opposing the bill. After the bill passed, nurses continued to deplore it (Kalisch & Kalisch, 1975).

Skipping to my own student days, I remember the pressure to "work extra" in the hospital on weekends, even though I was exhausted by a long week of classes and clinicals and longing for the frivolity of a night out with a date or friends. On many occasions, a supervisor urged me to cancel my personal plans because the hospital needed me. My needs for rest and restoration did not matter. I learned the concept of self-sacrifice well, and it is still with me. For nurses who are women, this merely reinforced the lessons we had learned in our socialization to femininity. Nurses in our research tell us that administrators continue to expect (or even mandate) excessive hours of work, appealing to nurses' compassion for the patients who need care: "We can't find anybody for night shift. Please say you'll come in."

When our roles as partners and parents are added to our professional caregiving responsibilities, time for self-care can be virtually extinguished—unless we deliberately carve it out. The consequences of self-sacrifice can be serious. In 1991, researchers reported an interesting follow-up study of married female nurses who had received a master's degree from Yale during the years 1941 to 1965 (Dixon, Dixon, & Spinner, 1991). The tension between family and work commitments was examined in relation to the development of cardiovascular disease. *Sacrifice* was a key variable, both in terms of (a) career limitations that women thought necessary because of family commitments, and (b) difficulty in relationships as a result of career involvement. The researchers found that scoring high on sacrifice—trying to do everything for everybody—was a significant predictor of major cardiovascular disease (Dixon et al., 1991). The conclusions of this study remain relevant today. The words of Eunice Adams, a participant in our own research, depict the continuing tension between family and work:

If I'm not pulled in that direction I'm pulled in the other, and they're going to pull me apart one of these days. I just can't keep up with all their needs. I'm about tired. You do and you do and you do, and sometimes I think I'm just going to walk away and not come back.

Nursing does not mean sacrificing the self for others. It's time for nurses to care for themselves. Self-care is not selfish.

Stressed, angry nurses who feel like running away from all the demands cannot be a healing presence to the patients they see. Honoring our own needs for rest and play is not only crucial for our health, but also enhances our capacity to give to others. Erich Fromm believed that caring about oneself *precedes* caring about others. The empathic self can maintain its integrity and not be consumed by others. The process of learning to achieve a balance between engagement and detachment in caregiving has been studied by Carmack (1997) in both formal caregivers (nurses, social workers, priests, et cetera) and informal caregivers (friends or family of ill individuals). Almost all of the study participants had been overinvolved at some point and had suffered the consequences. They had learned through experience how to achieve balance in order to survive. One study participant found it helpful to hold an image of a scale or seesaw in her head. During the process of achieving a balance, caregivers became more realistic about their own inability to fix everything. They no longer took on the problems of the people they were helping, but instead allowed self-determination. They set limits and boundaries, such as refusing to work overtime or give their home phone numbers to patients. And all of them recognized the importance of practicing self-care.

Caring for the self involves:

- Reflection on your purpose in life and goals
- Reining in stress
- Building more pleasure into your life
- Turning to literature and music
- Laughing more
- Crying more
- Exercising
- Meditating
- Improving your time management
- Immersing yourself in the sacred

Reflection on Your Purpose in Life and Goals

Caring for the self begins by assessing both the work and nonwork dimensions of your life. We begin with work, because work represents nearly half of waking life for most adults. If we deprive ourselves of time for contemplation, life can be like a speeding train, hurtling past forests, valleys, and rock formations (but, of course, we're going way too fast to appreciate the varied topography). One day blends into another, weeks fold into the next weeks, and before you know it, a whole year has whizzed by. We're not sure of the destination, but we seem to be thrust forward toward something. I challenge you to step off the train for a bit. If you don't step off from time to time, physical illness or depression may bring you to a halt, especially if your itinerary needs some correction. I am concerned about nurses who seem to be unclear about where they are going. For example, Dawn Perkins, who was highly stressed and angry when interviewed for our research, is studying to be a nurse practitioner because her husband wants her to:

> *If you asked me what is my primary reason for going back to school, I'd tell you it's because my husband wants me to. Right now, that's my only interest. I know that's not a good reason to do it, but when I start something I finish it. I'm not going to quit. If I quit, I'd have less stress. He's putting a lot of pressure on me. He says things like, "Well, you can quit," but I know that he didn't really mean that. I feel like if I make a B, he gets disappointed. I have no plans to know what I'll do as an NP. I have no concept right now of what I want to do in that role.*

Why are you doing what you're doing, and is it getting you what you want out of life?

The great myths and religious traditions all contain sagas of heroes journeying to find their personal destinies. A Greek-derived word for fulfilling one's essential purpose in life is *entelechy*. It is the entelechy of an acorn to be an oak tree, and likewise the entelechy of each human to be uniquely who he or she is (deQuincey, 2002). David Bohm might speak of the implicate order, Abraham Maslow of self-actualization, a Buddhist of his karma. In some sense, an inner force is creating and shaping us, but we are modifying it as well by the choices that we make: "it is as if we were each dealt a specific hand of cards, and our task in life . . . is to exercise our consciousness in how we 'play' our hand" (deQuincey, 2002, p. 42). One of life's major choices, is, of course, our profession. But in today's turbulent times, this is not a choice made just once when we are in early adulthood. Professional directions must be renegotiated many times during a career. Many potentials of the self become evident only in middle or later adulthood. Many opportunities are not offered to us until we obtain additional experience or credentials.

Maslow, in describing self-actualizing people, said that work becomes a defining characteristic of the self, becomes part of the self. When you have found your niche, you are getting paid to do what you love to do. Is this true of you at the present time? Here are some questions from nurse consultant Jo Manion (2008) to ask yourself:

- Does my work use my strengths and talents?
- To what degree am I engaged in and by my work?
- Does my work have meaning?
- Do I find pleasure and joy in my work?

If you could not answer these questions in the affirmative, what would excite and challenge you? Where do you want to be in your career 5 years from now? What would it take for you to get there? Do you need to go back to school? Do you need to pursue certification? Resolve to take control of your career plan, instead of allowing it to unfold in a haphazard manner. Continuing to do work that is no longer engaging and satisfying is to some extent a death of the self (Levinson, 1996).

Are You a Workaholic?

Perhaps you are not at all like Dawn Perkins, who told us she is becoming an NP because of her husband's pressure. Perhaps you *are* fully engaged in your work—so much so that work has come to dominate your existence. I have known some nurses whose entire life was nursing: They ate, they slept, they worked. Could the word "workaholic" be used to describe you? If not, you can skip right to the next section. Unfortunately, this noun is a good descriptor not only for nurses but also for many other Americans who do professional work. Heavy investment in work is admired and rewarded in Western culture—even more so in the United States than in Western Europe. In fact, Americans work nearly 9 full weeks (350 hours) longer per year than our European counterparts ("Take Back Your Time," 2008). We work more than citizens of any other industrialized nation. And we're working longer hours now than we did in the 1950s ("Take Back Your Time," 2008). Workaholism can lead to fatigue, burnout, and other adverse sequelae.

You may be a workaholic if:

- You have a huge investment of identity and self-worth in your job.
- You stay connected with work via e-mails, beepers, pagers, or cell phones, even during "leisure" and vacations.
- Your family and friends complain that they are being short-changed.

Sociologist Arlie Hochschild, in a book called *The Time Bind*, drew some disturbing conclusions about workers who display these characteristics. She states, "Although work can complement—and indeed, improve—family life, in recent decades it has largely competed with family, and won" (Hochschild, cited in Bourke, 1997). Working parents drop their children off at day care in the wee hours of the morning and pick them up at the last possible moment at night. Dinner is fast food, family rituals go by the wayside. Work is the place to see friends, work toward goals, reap rewards for performance, and escape the stresses of home. In contrast, home is the source of irritation and conflict. In effect, work has become home and home is work, according to Hochschild. It's a sobering analysis, isn't it?

Victor Frankl survived horrendous treatment in a World War II concentration camp and went on to become a shrewd observer of society as it became more materialistic in the succeeding decades. He knew that we were going astray when we began to put more emphasis on materialism than on the meaning of life: "For too long we have been dreaming a dream . . . that if we just improve the socioeconomic situation of people, everything will be okay, people will become happy. The truth is that as the struggle for survival has subsided, the question has emerged: survival for what? Ever more people today have the means to live, but no meaning to live for" (Frankl, 1978, p. 21). Along the same vein, another giant of our times, Carl Jung, warned against preoccupation with the outward trappings of success while neglecting the inner life: "I have frequently seen people become neurotic when they content themselves with inadequate or wrong answers to the questions of life. They seek position, marriage, reputation, outward success or money, and remain unhappy and neurotic even when they have attained what they were seeking. Such people are usually confined within too narrow a spiritual horizon. Their life has not sufficient content, sufficient meaning" (Jung, 1965, p. 140).

I, as a recovering workaholic, now know that work cannot be all of one's existence. Urges RN Karen Roush: "Don't let nursing define your whole being. Be a baker, a runner, a book club member, a father, a wife. Whatever it is, be it totally, ferociously, and separate from nursing. . . . Shelter that part of you that is away from nursing and it will energize your presence as a nurse" (Roush, 2008, p. 9). We turn our attention now to other self-care strategies that will recharge your batteries and enhance your well-being.

Reining in Stress

It is indisputable that nursing is a stressful line of work. Thus, decreasing the level of stress we are feeling is a crucial element of self-care. I know that you, like I, have been bombarded with simplistic suggestions for good "stress management." When told to "take one day at a time," I feel like Ashley Brilliant, who responded: "But sometimes several days attack me at once!" So, I won't bore you with simplistic advice. It is important, however, to take a look at how views of stress have changed over the years, moving away from the early conceptualizations of Hans Selye and others.

The concept of *homeostasis* has been replaced by *allostasis*, a term that means continual adjustment of our bodies to the physical and psychological stressors we face (McEwen & Stellar, 1993). The marvelous system that permits us to "roll with the punches" of daily life can begin to wear down organs and tissues with chronic provocation. Allostasis can slide into damaging *allostatic load* when (a) the stress is unremitting/lasts too long; (b) the body's response is too strong; (c) the body doesn't hear the "all-clear," and fails to return to baseline; and/or (d) the body's protective response is insufficient (McEwen & Lasley, 2003; Sapolsky, 1998). The good news is that the stress response can be modulated by psychological factors, such as believing that you have some control, marshalling some social support, or choosing to perceive a situation differently (Sapolsky, 1998).

Let's take a moment to focus on *perception*. Gone are the days when we believed that the Holmes and Rahe scale (1967) measured stress. You probably remember the list of life events in that scale, because it was published in every nursing textbook. The scale included events such as divorce and assumption of a mortgage, each event being assigned a numerical weight. Supposedly, you could just tally up the number of events and discover your stress score. The higher it was, the more you were at risk for health problems. But something interesting happened as studies continued. Researchers discovered that the very same event could produce profoundly different responses. We know now that an event such as a financial crisis will produce a mild reaction in one individual and a severe, even debilitating, reaction in another. Thus, reducing stress often involves a *shift in perception*. What if you decided not to become so perturbed by life's minor daily hassles—the traffic, the rude salesclerk, the slow line at the bank? What if you began to shift your thinking to consider negative life events as challenges to be mastered? Even negative life events can stimulate psychological growth and development (Wethington, 2003). Psychologist Carolyn Aldwin (1994) pointed out that stress can lead to an "inoculation effect" whereby similar events are not so distressful.

What if you did something specific to unwind from the day's work rather than just expecting your stress level to gradually diminish on its own? Repetti (1992) took an original approach to stress management, recommending *social withdrawal* as a short-term coping response to daily stressors. She asserted that social withdrawal can assist in restoration of a more positive emotional state. This approach may not appeal to you, because you may want to vent your gripes about the day to a sympathetic listener. If that's your choice, that's okay, too. But Repetti's proposal makes sense to me, because nurses so seldom have downtime when they are not with patients, partners, or other family members. We are prone to sensory and interpersonal overload. Whatever happened to the idea of "repose?" Have you heard the word "solitude" lately? These words do not seem to exist in our contemporary lexicon. Perhaps bringing them back has merit. I recommend making space for reflection in a "hermit spot" at the end of a trying workday. You may want to employ Benson's relaxation procedure, which we introduced in Chapter 4. Your goal is to give your body the "all-clear," so that it returns to baseline rather than remaining in a state of prolonged physiological arousal. Read on for other efficacious stress reduction strategies.

Building More Pleasure Into Your Life

Barasch (1994) has pointed out that the "work week" of our tribal ancestors was only about 20 hours; the remainder of their time was spent in conversation and play (singing, dancing, games, etc.). It's ironic that we, their sophisticated descendents, with our self-cleaning ovens and store-bought bread, can't find the time for play. We do have conversation, with our e-mail, voice mail, and text messaging, but not long, deep, dialogue before a great fire, talking far into the night as the flames grow low and the embers turn gray. Deep conversation can be highly pleasurable, filling our need for meaningful connections with other humans.

Even when you're still steaming from an unpleasant confrontation just before you left work, the research of Zillman (1988) suggests that your anger can be diminished or terminated by highly absorbing, pleasant entertainment. A movie can quickly transport you to the breathtaking vistas of Alaska or the Alps, or to the vast Arabian desert or the canyons of the American West. Caught up in the visual images and the story, it becomes impossible for you to continue to dwell on your problems. Dance performances, plays, concerts, and poetry readings await you in any medium-sized city. Even small towns usually have theater troupes and choral groups. I hesitate to recommend television because I think that most

Americans spend too much of their free time in front of their TV sets, in a kind of bland, anesthetized stupor. But obviously my bias is glaringly evident! TV may be incredibly pleasurable to some of you, and if so, pop the popcorn and plop down in front of it!

I can hear some of you—especially the women—saying that all these recreational activities sound great, but how will the housecleaning and laundry get done? One of women's biggest dissatisfactions in the Women's Anger Study (Thomas, 1993a, Thomas, et al., 1998) was the failure of their partners to take on a fair share of the household chores. This segment of a phenomenological interview is illustrative:

> *I felt like my weekends were spent cleaning the house while his weekends were spent playing, and I resented that. . . . Like I told him when I was angry, "You don't want to compare what you do and what I do because you'll lose, trust me. How many times do you do the laundry, and how many times do you fold and put up clothes, and cook the meals and run the kids?" He knows he doesn't do that. He knows I do most of it, and he likes it that way, and he wants to keep it that way.*

When women in my anger workshops begin making *specific assertive requests* ("I need you to run the vacuum in the family room"), their husbands/partners are willing to help out. Instead, many women are sighing heavily and fuming inside about the inequitable division of labor, expecting their partners to intuit that they need assistance. This is an irrational expectation. As unbelievable as it may sound, your spouse may not *see* the cobwebs and dustballs. And your children are probably oblivious as well. All children should be given age-appropriate chores, such as picking up their toys or setting the table. Link your assertive requests to outcomes that will be pleasurable for the whole family: "If we finish the chores by 11:00, there's still time to get to the mountains for a picnic." Try it, you'll see. Have a nice picnic, and don't forget the pickles.

Turning to Literature and Music

RN Cortney Davis (2003) proposes that reading novels and poetry could help nurses reduce stress: "Many of the nurses and students I talk to, at work and in my travels, tend to sicker-than-ever patients and make complex ethical decisions with little opportunity to defuse stress or develop any 'narrative sensibility' about their daily routine" (p. 13). Davis has been heavily involved in compiling volumes of nurses' prose and poetry, and believes that reading these materials can help other nurses as they grapple with human suffering and death. Moreover, claims Davis, literature and art could help nurses internalize what is valuable about our profession.

I am particularly drawn to poetry, because it deeply touches my emotions. So, I did something to remind myself to read poetry regularly. I bought an inexpensive basket, filled it with 10 or 12 of my favorite books of poetry, and placed it right by my reading chair. Now, I delve into my poetry basket as part of my nightly wind-down. At random, I select a volume. Sometimes I read one poem, and just quietly reflect upon it for awhile. Sometimes I'm too tired to think much about a poem's meaning, especially if there are obscure allusions, but I still enjoy the words themselves as they dance across the page. You might prefer to read poetry online. There are many excellent web sites, such as "Words Without Borders." Web magazines ("zines") publish unknown poets and writers as well as established ones.

Great literature provides much more than distraction from stress. We gain understanding of other people, ourselves, and our world. You may enjoy both the socialization and intellectual stimulation of participating in reader groups at your local libraries or book clubs in your neighborhood. Some cities are choosing classic literary works, such as *To Kill a Mockingbird* by Harper Lee, and urging all residents to participate in discussion groups about the book.

Music can be one of the best stress-busters after a grueling workday. Take off your uniform—or your dress-for-success business suit—and slip into the happy hedonism of Jimmy Buffett. Make a margarita—nonalcoholic if you choose—and put some shrimp on to boil. Let the music take you to the Caribbean, where the sun slowly bakes everyone into a slowed-down lethargy, and your only decision is when to turn over and let the sun bake your other side. Or, perhaps you'd rather go to San Francisco, where you left your heart, or New Orleans, where the saints go marching in. Mozart could take you to snowy Salzburg, mariachis to Mexico. In short, music can provide a delightful mini-vacation.

Humor

Yes, I know there are days when the only way you can put a smile on your face is by putting a coat hanger in your mouth! But if that's what it takes, do it! Humor is inexpensive, widely available, and heaping doses of it can be self-administered by nurses ad lib. It's even better when it's shared with other nurses. Laughing with one another alleviates the seriousness that permeates our work settings and counters our sense of isolation, providing important moments of genuine connection. Everyone in your work group will identify with you—and surely chuckle—when you report, "I'm selling T-shirts that say, 'I used up all my sick days, so I'm calling in dead.'" You can probably gauge the emotional health of a work group by the amount of laughter they share: People are most likely to be humorous and playful in the presence of people who like and enjoy them (Saussy, 1995). Here is an example of an unexpected humorous situation, in which oncology nurses shared laughter with their patient:

> We heard a scream coming from her room. We ran in there, and everyone in the station ran into the room to see what was wrong. And she said, "I'm falling, I'm falling." She had not been confused to this point. She really thought she had fallen to the floor and we were, you know, trying to comfort her, and I noticed that the air hose had come out of the mattress. To her, she really had fallen. The air mattress was completely flat. So I said, "Here's our problem." I hooked it back up, and it floated her back up in the air and she absolutely loved it. She said, "Oh, this is nice," and laughed. She wanted me to do it again, and so she made me unhook it and plug it back in. So we did this for about 30 minutes to an hour. (Gunther & Thomas, 2006, p. 372)

Did you know that laughing actually confers health benefits?

Research shows that laughing increases the efficiency of the respiratory system. Furthermore, the cardiovascular and muscular systems relax (Kennedy, 1995). Laughter has also been linked to higher levels of immunoglobulin A and lower levels of cortisol (Berk et al., 1989). As shown in studies of prisoners of war and concentration camps, laughter can provide moments of grace even in the most extreme misery. Not long ago, my colleague Howard Pollio, a psychology professor, showed me the Jewish jokes that were circulated during the Holocaust. What a remarkable manifestation of the indomitable human spirit!

Humor can be used to dispel anger at a provocation you don't want to dwell upon. Laughing and fuming are simply impossible to enact simultaneously. A few years ago, when the first reports of our research on women's anger hit the press, I was inundated with calls from reporters and gave a number of interviews. Most of the journalists were responsible individuals who read at least some of the book before conducting their interviews, asked me intelligent questions, and prepared stories that were reasonably accurate. Some of the journalists, such as Jane Brody with the *New York Times,* did a superb job describing the study and its findings. Not so Rush Limbaugh. Without interviewing me or taking any other steps to verify the accuracy of his story, he went on the radio and trashed the research. The first I knew of Rush's diatribe was about 15 minutes after his show went off the air. A professor from the College of Education had heard the broadcast while driving to the university, and outraged on my behalf, he came straight to my office to tell me about it. My first response was anger, but then I considered the source and became amused. By the time other friends were calling to express their dismay about the unfair comments, I was laughing and saying that I planned to add "trashed by Rush Limbaugh" to my resume.

Tears

Tears get a bad rap in our society. They are only acceptable in young children and only until a certain age, after which they are disparaged. No one wants to be called a *crybaby.* Although in adulthood, tears are somewhat more permissible for women than for men, women who freely cry still run the risk of being labeled overly emotional or hysterical. Crying for men receives even more pejorative labeling. My husband grew up in the Mediterranean culture, and he finds Americans far too uptight about crying. It's not unusual for him—and other men from his part of the world—to cry.

I believe that crying can be very therapeutic, releasing emotional tension and leaving in its place a cleansed, quiet state. The first major study on crying in adults (Frey & Langseth, 1985) was devoted to a chemical analysis of tears and the physiological function of tears. I found the study results quite interesting. Emotional tears were chemically different than irritant tears (caused by air pollution or cutting onions), in that they serve an excreting function. Analysis showed that emotional tears contain chemicals that may mediate the immune system's response to stress. This research raises an intriguing question: By stifling our tears, are we depriving ourselves of a natural healing mechanism that could combat the ill effects of angry, stressful situations? I say that having a good cry at the end of a frustrating workday is a healthy way of caring for oneself. Go ahead and let those tears flow.

Exercise

You already know that you need to exercise. I'm not going to reiterate all of the reasons why, because you are well-educated readers. You've read the studies showing that exercise lifts your spirits for as long as 2 to 4 hours (Kaplan, 1997). But did you also know that the greatest improvements in emotional state occur when people feel *worst* before they engage in exercise (Gauvin, Rejeski, & Norris, 1996)? Given these demonstrated benefits for droopy spirits, coupled with what you already know about heart health, muscle tone, and so on, what's getting in your way of exercising? A common excuse I hear from nurses about their failure to exercise is "no time to get to the health club." I always chuckle a bit, wondering how so many of us have gotten the idea that fitness can only be achieved if one has a health club membership—or a personal trainer. True enough, health clubs offer all those snazzy rowing machines, treadmills, weight contraptions, and other devices to make you puff, sweat, and groan. But what would our parents' generation think about trotting off to the health club instead of just attacking some chores at home? After a day of hoeing and milking and chopping cotton, I doubt if any of my rural West Tennessee relatives ever had to worry about fitness.

Those of us who are suburban couch sitters do. Television keeps many of us sedentary for hours (an average of 11 hours per week) along with other popular leisure activities such as reading, sitting around socializing, talking on the telephone, surfing the Internet, and playing computer games. Altogether, such sedentary pursuits total around 37 hours per week for most of us (Salmon, Owen, Crawford, Bauman, & Sallis, 2003). In contrast, time spent walking averages only 3 hours or less. Although I sped down the hospital halls in my "duty shoes" with the best of them when I was younger, my current work in the university is largely sedentary. Nurses who are therapists, middle managers, and administrators spend much of their day sitting as well.

Even RNs whose work is entirely in fast-paced settings such as emergency departments or intensive care units cannot count on getting enough aerobic exercise during the workday. Remember that, for aerobic benefit, you have to be doing something that gets your heart rate to within 50% to 70% of its maximum (for a man that is 220 beats per minute minus his age, for a woman 200 minus her age). If you are turned off by intensely competitive sports and pumping iron for massive muscles, the good news is that it's relatively easy to build many health-promoting activities into your daily routine. I think the best way to begin is by shelving all those labor-saving devices in the kitchen and the garage, and start burning calories doing work the way we used to do. Why do we need riding mowers to take care of postage-stamp-size lawns? Why do we need to pay somebody else an exorbitant amount to wash and vacuum the car? Writer Harry Chipkin devised a list of such activities and the amount of calories they burn, as compared with calories expended in vigorous sports like squash. According to Chipkin's Sports-haters, Nonathletic, Easy-does-it, Kiss-your-sweatsuit-goodbye Equivalency Rating, or SNEAKER, washing the car for an hour is equivalent to swimming for an hour, and mowing the lawn with a manual mower for 75 minutes is roughly the same as playing racquetball for 35 minutes. Ironing for 3 hours is about the same as cross-country skiing for 30 minutes, and heavy scrubbing burns 250 to 350 calories per hour. One of my favorite facts from SNEAKER is that climbing stairs burns 250% more calories than swimming for the same amount of time, 150% more than tennis, 94% more than racquetball, 63% more than cycling, and 23% more than running. See, you really don't have to jog down the boulevard, pounding the asphalt in freezing weather while breathing in all that carbon monoxide. You can run up and down the stairs in the warm comfort of your own home instead.

Dr. Richard Stein, a spokesman for the American Heart Association, points out that dusting works your shoulders, chest, and triceps, burning 180 calories an hour; vacuuming works your back and biceps, burning 230 calories an hour; and window-washing works your chest, shoulders, back, and legs, burning 280 calories an hour. You may be thinking that vacuuming, ironing, and scrubbing are extremely unappealing ways to get your exercise. Whether or not any of these ideas appeal to you, resolve to get your body moving. Fitness does not mean just cardiac fitness but also greater flexibility, endurance, and strength; improvements in metabolism of sugar and lipids; and decreased tension and stress. The latter benefit is particularly important during times of emotional turmoil at work. Research shows that biking at a moderate rate for 1 hour reduces depression, anger, and confusion. However, the same research shows that moderation is the key. When individuals who were upset cycled more intensely or strained to their absolute limit, they actually felt worse afterward (Motl, cited in Kaplan, 1997).

I find the tendency to push oneself to exhaustion a uniquely American phenomenon. We exercise like we work: in obsessive type A fashion. Nowhere else in the world have I seen so many grim-faced, driven runners. Examples of a healthier approach to body movement abound in other cultures. One of the fondest memories of my 1985 visit to China was the sight of thousands of people outdoors in the early morning doing their exercises—graceful octogenarians included. Even in the hospitals that I visited, all patients who could be ambulatory were exercising, out on the roof garden in the fresh air wherever possible. In China, movement is considered as important for health as eating, sleeping, and drinking fluids. We can learn from the wisdom of the East.

Perhaps one secret of the Chinese dedication to exercise is the communal nature of the activity. People are doing the Tai Chi movements—different ones, to be sure—*together* in public parks and other community gathering places. In our country, too, many of us are more likely to engage in physical activity if we are enrolled in a class or have a neighbor to walk with. California nurse researchers Bonnie Raingruber and Carol Robinson (2007) offered Tai Chi, meditation, and Reiki healing classes to nurses at a large medical center. The nurses attended the group sessions either before or after their work shifts for a 3-month period. Journals kept by the nurses documented benefits they perceived, such as letting go of worry and the need to be perfect (see 9.1).

> *9.1.* *I enjoy the flow of the Tai Chi exercises, how one movement transitions into another. I feel a sense of peace, calm, and warmth all over my body . . . a tingling feeling that flows like a stream over me. That's odd because I've been to a lot of meetings in the same room, and I never felt that sense of peace that I notice in the room during the Tai Chi class. (journal entry of RN in study by Raingruber & Robinson, 2007, p. 1146)*

Unanticipated by the researchers, the nurses in the study not only reported personal health benefits, but also an enhanced ability to focus on their patients' needs and solve clinical problems. You could use these research findings to convince management to offer classes like this at your workplace.

Simply increasing the amount of time you walk each week is probably the easiest way to "ease" into a more active lifestyle. Nearly everyone can find a safe place to walk, such as a shopping mall. Research consistently demonstrates that walking provides nearly all of the benefits of more vigorous activity and requires no equipment or fees (Norman & Mills, 2004). Owning a dog provides regular impetus for walking; your dog is impossible to ignore and will not accept your excuses. Writer Carol Krucoff (1997) says she has even learned some "health secrets" from exercising with her beagle: (a) greet everyone you meet, but keep your ears cocked until you determine friend or foe; (b) lap up water every chance you get; (c) enjoy nature in all her moods; (d) stretch frequently; (e) live in the moment; (f) rely on more than just your eyes (sniff, listen, etc.); (g) always take time to roll on the floor and play; and (h) never become too busy to stop and smell the rabbit holes. Terrific advice, in my opinion! Get off the couch—with or without a dog—and go move your body. You'll live longer, look better, feel great, and be an excellent example for your patients.

Improving Your Time Management

Many of the stressed-out people I know have poor time management skills. They procrastinate, fail to delegate, and try to catch up through frantic multi-tasking or pulling "all-nighters." RN Diana Taylor suggests an exercise called "Slicing Your Time Cake," to help you see what you really do with the 24 hours of your day. It's easy: Draw a circle, representing a cake. Mark a slice for hours of sleep, a slice for work, then smaller slices for household chores, errands, child care, commuting to and from work, and so forth. Next, make a list of your 10 favorite activities (such as hanging out with friends, reading a novel, or playing a musical instrument). Finally, assess how many of your favorite activities are reflected in your time cake. Chances are, you may be giving yourself a very thin slice of time. Here's how you can learn to allocate time more wisely:

- *Decide which of your daily tasks you must do personally* and which you could delegate to a family member or coworker, then start delegating!
- *Practice saying "no,"* gently but assertively, to supervisors, colleagues, neighbors, and family members when you truly cannot take on another thing. Saying "no" is especially hard for people-pleasers, but essential in managing time and reducing stress.

- *Conquer the habit of procrastination.* This habit not only escalates stress; it detracts from your professional effectiveness. Make lists and schedules, and stick to your self-imposed deadlines. Reward yourself for doing so.
- *Build in a specified time each day to reflect on the day* that is ending and plan ahead for the new one. Include some flexibility in your plan to deal with unexpected events (e.g., heavier traffic, meetings that may run past the allotted hours, etc.), so that you don't become frazzled when your plans go awry.

Meditation

Another useful self-care strategy is the practice of meditation. Meditation has many proven benefits, including the reduction of nurses' stress levels (Tsai & Crockett, 1993). Some people are leery of the practice, however, perhaps because of its association with misguided hippies who dropped out to wander aimlessly on the fringes of society. Another objection, sometimes raised by my students, has to do with the connection between meditation and Eastern religions. Some students think meditation would be inappropriate for them to do because of their religious beliefs. I give them readings containing accurate information, but the decision to meditate is, of course, ultimately theirs. What is meditation, really? "Meditation refers to a family of techniques which have in common a conscious attempt to focus attention in a non-analytical way and an attempt not to dwell on discursive, ruminating thought" (Shapiro, 1982, p. 268).

Breathing Meditation

Breathing meditation is perhaps least likely to provoke objections on the grounds of religion, because concentration on breathing is a part not only of Buddhist and Hindu practices, but also of Jewish and Christian traditions. Kornfield (1993) says that the breath is a great teacher, from whom we can learn about opening and letting go. Here is his recommended procedure for breathing meditation:

- To begin, find a quiet place to sit and arrange its furnishings (cushion or chair, vase of flowers, candle, books).
- Select a regular time in the morning or evening.
- If you like, read something inspirational first.
- Then begin your period of meditation by bringing attention to your breathing.
- Let your breath change rhythms naturally.
- When your mind wanders, simply come back to the next breath.
- When you return, acknowledge where you wandered with a soft word: "thinking, " or "planning."
- At first, keep your sessions to 10 to 20 minutes.

Meditation is very much like training a puppy, according to Kornfield. Imagine a playful puppy you have told to "stay," but the puppy scampers off in a flash.

Again, you sit the puppy down and say "stay." And the puppy runs away over and over again. Likewise, in training oneself to meditate, be prepared for an unruly mind that just will not stay focused. Infinite patience will be required before you end up with the puppy as your lifelong friend. But you will gradually learn to calm and center yourself using the breath.

Walking Meditation

Walking meditation is a variant that I find appealing. I hope you will give it a try. Here's how: Select a place where you can walk back and forth, indoors or out, about 10 to 30 paces. Begin by closing your eyes and centering yourself, feeling your body standing on the earth. Then open your eyes and begin to walk slowly, easily, paying attention as you place each foot on the earth. When you reach the end of your path, pause, carefully turn, and start back. Walk for 10 or 20 minutes. When the mind wanders, follow the same procedure as above. After you have some practice with walking meditation, you can do it informally when walking down a street or to and from your car. It is a simple, but profoundly different, way of walking than you usually do when your mind is preoccupied with thinking and planning (Kornfield, 1993).

Mantram Repetition

Although both of the meditative procedures that I just described require that you leave the workplace, you can use this variant throughout the workday. Nurse researcher Jill Bormann reported statistically significant reductions in stress and anger when nurses and other health care workers were trained to use *mantram repetition* (Bormann et al., 2006). A *mantram* (also called mantra) is a word or phrase with spiritual meaning, chosen for its calming and comforting effect. A Jewish person might choose *Shalom* (peace), a Native American *O Wakan Tanka* (Oh, Great Spirit), and a Christian *Lord Jesus Christ*. The mantram is repeated silently in times of distress (Bormann, 2005). High mantram users in Bormann and colleagues' (2006) study reported mantram repetition an average of eight sessions per day; low users averaged three sessions per day. In addition to stress and anger reduction, study participants also experienced improved spiritual well-being. If you are interested in trying mantram repetition, see Bormann (2005) for additional information.

Immersing Ourselves in the Sacred

Caring for the self also involves taking time to immerse yourself in whatever you find sacred. Doing what is sacred to you is not necessarily what your parents, or theologians, or society may consider sacred; the sacred is that which has the power to move you deeply and help you cope with the demands and struggles of life's journey. You may or may not get in touch with that power within formal church services. Many Americans are hungry for new ways to care for the soul, as shown by the popularity of the books by Thomas Moore on this topic. Perhaps you care for your soul when you are gardening or listening to music. Alice Walker calls her writing a prayer. I recommend keeping a gratitude journal or log, focusing on the good things about your work and family life. You need not spend a lot of time on this; simply recall how thankful you were to hear from a long-lost classmate, or to learn that your high-risk pregnant patient delivered a healthy son. In other words, regularly count your blessings. Research shows that people who make it a habit to focus on blessings (rather than hassles) are happier and feel better about their lives (Norville, 2007). Some nurses in our study described work-related experiences that made them feel blessed or grateful. For example, an ICU nurse appreciated a patient who came back to visit after his recovery:

Nobody thought he would make it out of the hospital [but] this little man finally started getting better. He was a joy to take care of. You know, sometimes after they have been in the ICU for quite a while they get psychosis. Sometimes that psychosis can be violent. Well, he had a real cute psychosis. He was just a little goofy . . . A few weeks later, he came to visit me. I was like, "Wow!" I didn't even recognize him. He said of all the people in the unit, he remembered me, and that was just real special to me.

An oncology nurse focused on the privilege of being with her patients throughout the cancer trajectory:

We're there with them at the most dreadful moment [when] they've found out. We're with them when they've accepted it, and if we're lucky, we're there with them at the end. We're the last caring face they see. That's when I realize I have been given a gift, to be there at the moment when the light goes out and they've gone on their journey.

If you keep a gratitude journal, recording vignettes such as these; you can savor them again and again—especially on awful days when you are heavily discouraged.

Being in nature fills me with gratitude for life itself, and for all of the living things that populate the world around me. I find a cathedral of trees more awe-inspiring than a man-made one, a rainbow more spectacular than a stained glass window. I live in a beautiful part of the world, with gently curving hills, so lovely in the spring with new vegetation softening their creases, smoothing out the corrugated evidence of erosion. Taking a drive, I am immersed in a vast sea of green fields and blue-gray hills. Ride along with me and see the wispy, tentative, fragile green of willow wands waving in the breeze . . . richer yellow-green vista in the background, the texture of velvet, like a pillow cover tightly stretched to cover a fat round cushion of soil . . . darker green of spiky pines punctuating all this softness and roundness . . . and then flamboyant forsythia thrusting itself into my line of vision, Bradford pear trees in their lacy bridal white, pearly gray rock families clustered like mushrooms on the hillsides, a random daffodil here and there . . . in the sky, ephemeral cloud curls suffused with pink-rose of early morning sun . . . the clouds patterning and repatterning: now a herd of droll woolly sheep, now a nest of elegant white birds with primly folded feathers, now frothy peaks of meringue . . . the sun becoming more brilliant in a sky that is the color of Lake Louise . . . the hills light-dappled, serene, solid, wise, eternal. Hear the hum of the universe and the heartbeat of God.

A Last Word

Unlike some of the chapters in this book, this one homed in on matters that are entirely within your control. Only you can provide proper care for yourself. Only you can make the decision to allocate your time differently, so that you can play more, laugh more, and exercise more. To the extent that you adopt some of the suggestions in the chapter, you will feel less stressed and experience more pleasure in your life. You will also have more energy to tackle the continuing challenges of the work environment.

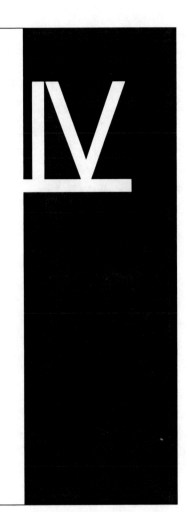

Claiming Our Power and Using It

10

Taking a New Stance Toward the Concept of Power

Personal power is a flame within me that I have to follow to be me. It looks like a tiny flame that could be easily blown out but really it's one of those perpetual lights. I can go off and leave it or give some of it to others and feel confident that it won't go out. In fact, the more I give my flame to others, the brighter my flame gets, until I don't have to worry about its going out at all. It comes from inside of me but it's brightened by others so that I can proudly say, "Look, this is my flame," and I can follow it. All of my important life decisions are made by the light of this flame. It's the light of integrity, of being true to myself.

—Stratman, 1990

For a long time now, I have been using the word *empowerment* in my speeches and workshops. The term is used in different ways in the hundreds of papers on the topic. Let me explain what I mean by it. I define empowerment as *the enhanced ability to take action and resolve problems.* Empowerment theory and praxis have roots in feminist scholarship, adult education techniques, and community and political organization methods (Gutierrez, 1990). Self-empowerment, which this book is designed to facilitate, means having the power to influence and control one's own life (Heide, 1988). But beyond controlling their own lives, nurses must become empowered to make a greater impact on institutional and health care policies. Too many nurses remain marginalized or silenced, chafing at short-sighted policies, but excluded from the decision-making circle. Davies (1995) contends that nurses are usually excluded from policy debates because they are considered "incompetent" or "divided," and when they do enter the arena of debate, they often feel "bruised and confused."

I contend that *nurses' anger can be empowering, if it is used constructively.* When we get "good and angry," we marshal the courage to act. I was greatly moved, while reading a *National Geographic* article about India's "untouchables" (those individuals at the bottom of the Hindu caste system) by the newfound assertiveness of these persecuted people. I cannot imagine a more miserable existence than that of the untouchables. They do the country's dirtiest jobs, such as cleaning the latrines and cremating the dead. Article author Tom O'Neill (2003, p. 9) reports that the untouchables are "shunned, banned from temples and higher caste homes, made to eat and drink from separate utensils in public places, and in extreme but not uncommon cases, are raped, burned, lynched, and gunned down." But there is a small grassroots movement led by a man named Martin Macwan. He trains people to take cases of discrimination and violence to police, human rights organizations, and the courts. How does he enlist his recruits? As he searches among the villages of the untouchables for potential activists, Macwan says "I look for anger" (p. 27). He knows that when anger is ignited, dispirited people finally begin speaking out.

Strong emotion can galvanize dispirited nurses too—to challenge sex discrimination, harassment, inequitable work assignments, and ill-conceived policies (Thomas & Droppleman, 1997). We need look no further than the founder of modern nursing for corroboration of my premise. Recall that Florence Nightingale said "I do well to be angry" (Strachey, 1918/1996, p. 31). It was her chafing at the uselessness of the Victorian lady's social role and the "petty grinding tyranny of a good English family" (cited in Smith, 1982) that fueled her resolve to "strive after a better life for women" (Cook, 1913). It was her outrage at the deplorable sanitation, nutrition, and medical care of the British soldiers that brought about her campaign for massive reforms, not only in the Crimea but also back home in England. It was her passionate commitment to education for nurses that banished Sairey Gamp and brought modern professional nursing into existence. It was her righteous anger that propelled her into the public policy arena to address prostitution, crime, infant mortality, urban slums, workhouse conditions, and the problems of the rural poor.

Do We Really Want Power?

It is an old truism that no one gives away power. Nurses themselves are going to have to make an effort to take it. But nurses are ambivalent toward the concept of power, perhaps because nursing has remained a woman's profession. Nightingale was an unusual woman who defied Victorian society's rules for her gender, but too few of the nurse leaders who followed her displayed similar courage. The relationship between nursing and feminism remains strained, with many nurses disavowing feminism and many feminists disparaging nursing (Kane & B. Thomas, 2000). Nurses often view power as something unfeminine or coercive (Carlson-Catalano, 1994). In a study by Valentine (1992), five out of six nurses regarded power and ambition *negatively.* Nurses who fought for their rights were viewed as uncaring and undeserving, "not having the qualities that nurses should have" (p. 20). Presumably, those qualities that nurses *should* have were humility, self-sacrifice, and bearing one's burden in silence. Not long ago, I was fascinated to learn that the motto chosen for the first school of nursing in Canada, St. Catherine's was, "I see but I am silent" (George, 1997). How accurately this motto captures the traditional role socialization of the student nurse! We recited the Nightingale pledge, but we sure weren't encouraged to behave like Nightingale.

The sense of powerlessness that permeated our nurse interview data (see Chapter 1) was one of the most disturbing aspects of this research. Powerlessness was identified in other studies of nurses too (e.g., Jacobs, Fontana, Kehoe, Matarese, & Chinn, 2005). Bush (1988) found that powerlessness was a major cause of job dissatisfaction in hospital nurses. Erlen and Frost (1991) had set out to study nurses' experience in influencing ethical decisions. However, what they found was pervasive powerlessness described by nurses of all ages, educational levels, and years of nursing experience. Nurses were unable to effect resolution to situations, resulting in anger, frustration, and exhaustion. As in our own study, the nurses had knowledge and responsibility but lacked the corresponding authority.

I know you've heard the old maxim about power corrupting (and absolute power corrupting absolutely). Heide (1988, p. 259) proposed a corollary: that *powerlessness corrupts and absolute powerlessness corrupts absolutely!* The "corruption" takes many forms, including decreased self-confidence, inhibited personal and professional growth, competition with other powerless nurses for a modicum of power, and identification with the powerful oppressor as we discussed in Chapter 5. When a group has been powerless for a long time, its members come to believe that "this is the way things are." They have learned to view attempts to escape aversive stimuli as futile, like the dogs in Seligman's famous experiments on learned helplessness (Seligman & Weiss, 1980).

Power: We Have to Want It Before We Can Have It

It's time for nurses to take a new stance toward the concept of power. You and I need to *claim our power*. Each individual nurse, by taking a new stance toward power, contributes ultimately to the advancement of our profession. As the saying goes, why not decide for yourself that martyrdom is dumb? Let's strive for horizontal power instead of horizontal violence—the power derived from building strong connections with our colleagues. Power may be as fundamental to human existence as anxiety, self-concept, and self-esteem (Pieranunzi, 1997). In her book *Paths to Power* Josefowitz (1980) distinguishes between power as forcefulness and power as effectiveness. It is *effective power* that I advocate: power that enables us to make positive, proactive changes.

We have to want power before we can have it. We have to believe that there is enough of it to go around, so that we can stop hoarding our little thimblefuls of it. We have to deliberately build power by forging coalitions with other nurses and pooling our talents and resources.

When each of us as individuals becomes empowered, the power quotient of the group increases, and likewise the group's power can enhance the development and functioning of its individual members. Power is a network of practices carried out by many people. There is creativity in power, as shown in a study of African tribal societies. Rejecting conceptions of power as subjugation and domination, these tribal societies see power as a means to "create new forms of experience and activity" (Arens & Karp, cited in Pieranunzi, 1997). Surely there has never been a more critical time for the nursing tribe to create new forms of activity.

The empowerment process involves four interrelated psychological changes that take place, not necessarily in a precise sequence. Developing a personal sense of *self-efficacy* or mastery is essential in moving from apathy to action. Next, it is necessary to develop a *group consciousness*—a keen awareness of the *shared* powerlessness of nurses and the factors that have created it. We must be clear that there is no need for *self-blame,* because nurses are not responsible for the inequitable power arrangements in our work settings that have long oppressed us. Finally, each of us must assume *personal responsibility for change* (Gutierrez, 1990).

The Power of the Pen

The power of the written word was Nightingale's forté, and her tactics are still worthy of emulation today. For example, she often wrote to the same individual numerous times until the desired action had been completed. She also used the technique of repeating key points within the body of a letter (Monteiro, 1985). In addition to her persuasive letters—at least 15,000 of which have been found—she published 147 books and pamphlets, and submitted numerous reports to Queen Victoria, Parliament, government commissions, and newspapers. Many of these documents included skillfully prepared graphs, charts, tables, and figures based on statistics she had gathered to bolster her arguments. Clearly, Nightingale had "fire in the belly" for her causes and used it to great effect. Likewise, I think that anger can ignite the "fire in the belly" that contemporary nurses need to take bold actions in this critical time. It can propel us into the societal debates regarding who should get what health care services, from whom, and where. One way we can enter these debates is via the power of the pen.

Not enough attention is given in nursing education to the power of the pen—or, in more contemporary parlance, the power of the word processor. Students write a lot of papers in nursing school, but they don't learn to write for the general public. Bernice Buresh and Suzanne Gordon (2000) have written a helpful book, *From Silence to Voice,* about communicating to the public through newspaper columns, letters to the editor, magazine articles, and op-eds. Specific guidelines and examples, such as op-eds by Linda Aiken, Claire Fagin, and Ellen Baer, are provided. An op-ed can propose a solution to a problem, depict a personal experience, or present the nursing perspective on a current issue. What I learned from this book is how much information can be packed into a 750-word op-ed! When publication is achieved in a newspaper like the *New York Times*—where Claire Fagin is often successful with pieces she's penned—nursing issues command a national audience. I'm going to give it a try. How about you?

The Power of the Media

We need to communicate to the public through other media, too. The media stretch their tentacles into every aspect of American life, to the extent that millions of people talk about the participants on "American Idol" or "Survivor" or the latest info from CNN Headline News as they have their morning coffee break. How many times have you heard your friends or family talking about the nurse they saw on TV that morning? Probably not very many. Buresh and Gordon (2000) called attention to the invisibility of nurses in the media. Not only must we write more letters to newspaper editors, but we must garner more TV and radio spots, too. In a profession of nearly 3 million members, why aren't more nurses hosting talk shows? Why are so few nurses being interviewed about health-related topics?

Donna Zazworsky is a media-savvy nurse. Donna says, "When the media asks you to do a story, your response is, 'Yes. When?'" (2002, p. 175) (see 10.1). You may have to juggle your schedule to have time to squeeze in an interview. When I am busy, I ask that television interviewers come to film me at my university office or my home. I often receive calls from radio show hosts at home as well. If necessary, of course, I will travel to a TV or radio station, too. I don't remember ever turning down an opportunity, because I want to contribute to the greater visibility and influence of nursing.

10.1. Using the Power of the Media

Donna Zazworksy (2002) has worked to establish good relationships with news anchors and medical reporters in her community by being regularly available for interviews. She is the only nurse on a team of medical experts on Channel 4 in Tucson, and she knows how to use the power of the media to get something accomplished. For example, she was involved in a community coalition to build an aquatic center for disabled individuals. A bond issue to fund the facility was coming to a taxpayer vote. Donna carefully crafted a TV story on the water exercise classes she was leading for people with multiple sclerosis and arthritis. Her story counteracted the misinformation being circulated by the opposition. The story was aired on both morning and evening news programs, reaching over 15,0000 people. Voters approved the bond.

As in learning all other skills, there are some things to learn about appearing on television or radio. I never had a media coach, so I have learned through making mistakes. By viewing a tape of one of my TV appearances, I learned that I moved my eyes too often, instead of maintaining a steady, even gaze. From another tape, I learned to put my hands in my pockets, out of sight except for occasional gesturing to add emphasis to a specific point. Perhaps the biggest lesson I learned was not to be disappointed when a 30-minute interview is cut to a short sound bite on the evening news. Even when cut to a sound bite, I have been glad that my voice was heard.

Steps Toward Confident Media Interviews

- *Always return calls from reporters or radio and TV stations.* Even if you do not have the proper expertise to address the topic at hand, you can refer them to a colleague.
- *Be flexible and adaptable when the media call.* They can't put off your interview until next week; the news item they want your reaction to is "hot" right now.
- *Before your interview, prepare a short human interest story* about the topic, if possible (the media prefer stories to recitations of facts and numbers).
- *Avoid jargon.* If you will be asked during the interview to explain complicated medical procedures, or statistical computations in your research, practice translating the information to layman's language beforehand (family members can give you feedback). Strive for clarity and conciseness.
- *Don't be handicapped by bashfulness or fear* of not knowing the answer to a question. Believe me, you know a lot more about nursing and health care than your interviewer.
- *Be sure that the interviewer identifies you as an RN.* I have found it best to specify this in advance.

What Nurse Administrators Can Do

The nurse administrator can play a number of vital roles in empowering staff: model, mentor, challenger, facilitator, problem-solver, supporter. It does not diminish one's power to lift others on their climb up the ladder. To the extent that autonomy of staff can be increased through decentralization, self-scheduling, and other innovations, the anger "titer" of the institution will decrease. A number of new unit-level governance structures have been tried, and evaluation data about their impact on staff nurse job satisfaction and clinical outcomes are positive (Hastings & Waltz, 1995; Porter-O'Grady, 2005). The data indicate that some nurse managers have difficulty "letting go" and allowing their staff to participate in decision making. However, involvement in decision making is one of the strongest predictors of staff nurse job satisfaction. In participative management strategies, individuals throughout the organization are given more information and power. The result? A true win–win situation. Not only do the staff appreciate the freedom to make decisions, but studies also show that the managers who work in decentralized hospitals have higher job satisfaction (Acorn, Ratner, & Crawford, 1997; Armstrong, 2005). Likewise, nursing faculty have greater job satisfaction in institutions practicing less formalization and centralization (Mansen, 1993).

What kinds of empowering behaviors are staff nurses really looking for in their leaders? And how do leader behaviors impact staff nurses' work effectiveness? These questions prompted a series of studies by Heather Laschinger and her research team. Five leader behaviors received special scrutiny: (1) enhancing the meaningfulness of work, (2) fostering participation in decision making, (3) facilitating goal accomplishment, (4) expressing confidence in high performance, and (5) providing autonomy from bureaucratic constraints. Of these five behaviors, staff nurses in a 1999 study rated the last two behaviors as most empowering. A strong positive correlation was noted between empowering behavior of the leader and staff nurses' perceptions of their own empowerment. Staff who felt empowered showed increased work effectiveness and had lower job tension (Laschinger, Wong, McMahon, & Kaufmann, 1999). In a second study, involving a random sample with better than usual gender balance (195 males, 217 females), the researchers found that staff nurse empowerment directly affected job satisfaction (Laschinger, Finegan, & Shamian, 2001). Empowerment also strongly affected staff trust in management. Unfortunately, nurses in this study weren't very satisfied with their jobs, and perceived their work setting to be only moderately empowering. It appears that leaders still have work to do. Some don't yet realize that "power begets power" (Kanter, 1977).

Fostering staff *intrapreneurship* is one proven way of empowering staff. Intrapreneurs have creative ideas and implement them *within* their place of employment, instead of establishing a separate business as entrepreneurs do. For example, intrapreneurs at 3M developed those indispensable yellow Post-It notes. In a pilot program at the University of Michigan Hospitals, two-page proposals from nursing service personnel are solicited for new products, processes, or programs and then evaluated by a senior management team. When a proposal is selected for further development, the intrapreneur is matched with a mentor-coach to prepare a business plan. Innovators are honored at a reception given by the hospital CEO (Marszalek-Gaucher & Elsenhans, 1988).

Increasing nurses' power was an explicit goal in one study. The researchers assigned 170 nurses from nine metropolitan hospitals to either an experimental group (which participated in the training activities) or a control group (which went about their usual nursing practice activities). Nurses in the experimental group were taught to apply their analytic skills to organizational problems, to work in teams on planned change projects, to use their colleagues for consultation and support, and to function in a complex bureaucracy. The directors of nursing services in the nine hospitals played key roles in the project. They provided access to resources, information, and support systems. And they interacted with the staff nurses as professional colleagues. Many of the nurses had had no previous contact with nursing leadership, even after working for their institutions for an extended period of time. Findings of the 3-year study showed that members of the experimental group scored higher on outcome measures of nursing power (Gorman & Clark, 1986). This successful and worthwhile project could be replicated in other settings by enlightened nurse administrators.

A Clarion Call for Mentors

A key element of the Gorman and Clark project was the mentoring provided by the nursing directors. Sadly, many RNs say they lack mentors. In July, 2001, Diana Mason, Editor of *American Nursing Journal* wrote an editorial entitled "On Mentorship and Scotch on the Rocks." She fondly recalled two mentors who "took me under their wings . . . and wrapped me in their warmth . . . their laughter nurtured me, their disagreement challenged me, and their guidance encouraged me" (Mason, 2001, p. 7). The response to Mason's editorial was an outpouring of angry letters to the editor from RNs who had experienced horizontal violence instead of mentoring. One aspect of my present job is interviewing prospective PhD students. I often ask them about their mentors. The applicants almost never say that another *nurse* recognized their intellect and encouraged pursuit of a doctoral degree. Occasionally, a family member or a professor from another discipline will be acknowledged. I am left to wonder why the former instructors and managers of these bright men and women did not offer them career guidance. Clearly, we need to do more mentoring in nursing.

RN Connie Vance has devoted a number of years to studying and writing about mentoring (Vance & Olson, 1998). She reminds us that the word *mentor* dates back to Homer. Odysseus, whose travels took him far from home, became worried about his son Telemachus and asked Mentor to take on the tasks of guiding and educating him. So, mentoring is something like parenting, in that one individual with greater life experience and wisdom unselfishly guides a less experienced protégé. The literature describes a continuum of mentoring, ranging from "peer pals" at the same level of the institutional hierarchy (two staff RNs or two middle managers) to "career guides" (seasoned RNs who give novices information and orientation) to *mentors*, who have the most intense relationship with their protégés (Campbell-Heider, 1986).

The mentor–mentee relationship is a special one, characterized by mutual trust and caring. Although some institutions have tried to *assign* mentors—somewhat like an arranged marriage—I question the feasibility of this. The mentor–mentee relationship only works when attitudes, beliefs, and values are compatible (Slagle, 1986). For example, I value (a) meeting deadlines, (b) attention to detail, and (c) straight talk. Mentees that I work best with share these values. In the past, I have been greatly frustrated when I had mentees who procrastinated, made lame excuses, missed deadlines, and/or exhibited carelessness. Now, I make it clear in the beginning what I will expect from them.

Mentors generate power for their mentees by introducing them to people who can further their careers and by recommending them for positions, promotions, and honors. Nurses fortunate enough to have mentors allude to a variety of positive outcomes, including personal growth, heightened awareness of organizational and political systems, greater career advancement, and enhanced career satisfaction (see Olson & Vance, 1993, for a compilation of 81 studies of mentoring). Nurses who have been mentored also assume the responsibility to "pay it forward" by mentoring others.

"If you're not mentoring a nurse or a student, what are you waiting for?" (Diana Mason, 2001, p. 7)

What You Can Do to Mentor Your Peers, Supervisees, or Students

▪ *Identify goals with your mentee.* What experiences and skills would your mentee like to acquire? What is the timeline for your work together?

- *Be clear about your availability* (e.g., hours per week). Some studies show that mentors spend 1 to 3 hours per week with their mentees; you may choose to spend more or less. A blend of role modeling, counseling, and socializing is common.
- *Be clear regarding your expectations.* Do not expect your mentee to become a clone of yourself. Appreciate talents and strengths that differ from your own. However, be clear that certain things are not negotiable (e.g., meeting the deadline for a draft of a journal article).
- *Provide honest, constructive feedback.* It is not a kindness to withhold feedback or "beat around the bush." If your mentee made a presentation, tell the truth about distracting mannerisms or the dozens of "you knows" that disrupted the flow of the talk.
- *Gradually nudge your mentee toward greater independence, visibility, and risk-taking.* For example, my doctoral students write one or more scholarly papers collaboratively with me. Then I nudge them to become first author, and ultimately, sole author. In other settings, such as hospitals or professional organizations, you can encourage your mentees to become involved in policy-making committees or task forces, then coach them until they are ready to serve as committee chair.

What You Can Do to Enhance the Powerful Self

While acquiring a mentor can give you a "leg up" in acquisition of power, there are many steps you can take on your own. Read on for some savvy strategies.

- *Engage in a power analysis.* If you are a researcher, you have learned an entirely different meaning of this term, but here I am using power analysis to mean *identifying potential sources of power* in your present work situation. For example, find out where decisions are made on your concerns. When you have completed your analysis, set some specific goals to work toward. Try to get yourself appointed or elected to a spot on the decision-making committee or board. Once appointed, show up for meetings. You don't have any power if you aren't there. Bring data with you to the meetings to document your arguments. If you've got the facts and figures, it's hard for an opponent to discount your proposal. When asked to assume a new responsibility, run with the opportunity instead of shrinking from it. Do a good job, because people will remember. Work on remembering names, analyzing group dynamics, cultivating a wider network of influential contacts. If you do not have a mentor, be proactive and find yourself one. Many people are pleased and honored to be asked to serve in the capacity of mentor. Then, make your mentor proud!
- *Acquire new knowledge.* Knowledge is power. In today's world, clinical expertise is not enough. Depending on your career trajectory, you may need to learn more about trending, budgeting, marketing, or cost–benefit analysis. Get on board the informatics revolution (see Angela Barron McBride's 2005 article in *Nursing Outlook*). Avail yourself of CE programs, seminars, and workshops. Build a unique repertoire of talents. Make yourself indispensable to your work unit and your institution.

One successful African American woman at our university recommends periodically asking ourselves, "If I leave the job tomorrow, will the show go on without a hitch? If the answer is 'yes,' then you haven't positioned yourself well." Good advice!

▪ *Take an assertiveness class.* This can be a great boost to your career if you have always been timid about standing up for yourself when someone is trying to manipulate you or take advantage of your good nature. Assertiveness is defined as "behavior which enables a person to act in his own best interests, to stand up for himself without undue anxiety, to express his honest feelings comfortably, or to exercise his own rights without denying the rights of others" (Alberti & Emmons, 1974). Assertive behavior is aimed at *equalizing the balance of power*, not putting another person down. A basic assertive statement when you are angry is a firm, clear statement "I am angry" followed by the reason "because ___," and then a request for what you would like to be different. The "broken record" technique can be used to calmly repeat the message several times if the other person doesn't seem to get it: Try this technique if someone is tuning you out or yelling while you speak.

▪ *Speak up.* When delivering an assertive message, lean forward confidently, keep direct eye contact, and don't hesitate, plead, or apologize. Keep your message short. If you are afraid you will become distracted or flustered (for example, when making a request to a supervisor), it may be helpful to prepare for the meeting with the supervisor by writing down in one sentence what you want to accomplish. Read the sentence several times before you go to the meeting. If you get off track during the discussion, remind yourself of that sentence and get back on track. No-no's while making your statement are a hostile, sarcastic tone, accusations, or blaming the other person for your feelings. Assertiveness is a skill that must be practiced. I highly recommend a class that involves role playing and feedback. Classes are frequently offered by university counseling centers and mental health facilities. If you are a faculty member, consider conducting a class for your nursing students after you are comfortable with your own skills. Some years ago, I developed an 11-week plan and conducted the assertiveness training sessions concurrently with the psychiatric-mental health nursing course I taught (Thomas, 1982). Assertiveness instruction is also valuable in leadership and management courses.

▪ *Make your "bubble" bigger.* Your assertive words will have greater impact if they are accompanied by assertive body language. I have used an exercise called "Making Your Bubble Bigger" with students for years. I got the idea from the "First Venusian Anthropological Expedition to Earth" by Nancy Henley. In Henley's (1977) story, Venusians visiting the Earth observe that "all earthlings have a space bubble around them, the amount of space belonging to their own bodies. Dominants have larger space bubbles. . . . One need only watch the Earthlings move about in their bubbles of different sizes, approaching bubble to bubble, to know immediately who is the superior, and who the inferior, in any interaction." You can watch the powerful earthlings—CEOs, doctors, lawyers—and see for yourself how big their bubbles are. You can make your bubble bigger too. Here's how:

> *First, pick a private time and place where you can concentrate, uninter-rupted, on expanding your bubble. Stretch out from the tips of your toes up through the top of your head. Stand tall and straight, make huge, expansive arm and hand gestures, walk around the room like you're royalty. Feel your bubble growing bigger, taking up more space. Sense the increased power and self-confidence that you have as a regal leader. If you like, practice in front of a mirror, paying particular attention to your posture, effective hand gestures, and walking with a determined gait. Then try out your new body language in a low-risk situation, like with a store clerk or waiter who's ignoring you. Later, try making your bubble bigger in increasingly complex situations.*

- *Never acquiesce to the status quo* when you are in a frustrating work situa-tion in which you feel powerless. Unfortunately, women are more likely to do so than men. Mainiero (1986) talked to men and women about work sit-uations of powerlessness and found a much higher percentage of women responding by acquiescence. That is, they acted in a helpless, dependent manner, like the nurses in our sample who had avowed that there was nothing they could do. In contrast, men were more likely to adopt a strat-egy of *persuasion*, discussing the frustrating situation persistently with the person who could supply a remedy. My motto is "Doing something always feels better than doing nothing." I am enough of a realist to know that none of us will ever achieve a perfect work situation. But you will feel better that you acted on your concerns.
- *Master the art of persuasion.* You cannot acquire or exert power unless you are verbally articulate. Classes in speech-making or debate tech-niques can be helpful in learning how to mount an argument and deliver it with maximum impact. Such classes frequently involve videotaping, so that you can see yourself as others see you. Classmates can be help-ful in critiquing your hand gestures and other mannerisms that detract from your overall effectiveness. Linguist Deborah Tannen (1994) points out that *how* you deliver your message is of crucial importance. Don't preface your remarks with disclaimers such as "I don't know if this will work, but..." or "You may have already tried this, but..." Speak with certainty and repeat key points. This way of speaking is more difficult for women, who tend to lower their voices, hesitate, and make disclaimers when arguing a position (Tannen, 1994).
- *Collect—or locate—data to support your arguments.* Ever since Nightingale presented soldier mortality data in skillfully prepared graphs, we have understood the power of data. It is encouraging that so many contempo-rary nurse researchers are collecting data on *nursing-sensitive outcomes*; that is, measurable changes in patients' conditions or behaviors because of nursing actions. Nurses are studying outcomes such as the number of patient infections and pressure ulcers, as well as significant decreases in patient symptoms such as fatigue, pain, or dyspnea. Thus, it will be easier

in the future to convince policy makers and decision makers that nursing makes a difference (Doran, 2003). This rapidly accumulating empirical evidence is invaluable in our ongoing efforts to demonstrate the need for safe hospital staffing.

- *Become involved in organizations.* Join your district nurses association and community groups, taking the microphone to practice your skills in speaking to a main motion or defending a position. My district nurses association was definitely a leadership training ground for me over the years. I am an introvert by nature, and I used to be very hesitant to speak before a group. After my first trip to the state convention as a delegate, I was nervous about having to give a report at the district meeting. My knees were actually shaking when I stood at the podium to report. Who would have dreamed that someday I would be appearing on "Good Morning America" and making speeches to hundreds at the American Nurses Association (ANA)? But, as I became more involved in organizational work, I became much more comfortable in speaking, proposing actions, persuading others to support a plan I had concocted, debating without being overly emotional, convening caucuses to negotiate compromises, and other vital skills. I watched ANA leaders who had these skills and emulated them.

- *Extend your networking to the national (and/or international) levels*, and don't confine your conference attendance solely to those offered by nursing organizations. Interdisciplinary collaboration is increasingly important. After you are registered to attend a prestigious conference, do some homework to find out who will be present. You can Google prominent leaders to learn more about their current foci before you go. Introduce yourself to leaders during coffee breaks, and mention your own goals and interests. Carry business cards and distribute them freely. Jot notes on the back, such as "interested in serving on legislative committee." You may be pleasantly surprised to receive a call or e-mail later about an opportunity to serve on that very committee.

- *Aspire to leadership roles*—not because you need to collect a batch of titles such as President, Director, or Board Member—but because you want to make a difference. At a Sigma Theta Tau International conference in Indianapolis, I was given a little book called *You Don't Need a Title to Be a Leader* (Sanborn, 2006). The author emphasizes that each of us, every day, can display leadership behaviors. I like the story of the window-washer at the World Trade Center who became a leader on 9/11. Jan Demczur, with his bucket and squeegee, was stranded at the fiftieth floor of Tower One after the terrorist attack. He, along with five other men, was on an elevator—and the electricity had gone out. Although most of his fellow elevator passengers were executives, it was the window-washer who assumed the role of leader. First, he used his squeegee to pry open the elevator door, then directed the efforts of the other men in chopping a hole through the layers of drywall that greeted them once the door was open (the elevator was an express with no opening at the fiftieth floor). All the men escaped death that day because of the leadership exhibited by the window-washer (Goleman, 2002).

A Last Word

I hope that this chapter has persuaded you to take a new stance toward the concept of power. What clout our profession could wield if we achieved horizontal power, not horizontal violence! If you are an administrator or a seasoned nurse, I hope you are reaching out to novices who need mentoring. If you are not yet in a leadership role, I hope you are undertaking some steps toward a more powerful self. How will you know when you have achieved empowerment? According to psychologist Judith Worell (1996), an empowered individual has the characteristics listed below. Assess yourself on each:

- Positive self-esteem, self valuing
- Positive comfort–distress quotient
- Internal personal control
- Avoidance of self-deprecation
- Flexibility in gendered beliefs and behaviors
- Assertiveness
- Knowledge of important resources

These characteristics should look familiar, as much of this book has been devoted to actions to improve your self-esteem, lessen distress, and enhance control and assertiveness. But we're not quite finished. Worell says—and I heartily agree—that an empowered individual also has competence in problem-solving and acts as a change agent and social activist. Empowerment is an empty concept unless linked to a commitment to challenging oppression (Ward & Mullender, 1991). "The mouse has to know what to do after it roars." Once empowered, nurses must use their intelligence, creativity, and political savvy to address the problems in the profession.

Solving Problems

We are all faced with a series of great opportunities—brilliantly disguised as unsolvable problems.

—John Gardner

There is an old saying about the three kinds of people: those who make things happen, those who watch things happen, and those who don't know what's happening. This chapter is for those of you who want to make things happen—to solve the problems that interfere with your ability to practice your profession in the way that you want. In this chapter, we look at a dozen problems that nurses told us about and strategies to solve them. Stressful, emotionally upsetting events come with the territory in nursing. But research shows that problem-focused coping is significantly correlated with a reduction in psychological stress symptoms (Hedin, 1994) and better mental health (Chang, Bidewell, Huntington, Daly, Johnson, Wilson, Lambert, & Lambert, 2007). As politician Pat Schroeder puts it, "You can't roll up your sleeves and wring your hands at the same time." Throughout the chapter, nursing leaders candidly share their experiences of rolling up their sleeves and grappling with some tough situations. As you read their stories, keep the following principles in mind:

Principles of Problem-Solving

- *Learn to view problems as a natural part of life.* It is not bad to have problems, nor does their presence imply weakness.
- *Think before jumping to a solution.* It is more adaptive to do some thinking about the problem before attempting to solve it.
- *Engage in the process of problem-solving* with the conviction that most problems can be solved.
- *Take responsibility for problems that can be attributed (at least in part) to yourself.*
- *State what you can do, not what you can't do.* Having a goal provides direction and incentive
- *Consider whether your solution to the problem is legally and socially acceptable.*
- *Consider whether your solution to the problem is within your power and ability.* The most common error people make when problem-solving is forgetting that they can control only their own behavior (Bedell & Lennox, 1996).

Problem 1: If Your Workplace Is Unsafe

RN Karen Daley received exposure to both HIV and hepatitis C virus through a needlestick injury in the emergency room where she worked. This injury could have been prevented if her employer had provided safer sharps protection devices. But in 1998, when this happened to Karen, less than 15% of employers did so. The needlestick injury forced her to leave the work she loved and plunged her into a rigorous regimen of medical treatment. It was a nightmare. Karen displayed incredible courage, not only in fighting for her own health but also in undertaking 2 years of passionate testimony across the nation, so that legislation would be enacted to mandate safer sharps protection devices. She moved beyond anger to constructive action, as she explains:

> I struggled for some time to come to terms with the anger I felt and to understand why this had happened to me. But I've also always believed that things happen for a reason, regardless whether it appears to make sense at the time. Once I moved beyond the anger, I was able to see more clearly that... I could perhaps use my experience and position within the nursing community to prevent an injury like mine from happening to others. (Daley, 2002, p. 414).

Although Karen was thrilled to be invited to the Oval Office to witness President Clinton's signing of the Needlestick Safety Prevention Act in 2000, she warned that "Challenges remain with regard to every aspect of health and safety in the workplace" (2002, p. 419). Prevention of injury must become a national priority. It is incumbent on every nurse to speak out about unsafe practices and equipment. Many issues are deserving of activism like Daley's. For example, back injuries are still far too common—affecting 38% of nurses—but many facilities have yet to employ newer types of lift devices or lift teams (Allen, 2003). As the obesity epidemic widens, the need for lift devices assumes even greater urgency. On a typical day at one urban hospital, 15 patients required "big boy beds" (for people weighing over 350 pounds) (Allen, 2005, p. 6). When you realize that nurses already lose more days of work from back injuries than construction workers, it's clear that much remains to be done (Nelson, Fragala, & Menzel, 2003). Bearing in mind that 40% of working RNs will be over age 50 by the year 2010, smart institutions will design safer and more ergonomically sensitive work processes—or they won't be able to retain mature nurses (Buerhaus, Staiger, & Auerbach, 2000).

Problem 2: If You're Beaten Down by Bureaucracy

A host of studies show that it is not nursing work that causes RNs to burn out, but the impediments to self-determined practice. The restrictions of bureaucratic institutions stifle nurses' creativity and independence. But I am going to share with you a terrific example of how to transform a workplace. As the nurses themselves described their situation, they were part of a "fiercely patriarchal and autocratic hospital culture" (Breda et al., 1997). Fortunately, they understood that if changes were to occur, their own actions would have to be the catalyst. So, a small group of psychiatric nurses at this hospital undertook a project to increase the autonomy of nurses there. The project involved a number of elements, including formation of a study group to prepare for certification, incorporation of new holistic healing interventions into their nursing practice, presentation of educational sessions and retreats for the staff, and increased participation in multidisciplinary teams. From an oppressed group, these nurses evolved to become increasingly confident, outspoken, and articulate:

> The... project allowed us to experience a new sense of dignity about ourselves as professionals, which we call "ownership of practice." Ownership of practice includes many of the dimensions of autonomy—control over our practice, the freedom to make decisions, and the quality of professional exchange with colleagues that we always sought. We also [became] mentors and role models for less experienced and new nurses. Above all, we developed a firm sense of making a difference with clients and within the organization as a whole. We had become secure in our knowledge base, and were no longer willing to be subordinated by others. We recognized that autonomy is linked to power and that the many limits placed on our practice were simply a way to keep nurses in line. (Breda et al., 1997, p. 79)

The story has a happy ending. Physicians and social workers responded positively to the newly empowered nurses. In fact, the only resistance they encountered was from a few nurses who did not *want* to become more autonomous (these nurses had been well indoctrinated to believe that "the hospital knows what's best for us," and they saw no benefit of change). This successful project shows that nurses can challenge institutional rules and norms that limit nurses' autonomy. Instead of leaving for greener pastures, like so many nurses opt to do, Breda and her colleagues stayed put in the same system and transformed it.

Another way to transform a hospital is pursuing the prestigious "magnet" accreditation status conferred by the American Nurses Association (ANA).

Nursing autonomy and control over practice are the keys to the success of magnet hospitals (Kramer & Schmalenberg, 2003). The magnet movement began after the first study was reported in 1983 (McClure, Poulin, Sovie, & Wandelt). The study highlighted the importance of a powerful nursing leader, adequate support services, good relationships among colleagues, and opportunities for RNs to participate in policy decisions. Hospitals exhibiting these features are able to attract and retain staff even in times of nurse shortage: Nurse researcher Linda Aiken calls the magnet program "the single most effective and evidence-based reform of the hospital workplace in the last two decades" (cited in Armstrong, 2005, p. 17). Before a hospital can earn magnet status, it must offer opportunities for RN recognition, advancement, and additional education. Also, it must invest in technologies that nurses find useful (Pekkanen, 2003). You could be a catalyst in starting a movement toward "magnetism" in your hospital. For additional details, see the new book by McClure and Hinshaw, *Magnet Hospitals Revisited*.

Problem 3: If You're Being Sexually Harassed

As shown in our research data, both male and female nurses still endure sexual harassment, despite greater societal consciousness-raising about harassment. RNs will continue to be harassed until more of us take action to report—and prevent—its occurrence. Even though there have been some highly publicized lawsuits in recent years, statistics show that 90% of episodes of harassment in this country are not reported to anyone in authority in the organization where they occur (Rutter, 1996). The first step that must be taken when someone invades your space, touches you, or makes a suggestive remark, is to make a clear, direct verbal response: "I don't appreciate that." The harasser often feigns surprise and acts as though you are making something out of nothing. If you get such a reaction, stand your ground and describe very specifically what bothered you: "You were standing too close to me" or "I find your language offensive." It is important that you call attention to the inappropriate behavior early on, because studies show that harassment on the job is seldom a one-time thing. Sexual remarks and pressure for dates often go on for 6 months or more (Fitzgerald, 1993). If the harassing behavior continues, warn the individual that you may have to discuss the matter with his supervisor or with the human resources department. Many institutions have someone designated to deal with cases of harassment. Keep written records of incidents and warnings that you have given. Include the names of witnesses to the egregious behavior. Send a registered letter to the offender asking that the harassment stop, keeping a file copy for yourself. If none of your initial limit-setting efforts are successful in stopping the harassment, filing a formal complaint or seeking legal counsel may be necessary. Although going to court can be a time-consuming and expensive undertaking, many lawyers collect no fee if the case is lost or if no money is awarded for damages. Guidance in dealing with sexual harassment issues can be obtained by calling a toll-free hot line: 1-800-522-0925. Do be aware of the Equal Employment Opportunity Commission's requirement that a complaint must be filed within either 180 or 300 days from the date of the incident, depending on the state where you live (Rutter, 1996). Of course, far better than these last-resort remedies is prevention of the harassment in the first place. Its incidence will surely begin to decline when all nurses are the strong, empowered individuals that this book is devoted to developing.

Problem 4: If You're the Recipient of Horizontal Hostility

As discussed in Chapter 5, there are several effective ways to deal with the problem of horizontal hostility, including direct confrontation of the other nurse as soon as you learn of his destructive gossip or sabotage. Here, Luther Christman provides an example of another approach: using humor.

> *As many probably are aware, I was the first man in the profession to be appointed as a dean of nursing. Two years after this appointment, I was attending a meeting of deans of nursing. After the opening plenary session, the dean of one of the major university schools walked to a floor microphone and asked everyone to remain until she made an important statement. She announced, "All those wonderful things you have heard about what is happening at Vanderbilt School of Nursing have nothing to do with Luther Christman's competence because he doesn't have any. The only reason the programs are taking place is because every man on the entire faculty automatically gives in to any request he makes whenever he makes it." A dead and strained silence ensued as she stood at the microphone with her hands on her hips. I sensed the great uneasiness and moved to the floor microphone that was closest to me. Even though I was somewhat irked, I merely commented, "She just says that because it is true." Titters, then roars of laughter followed. The dean stood somewhat stunned and annoyed as everyone left the room. All those who approached me were jovial in their interactions with me.*
>
> *Perceiving events with a humorous slant helps to keep blood pressure at normal levels. I had a very early experience that helped me understand behavior. When I was a first-year student in nursing, I established a pleasant relationship with the chief of psychiatry. One day I said to him, "Dr. Bond, you appear to be different from any other person in this hospital. I have never seen you upset or disturbed by anything that happens." He replied, "Young man, you too can be that way. Whenever I am interacting with other people, I always treat them as if they were paranoid schizophrenics. Who can become upset over what a paranoid schizophrenic says or does?" I have used this concept all my professional life, and it has enabled me to be relaxed and not as irritated as many. A few months after that incident with the dean, I learned that that very morning she had been called into the chancellor's office and given 5 minutes to resign or be discharged. This helped explain why she had projected her anger at me.*

Problem 5: If You're Unfairly Blamed

Linda Harvey, a med-surg nurse, was angry that she alone was unfairly blamed for a medication error for which at least one other person should have been held responsible. In this incident, Linda used her anger productively to advocate for herself. She explained to the director of nursing that, although she was in error when she administered potassium to a patient who'd been taken off the supplement, the outgoing nurse hadn't flagged the change in orders in the Kardex or the chart—and she'd forgotten to tell Linda about it at shift report. The hospital's medication error report form was subsequently revised to accommodate shared responsibility. And hospital policy was modified to put more red flags into effect when changes were made to a patient's medication regimen. Because of Linda's actions, nurses who make a medication error at that hospital now experience a less punitive aftermath.

Problem 6: If Others Are Not Responsive to Your Concerns About a Patient

Advocating on behalf of a patient is an important aspect of good nursing. In previous chapters, we included some short vignettes in which anger empowered nurses to go to bat for their patients. The following is a longer, more complex account, involving anger not only at the patient's doctors, but also at his nurses, and requiring a number of strategies on the part of this nurse. First, she explains the problem:

> The patient was in cardiac intensive care with complications after open heart surgery. A protracted hospitalization involving postoperative bleeding, a nosocomial infection, and extended ventilator dependence, left him anxious and depressed. Part of my anger was related to staff, who seemed to have a much lower idea of a standard of care than I did. For instance, immediately after surgery, the clinical specialist called to tell the family to say "he is okay," and was ready to hang up. When I said we needed more details about blood loss and the surgical procedures, the clinical specialist had no idea and did not propose to do anything else. My anger grew as staff skipped some informed consents, ignored suggestions for a communication board for the vent-dependent patient, disregarded the need to treat anxiety and depression, and failed to order some important lab tests. When I asked the staff what communication aids they used for these patients, they thought a communication board was a good idea. They said they used to have one, but it disappeared. I was irritated when staff did not explain problems to the patient. The patient became more depressed as the surgical team delayed removing the ET tube, never clarifying why, and avoided speaking with him for several days.

The nurse used diverse tactics to problem-solve on this patient's behalf:

> I've rarely been so angry that colleagues did not provide a standard of care, and yet I needed to contain the anger and negotiate with staff to improve patient care. In several instances where the proposed action seemed unwise, I asked the professionals for their rationale so I could explain it to the patient. This was effective because often I was told, "This is what we do," and I could inquire about their procedures for individualizing care. Initially, I offered suggestions, such as the communication board. Although staff thought this a good idea, nothing happened. I then brought the patient paper and pen. Next, I wanted to address the patient's anxiety. I gathered necessary data and determined the best person to approach. The chief resident did agree to order medications,

but ordered oral medications and did not order the necessary Haldol until the patient's agitation and confusion prompted him to pull out the tubes.

I ignored the small frustrations and focused on the patient's major issues, and I worked to form alliances with the staff. All the consultants encouraged removal of the ET tube, but they seemed impotent. I confronted the surgical team because the patient wanted the tube removed, but the surgeons avoided him and failed to do so. After paging, leaving messages, and other attempts to speak with the surgeon, I decided to stay with the patient until rounds. However, the evening RN asked me to leave. I agreed, provided that she would communicate the patient's wishes to the surgeon. She replied that she did not think she could. I stared at her in amazed silence and anger. I did not raise my voice as I said, "You do not believe it is the nurse's role to advocate and communicate for a patient on a ventilator?"

I conveyed the patient's distress and frustration to the surgical resident, and asked that the surgeons talk with him daily and provide a clear answer about when the ET tube would be removed. After this, the surgical team did talk with him daily, but days passed without explaining to the patient the continued ET tube. The surgeon refused my request for a team conference with family, surgeons, and consultants. The patient lost about one-fifth of his body weight before finally, after much nudging, nutritional supplements were ordered. And finally, the surgeons agreed to extubate, oxygenation was adequate, a defective ET tube was discovered, and the patient left intensive care.

Although this nurse, through constant vigilance and persistent advocacy, was able to get staff to address her concerns, what other avenues are available to you? If you fail to resolve a concern about patient care quality or safety through workplace channels, what can you do? Your options include filing a complaint with your state's Board of Nursing, Department of Health, Insurance Commissioner, or elected representatives (look in the state government pages of your telephone book). Written complaints about a health care organization can also be made to the Joint Commission for Accreditation of Health Care Organizations. The address is 1 Renaissance Blvd., Oakbrook Terrace, Illinois, 60181. The telephone number for complaints is 800-994-6610, or you can send an e-mail complaint to complaint@jointcommission.org. Be sure to document inadequate staffing, unsafe practices, accidents, injuries, and missed treatments; make notes about dates, times, and personnel. You can report potential problems as well as actual ones. Send a copy of your written complaint to your state nurses association (now called a *constituent member association*) to assist in tracking problems (American Nurses Association, 1995).

Problem 7: If Your Unit Is Experiencing Intergenerational Conflict

How many generations are working together in your workplace today? Do you work among a disparate mixture of "Veterans" (born 1925–1945), "Baby Boomers" (born 1946–1964), "Generation X'ers" (born 1965–1980), and "Millenials" (born 1980–2000)? If so, your workplace may be rife with misunderstandings—simply because these four cohorts can be very different in work ethic, communication style, and other characteristics (Duchscher & Cowin, 2004b). To cite just one example, Veterans and Boomers may be uncomfortable with the increased computerization being introduced in health care, whereas it is "duck soup" to younger cohorts. If your unit is experiencing intergenerational conflict, heed Marge Pike's sage advice in 11.1 (reprinted with permission from Sigma Theta Tau International):

11.1 Who are you—Andy, Opie, or Aunt Bea?

Many of our new and junior nurses (in practice only a few years) state that no one helps or mentors them! They feel isolated and unvalued. Senior nurses, on the other hand, those in practice for 10 or more years, relate that younger nurses are not willing to recognize and learn from their knowledge and years of experience.

At times, it is hard for junior nurses to understand that things were different in nursing, not only decades ago, but just a few years ago. It might be time to better understand what experienced nurses have accomplished. These nurses worked during wars and international conflicts, the civil rights movement, and the women's movement and have worked hard to establish university-based nursing schools with undergraduate and graduate degree programs. It was for their future, and indeed, for future generations of nurses that they worked to make things better. These senior nurses, on the other hand, should not forget their early years of practice and the support and understanding they needed from senior staff. Also, they need to remember that they, too, at times felt brighter and smarter than more senior nurses.

A story was told to me the other day, and it made me think of our nursing profession. It had to do with "The Andy Griffith Show" from the 1960s. One of the initial shows, if not the very first, had Aunt Bea coming to live with the recently widowed sheriff, Andy, and his young son, Opie.

Andy invited Aunt Bea to live with him and Opie in the hopes of keeping the family together and providing a loving, homelike atmosphere. Opie made sure that Aunt Bea knew he didn't care for any of her recipes; his mother had cooked everything better. Any of Aunt Bea's rules were not ones his mother would have enforced. She couldn't do the things Opie's mother used to do with him, such as frogging, fishing, and throwing a baseball.

Aunt Bea decided things were not working out and told Andy it was best for her to leave. Andy begged her to stay, but she said it just wasn't going to work out. She said it was best for her to leave quickly and quietly after Opie was asleep, and that somehow, they would be able to manage without her. The night arrived for Aunt Bea's silent departure, and as Andy was loading the car trunk with her possessions, the noise woke Opie. As he went to the window and peered out, a look of horror came across his face when he realized what was happening. He rushed down the stairs and out to the porch yelling to his father, "Aunt Bea can't leave. She needs us!"

When I heard this story, I thought about families and all the different roles, each member bringing strengths and flaws, each perceiving one another differently. How could Aunt Bea replace Opie's mom, tucking him in at night, hugging him in his mom's special way? Here was Aunt Bea, unable to do all the things little boys like to do—catch a fish, a frog, a high fly ball. Aunt Bea brought all her love, wisdom, and experience, but at this point and time in Opie's life, it was not recognized or desired. Andy, of course, just wanted everything to work out! The one thing he forgot to do was bring his little son and his aunt together to discuss the issues openly and honestly.

I loved the retelling of this episode of the show! My mind began to think beyond our personal families to community or work groups that are family to us. In these groups, I think we also have Opies, Aunt Beas, and Andys.

Let's take a look at our own nursing profession. Are there times when we have young nurses feeling like Opie? No one can do things the way they want or think it should be done. The senior nurses might feel like Aunt Bea. They can't quite get the knack of "frogging and fishing," so they pack their bags and leave. There are the Andys, who are caught up in the hardship of the work environment and can't figure a way to bring the Opies and the Aunt Beas together.

I believe we are, at times, one of these three characters, depending on the situation. As young nurses, we hate things because it isn't what we thought it would be. The senior nurses are weary because it isn't like it used to be. Both new and experienced nurses can't understand why some nurses find it hard to learn new ways of doing things or find no value in acquired wisdom and experience.

And so the challenge to us as nurses, both senior and junior, is to have the ability to peer through the window and cry out, "You can't go! You need us!"; or "You can't go! We need you!" We have to run down the stairs, unload the trunk and together figure out how to keep the nursing profession wise, innovative, on the cutting edge and the best it can be (Pike, 2003).

Problem 8: If You're Working for Cruella DeVil

What if your problem is an unreasonable manager, supervisor, or dean? It is no secret that individuals with personality disorders and other kinds of mental pathology can and do achieve leadership positions in organizations. Having to work under such an individual can be pure hell. Here's one nurse's story:

Twice in my career, I have been deeply involved in the removal of a key person in a school of nursing. In the first instance, the individual attempted the divide-and-conquer approach. She got the weakest members of the faculty on her side through showing favoritism. At the same time, she attempted to make life hell for those of us she perceived as threats or as strong persons. One favorite tactic was to call me into her office and scream at me. Needless to say, the stress was unbearable. Much as I was angry at the perpetrator of this misery, I was even angrier at colleagues who, behind her back, would go on and on about how bad things were but, to her face, and to outside evaluators who were brought in, would say everything was wonderful. Six of us—three tenured and three nontenured—went to administration. I felt we stuck our necks out and then did not get support.

I decided, however, that it would be self-destructive to let the stress and anger eat at me, so I channeled it into scholarly work. I wrote a number of books, articles, did presentations, collaborated with clinical and academic colleagues on research projects. When it became clear that the top administration at the university was too afraid of the legislature to act, I made plans to leave. Having built up my scholarship, service, and teaching records significantly, I was able to use my work to negotiate for the position I wanted. Furthermore, among those of us who left, as well as those who stood strong, there grew a camaraderie and a feeling that justice would win out eventually.

When a new president was appointed, he examined the data, looked at the accomplishments of those of us who had left, and acted swiftly to end the reign of terror. Not only did I take away my integrity as a faculty member intact, but I also learned from the experience how to handle another, should it arise—and it did. The style was in some ways different, but many of the tactics were the same. This time I rallied all the tenured faculty and insisted that the only way we would eventually win would be to stand together. We did, and the administration acted.

One of the most valuable tactics I learned was to turn negative energy and anger into positive activities. Secondly, I learned to consult wise persons from other disciplines. Third, I learned how to counter the divide-and-conquer tactics used by many destructive and insecure leaders. What was not so evident to me the first time around was crystal clear the second.

Problem 9: If You're Incensed by Offensive Portrayals of Nurses in the Media

Weary of the portrayals of nurses on "Grey's Anatomy" and "House," not to mention irritating commercials using sexy nurses to sell products? These offensive portrayals of nurses in the media won't decrease until thousands of us make our displeasure evident. Strategies include boycotting products promoted in offensive advertisements and writing letters to editors of newspapers and magazines. The Center for Nursing Advocacy (www.nursingadvocacy.org) has been particularly vigilant with regard to television and advertisements. For example, within the past year, the nonprofit Center has led letter-writing campaigns in response to:

- Television character Dr. House suggesting to another doctor that they could rank nurses in order of "do-ability."
- On another TV show, Dr. Steve-O's nurse "hot babe Trishelle" offering sexual attention to Dr. Steve-O.
- A TV ad for Dentyne gum showing female RNs being lured into bed with male patients.
- A marketing campaign for Coors beer featuring models dressed as "naughty nurses."
- A radio commercial for Bloomingale's department store in which a sultry nurse was seducing a doctor with a cashmere sweater.

The Center's letter-writing campaigns have convinced many advertisers and scriptwriters to depict nurses more accurately. You can join the Center for Nursing Advocacy or donate money to support its work. You can also help by monitoring the media and alerting staff when you see negative or inaccurate portrayals of nurses and their work. For more information, contact RN Sandy Summers, the executive director, at ssummers@nursingadvocacy.org.

Problem 10: If Your Task Seems Impossible

Distinguished nursing leader Angela Barron McBride has always seemed un-flappable to me, calmly taking on the presidency of nursing's largest organization (Sigma Theta Tau International) and later the deanship of the nation's largest nursing school (Indiana University). Here, McBride tells us about a seemingly impossible task that provoked anger, and how she dispelled the anger:

I am a great believer in the extent to which explanations of events consequently shape feelings, behavior, and future expectations. When I became Dean of In-diana University School of Nursing—one school of nursing but with offerings on eight campuses—I was angry not to find much of a paper trail in the files that described what was intended in the development of a so-called univer-sity school. I was expected to manage a structure that had only been vaguely defined, but required me to interact not only with a president, but eight chan-cellors and eight academic vice-chancellors. I wanted principles spelled out to use in guiding future actions, and was angry that mine was an impossible task: to manage an entity about which there were no common agreements, either at the university or school levels.

It is not uncommon for new administrators to want to bring down the fu-ries of the gods on those who have gone before, and seem to have created what does not make sense by today's standards. The trouble with such anger is that it leaves one sulky instead of action-oriented. What helped me was to recon-ceptualize the situation.

First of all, what the university was experiencing was generally true for other schools operating university-wide. In a matrix organization where dis-cipline interacts with campus mores, matters will never be clear because of the organizational complexity. Second, I began to see that the school was at a different developmental stage. The issue was no longer the establishment of basic programs but moving existing programs forward so they could address the needs of quickly changing health care delivery systems. I always feel better when I conceptualize a problem as generic or developmental rather than per-sonal, because the former makes me feel as if I'm dealing with the issues of the day while the latter makes me feel negative about my institution and my own abilities.

Finally, I came to realize that the university probably was only now ready to have the various chancellors, academic vice-chancellors, and nursing leaders go through the task of forging common understandings, because some trust had been established, and we were now capable of higher-order thinking. Since one of my talents is bringing people together for a common purpose, I began to feel as if there might be a fit between my person and the place. My generalized anger began to dissipate as I got down to the task at hand.

Problem 11: If You've Gotten a Pink Slip

What if the unthinkable happens, and you find yourself the recipient of a pink slip?

Barry Adams was a whistle-blower. He got his pink slip when he spoke out about his concerns about patient safety. He did all the right things when he went to meet with his director of nursing. He had the data to document errors and injury. But the director told him, "There are no unsafe work environments, only unsafe nursing practice" (Adams, 1997, p. 80). He was terminated for "insubordination." After Adams was fired, he filed a wrongful termination suit against the hospital. In a chilling coincidence, the same day that an article about his lawsuit appeared in the *Boston Globe*, the newspaper also reported the accidental death of a patient at the hospital that had fired him. The nurse who had given the lethal morphine overdose had had no previous training in infusion pumps—exactly the dangerous kind of situation Adams had placed his job on the line to protest.

Adams filed a complaint with the National Labor Relations Board (NLRB) and a complaint against the director of nursing and the hospital administrator (also a nurse) with the Massachusetts Board of Registration in Nursing. He won his NLRB case, with the judge ruling that his firing was an "illegal attempt to silence and retaliate against him" (Buresh & Gordon, 2000, p. 198), and he won national attention by courageous media appearances and an article in *Newsweek*. Legislation protecting whistle-blowers like Adams was passed in Massachusetts in 1999. I wish I could say that the Board of Nursing ruling was favorable as well. Unfortunately, his complaint against his nursing director and administrator was dismissed. Adams, understandably, felt a deep sense of betrayal, but says, "If I had to do it all over again, I would" (cited in Buresh & Gordon, 2000, p. 200).

Ageism was the culprit in the next nurse's unfair termination. Internationally known nursing scholar Phyllis Stern received a pink slip from her university at the age of 65. The Canadian Supreme Court had ruled that forced retirement is *not* a violation of an individual's human rights, and the financially strapped university saw an opportunity to cut the faculty complement with impunity. But Phyllis was not prepared for this development, and not ready to retire. Having earned her doctorate in mid-life, she was chronologically in mid-career and thriving on a busy schedule of teaching, research, and professional society leadership. Furthermore, she had not taught at the institution long enough to accrue a livable pension and feared running out of money in her forced retirement. To put it mildly, Phyllis was angry at becoming just a number—65. Here's what happened:

> We got 2 weeks' notice after the Supreme Court decision that our services would no longer be needed after June 30. Most faculty in Canadian universities are unionized, and mine was no exception. So, I went to a union meeting, and here were nine old guys and the lone woman. Their chins were dragging on the table. They were feeling used up and cast out. I felt that way for about a week. But I found my mouth too crowded with my thumb stuck in it. So I got busy.
>
> Although I was a Canadian citizen, I had kept my U.S. citizenship. So, unlike the nine old guys, I had options. I started calling around to my U.S.

network. I looked at the ads, but glossed over most. I applied for a chair position at IUPUI. I wasn't hot about living in Indianapolis, but my husband gave me his usual line, "Keep an open mind." Well, it turned out to be a nifty place, and I've been happier in this job than any I've had until now. I am the oldest person working here at the school. I'm still trying to decide what I want to be when I grow up.

For each of these individuals, and for you, if you lose your job, the concept of *transition* is useful. The word means a change from one thing to another. Even when the change is viewed as positive (marriage, childbirth), there is a loss of the way things were. We cannot ever go back again to the way things were. What do we know from research about transitions? Certainly, they are more difficult when they occur suddenly and you have no choice—like a pink slip with no warning. Transitions are also more difficult if you customarily view change as scary rather than challenging. And, without a doubt, any transition will be more difficult if you do not have adequate support from significant others. The timing of events in relation to the life cycle is important too: A career transition will be more stressful if you are simultaneously involved in your mid-life crisis (or another of life's developmental transitions). Having undergone a number of life transitions, including death of my parents, mid-life divorce, becoming a single parent, remarriage, and becoming a stepparent, as well as numerous career peregrinations, I have always taken comfort in the maxim that all change *requires* the death of something in order that something new may develop.

One of the best empirical examinations of life transitions has been completed by Levinson (1978, 1996). Through in-depth study of the lives of men and women, he learned that the life structure evolves through a sequence of alternating stable periods and transitional periods. Each of the transitional periods ordinarily lasts about 5 years. Therefore, if you tally them up, almost half our adult lives is spent in transitions (Levinson, 1996). If we can wrap our minds around this fact, I believe it is reassuring. After we complete necessary tasks of terminating, questioning, and exploring new options, we build a new life structure that will serve us well—until the next transition.

Transitions are inevitable, and most of us endure them and grow because of them—even if initially the disruption was of great magnitude.

As you problem-solve to deal with a job layoff or termination, consider a radically new career direction. If you have always been a provider of clinical services, perhaps you would enjoy teaching. There is a huge shortage of nursing faculty, causing schools of nursing to turn away qualified applicants. You could help educate the next generation of nurses. Perhaps the prospects of doing research sound appealing. Maybe you're ready for a leadership role. It's not too late for you to go to graduate school. I teach students in their thirties, forties, and fifties every day. They are excited about their new trajectory. You could also consider opening an independent practice. More and more nurses are doing so.

Problem 12: If Action by an Individual Is Not Enough

Some thorny problems cannot be solved by individual action; the power of the collective is required. Recall the words of Helen Keller: *"Alone we can do so little; together we can do so much."* System problems require system solutions. Nursing's best thinkers and strategists must unite to lobby, persuade, and negotiate. Think of geese that fly in V formation. As each goose flaps its wings, it creates an uplift for the birds that follow. By flying in V formation, the flock adds 71% greater flying range than if each bird flew alone. Fortunately, nurses are recognizing that we need to flock together to be successful. Read on to consider some of the possibilities.

Collective Bargaining. Collective bargaining is one strategy that nurses have used to gain control of their work environments and their practice. Erroneously, you may presume that collective bargaining inevitably means going on strike. Strikes by RNs are actually rare. More often, when nurses organize, negotiations are successful in achieving a contract that ensures better working conditions. A strike is the last resort, when management fails to respond to nursing concerns, such as insufficient staffing or required floating to unfamiliar units. A crisis point had been reached at St. Catherine of Siena Medical Center in New York in November, 2001. Explains Barbara Crane, the RN who heads the hospital bargaining unit, "the issue of mandatory overtime had come to a crisis point. . . . We were no longer able to keep our new nurses due to the demands of mandatory overtime" (cited in Martin, 2002, p. 8). Four-hundred seventy-four nurses went out on strike November 26. They organized outreach efforts to the community, including parades and distribution of informational leaflets. The strike was prolonged, but the nurses were unified. They won strong contract language prohibiting mandatory overtime except in the case of emergency. Although salary was not the primary issue precipitating the strike at St. Catherine's, the new contract did provide for a salary increase as well.

Collective bargaining clearly gave these nurses clout that they would not otherwise have had. Only a few nurses choose this route, however. Only 18.5% of RNs are covered by a collective bargaining agreement (United American Nurses/American Nurses Association, 2001). Some of them are represented by trade unions (e.g., Service Employees International Union) and others by nurses' unions such as the National Nurses Organizing Council (NNOC) and the United American Nurses (UAN). There have been reports of NNOC engaging in "raids" on staff RNs who already belong to UAN (Barey, 2005). According to Foley (2002), exaggerated promises are often made by unions that are trying to entice people to decertify their existing union and join another. If you are considering union membership, or a switch in unions, I encourage you to interview current members about their satisfaction with the representation they receive.

Workplace Advocacy. What alternative is available to nurses who view unionization as "unprofessional?" One alternative route to address deplorable job conditions is through the services of a workplace advocacy organization. Individuals who do not live in collective bargaining states should contact the Center for American Nurses. The Center equips nurses to advocate for themselves and their patients. Audio conferences have been held on topics such as improving the workplace and legal aspects of delegation. Please see the Center's web site (www.centerforamericannurses.org) for further information, including educational and self-assessment tools.

Professional Organizations. I am a firm believer in joining together in professional organizations to build a base of power. However, only a small percentage (20%) of RNs belong to any nursing organization (Foley, 2001). Roberts (1983) attributes nurses' lack of participation in their professional organizations to the self-hatred common in oppressed groups. Because nurses do not feel proud or powerful, they refuse to join with others whom they perceive as powerless. They have internalized their oppressors' view of them. I will be very specific here and state my own conviction that every single nurse should join the ANA. The fragmentation of nurse power into a multiplicity of organizations—now numbering more than 100—keeps us from speaking with one strong voice. If you don't like positions that the ANA is taking, let your voice be heard *within* its deliberations, not outside it. If you don't want to come to meetings, send your dues money to contribute to the work that the association does on your behalf.

Fortunately, efforts of our professional organizations—undertaken on behalf of nonmembers and members alike—are going forward on a number of fronts. Safe staffing is the dominant issue in ANA as this book goes to press. A national campaign, "Safe Staffing Saves Lives," publicizes compelling research evidence about the impact on patient outcomes when there are more hours of RN care per patient day and a higher proportion of RNs in the staffing mix (the website is a storehouse of good information: visit www.safestaffingsaveslives.org).

Coalition Forming. Coalitions of organizations may be needed to address the big issues. For example, a coalition involving the American Association of Retired People (AARP) and the Robert Wood Johnson Foundation launched the Center to Champion Nursing in December, 2007. The Center's ambitious goals include raising public awareness about the nursing shortage, finding funding to expand nursing education, and improving RNs' job satisfaction, so that they remain in the workforce. Another example of collaboration among organizations is the "Handle With Care" campaign mounted by ANA with Johnson & Johnson corporation, aimed at reducing musculoskeletal injuries among nurses (deCastro, 2006). Nursing needs to continue developing and mobilizing powerful coalitions, partnering with diverse organizations, such the Children's Defense Fund, National Alliance for the Mentally Ill, and environmental groups, to mention just a few possibilities.

Federal and State Legislation. It is through legislation that much of nursing's agenda will be accomplished. A plethora of problems await the enactment of laws. For example, assault on nurses is not yet a felony, as it is for bus drivers, lifeguards, and umpires. Another unresolved problem requiring legislative action is mandatory overtime. The ANA has vigorously opposed this nefarious practice—after all, even truck drivers are protected from it by law! Only a few states have followed the lead of the Minnesota Nurses Association, which succeeded in obtaining passage of the Mandatory Overtime Prevention Act in 2002. This law gives nurses the right to refuse overtime when, in their professional judgment, they are too tired to continue (Brodeur & Laraway, 2002). If overtime is worked, it should be strictly voluntary. Legislation is pending in other states as this book goes to press. Check the ANA web site (www.nursingworld.org) for updates, so that you can support the efforts in your own state.

Legislation to ensure safe staffing is being sought on both federal and state levels, with greater initial success at the state level. This legislation would hold hospitals accountable for adhering to valid and reliable staffing plans that are created with RN input. We need to convey to our lawmakers: Patients suffer when RN staffing is inadequate. Show them the data. In addition to studies conducted or commissioned by nursing organizations, a study funded by the Agency for Healthcare Research and Quality, involving data from 6 million patients and 799 hospitals, clearly demonstrated that *lower* RN staffing levels are associated with *higher* rates of patient complications. Medical patients being cared for in hospitals with a smaller proportion of nursing hours from RNs had higher rates of urinary tract infections, gastrointestinal bleeding, pneumonia, shock, cardiac arrest, and failure to rescue. Conversely, patient length of stay was 3% to 5% shorter, and rate of complications was 2% to 9% lower in hospitals with high RN staffing (Needleman, Buerhaus, Mattke, Stewart, & Zelevinsky, 2002). In 2002, California became the first state to legislate minimum nurse-to-patient ratios for acute care hospitals. Some nurses hailed this law as a great victory, whereas others sensed a danger in laws mandating a certain number of nurses because technology, treatments, and information systems change so rapidly (Kovner, 2000). Noted Brodeur and Laraway: "Not all nurses believe that staffing ratios are the answer. . . . They fear that the ratios will become ceilings for staffing and that they will be taken too literally" (2002, p. 230). Undoubtedly, controversy on the best way to ensure safe staffing will continue. But without legislation, what would motivate hospitals to work harder to recruit and retain registered nurses?

You will also want to monitor the legislation in the works to protect whistle-blowers, like Barry Adams, who speak out about unsafe conditions for patients. Some states, like Massachusetts, have already passed laws to protect those who speak up, and attempts to pass bills are ongoing in many others. Once enacted into law, nurses who report dangerous conditions cannot be suspended, demoted, harassed, or discharged.

Beyond the aforementioned legislation concerned with our own welfare as nurses, we must monitor an ever-changing array of issues affecting the health and welfare of the public. Nurses must make their voices heard on these critical issues. What could you do in your state to gain the ear of legislators and policy makers? With whom could you join hands to craft an action agenda? Who else cares about the issues you care about? How can you become more involved in health policy activism? Here are some suggestions.

Steps Toward Becoming an Effective Health Policy Activist

- *Marshall information and tools.* Mason, Leavitt, and Chaffee's (2002) textbook on policy and politics provides a wealth of information and impressive examples of nurse activism. The ANA web site (www. nursingworld.org) and the National League for Nursing's government affairs action center (www.capwiz.com/nln/home/) provide updates on priority issues and pending legislation. Also check out the web site of the Nightingale Policy Institute (www.policynurses.org).

- *Become involved in a political party* and the legislative committee of your state nurses' association. It is unfortunate that many nurses consider politics unsavory (J. Leavitt, Cohen, & Mason, 2002). It is past time to abandon this attitude.
- *Build, and nurture, relationships with legislators* (see 11.2 about Maine RNs). Remind your legislators that one in 44 registered female voters is a nurse. Make your views on pending legislation known quickly and easily via e-mail (see Ray & Roberts [2002] for helpful pointers).
- *Nurture relationships among nursing organizations* as well, so that all are "on the same page." As noted in Chapter 5, sometimes groups of RNs align themselves with hospital or medical associations to oppose the efforts of other RNs to obtain changes in state nurse practice acts. In response to our disunity, I have seen legislators wearily yawn, saying "You girls come back when you get your act together."
- *Remember that success depends on persistence.* Securing desired legislation or policy change can be a slow process, involving a lot of delay and compromise. For example, it took 10 years for advanced practice nurses to receive Medicare reimbursement. It took 18 years to obtain passage of the Family and Medical Leave Act (J. Leavitt, Cohen, & Mason, 2002). New leaders—and followers—may have to step up along the way.

11.2. During a campaign for a specific piece of legislation, Maine nurses hosted "Nurse Day" at the State House, featuring blood pressure, cholesterol, and blood sugar checks, as well as information about their legislative agenda. They even provided lawmakers a catered lunch—"fish chowdah" (P. Leavitt, 2002). This approach was so successful that it has become an annual event. "Feed them, they will come" is a time-honored strategy to motivate attendance.

A Last Word

Perhaps the most fitting way to close this chapter is with the simple aphorism of folk singer and activist Pete Seeger: "The establishment never moves unless they are pushed by the people." In this chapter, you heard story after story of people who claimed their personal power and joined with others to shake up "the establishment": whistle-blowers, letter writers, patient advocates, and crusaders for workplace safety. What role will *you* play in solving nursing's problems?

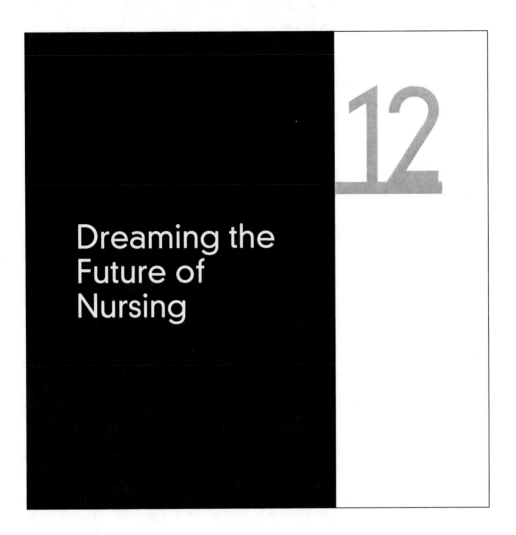

Dreaming the Future of Nursing

Heal the past, live the present, dream the future.
—Mary Walker, PhD, RN, FAAN

What is your dream of nursing's future? The first decade of the 21st century will soon end. Futuristic prognostications about health care fill the pages of both professional and popular books and magazines. Let's look at a few of the more intriguing predictions that are being made. Well-known lecturer and consultant Tim Porter-O'Grady says that nurses are at the outset of a new paradigm for practice, because patients will not need the kind of care that nurses were accustomed to giving. Through genomic typing, anomalies will be diagnosed in the earliest stages. Portability of medical hardware will permit cheaper, short-term ambulatory delivery of services for the majority of patients. The nursing role will mainly involve advising, guiding, and educating (Porter-O'Grady, 2001). Eleanor Sullivan, editor of *Journal of Professional Nursing,* foresees that eradicating entire diseases via genetic engineering is a possibility. Sullivan also predicts therapeutic cancer vaccines, advances in noninvasive diagnostic and treatment procedures, expanded communication technologies, and greater use of nanotechnology (Sullivan, 2002). Nursing visionary Luther Christman speaks of a device to instantly translate languages that will enable scientists across the globe to communicate easily: "Each will be able to raise questions in their respective language, the recipient will hear it in his or her own language, and responses will be similarly translated" (2000, p. 14). Thus, the growth of scientific knowledge will be even more swift and dramatic, with profound impact on the health care system.

Dan Pesut, educator and former president of Sigma Theta Tau International nursing honor society, foresees a renewal in nursing and the creation of a caring society. In Dan's vision, reflective practice provides a means for renewal. Reflection is a form of "inner work" that results in the energy for engaging in "outer service." Pesut explains what happens when self is renewed:

> As self is renewed, commitments to service come forward more easily. Renewed commitments to service require attention to mindfulness and reflective practice. Mindful reflective practice begets questions that support inquiry. Such inquiry guides knowledge work and evidence-based caregiving. Caregiving supports society as knowledge, values, and service intersect. Knowledgeable people and especially knowledgeable nurses provide care that society needs. Creating a caring society is the spirit work of nursing. Creating a caring society starts nurses caring for themselves and becoming, through reflection, more conscious and intentional in their being, thinking, feeling, doing, and acting.

Here are my predictions. We are certainly in for a dizzying roller coaster ride of changes, some of them unwanted and unpleasant. But we're going to ride it out and avail ourselves of the new opportunities. The public will demand that the government break up corporate monopolies in health care. Insurance companies will no longer own HMOs, hospitals, and drug manufacturers. Wasteful administrative costs—such as the enormous salaries, bonuses, and stock options paid to executives of HMOs and for-profit hospitals—will be drastically curtailed. National licensure will replace state licensure for all clinical professions. Workplaces will not be free of stress, but nurses will be hardier and more stress-resistant. New graduates will be nurtured in well-designed residency programs that smooth their transition from student to RN. The American Nurses Association (ANA) will be more than a million strong, and we will have the most powerful political action committee in the nation's capital. Nurse researchers will be cited in the daily newspapers as frequently as medical researchers.

Greater gender, ethnic, and racial diversity will be achieved in nursing. Enrollment of men has been increasing (Trossman, 2003); when I look out at a roomful of students to deliver a lecture, more men are sprinkled throughout the lecture hall—it's nice to see. Many mid-life men are choosing nursing as a second career, and not all young men are finding the get-your-MBA-and-then-a-BMW route appealing. As the numbers of men and women equalize, men will not feel marginalized, excluded from the female "sorority," as one of our research participants phrased it. Some evidence suggests that the social isolation of men in nursing is already decreasing, as shown in research by one of our doctoral graduates, Stephen Krau. He compared loneliness of female nurses, male nurses, and male ministers (ministers served as a comparison group of men in a helping profession that is traditionally male). No statistically significant differences were found among groups, refuting previous indications that loneliness is a problem for men who choose nursing as a career.

Loneliness will be less of a problem for minority nurses, too. The nursing school enrollment of racial/ethnic minority students was only 10% in 1992, but increased to 14% of entrants in 2000 (Sochalski, 2002). Associations such as the National Black Nurses Association, the National Association of Hispanic Nurses, and the Asian American/Pacific Islander Nurses Association are committed to mentoring these minority students. We need to continue aggressive recruitment of minorities into the profession. Many patients long to see a caregiver from their own ethnic group.

Supportive colleagueship, for which nurses in our studies yearned, will become a reality. _Horizontal hostility_ will become an obsolete term, because empowered nurses will have no need for self-deprecation or deprecation of their colleagues. Warm connection will replace isolation. Infighting will be a thing of the past that students will have to read about in the history books. No longer will we find in the biographies of our most esteemed leaders such sad admissions as that of Hildegard Peplau: _"I had exceedingly few real friends in nursing"_ (Calloway, 2002, p. 443).

Nurses will exhibit a new pride in who they are and what they do. Whether they are CEOs, family nurse practitioners (FNPs), or home health nurses, they will feel confident in their knowledge and comfortable in marketing their expertise. A heyday for nurse entrepreneurs is coming. More and more nurses will be presidents of their own businesses—everything from hospices, adult day care establishments, fitness emporiums, and holistic healing retreat centers, to software design firms and consulting firms of all types. Community nursing organizations (CNOs) will contract to provide primary care for groups of patients. Such organizations already proved their worth in Medicare demonstration projects funded by the Health Care Financing Administration. In a CNO, members are assigned to a nurse who works with them on health promotion or manages existing problems. The nurse may meet with them in a clinic, community center, or their homes (Schraeder, Lamb, Shelton, & Britt, 1997). The success of these projects should not surprise us, for after all, nurses know more about holistic health and wellness than any other group of professionals, and we excel in the management of chronic diseases and eldercare.

Nontraditional practice sites will continue to proliferate. Already, RNs are proving well suited to staffing those retail clinics that are springing up like mushrooms inside supermarkets and pharmacies across the country. The public finds that the care given by nurse practitioners at these clinics is excellent and economical. Suzie Cole, an advanced practice nurse (APN) interviewed for a magazine article, says, "I see a lot of moms who don't have time to wait in a doctor's office with their sick kids. They love the convenience and the speed" (Patzer, 2008, p. 13).

And let's not forget the acutely ill. Hospitals will always need highly skilled nurses because they are really giant intensive care units. Unlicensed assistive personnel cannot be safely utilized for direct patient care in such facilities. In fact, the need for unskilled workers will disappear, because robots will do the manual chores such as cleaning. Increased use of information technology will contribute to more efficient hospital work processes. Patient acuity will determine safe staffing levels, and nurses themselves will decide if admissions must be curtailed because of insufficient staffing. The morale of hospital RNs will be high because their workloads are reasonable, and they receive appreciative e-mails from their CEOs and VPs.

My final prediction? All nurses will share their expertise and concern in the communities where they live. They will be heavily involved in health councils, citizens groups, and politics. They will wield their power in the boardroom and at the ballot box. Virginia Henderson once said, "It seems hardly possible to me that an excellent nurse can be at the same time an indifferent or socially inexperienced citizen."

Extinction? Not a Chance!

Some years ago, I wrote a futuristic story about Joey, a child hospitalized in the year 2040 after the profession of nursing had become extinct (Thomas, 1980). Joey was cared for in an efficient, fully computerized, facility with a fleet of efficient, speedy, technicians. But he was lonely, and quite delighted when Grandma, a former nurse, came to visit. Enthralled, he listened as she told him about nurses (he had never heard of them). "What happened to nurses, Grandma? Why don't we have them anymore?" asked Joey. Grandma looked sad, and maybe a little bitter too. She was slow in formulating her answer, as if, after all this time, she still could not understand what had happened: "I guess nurses couldn't decide what they were and what they wanted to do, Joey. They just couldn't get together. . . . organizations held conferences, conventions, meetings, seminars, task forces, and workshops. But after all the talking, there was still no agreement on anything. . . . No one listened to anyone else, Joey. People were too emotionally upset. . . . And while all of this was going on, technicians took care of the patients. Eventually, nurses weren't needed any more. The end was really not very dramatic, as a matter of fact everyone just forgot about nurses. To use the words of a 20th century poet named Eliot, nursing ended 'not with a bang but a whimper.'"

I wrote this little story as a wake-up call, not a prediction of what would actually come to pass. Neither then, nor now, have I been pessimistic about nursing's prospects for the future. Nurses are not an endangered species *if we unite*, and history shows that when groups are threatened by outside forces, they become more cohesive within their own ranks. I have the privilege of teaching the individuals who will be the profession's future leaders, and I can tell you that they are a fantastic cohort of men and women. They are critical thinkers and competent, creative caregivers. They are excited and proud to contemplate taking part in nursing's bright new future. They fill me with hope. But *all of us* are in charge of our future. Like Nightingale, we must tackle obstacles with determination, adopting her conviction that "never to know that you are beaten is the way to victory" (Nightingale, cited in Cook, 1913).

The Butterfly Effect

In a rut of apathy and cynicism, you may feel that the actions of one individual cannot possibly make a difference. Let me remind you of the Butterfly Effect.

According to chaos theory, when a butterfly moves its wings deep in the Amazon forest, tiny air currents result. These currents affect larger eddies—and circumstance compounds circumstance, until the barely perceptible movement of that particular butterfly at that particular time changes the course—weeks later—of a tornado (Leach, 1990). I think of human examples like Rosa Parks, who refused to move to the back of the bus where African Americans were assigned to sit. One woman, one act of quiet protest against the idiocy of racist seat assignment in a public bus. I also think of Rosli Naf, whose name is not nearly so well known as that of Rosa Parks. Naf was a Swiss Red Cross nurse. She was 30 years old when sent to Nazi-occupied France in 1941 to care for 100 Jewish children and adults. She had never had contact with Jews, and had heard much anti-Semitic propaganda about them in Switzerland. But she quickly came to love the children and was horrified when 42 of the teenagers were forcibly taken away to a transit camp that was a stop on the way to the Auschwitz death camp. Over the next 2 days, she made her way by bicycle, bus, and taxi to the transit camp. She marched in and began to badger the guards to release the children. She got them out of the camp, but was refused permission to take them to safety in Switzerland. So Naf decided that she must help the youngsters escape. She made them fake IDs and gave them train fare, having arranged an escape route with the help of the French underground and some Swiss citizens. The first five teenagers were caught at the French–Swiss border. Two served jail time but survived, and the other three were sent to Auschwitz where they were gassed. The rest made it to safety. Naf was fired for her actions, because she acted without Red Cross approval. But years later, when interviewed in a Swiss nursing home, her only regret was that she was not able to save more children. One woman, one courageous act during the insanity of the Holocaust (Kelley, 1997).

All of us who learn of Rosa Parks and Rosli Naf are profoundly affected and inspired by their heroism. Likewise, the assertive actions of one nurse in her workplace become linked to empowering actions of other nurses. We, and the butterfly, are part of the organic whole of the universe. Not all of us will display the uncommon heroism of Rosa Parks and Rosli Naf. Nor will all of us run for political office or work at the national level in our professional organizations. But what we do each day, blooming where we are planted, *can* make a difference. William James once said: "I am done with great things and big things, with great institutions and big success. And I am for those tiny, invisible molecular forces that work from individual to individual, creeping through the crannies of the world like so many soft rootlets, or like the capillary oozing of water; but which, given time, will rend the hardest monuments of men's pride."

A Last Word

The seeds of wisdom, peace, and wholeness are within each of our difficulties.
—Jack Kornfield, 1993, p. 80

Although this book plumbed nurses' collective difficulties and private suffering, I do believe that wisdom, peace, and wholeness are possible. The practice of nursing will always be needed by society and will always attract individuals who have a vocation to give loving care. Nursing yields great joys. That is why so many of us remain devoted to it, even though we've been "ordered to care in a society that [does] not value caring," as historian Susan Reverby (1987) once stated. What sustains us is the intimate connection with our patients. When Nightingale was faced with filthy conditions, woefully inadequate supplies, and opposition from male army medical officers at Scutari, she found her sustenance in the one-to-one interactions she had with the soldiers themselves (Thomas, 1993b). In Nightingale's later years, when she was an elderly invalid, what she remembered most about Scutari were the soldiers who were her patients. She was still corresponding with the survivors of the Balaclava Charge in 1900, more than 40 years after the Crimean War had ended.

I asked some nurse colleagues to share what keeps them enthused about this profession, and this is what they said:

> *I think of that woman who was so grateful that she could get a reliable method of birth control or the scared pregnant adolescent who didn't know what to do next. I remember the teenage couple who was so afraid that their new baby's cord had become infected. And the 150 older members of the community who brought their smiles and stories of earlier times with them to get their flu shots. And all those parents who brought their children for gamma globulin after they had been exposed to hepatitis at their day care. These are the things that make my anger fade. I forget about my feelings of powerlessness. I know that I make a difference.* —Belinda McCall

> *I am a person who needs to know that what I do makes a difference. Nursing has met this need for almost 40 years. I remember the wrenching pain of being with an elderly man on discharge day, and we both knew he was going home to die. I remember the student who sat at my office door early one morning waiting to tell me she was pregnant. I have always been inspired by other nurses. Nurses are not compensated commensurate with the contribution they make to the nation's health. Luckily for society, nurses are motivated more by satisfaction than by the bottom line. Nursing makes me proud. It is a rare privilege for me to know I am part of a worldwide force that exists to improve the quality of people's lives. Nursing is who I am.* —Carol Seavor

> *I was only 5 years old when I decided I wanted to be a nurse. I did not have support from my family, quite the contrary. They told me that I did not have the physical, intellectual, or character strength to meet this goal. They thought that nursing embodied a life of drudgery, and furthermore, they were convinced I would not succeed. . . . I received a 3-year scholarship to a diploma program when I was 17. . . . At only one point in my life did I think of changing careers; this was when I received my first master's degree in child development. I continued my life in nursing because of the variety of experience that nursing offered and because of the soul satisfaction it brought to me. Through the years, I have never lost my enthusiasm for assisting families to whatever level of wellness they are capable of. . . . Given the present climate in which females are socialized to believe that all professional avenues are open to them, I ask myself the obvious question: Would I still choose nursing? My answer is a resounding "yes."* —Patricia Droppleman

Compare the testimony of these nurses about "making a difference" and "soul satisfaction" with the rueful remark of Michele Proto, a subject in Levinson's study who has spent her career in business: "I wish I had a feeling that what I do is important. My work is geared toward making a lot of rich people richer. There is not one social benefit in anything I do, not one redeeming thing. Let's face it, there are no redeeming factors. What the hell am I doing this for? My tombstone will read: 'She delivered projects on schedule'" (Levinson, 1996, p. 399).

Nursing, with all its stress and frustrations, is still a wonderful way to make one's living. I have never once regretted choosing nursing. My nursing work has been a hugely important part of my life, bringing me great pleasure and satisfaction. Although I have done a number of different things—including med-surg floor nursing, inpatient and outpatient psychiatric nursing, administration, research, journal editing, and teaching students at the diploma, baccalaureate, master's, and doctoral levels—I've enjoyed each and every one of them. What a marvelous profession that so many different directions can be taken as one's interest change through the years! I've worked 7–3, 3–11, and 11–7—and double shifts. I've been employed in places where I had to clock in and in places where I had academic freedom. I've worked in uniform and in street clothes, with lab coat and without. I've been poorly paid and well paid. I've toiled alongside humble nurse's aides who exemplified dignity and compassion as well as stellar leaders of the profession who shared their sophisticated theories, vision, and political savvy. I've nursed innocents and murderers. I've sat on dilapidated sofas in drug-infested housing projects and plush chairs in tastefully decorated board rooms. I've made mistakes as well as contributions. But I've *never* been bored or burned out. I hope to meet my demise continuing to do the work I love. While visiting Victoria for a conference, I saw an obituary that I really liked. It said, "On Friday, June 13, 2003 in his 53rd year, R___ passed away suddenly on the 17th hole (after a birdie on 16)." What a way to go! But I'm not quite ready. I would like to be here to see my dreams of nursing's future become actuality.

Just as I began this book, drawing inspiration from Nightingale's admonition to "Charge on!", I close with her inspiring words about doing all that we do as professional nurses as well as it can be done. I find her words more meaningful than our trendy buzzwords of continuous quality improvement, benchmarking, and the like. Nightingale was quite demanding of herself, as well as others. She yearned for others to share her passion, urgency, and commitment to better health for all people. Her standards for nursing were exacting. Out of 1,000 to 2,000 applicants to the Nightingale Training School each year, she selected only 15 to 30 students of the highest moral character (Smith, 1981). She viewed the graduates of the school as "nursing missioners" and kept up a voluminous correspondence with them as they sailed off to America, France, Australia, and the far corners of the earth to start new schools and upgrade nursing. In her missives to them, she continually exhorted them to display the highest professionalism and devotion to the art of nursing. Even though there was a nursing shortage in her time, Nightingale was adamant that individuals with inferior preparation could not be substituted for educated nurses—even with good intentions. "There is no such thing as amateur nursing," said Nightingale (Monteiro, 1985). We still carry her legacy into the minds and hearts of people everywhere when we deliver superb professional nursing care. We must continue to fight for the rights of all people to have access to that care. Let us dedicate our efforts to our founder, who said:

> *The professional motive is the desire and perpetual effort to do the thing as well as it can be done, which exists just as much in the Nurse, as in the Astronomer in search of a new star, or in the Artist completing a picture.* (Florence Nightingale)

Epilogue

I realize that some of my readers would like to have more detail about the anger research alluded to in this book. In 1989, I put together a 14-member research team (all female, all nurses except for one psychologist) to conduct a descriptive study of women's anger. Unlike previous studies of women aroused to anger in artificial laboratory experiments or deeply troubled women discovering long-buried anger in psychotherapy, our study aimed to examine anger in everyday situations at home and at work. We wanted to know what provoked women's anger and how they expressed or inhibited it. Given the scant research and conflicting advice about anger management in both professional and popular literature, we wanted to know what ways of dealing with anger were health-promoting. There was plenty of advice about health-damaging thoughts and behaviors, but virtually no databased information about constructive anger.

Data were collected over a 3-year period in a variety of community settings, including work sites, schools, and women's organizations. More than 500 women, between the ages of 25 and 66, participated in this initial phase of the study. The women represented a wide range of educational backgrounds, marital status, occupations, and income brackets. The racial composition of the sample closely approximated the racial composition of the U.S. population, with the exception of fewer Hispanics. Seventy-five of the women were nurses, and we found that the nurses—along with other human service professionals—scored highest among occupational groups on overall anger proneness.

Phase I of the Women's Anger Study was primarily quantitative. We used well-established and validated questionnaires to measure the anger variables as well as other variables related to anger, such as stress, self-esteem, and depression. The test battery included Spielberger's Trait Anger Scale, the Framingham Anger Scales, the Cognitive-Somatic Anger Scale, the Perceived Stress Scale, Rosenberg's Self-Esteem Scale, the Beck Depression Inventory, the Current Health Scale from Ware's Health Perceptions Questionnaire, Norbeck's Social Support Questionnaire, and a researcher-developed questionnaire assessing health indicators and demographics. A small qualitative component of the study consisted of open-ended questions about the precipitants of women's anger, its targets, and its duration. Study participants wrote their responses to these questions. The Phase I findings were reported in the book *Women and Anger*, published in 1993 by Springer Publishing.

The second phase of the Women's Anger Study took place over the next 4 years and involved collection of several data sets from specific groups of women. What prompted further study was the need to know more about the situational context in which anger episodes occurred and the meaning of these experiences for women. The large quantitative investigation had provided useful data—quite useful, in fact, because our study was the first large, comprehensive examination of women's anger. But we found the written responses to our questions about anger incidents tantalizing in their brevity. We needed to conduct in-depth interviews with women to obtain richer, more complete descriptions of the anger incidents. Therefore, we chose existential phenomenology as our method.

Because Phase II was a phenomenological study, it differed significantly from Phase I not only with regard to method but also in sample size and other aspects. Details of the research method may be found in our published papers and in our 2002 textbook *Listening to Patients: A Phenomenological Approach to Nursing Research and Practice* (Thomas & Pollio). Interviews were conducted by members of the research team with 29 Caucasian women, ranging in age from 21 to 66. Illustrative occupations ranged from homemaker, student, waitress, to business executive, college professor, and human service professional. Participants were selected on the basis of having experienced the phenomenon of anger and being willing to discuss it at length. Findings of this study were reported in an article in *Journal of Advanced Nursing* (Thomas, Smucker, & Droppleman, 1998). Because we had collected data only from Caucasian women, we embarked almost immediately on recruitment of a sample of African American women. In-depth phenomenological interviews were subsequently conducted by two African American members of our research team with nine women. Preliminary findings from this study were reported in 1997 at the Southern Nursing Research Society and the American Psychological Association, and the journal article came out in 1998 (Fields et al.).

In both of these samples of women, some nurses were included. And again, as we had seen with the quantitative data, it was clear that nurses were very angry. Although we did not pull out the data from the nurse interviews for separate analysis, my research team was struck and disturbed by nurses' distress and powerlessness. I felt the need to focus more specifically on individuals in my own profession. Because the earlier studies were not designed solely to investigate *work-related anger*, a new project (the Nurses Anger Study) was launched, and new interviews conducted. In conjunction with my colleague Pat Droppleman and doctoral student Marilyn Smith, data from nine female registered nurses were collected and analyzed. The sample included staff nurses, nurse managers, nurse practitioners, a midwife, and a nursing instructor. Educational preparation of the nurses ranged from associate degree (AD) to PhD, ages from 29 to 56, and years of practice from 7 to 34 years. Two participants were African American and seven were Caucasian. The findings of this study were reported in *Nursing Forum* (Smith, Droppleman, & Thomas (1996).

But we did not feel that we had finished examining nurses' anger, because we had not studied any males. At that time we were fortunate to have a male master's student, Aaron Brooks, who wanted to work with us to fulfill his research requirement. He was excited about interviewing men about their anger. Almost immediately, we launched the next project, which involved five male nurse participants. Their ages ranged from 28 to 38, and their nursing experience from 3 to 17 years. One nurse had a master's degree, two a bachelor's, one a diploma, and one an associate degree. Findings of this phenomenological interview study were also reported in *Nursing Forum* (Brooks, Thomas, & Droppleman, 1996).

Fresh data from nurses working in hospitals are included in this book. My faculty colleague, Mary Gunther, and I supervised an excellent team of master's students who collected interviews with 46 nurses during an 18-month period. As with our previous samples, education level of the nurses varied, ranging from diploma or AD to master's (MSN). Ages ranged from 20s to 60s, and this sample did include males, although most nurses were female.

Altogether, researchers at the University of Tennessee have accumulated a vast amount of data on nurses. We have hundreds of pages of interview transcripts from RNs whose present or past work settings include intensive care, coronary care, behavioral health, orthopedics, neurology, oncology, med-surg, home health, emergency, primary care, long-term care, maternity, pediatrics, and public health (not an exhaustive list). These nurses have held a variety of staff, management, and teaching positions, and some were in advanced practice roles such as nurse practitioner and clinical specialist. While we would not claim that we have assessed a representative sample of the population of American nurses, we certainly claim a diverse sample. In a 2005 paper, McNeely deplored the lack of research on the employee frame of reference because "the bulk of nursing studies [are] driven from the perspective of the organization" (p. 295). Our program of research most definitely elucidates the RN frame of reference. You have heard the voices of dozens of nurses throughout this book. You, the readers, can judge the validity of our findings. In phenomenology, a study is considered valid if it provides a compelling, thorough description of the phenomenon. The validity of our work is further substantiated if the findings resonate with readers' own experience of anger in the workplace. In qualitative research, the criterion of "fittingness" is met when the findings of a study "fit" contexts other than the study situation, and when people in those contexts view them as applicable to their experience (Sandelowski, 1986).

Members of the research team certainly found that nurses' stories were similar to our own lived experience. Analyzing the data aroused strong emotion. Members of the research teams grappled with the pain of our study participants as the transcripts were read aloud and discussed. The nurses' words hung in the air, and our stomachs knotted as we listened to them. We resonated with the pain because we, too, had been in the hostile environment they described. We too had sometimes screamed, or seethed silently because we dared not speak. It was hard to "bracket" (set aside) our own biases, as the method of phenomenological research requires. For that reason, we took many of the interviews to an interdisciplinary phenomenology research group for assistance with the data analysis. We also took the final themes back to some of our participants to ascertain if we had accurately captured their experience. Many have encouraged us to publish something that would help nurses when we finished the research.

Over the years, I became convinced that beyond reporting our research findings there was a moral imperative to propose strategies for channeling nurses' anger into positive interventions. That is, of course, the purpose of this book. I am also doing many talks and workshops for groups of nurses. Research is ongoing, focusing presently on the anger experiences of junior students during their clinical experiences. Renee Burk is working with me to analyze these data. As always, there are new questions and new directions to take. I also want to acknowledge the wonderful people who have collaborated with me on the earlier projects. Phase I team members were Kaye Bultemeier, Gayle Denham, Madge

Donnellan, Patricia Droppleman, June Martin, Mary Anne Modrcin-McCarthy, Sheryl Russell, Pegge Saylor, Elizabeth Seabrook, Barbara Shirk, Carol Smucker, Jane Tollett, and Dorothy Wilt. I am particularly indebted to Dorothy Wilt, from whom I learned much about helping women who suppress their anger or vent it inappropriately. Dorothy is a nurse psychotherapist and my dear friend for more than 25 years. We went through the mental health master's program together.

The team that worked with me on the Phase II data of Caucasian women were Janet Crooks, Janet Deese, Lucy Gasaway, Mary Pilkington, Donna Saravi, Patricia Droppleman, and Carol Smucker. Team members for the African American anger project were Becky Fields, Kelli Edwards, Angela Sims, Karen Reesman, Carolyn Robinson, Blair Short, and Belinda McCall. Contributors to the study of female nurses were Marilyn Smith, Patricia Droppleman, Janet Secrest, Linda Mefford, Tom McKay, and Phyllis Smith. Research group members at the time of the male nurses study were Aaron Brooks, Susan Blair, Lutie Culver, Mitzi Davis, Jane Dozier, Patricia Droppleman, Phyllis duMont, Nancy Kile, Jerry Kline, Linda Mefford, Alicia Richardson, Marilyn Smith, Carol Smucker, and Susan Stuber. Contributors to the 2003 study, in addition to Mary Gunther, were Debra Achenbach, Amy Allen, Rebecca Brown, Colleen Cole, Alvinia Ziegenfuss, Regina Conard, Kevin Douglass, Melanie Hill, Amber Hobbs, Stephanie Sharp, and Sandi Walker. Professor Howard Pollio's contribution to my understanding of phenomenology has been immeasurable, and I feel privileged to have attended his weekly research group—and eventually assumed the role of co-chair of the group—over the past 15 years.

Finally, we must honor all of the courageous RNs who shared their work lives with us. Along with the rage and tears were many success stories of advocating for patients, using anger for self-empowerment, and lobbying for changes in ill-conceived institutional policies. This program of research has been rewarding and enlightening to all of us on the investigative team. I know the study participants will be pleased if you benefit from what they shared with us.

References

Abramson, H. S. (1996). A patient's view. In E. D. Baer, C. M. Fagin, & S. Gordon (Eds.), *Abandonment of the patient: The impact of profit-driven health care on the public* (pp. 25–30). New York: Springer.

Adams, B. L. (1997). Why must nurses risk their careers for safe care? *American Journal of Nursing, 97*(7), 80.

Acorn, S., Ratner, P., & Crawford, M. (1997). Decentralization as a determinant of autonomy, job satisfaction, and organizational commitment among nurse managers. *Nursing Research, 46*, 52–58.

Adkins, S. (1997). The privilege of intimacy. *Tennessee Nurse, 60*(2), 4.

Adler, A. (1956). *The individual psychology of Alfred Adler.* New York: Basic Books.

Adriaanse, H., Van Reek, J., Zandbelt, L., & Evers, G. (1991). Nurses' smoking worldwide: A review of 73 surveys on nurses' tobacco consumption in 21 countries in the period 1959–1988. *International Journal of Nursing Studies, 28*(4), 361–375.

Aiken, L. (1992). Charting nursing's future. In L. Aiken & C. Fagin (Eds.), *Charting nursing's future: Agenda for the 1990s* (pp. 3–12). Philadelphia: Lippincott.

Aiken, L., Clarke, S., Sloane, D., & Sochalski, J. (2001). An international perspective on hospital nurses' work environments: The case for reform. *Policy, Politics, and Nursing Practice, 2*, 255–263.

Aiken, L., Clarke, S., Sloane, D., Sochalski, J., & Silber, J. (2002). Hospital nurse staffing and patient mortality, nurse burnout, and job dissatisfaction. *Journal of the American Medical Association, 288*(16), 1987–1993.

Alberti, R., & Emmons, M. (1974). *Your perfect right: A guide to assertive behavior.* San Luis Obispo, California: Impact Publishers.

Aldag, J., & Christensen, C. (1967). Personality correlates of male nurses. *Nursing Research, 16*, 375–376.

Aldwin, C. (1994). *Stress, coping, and development.* New York: Guilford.

Aldwin, C., Sutton, K., & Lachman, M. (1996). The development of coping resources in adulthood. *Journal of Personality, 64*, 837–871.

Allen, J. E. (2003, June 16). New variety of caretaker lifts patients, spirits. *Knoxville News Sentinel*, p. E10.

Allen, S. (2005, October 23). Critical care: The making of an ICU nurse. *Boston Sunday Globe*, pp. 1–8.

American Nurses Association. (1993). *Sexual harassment: It's against the law.* Washington, DC: Author.

American Nurses Association. (1995). *Protect your patients, protect your license.* Washington, DC: Author.

American Organization of Nurse Executives (AONE). (2002). *Acute Care Hospital Survey of RN Vacancy and Turnover Rates in 2000.* Washington, DC: Author.

American Psychiatric Association. (1994). *Diagnostic and Statistical Manual of Mental Disorders, Fourth Edition (DSM-IV).* Washington, DC: Author.

Anderson, N. B. (2008). Toward reducing work stress. *Monitor on Psychology, 39*(2), 9.

Anderson, S. F., & Lawler, K. A. (1994, April). *Type A behavior in women and the anger recall interview: What are Type A women angry about and how do they express it?* Paper presented at the annual meeting of the Society of Behavioral Medicine, Boston.

Andrews, D. R., & Dziegielewski, S. F. (2005). The nurse manager: Job satisfaction, the nursing shortage and retention. *Journal of Nursing Management, 13*, 286–295.

Angelou, M. (1993). *Wouldn't take nothing for my journey now.* New York: Random House.

Antonuccio, D. O., Danton, W. G., & DeNelsky, G. Y. (1995). Psychotherapy versus medication for depression: Challenging the conventional wisdom with data. *Professional Psychology Research and Practice, 26,* 574–585.

Antonovsky, A. (1987). *Unraveling the mystery of health: How people manage stress and stay well.* San Francisco: Jossey-Bass.

Armstrong, F. (2005). Magnet hospitals: What's the attraction? *Australian Nursing Journal, 12*(8), 14–17.

Arnetz, J. E., Arnetz, B. B., & Soderman, E. (1998). Violence toward health care workers. *American Association of Occupational Health Nurses Journal, 46,* 104–114.

Asher, R., & Hilton, I. (1996, September). *Security and investment in relationships: The impact on women's and men's anger.* Paper presented at the American Psychological Association Conference "Psychosocial and Behavioral Factors in Women's Health: Research, Prevention, Treatment, and Service Delivery in Clinical and Community Settings," Washington, DC.

Ashley, J. A. (1976). *Hospitals, paternalism, and the role of the nurse.* New York: Teachers College Press.

Ashley, M. J., Olin, J. S., Le-Riche, W., Kornaczewski, A., Schmidt, W., & Rankin, J. G. (1977). Morbidity in alcoholics: Evidence for accelerated development of physical disease in women. *Archives of Internal Medicine, 137,* 883–887.

Ausbrooks, E., Thomas, S. P., & Williams, R. (1995). Relationships among self-efficacy, optimism, trait anger, and anger expression. *Health Values, 19*(4), 46–53.

Averill, J. R. (1982). *Anger and aggression: An essay on emotion.* New York: Springer-Verlag.

Averill, J. R. (1983). Studies on anger and aggression: Implications for theories of emotion. *American Psychologist, 38,* 1145–1160.

Babor, T. F., Lex, B. W., Mendelson, J. H., & Mello, N. K. (1984). Marijuana, effect and tolerance: A study of subchronic self-administration in women. In L. H. Harris (Ed.), *Problems of drug dependence (NIDA Research Monograph No. 49,* pp. 199–204). Washington, DC: U.S. Government Printing Office.

Bach, G., & Goldberg, H. (1974). *Creative aggression.* Garden City, NY: Anchor Books.

Barak, Y., Achiron, A., Kimh, R., Lampl, Y., Gilad, R., Elizur, A., & Sarova-Pinhas, I. (1996). Health risks among shift workers: A survey of female nurses. *Health Care for Women International, 17,* 527–533.

Barasch, M. (1993). *The healing path: A soul approach to illness.* New York: Penguin Books.

Barey, P. T. (2005). Beware of strangers making promises: California Nurses Association/NNOC *Connecticut Nursing News.* Retrieved June 5, 2008 from http://findarticles.com/p/articles/mi_qa3902/is_200506/ai_n13643819

Bargmann, J. (2002). The top hospital in America. *AARP, 45*(3), 44–47, 51–53, 77–78.

Barnum, B. (1989). Anger and creating one's world. *Nursing and Health Care, 10*(5), 235.

Barritt, E. R. (1984). Inbreeding, infighting, and impotence. *American Journal of Nursing, 84,* 803–804.

Bartholomew, K. (2006). *Ending nurse-to-nurse hostility: Why nurses eat their young and each other.* Marblehead, MA: HCPro.

Bass, B. M. (1997). Does the transactional-transformational leadership paradigm transcend organizational and national boundaries? *American Psychologist, 52,* 130–139.

Bateson, M. C. (1990). *Composing a life.* New York: Plume.

Baumeister, R. F., Stillwell, A., & Wotman, S. R. (1990). Victim and perpetrator accounts of interpersonal conflict: Autobiographical narratives about anger. *Journal of Personality and Social Psychology, 59,* 994–1005.

Beard, R. O. (1913). The trained nurse of the future. *Journal of the American Medical Association, 61,* 2149–2152.

Beck, A. (1976). *Cognitive therapy and the emotional disorders.* New York: International Universities Press.

Beck, C. T. (1991). How students perceive faculty caring: A phenomenological study. *Nurse Educator, 16*(5), 18–22.

Bedell, J. R., & Lennox, S. S. (1996). *Handbook for communication and problem-solving skills training.* New York: John Wiley.

Bell, R. (1984). Over-the-counter drugs: Factors in adult use of sedatives, tranquilizers, and stimulants. *Public Health Reports, 99,* 319–323.

Bennett, E. M. (1991). Weight loss practices of overweight adults. *American Journal of Clinical Nutrition, 53,* 1519S-1521S.

Benson, H. (1993). The relaxation response. In D. Goleman & J. Gurin (Eds.), *Mind/body medicine: How to use your mind for better health.* (pp. 233–257). Yonkers, NY: Consumer Reports Books.

Berk, L., Tan, S., Fry, W., Napier, B., Lee, J., Hubbard, R., Lewis, J., & Eby, W. (1989). Neuroendocrine and stress hormone changes during mirthful laughter. *The American Journal of the Medical Sciences, 289,* 390–396.

Bernard, J. (1981). *The female world.* New York: Free Press.

Bernardez, T. (1987). Women and anger: Cultural prohibitions and the feminine ideal. *Work in progress: Stone Center for Developmental Services and Studies.* Wellesley, MA: Wellesley College, Stone Center.

Biener, L. (1987). Gender differences in the use of substances for coping. In R. C. Barnett, L. Biener, & G. K. Baruch (Eds.), *Gender and stress* (pp. 330–349). New York: The Free Press.

Birnbaum, D. W., & Croll, W. L. (1984). The etiology of children's stereotypes about sex differences in emotionality. *Sex Roles, 10,* 677–691.

Bishop, W. (1957). Florence Nightingale's letters. *American Journal of Nursing, 57,* 607–609.

Blegen, M. A. (1993). Nurses' job satisfaction: A meta-analysis of related variables. *Nursing Research, 42,* 36–41.

Bleich, M. R., Hewlett, P. O., Santos, S. R., Rice, R. B., Cox, K. S., & Richmeier, S. (2003). Analysis of the nursing workforce crisis: A call to action. *American Journal of Nursing, 103*(4), 66–74.

Block, J. (1973). Conceptions of sex role: Some cross-cultural and longitudinal perspectives. *American Psychologist, 28,* 512–526.

Block, K. (1997). The role of the self in healthy cancer survivorship: A view from the front lines of treating cancer. *Advances: The Journal of Mind-Body Health, 13*(1), 6–26.

Bohm, D. (1990). *On dialogue.* Ojai, California: David Bohm Seminars.

Boltwood, M. D., Taylor, C. B., Burke, M. B., Grogin, H., & Giacomini, J. (1993). Anger report predicts coronary artery vasomotor response to mental stress in atherosclerotic segments. *American Journal of Cardiology, 72,* 1361–1365.

Bormann, J. E. (2005). Frequent, silent mantram repetition: A Jacuzzi for the mind. *Topics in Emergency Medicine, 27,* 163–166.

Bormann, J. E., Becker, S., Gershwin, M., Kelly, A., Pada, L., Smith, T. L., & Gifford, A. L. (2006). Relationship of frequent mantram repetition to emotional and spiritual well-being in healthcare workers. *The Journal of Continuing Education in Nursing, 37,* 218–224.

Bourke, D. H. (1997, May 17). Today's work has become hearth, altar. *St. Petersburg Times,* 8B

Brandman, W. (1996). Intersubjectivity, social microcosm, and the here-and-now in a support group for nurses. *Archives of Psychiatric Nursing, 10,* 374–378.

Breda, K. L., Anderson, M. A., Hansen, L., Hayes, D., Pillion, C., & Lyon, P. (1997). Enhanced nursing autonomy through participatory action research. *Nursing Outlook, 45*(2), 76–81.

Briles, J. (1994). *The Briles report on women in health care.* San Francisco: Jossey-Bass.

Brodeur, M. A., & Laraway, A. S. (2002). States respond to nursing shortage. *Policy, Politics, and Nursing Practice, 3,* 228–234.

Brody, J. (1994, Sept. 5). Smoking halt tough for depression-prone. *The Knoxville News-Sentinel,* pp. B1, B2.

Brody, L. R. (1985). Gender differences in emotional development: A review of theories and research. *Journal of Personality, 53,* 102–149.

Bromberger, J. T., & Matthews, K. A. (1996). A "feminine" model of vulnerability to depressive symptoms: A longitudinal investigation of middle-aged women. *Journal of Personality and Social Psychology, 70*(3), 591–598.

Brondolo, E., Bendetto, Storrs, Baruch, & Contrada, R. (1993, March). *The effects of conflict management style on ambulatory blood pressure among NYC traffic agents.* Poster presented at the meeting of the Society of Behavioral Medicine, San Francisco, CA.

Brondolo, E., Rieppi, R., Erickson, S., Sloan, R., & Bagiella, E. (2002, April). *Hostility and ambulatory diary measures of mood and interpersonal interactions.* Poster presented at the meeting of the Society of Behavioral Medicine, Washington, DC.

Bronner, G., Peretz, C., & Ehrenfeld, M. (2003). Sexual harassment of nurses and nursing students. *Journal of Advanced Nursing, 42,* 637–644.

Brooks, A., Thomas, S. P., & Droppleman, P. (1996). From frustration to red fury: A description of work-related anger by male registered nurses. *Nursing Forum, 32*(2), 13–21.

Brooks, D. (2002). Lions and foxes. *The Atlantic Monthly, 290*(3), 28–30.

Broom, B. (2002). Somatic metaphor: A clinical phenomenon pointing to a new model of disease, personhood, and physical reality. *Advances, 18*(1), 16–29.

Brown, B. J. (2003). NurseWeek/AONE National Survey of Registered Nurses. *Nursing Outlook, 51,* 47–48.

Brown, H. J. (2003). *Life's little instruction book.* Nashville, TN: Thomas Nelson Publishing.

Brown, L., & Gilligan, C. (1992). *Meeting at the crossroads: Women's psychology and girls' development.* Cambridge, MA: Harvard University Press.

Browne, A., & Finkelhor, D. (1986). Impact of child sexual abuse: A review of the research. *Psychological Bulletin, 99*(1), 66–77.

Browning, L. (1994). Government affairs. *Tennessee Nurse, 57*(1), 9.

Buber, M. (1965). *Between man and man.* New York: Macmillan.

Buerhaus, P. I., Staiger, D. O., & Auerbach, D. I. (2000). Policy responses to an aging registered nurse workforce. *Nursing Economics, 18,* 278–284.

Bullough, V. L. (1990). Nightingale, nursing and harassment. *Image: Journal of Nursing Scholarship, 22*(1), 4–7.

Bullough, V. L., Church, O. M., & Stein, A. (1988). *American nursing: A biographical dictionary.* New York: Garland.

Bunde, J., & Suls, J. (2006). A quantitative analysis of the relationship between the Cook-Medley Hostility Scale and traditional coronary heart disease risk factors. *Health Psychology, 25,* 493–500.

Buresh, B., & Gordon, S. (1996). Subtle self-sabotage. *American Journal of Nursing, 96*(4), 22–24.

Buresh, B., & Gordon, S. (2000). *From silence to voice.* Ottawa, Canada: Canadian Nurses Association.

Burns, J. M. (1978). *Leadership.* New York: Harper & Row.

Bush, J. (1988). Job satisfaction, powerlessness, and locus of control. *Western Journal of Nursing Research, 10,* 718–731.

Cafferata, G., Kasper, J., & Bernstein, A. (1983). Family roles, structure, and stressors in relation to sex differences in obtaining psychotropic drugs. *Journal of Health and Social Behavior, 24,* 132–143.

Calloway, B. J. (2002). *Hildegard Peplau: Psychiatric nurse of the century.* New York: Springer Publishing.

Campbell, A. (1993). *Men, women, and aggression.* New York: Basic Books.

Campbell-Heider, N. (1986). Do nurses need mentors? *Image: Journal of Nursing Scholarship, 18,* 110–113.

Canavan, K. (1997). Media embraces ANA's concerns about unsafe patient care. *The American Nurse, 29*(3), 1, 12.

Carlson-Catalano, J. (1990). Hospital nurse experiences. In L. Gasparis & J. Swirsky (Eds.), *Nurse abuse: Its impact and resolution* (pp. 125–174). New York: Power Publications.

Caring for criminals. (2008, Spring). *Salute to Nurses,* 10, 12.

Carmack, B. J. (1997). Balancing engagement and detachment in caregiving. *Image: Journal of Nursing Scholarship, 29,* 139–143.

Caroline, H., & Bernhard, L. (1994). Health care dilemmas for women with serious mental illness. *Advances in Nursing Science, 16*(3), 78–88.

Carroll, V. (2003). Verbal abuse in the workplace: How to protect yourself and help solve the problem. *American Journal of Nursing, 103*(3), 132.

Carroll, V., & Morin, K. (1998). Workplace violence affects one-third of nurses. *The American Nurse, 30*(5), 15.

Casey, K., Fink, R., Krugman, M., & Probst, J. (2004). The graduate nurse experience. *The Journal of Nursing Administration, 34,* 303–311.

Cautela, J. (1969). Behavior therapy and self-control: Techniques and implications. In C. M. Franks (Ed.), *Behavior therapy: Appraisal and status* (pp. 323–340). New York: McGraw-Hill.

Centers for Disease Control and Prevention. (1999). *Youth Risk Behavior Surveillance—United States, 1999.* Atlanta, GA: U.S. Department of Health and Human Services, CDC.

Chang, E. M. L., Bidewell, J. W., Huntington, A. D., Daly, J., Johnson, A., Wilson, H., Lambert, V., & Lambert, C. E. (2006). A survey of role stress, coping and health in Australian and New Zealand hospital nurses. *International Journal of Nursing Studies, 44,* 1354–1362.

Cheng, Y., Kawachi, I., Coakley, E. H., Schwartz, J., & Colditz, G. (2000). Association between psychosocial work characteristics and health functioning in American women: Prospective study. *British Medical Journal, 320,* 1432–1436.

Chernin, K. (1985). *The hungry self: Women, eating, and identity.* New York: Harper & Row.

Cherniss, C. (1995). *Beyond burnout: Helping teachers, nurses, therapists, and lawyers recover from stress and disillusionment.* New York: Routledge.

Chesler, P. (2001). *Women's inhumanity to women.* New York: Thunder Mouth's Press/Nation Books.

Chesney, M. A., Darbes, L. A., Hoerster, K., Taylor, J. M., Chambers, D. B., & Anderson, D. E. (2005). Positive emotions: Exploring the other hemisphere in behavioral medicine. *International Journal of Behavioral Medicine, 12,* 50–58.

Chinn, P. L. (1991). Looking into the crystal ball: Positioning ourselves for the year 2000. *Nursing Outlook, 39,* 251–256.

Chinn, P. L. (2008). Lesbian nurses: What's the big deal? *Issues in Mental Health Nursing, 29,* 551–554.

Christen, A. G., & Cooper, K. H. (1979). *Strategic withdrawal from cigarette smoking.* New York: American Cancer Society.

Christman, L. (1988). Luther Christman. In T. Schorr & A. Zimmerman (Eds.), *Making choices, taking chances: Nurse leaders tell their stories* (pp. 43–52). St. Louis: C.V. Mosby.

Christman, L. (2000). Management adjustment—A glimpse into the future structure of care. *Nursing Administration Quarterly, 25*(1), 14–17.

Clark, C. (2008). Student perspectives on faculty incivility in nursing education: An application of the concept of rankism. *Nursing Outlook, 56*(1), 4–8.

Cleary, D. M. (1975). A nonstrike for patient care. *Modern Healthcare, 3*(6), 43–44.

Colgrove, M., Bloomfield, H., & McWilliams, P. (1991). *How to survive the loss of a love.* Los Angeles: Prelude Press.

Constable, J., & Russell, D. (1986). The effect of social support and the work environment upon burnout among nurses. *Journal of Human Stress, 12*(1), 20–26.

Cook, E. (1913). *The life of Florence Nightingale.* London: MacMillan.

Cooper, S. S. (1997). Men who choose nursing. *Nursing Dimensions, 8,* 24–26.

Cooperstock, R. (1978). Sex differences in psychotropic drug use. *Social Science and Medicine, 12B,* 179–186.

Corbett, S. (2003, March 16). The last shift. *New York Times Magazine,* 58–61.

Corley, M. C. (2002). Nurse moral distress: A proposed theory and research agenda. *Nursing Ethics, 9*(6), 636–650.

Corley, M. C., Minick, P., Elswick, R. K., & Jacobs, M. (2005). Nurse moral distress and ethical work environment. *Nursing Ethics, 12,* 382–390.

Cox, D. L., Stabb, S. D., & Hulgus, J. F. (2000). Anger and depression in girls and boys: A study of gender differences. *Psychology of Women Quarterly, 24,* 110–112.

Cox, D. L., Van Velsor, P., Hulgus, J. F., Weatherman, S., Smenner, M., Dickens, D., & Davis, C. (2004). What's the use in getting mad? Anger and instrumentality in women's relationships. *Health Care for Women International, 25,* 813–834.

Cox, H. (1991, January). Verbal abuse nationwide, Part I: Oppressed group behavior. *Nursing Management, 22,* 32–35.

Cox, K. B. (2003). The effects of intrapersonal, intragroup, and intergroup conflict on team performance effectiveness and work satisfaction. *Nursing Administration Quarterly, 27,* 153–163.

Crawford, J., Kippax, S., Onyx, J., Gault, U., & Benton, P. (1990). Women theorizing their experiences of anger: A study using memory-work. *Australian Psychologist, 25,* 333–350.

Crick, N. R., & Grotpeter, J. K. (1995). Relational aggression, gender, and social-psychological adjustment. *Child Development, 66,* 710–722.

Crouch, M. A., & Straub, V. (1983). Enhancement of self-esteem in adults. *Family and Community Health, 6*(2), 65–78.

Cummings, S. H. (1995). Attila the Hun versus Attila the hen: Gender socialization of the American nurse. *Nursing Administration Quarterly, 19*(2), 19–29.

Currie, D. M. (2003). *Becoming a radical poet: Transforming anger into freedom.* Unpublished master's thesis, Trinity Western University, Canada.

Dafter, R. E. (1996). Why "negative" emotions can sometimes be positive: The spectrum model of emotions and their role in mind-body healing. *Advances: The Journal of Mind-Body Health, 12*(2), 6–19.

Daley, K. A. (2002). Needlestick injuries in the workplace: Implications for public policy. In D. J. Mason, J. K. Leavitt, & M. W. Chaffee (Eds.), *Policy and politics in nursing and health care* (pp. 412–419). St. Louis: Saunders.

Dattilo, A. M., & Kris-Etherton, P. M. (1992). Effects of weight reduction on blood lipids and lipoproteins: A meta-analysis. *American Journal of Clinical Nutrition, 56,* 320–328.

Davidson, K. (2000, April). *Cost offset of an anger management intervention for CVD patients.* Paper presented at the annual meeting of the Society of Behavioral Medicine, Nashville, TN.

Davidson, K., MacGregor, M., Stuhr, J., Dixon, K., & MacLean, D. (2000). Constructive anger verbal behavior predicts blood pressure in a population-based sample. *Health Psychology, 19,* 55–64.

Davies, C. (1995). *Gender and the professional predicament in nursing.* Philadelphia: Open University Press.

Davis, C. (2003). Nursing humanities: The time has come. *American Journal of Nursing, 103*(2), 13.

DeCastro, A. B. (2006). Handle with care: The ANA's campaign to address work-related musculoskeletal disorders. *Orthopedic Nursing, 25,* 356–365.

Deffenbacher, J. (1992). Trait anger: Theory, findings, and implications. In C. D. Spielberger & J. N. Butcher (Eds.), *Advances in personality assessment* (Vol. 9, pp. 177–201). Hillsdale, NJ: Lawrence Erlbaum.

Deffenbacher, J. (1994, August). *Anger does not equal aggression.* Paper presented at the American Psychological Association, Los Angeles.

Deffenbacher, J. (1995a). Ideal treatment package for adults with anger disorders. In H. Kassinove (Ed.), *Anger disorders: Definition, diagnosis, and treatment* (pp. 151–172). Washington, DC: Taylor & Francis.

Deffenbacher, J. (1995b, August). *Assessing forms of anger expression.* Paper presented at the American Psychological Association, New York.

Deffenbacher, J., Oetting, E., Lynch, R., & Morris, C. (1996). The expression of anger and its consequences. *Behaviour Research and Therapy, 34,* 575–590.

Demand for nurses is high nationwide, according to *New York Times* Job Market research; Hospitals most in need of nursing talent. (2002, December 11). Retrieved July 10, 2003, from http://www.nytco.com

DeMarco, R. (2002). Two theories/sharper lens: The staff nurse voice in the workplace. *Journal of Advanced Nursing, 38,* 549–556.

DeMarco, R., Picard, C., & Agretelis, J. (2004). Nurse experiences as cancer survivors: Part I—Personal. *Oncology Nursing Forum, 31,* 523–530.

DeMarco, R., Roberts, S. J., Norris, A. E., & McCurry, M. (2007). Refinement of the silencing the self scale-work for RNs. *Journal of Nursing Scholarship, 39,* 375–378.

deQuincey, C. (2002). Entelechy: The intelligence of the body. *Advances, 18*(1), 41–45.

Derogatis, L., Abeloff, M., & Melisaratos, N. (1979). Psychological coping mechanisms and survival time in metastatic breast cancer. *Journal of the American Medical Association, 242,*1504–1508.

Diaz, A. L., & McMillin, J. D. (1991). A definition and description of nurse abuse. *Western Journal of Nursing Research, 13*(1), 97–109.

DiCicco-Bloom, B. (2004). The racial and gendered experiences of immigrant nurses from Kerala, India. *Journal of Transcultural Nursing, 15*(1), 26–33.

Diers, D. (2002). Research as a political and policy tool. In D. J. Mason, J. K. Leavitt, & M. W. Chaffee (Eds.), *Policy and politics in nursing and health care* (pp. 141–156). St. Louis: Saunders.

Dixon, J. P., Dixon, J. K., & Spinner, J. C. (1991). Tensions between career and interpersonal commitments as a risk factor for cardiovascular disease among women. *Women and Health, 17*(3), 33–57.

Doherty, R., Orimoto, L., Singelis, T., Hatfield, E., & Hebb, J. (1995). Emotional contagion: Gender and occupational differences. *Psychology of Women Quarterly, 19*, 355–371.

Doran, D. (Ed.). (2003). *Nursing-sensitive outcomes: State of the science.* Boston: Jones & Bartlett.

Dossey, B. (1995). Nurse as healer. In B. Dossey, L. Keegan, C. Guzzetta, & L. Kolkmeier, *Holistic nursing: A handbook for practice* (2nd ed., pp. 61–82). Gaithersburg, MD: Aspen.

Dossey, L. (1984). *Beyond illness.* Boston: Shambhala Publications.

Droppleman, P., & Wilt, D. (1993). Women, depression, and anger. In S. P. Thomas (Ed.), *Women and anger* (pp. 209–232). New York: Springer Publishing.

Dryden, W. (1990). *Dealing with anger problems: Rational-emotive therapeutic interventions.* Sarasota, Florida: Professional Resource Exchange.

Duchscher, J. E., & Cowin, L. S. (2004a). The experience of marginalization in new nursing graduates. *Nursing Outlook, 52*, 289–296.

Duchscher, J. E., & Cowin, L. S. (2004b). Multigenerational nurses in the workplace. *Journal of Nursing Administration, 34*, 493–501.

Duquette, A., Kerouac, S., Sandhu, B., & Beaudet, L. (1994). Factors related to nursing burnout: A review of empirical knowledge. *Issues in Mental Health Nursing, 15*, 337–358.

Durel, L. A., Carver, C. S., Spitzer, S. B., Llabre, M. M., Weintraub, J. K., Saab, P. G., & Schneiderman, N. (1989). Associations of blood pressure with self-report measures of anger and hostility among black and white men and women. *Health Psychology, 8*, 557–575.

Durkin, A. (2008). Educating nursing students about the dangers of drinking games. *Nursing Education Perspectives, 29*(1), 38–41.

Echternacht, M. (1999). Potential for violence toward psychiatric nursing students: Risk reduction techniques. *Journal of Psychosocial Nursing, 37*(3), 36–39.

Ehrenreich, B. (2002). The emergence of nursing as a political force. In D. J. Mason, J. K. Leavitt, & M. W. Chaffee (Eds.), *Policy and politics in nursing and health care* (pp. xxxiii–xxxvii). St. Louis: Saunders.

Eisenstein, H. (1988). On the psychosocial barriers to professions for women. In J. Muff (Ed.), *Women's issues in nursing: Socialization, sexism, and stereotyping.* (pp. 95–112). Prospect Heights, IL: Waveland Press.

Ekman, P. (1994). All emotions are basic. In P. Ekman & R. J. Davidson (Eds.), *The nature of emotion: Fundamental questions* (pp. 15–19). New York: Oxford University Press.

Elkind, A. K. (1988). Do nurses smoke because of stress? *Journal of Advanced Nursing, 13*, 733–745.

Ellis, A. (1973). *Humanistic psychotherapy: The rational-emotive approach.* New York: The Julian Press.

Emerson, C., & Harrison, D. (1990). Anger and denial as predictors of cardiovascular reactivity in women. *Journal of Psychopathology and Behavioral Assessment, 12*, 271–283.

Eng, P. M., Fitzmaurice, G., Zubzansky, L. D., Rimm, E. B., & Kawachi, I. (2003). Anger expression and risk of stroke and coronary heart disease among male health professionals. *Psychosomatic Medicine, 65*, 100–110.

Engebretson, T. O., Matthews, K. A., & Scheier, M. F. (1989). Relations between anger expression and cardiovascular reactivity: Reconciling inconsistent findings through a matching hypothesis. *Journal of Personality and Social Psychology, 57*, 513–521.

Epstein, A. H. (1989). *Mind, fantasy and healing: One woman's journey from conflict and illness to wholeness and health.* New York: Delacorte Press.

Eriksson, U., Starrin, B., & Janson, S. (2008). Long-term sickness absence due to burnout: Absentees' experiences. *Qualitative Health Research, 18*, 620–632.

Erlen, J., & Frost, B. (1991). Nurses' perceptions of powerlessness in influencing ethical decisions. *Western Journal of Nursing Research, 13*, 397–407.

Evans, P. D., & Edgerton, N. (1991). Life-events and mood as predictors of the common cold. *British Journal of Medical Psychology, 64*(1), 35–44.

Ewart, C. K., Taylor, C. B., Kraemer, H. C., & Agras, W. S. (1991). High blood pressure and marital discord: Not being nasty matters more than being nice. *Health Psychology, 10*, 155–163.

Ewashen, C. J. (1997). Devaluation dynamics and gender bias in women's groups. *Issues in Mental Health Nursing, 18*, 73–84.

Ex-teacher charged with murder in Georgia hospital shootings that killed three. Retrieved April 3, 2008, from http://www.foxnews.com/story/0,2933,343130,00.html

Extended Services Team, Visiting Nurse Association of Northern Virginia. (1997). Wellness for nurses, by nurses. *American Journal of Nursing, 97*(5), 67–68.

Fagot, B. I., Leinbach, M. D., & Hagan, R. (1986). Gender labeling and the development of sex-typed behaviors. *Developmental Psychology, 22,* 440–443.

Farrell, G. (1999). Aggression in clinical settings: Nurses' views—A follow-up study. *Journal of Advanced Nursing, 29,* 532–541.

Farrell, G. (2001). From tall poppies to squashed weeds: Why don't nurses pull together more? *Journal of Advanced Nursing, 35,* 26–33.

Feindler, E. L., & Ecton, R. B. (1986). *Adolescent anger control: Cognitive-behavioral techniques.* New York: Pergamon Press.

Felblinger, D. M. (2008). Incivility and bullying in the workplace and nurses' shame responses. *Journal of Obstetrical, Gynecological, and Neonatal Nursing, 37,* 234–242.

Ferguson, P., & Small, W. P. (1985). Further study of the smoking habits of hospital nurses. *Health Bulletin, 43*(1), 13–18.

Fields, B., Reesman, K., Robinson, C., Sims, A., Edwards, K., McCall, B., Short, B., & Thomas, S. P. (1998). Anger of African American women in the South. *Issues in Mental Health Nursing, 19,* 353–373.

Fiore, M. C., Novotny, T. E., Pierce, J. P., Giovino, G., Hatziandreau, E., Newcomb, P., Surawicz, T., & Davis, R. (1990). Methods used to quit smoking in the United States: Do cessation programs help? *Journal of the American Medical Association, 263,* 2760–2765.

Firth, H., McKeown, P., McIntee, J., & Britton, P. (1987). Professional depression, "burnout," and personality in longstay nursing. *International Journal of Nursing Studies, 24,* 227–237.

Fischer, A., Rodriguez Mosquera, P., van Vianen, A., & Manstead, A. (2004). Gender and culture differences in emotion. *Emotion, 4,* 87–94.

Fiske, S. T. (1993). Controlling other people: The impact of power on stereotyping. *American Psychologist, 48,* 621–628.

Fitzgerald, L. (1993). Sexual harassment: Violence against women in the workplace. *American Psychologist, 48,* 1070–1076.

Flanigan, B. (1992). *Forgiving the unforgivable.* New York: Macmillan.

Flegal, K. M., Carroll, M. D., Ogden, C. L., & Johnson, C. L. (2002). Prevalence and trends in obesity among US adults, 1999–2000. *Journal of the American Medical Association, 288,* 1723–1727.

Fletcher, C. E. (2001). Hospital RNs' job satisfactions and dissatisfactions. *Journal of Nursing Administration, 31,* 324–331.

Fleming, M. F., & Barry, K. L. (1992). *Addictive disorders.* St. Louis: C.V. Mosby.

Foley, M. (2001). ANA: Preserving the core while preparing for the future. *American Nurse, 33*(2), 5.

Foley, M. (2002). Collective action in health care. In D. J. Mason, J. K. Leavitt, & M. W. Chaffee (Eds.), *Policy and politics in nursing and health care* (pp. 387–397). St. Louis: Saunders.

Fondiller, S. H. (1995). Loretta C. Ford: A modern Olympian. *Nursing and Health Care: Perspectives on Community, 16,*(1), 6–11.

Force, M. V. (2005). The relationship between effective nurse managers and nursing retention. *Journal of Nursing Administration, 35,* 336–341.

Forest, K. B. (1991). The interplay of childhood stress and adult life events on women's symptoms of depression. *Dissertation Abstracts International, 51*(9–A), 3237.

Forster, J. L., & Jeffery, R. W. (1986). Gender differences related to weight history, eating patterns, efficacy expectations, self-esteem, and weight loss among participants in a weight reduction program. *Addictive Behaviors, 11,* 141–147.

Fowler, C. M. (1996). *Before women had wings.* New York: Fawcett Columbine.

Fox, C. M., Harper, A. P., Hyner, G. C., & Lyle, R. M. (1994). Loneliness, emotional repression, marital quality, and major life events in women who develop breast cancer. *Journal of Community Health, 19,* 467–482.

Frankl, V. (1978). *The unheard cry for meaning.* New York: Simon & Schuster.

Fredrickson, B., Mancuso, R., Branigan, C., & Tugade, M. (2000). The undoing effect of positive emotions. *Motivation and Emotion, 24,* 237–258.

Freiberg, P. (1991). Self-esteem gender gap widens in adolescence. *American Psychological Association Monitor, 22*(4), 29.

Frey, W., & Langseth, M. (1985). *Crying: The mystery of tears.* Minneapolis: Winston.

Frezza, M., DiPadova, C., Pozzato, G., Terpin, M., Baraona, E., & Lieber, C. (1990). High blood alcohol levels in women: The role of decreased gastric alcohol dehydrogenase and first-pass metabolism. *New England Journal of Medicine, 322*(2), 95–99.

Friedman, M., & Rosenman, R. (1974) *Type A behavior and your heart.* New York: Knopf.

Gabbay, F. H., Krantz, D. S., Kop, W. J., Hedges, S. M., Klein, J., Gottdiener, J. S., & Rosanski, A. (1996). Triggers of myocardial ischemia during daily life in patients with coronary artery disease: Physical and mental activities, anger and smoking. *Journal of the American College of Cardiology, 27,* 585–592.

Gallop, R., McKeever, P., Toner, B., Lancee, W., & Lueck, M. (1995). The impact of childhood sexual abuse on the psychological well-being and practice of nurses. *Archives of Psychiatric Nursing, 9*(3), 137–145.

Garmezy, N. (1991). Resiliency and vulnerability of adverse developmental outcomes associated with poverty. *American Behavioral Scientist, 34,* 416–430.

Gaskin, J. (1986). Nurses in trouble. *Canadian Nurse, 82*(4), 31–34.

Gauvin, L., Rejeski, W. J., & Norris, J. L. (1996). A naturalistic study of the impact of acute physical activity on feeling states and affect in women. *Health Psychology, 15,* 391–397.

Geiger, T. C., Zimmer-Gembeck, M. J., & Crick, N. R. (2004). The science of relational aggression: Can we guide intervention? In M. M. Moretti, C. L. Odgers, & M. A. Jackson (Eds.), *Girls and aggression: Contributing factors and intervention principles* (pp. 27–40). New York: Kluwer Academic/Plenum.

Gendlin, E. (1973). A phenomenology of emotions: Anger. In D. Carr & E. S. Casey (Eds.), *Explorations in phenomenology* (pp. 367–398). The Hague: Netherlands: Martinus Nijhoff.

George, T. (1997, June). *Mono-sexual tradition in philosophy, epistemology, and the work world of women.* Paper presented at the 8th International Congress on Women's Health Issues, Saskatoon, Saskatchewan.

Gerlock, A. A. (1994). Veterans' responses to anger management intervention. *Issues in Mental Health Nursing, 15,* 393–408.

Gianakos, D. (1997). Physicians, nurses, and collegiality. *Nursing Outlook, 45*(2), 57–58.

Giddings, L. S., & Smith, M. C. (2001). Stories of lesbian in/visibility in nursing. *Nursing Outlook, 49*(1), 14–19.

Glynn, L. M., Ebbesen, E. B., Christenfeld, N., & Gerin, W. (1998, March). *Recreating cardio-vascular responses with rumination: The effects of a delay between an emotion and its recall.* Paper presented at the annual meeting of the Society of Behavioral Medicine, New Orleans.

Godwin, G. (1983). *Mr. Bedford and the Muses.* New York: Ballantine Books.

Goertzel, V., & Goertzel, M. G. (1962). *Cradles of eminence.* Boston: Little, Brown.

Goffman, E. (1967). *Interaction ritual.* Garden City, NY: Doubleday.

Goldstein, D. J. (1991). Beneficial health effects of modest weight loss. *International Journal of Obesity, 16,* 397–415.

Goleman, D. (1995). *Emotional intelligence.* New York: Bantam.

Goleman, D. (2002). Could you be a leader? *Parade,* pp. 4–6.

Goodman, M., Quigley, J., Moran, G., Meilman, H., & Sherman, M. (1996). Hostility predicts restenosis after percutaneous transluminal coronary angioplasty. *Mayo Clinic Proceedings, 71,* 729–734.

Gordon, S. (1997). *Life support.* Boston: Little, Brown.

Gorin, S. S. (2001). Predictors of tobacco control among nursing students. *Patient Education and Counseling, 44,* 251–262.

Gorman, S., & Clark, N. (1986). Power and effective nursing practice. *Nursing Outlook, 34,* 129–134.

Greer, G. (1991). *The change.* New York: Fawcett Columbine.

Greer, S., & Morris, T. (1975). Psychological attitudes of women who develop breast cancer: A controlled study. *Journal of Psychosomatic Research, 19,* 147–153.

Greer, S., Morris, T., Pettingale, K. W., & Haybittle, J. L. (1990). Psychological response to breast cancer and fifteen-year outcome. *Lancet, 335*(1), 49–50.

Greif, E., Alvarez, M., & Ulman, L. (1981, April). *Recognizing emotions in other people: Sex differences in socialization.* Paper presented at the Biennial Meeting of the Society for Research in Child Development, Boston, MA.

Griffith. J. (1999). Substance abuse disorders in nurses. *Nursing Forum, 34*(4), 19–28.

Grilo, C. M., Shiffman, S., & Wing, R. (1989). Relapse crises and coping among dieters. *Journal of Consulting and Clinical Psychology, 57,* 488–495.

Gropper, E. (1994). Women supporting women: Are nurses really their own worst enemies? *Nursing Forum, 29*(3), 34–36.

Gross, J. J. (2006). *Handbook of emotion regulation.* New York: Guilford.

Grossarth-Maticek, R., Bastiaans, J., & Kanazir, D. (1985). Psychosocial factors as strong predictors of mortality from cancer, ischemic heart disease and stroke: The Yugoslav prospective study. *Journal of Psychosomatic Research, 29,* 167–176.

Grothgar, B., & Scholz, D. B. (1987). On specific behavior of migraine patients in an anger provoking situation. *Headache, 27,* 206–210.

Grover, S. M., & Thomas, S. P. (1993). Substance use and anger in mid-life women. *Issues in Mental Health Nursing, 14,* 19–29.

Groves, J. (1978). Taking care of the hateful patient. *New England Journal of Medicine, 298,* 883–887.

Gunther, M., & Thomas, S. P. (2006). Nurses' narratives of unforgettable patient care events. *Journal of Nursing Scholarship, 38,* 370–376.

Gut, E. (1989). *Productive and unproductive depression.* New York: Basic Books.

Gutierrez, L. (1990, March). Working with women of color: An empowerment perspective. *Social Work,* 149–153.

Hagberg, J. (1984). *Real power.* Minneapolis: Winston.

Hall, S. S. (1989, June). A molecular code links emotions, mind and health. *Smithsonian,* 62–70.

Hallstrom, T., Lapidum, L., Bengtsson, C., & Edstrom, K. (1986). Psychosocial factors and risk of ischemic heart disease and death in women: A 12-year follow-up of participants in the population study of women in Gothenburg, Sweden. *Journal of Psychosomatic Research, 30,* 451–459.

Halsey, J. (1985, Winter). The moderately troubled nurse: A not-so-uncommon entity. *Nursing Administration Quarterly,* 69–76.

Harburg, E., Blakelock, E., & Roeper, P. (1979). Resentful and reflective coping with arbitrary authority and blood pressure: Detroit. *Psychosomatic Medicine, 41,* 189–199.

Harburg, E., Julius, M., Kaciroti, N., Gleiberman, L., & Schork, M. (2003). Expressive/suppressive anger coping responses, gender, and types of mortality: A 17-year follow-up (Tecumseh, Michigan, 1971–1988). *Psychosomatic Medicine, 65,* 588–597.

Hart, P. D. (1990). *A nation-wide survey of attitudes towards health care and nurses.* Washington, DC: P. D. Hart Research Associates.

Hart, S. (1997). A gift disguised. *American Journal of Nursing, 97*(6), 54.

Hastings, C., & Waltz, C. (1995). Assessing the outcome of professional practice redesign: Impact on staff nurse perceptions. *Journal of Nursing Administration, 25*(3), 34–42.

Haynes, S., & Feinleib, M. (1980). Women, work and coronary heart disease: Prospective findings from the Framingham Heart Study. *American Journal of Public Health, 70,* 133–141.

Haynes, S., Feinleib, M., Levine, S., Scotch, N., & Kannel, W. (1978). The relationship of psychosocial factors to coronary heart disease in the Framingham Study: II. Prevalence of coronary heart disease. *American Journal of Epidemiology, 107,* 384–402.

Haynes, S., Levine, S., Scotch, N., Feinleib, M., & Kannel, W. (1978). The relationship of psychosocial factors to coronary heart disease in the Framingham Study: I. Methods and risk factors. *American Journal of Epidemiology, 107,* 362–383.

Haynes, S., Feinleib, M., & Kannel, W. (1980). The relationship of psychosocial factors to coronary heart disease in the Framingham Study. *American Journal of Epidemiology, 111,* 37–58.

Hazaleus, S., & Deffenbacher, J. (1985, January). Irrational beliefs and anger arousal. *Journal of College Student Personnel,* 47–52.

Hazaleus, S., & Deffenbacher, J. (1986). Relaxation and cognitive treatments of anger. *Journal of Consulting and Clinical Psychology, 54,* 222–226.

Hecker, M., Chesney, M., Black, G., & Frautschi, N. (1989). Coronary-prone behaviors in the Western Collaborative Group Study. *Psychosomatic Medicine, 50,* 153–164.

Hedin, A. (1994). *Perceived total workload stress, stress symptoms and coping styles of working women.* Unpublished doctoral dissertation. University of Maryland.

Heide, W. (1988). Feminist activism in nursing and health care. In J. Muff (Ed.), *Women's issues in nursing: Socialization, sexism, and stereotyping* (pp. 255–272). Prospect Heights, Illinois: Waveland Press.

Heim, P. (1995). Getting beyond "she said, he said." *Nursing Administration Quarterly, 19*(2), 6–18.

Helmlinger, C. (1997). A growing physical workload threatens nurses' health. *American Journal of Nursing, 97*(4), 64–66.

Henley, N. (1977). *Body politics: Power, sex, and nonverbal communication.* Englewood Cliffs, NJ: Prentice-Hall.

Hillhouse, J., & Adler, C. (1997). Investigating stress effect patterns in hospital staff nurses: Results of a cluster analysis. *Social Science and Medicine, 45,* 1781–1788.

Hochschild, A. R. (1979). Emotion work, feeling rules, and social structure. *American Journal of Sociology, 85,* 551–575.

Hoffman, M. L. (1989). Empathy and prosocial activism. In N. Eisenberg, J. Reykowski, & E. Staub (Eds.), *Social and moral values* (pp. 65–86). Hillsdale, NJ: Erlbaum.

Hollis, J. (1994). *Fat and furious: Women and food obsession.* New York: Fawcett.

Holmes, T., & Rahe, R. (1967). The Social Readjustment Rating Scale. *Journal of Psychosomatic Research, 11,* 213–218.

Holmila, M., & Raitasalo, K. (2005). Gender differences in drinking: Why do they still exist? *Addiction, 100,* 1763–1769.

Holz, K. (1994). A practical approach to clients who are survivors of childhood sexual abuse. *Journal of Nurse Midwifery, 39*(1), 13–18.

Hooper, W. (2003). Practicing safely in a non-safe environment. *Tennessee Nurse, 66*(2), 4–5.

Horton, J. A. (Ed.). (1992). *The women's health data book.* Washington, DC: Jacobs Institute of Women's Health.

Huesmann, L. R., Moise-Titus, J., Podolski, C-L., & Eron, L. D. (2003). Longitudinal relations between children's exposure to TV violence and their aggressive and violent behavior in young adulthood: 1977–1992. *Developmental Psychology, 39,* 201–221.

Hughes, J. R. (1985). *The relationship between smoking and mood: Role of smoking in affect regulation.* Symposium presented at the Society of Behavioral Medicine, New Orleans.

Hutchinson, S. (1986). Chemically dependent nurses: The trajectory toward self-annihilation. *Nursing Research, 35,* 196–201.

Ironson, G., Taylor, C. B., Boltwood, M., Bartzokis, T., Dennis, C., Chesney, M., et al. (1992). Effects of anger on left ventricular ejection fraction in coronary artery disease. *American Journal of Cardiology, 70,* 281–285.

Iribarren, C., Sidney, S., Bild, D. E., Liu, K., Markovitz, J. H., Roseman, J. M., & Matthews, K. (2000). Association of hostility with coronary artery calcification in young adults: The CARDIA Study. *Journal of the American Medical Association, 283*(19), 2546–2551.

Isler, C. (1970). Florence Nightingale: The call to war. *RN, 33*(5), 42–45, 74.

Jack, D. (1991). *Silencing the self.* Cambridge, MA: Harvard University Press.

Jack, D. (1999). *Behind the mask: Destruction and creativity in women's aggression.* Cambridge, MA: Harvard University Press.

Jacklin, C., & Maccoby, E. (1978). Social behavior at 33 months in same-sex and mixed-sex dyads. *Child Development, 49,* 557–569.

Jacobs, B. B., Fontana, J. S., Kehoe, M. H., Matarese, C., & Chinn, P. L. (2005). An emancipatory study of contemporary nursing practice. *Nursing Outlook, 53,* 6–14.

Jacoby, S. (2003, May). The nursing squeeze. *AARP Bulletin,* 6–8.

Jarratt, V. (1981, July). Why do nurses eat their young? *The Arkansas State Nursing Association Newsletter, 1*(2), 4, 10.

Johnson, C. L., Martin, S. L., & Markle-Elder, S. (2007). A national solution to patient handling injuries. *American Journal of Nursing, 107*(9), 73–75.

Johnston, D. W., Jones, M. M., McCann, S. K., & McKee, L. (2008). Determinants of negative affect in nurses during the working day: The role of demand, reward, control, and desire for more control. *Annals of Behavioral Medicine, 35,* S123.

Jones, J. W. (1982). *The burnout syndrome.* New York: London House.

Josefowitz, N. (1980). *Paths to power: A woman's guide from first job to top executive.* Reading, MA: Addison Wesley.

Josephson Institute of Ethics (2001, April). *The ethics of American youth: Violence and substance abuse: Press release, data and commentary.* Retrieved July 11, 2002, from http://www.josephsoninstitute.org/survey/2000/violence2000-commentary.htm

Jourard, S. (1971). *The transparent self.* New York: D. Van Nostrand.

Jung, C. G. (1965). *Memories, dreams, reflections.* New York: Vintage Books.

Kabb, G. (1984). Chemical dependency: Helping your staff. *Journal of Nursing Administration, 14*(11), 18–23.

Kagan, D. M., & Squires, R. L. (1984). Compulsive eating, dieting, stress, and hostility among college students. *Journal of College Student Personnel, 25,* 213–220.

Kalisch, B. J., & Kalisch, P. A. (1975). Slaves, servants, or saints? An analysis of the system of nurse training in the United States, 1873–1948. *Nursing Forum, 14,* 222–263.

Kane, D., & Thomas, B. (2000). Nursing and the "f" word. *Nursing Forum, 35*(2), 17–24.

Kanter, R. M. (1977). *Men and women of the corporation.* New York: Basic Books.

Kaplan, D. (1997). When less is more. *Psychology Today, 30*(3), 14.

Kawachi, I., Sparrow, D., Spiro, A., Vokonas, P., & Weiss, S. (1996). A prospective study of anger and coronary heart disease: The Normative Aging Study. *Circulation, 94,* 2090– 2095.

Kelley, J. (1997, May 5). Swiss nurse independently saved Nazis' youngest targets. *USA Today,* 2D.

Kenfield, S. A., Stampfer, M. J., Rosner, B. A., & Colditz, G. A. (2008). Smoking and smoking cessation in relation to mortality in women. *Journal of the American Medical Association, 299,* 2037–2047.

Kenna, G. A., & Wood, M. D. (2005). Family history of alcohol and drug use in healthcare professionals. *Journal of Substance Use, 10,* 225–238.

Kennedy, K. D. (1995). Invest in yourself: Have a laugh! Have a healthy laugh! *Nursing Forum, 30*(1), 25–30.

Kerfoot, K. M., & Ivy, S. S. (2004). Renewing the spirit: Sanctuaries for healing. *Reflections On Nursing Leadership, 30*(3), 20–23.

Kesey, K. (1973). *One flew over the cuckoo's nest.* New York: Picador.

Keyes, C. L. M. (2003). Complete mental health: An agenda for the 21st century. In C. L. M. Keyes & J. Haidt (Eds.), *Flourishing* (pp. 293–312). Washington, DC: American Psychological Association.

Kiecolt-Glaser, J., Malarkey, W., Chee, M. A., Newton, T., Cacioppo, J., Mao, H., et al. (1993). Negative behavior during marital conflict is associated with immunological down-regulation. *Psychosomatic Medicine, 55,* 395–409.

Kilbey, M., & Sobeck, J. (1988). Epidemiology of alcoholism. In C. B. Travis (Ed.), *Women and health psychology: Mental health issues* (pp. 91–107). Hillsdale, NJ: Lawrence Erlbaum.

Kittle, M. D. (2007, June 3). Whistleblowing nurse fights Finley hospital. *Telegraph Herald.* Retrieved June 5, 2008, from http://www.thonline.com/article.cfm?o=1&id=161002

Kleehammer, K., Hart, A. L., & Keck, J. F. (1990). Nursing students' perceptions of anxiety-producing situations in the clinical setting. *Journal of Nursing Education, 29,* 183–187.

Knaus, W. A., Draper, E. A., Wagner, D. P., & Zimmerman, J. E. (1986). An evaluation of outcome from intensive care in major medical centers. *Annals of Internal Medicine, 104,* 410–418.

Kolkmeier, L. G. (1995). Relaxation: Opening the door to change. In B. M. Dossey, L. Keegan, C. E. Guzzetta, & L. G. Kolkmeier. *Holistic nursing: A handbook for practice* (pp. 573–605). Gaithersburg, MD: Aspen.

Kollar, M., Groer, M., Thomas, S., & Cunningham, J. (1991). Adolescent anger: A developmental study. *Journal of Child and Adolescent Psychiatric Nursing, 4,* 9–15.

Kopper, B., & Epperson, D. (1991). Women and anger: Sex and sex-role comparisons in the expression of anger. *Psychology of Women Quarterly, 15,* 7–14.

Kornfield, J. (1993). *A path with heart.* New York: Bantam.

Kovner, C. T. (2000). State regulation of RN-to-patient ratios. *American Journal of Nursing, 100*(11), 61–63.

Kovner, C. T., Brewer, C. S., Fairchild, S., Poornima, S., Kim, H., & Djukic, M. (2007). Newly licensed RNs' characteristics, work attitudes, and intentions to work. *American Journal of Nursing, 107*(9), 58–70.

Kowalski, K. (1992). From failures to major learning experiences. *MCN: The American Journal of Maternal/Child Nursing, 17,* 9–10.

Kraegel, J., & Kachoyeanos, M. (1989). *Just a nurse.* New York: Dell.

Kralik, D., Koch, T., & Wotton, K. (1997). Engagement and detachment: Understanding patients' experiences with nursing. *Journal of Advanced Nursing, 26,* 399–407.

Kramer, M. (1974). *Reality shock.* St. Louis: C.V. Mosby.

Kramer, M., & Schmalenberg, C. (2003). Magnet hospital staff nurses describe clinical autonomy. *Nursing Outlook, 51*, 13–19.

Krucoff, C. (1997, May 6). Man's best exercise buddy: Secrets I've learned from my four-legged partner. *The Washington Post, Health, 13*(18), 20.

Kune, G., Kune, S., Watson, L., & Bahnson, C. (1991). Personality as a risk factor in large bowel cancer: Data from the Melbourne Colorectal Cancer Study. *Psychological Medicine, 21*, 28–41.

Kuper, H., & Marmot, M. (2003). Job strain, job demands, decision latitude, and risk of coronary heart disease within the Whitehall II Study. *Journal of Epidemiology and Community Health, 57*, 147–153.

Lancee, W. J., Gallop, R., McCay, E., & Toner, B. (1995). The relationship between nurses' limit-setting styles and anger in psychiatric inpatients. *Psychiatric Services, 46*(6), 609–613.

Lanza, M. L. (1983). The reactions of nursing staff to physical assault by a patient. *Hospital and Community Psychiatry, 34*, 44–47.

Lanza, M. L., Kayne, H. L., Pattison, I., Hicks, C., & Islam, S. (1996). The relationship of behavioral cues to assaultive behavior. *Clinical Nursing Research, 5*(1), 6–27.

Larson, D. G. (1987). Helper secrets: Internal stressors in nursing. *Journal of Psychosocial Nursing and Mental Health Services, 25*(4), 20–27.

Larson, E. L. (1995). New rules for the game: Interdisciplinary education for health professionals. *Nursing Outlook, 43*, 180–185.

Larson, M. R., Ader, R., & Moynihan, J. A. (2001). Heart rate, neuroendocrine, and immunological reactivity in response to an acute laboratory stressor. *Psychosomatic Medicine, 63*, 493–501.

Laschinger, H., Finegan, J., & Shamian, J. (2001). The impact of workplace empowerment, organizational trust on staff nurses' work satisfaction and organizational commitment. *Health Care Management Review, 26*(3), 7–23.

Laschinger, H., Shamian, J., & Thomson, D. (2001). Impact of magnet hospital characteristics on nurses' perceptions of trust, burnout, quality of care, and work satisfaction. *Nursing Economics, 19*, 209–220.

Laschinger, H., Wong, C., McMahon, L., & Kaufmann, C. (1999). Leader behavior impact on staff nurse empowerment, job tension, and work effectiveness. *Journal of Nursing Administration, 29*(5), 28–39.

Lazare, A. (2006). Apology in medical practice: An emerging clinical skill. *Journal of the American Medical Association, 296*, 1401–1404.

Leach, R. A. (1990, Sept. 6). Anecdote about butterfly's wings cures the blahs. *Nashville Banner*, A15.

Leavitt, J. K., Cohen, S. S., & Mason, D. J. (2002). Political analysis and strategies. In D. J. Mason, J. K. Leavitt, & M. W. Chaffee (Eds.), *Policy and politics in nursing and health care* (pp. 71–91). St. Louis, MO: Saunders.

Leavitt, P. (2002). Managed care mandated coverage in Maine: A grassroots success story. In D. J. Mason, J. K. Leavitt, & M. W. Chaffee (Eds.), *Policy and politics in nursing and health care* (pp. 379–385). St. Louis, MO: Saunders.

Leiter, M. P., Harvie, P., & Frizzell, C. (1998). The correspondence of patient satisfaction and nurse burnout. *Social Science and Medicine, 47*, 1611–1617.

Lerner, H. G. (1985). *The dance of anger*. New York: Harper & Row.

Lerner, M. J. (1980). *The belief in a just world: A fundamental delusion*. New York: Plenum.

Levant, R. (1995). Toward the reconstruction of masculinity. In R. Levant & W. Pollack (Eds.), *A new psychology of men* (pp. 229–251). New York: Basic Books.

Lever, J. (1976). Sex differences in the games children play. *Social Problems, 23*, 478–487.

Levey, G. A. (1994, November 13). What's your mood food? *Parade Magazine*, 16.

Levine, M. E. (1970). The intransigent patient. *American Journal of Nursing, 70*, 2106–2111.

Levinson, D. J. (1978). *The seasons of a man's life*. New York: Alfred A. Knopf.

Levinson, D. J. (1996). *The seasons of a woman's life*. New York: Ballantine Books.

Levinson, H. (1980). Power, leadership, and the management of stress. *Professional Psychology, 11*, 497–508.

Lex, B. W. (1991). Some gender differences in alcohol and polysubstance users. *Health Psychology, 10*, 121–132.

Lexicon Publications. (1989). *The new lexicon Webster's dictionary of the English language.* New York: Author.

Libbus, M. K., & Bowman, K. G. (1997, June). *Sexual harassment: Development of an instrument to assess staff nurse sensitivity.* Paper presented at the 8th International Congress on Women's Health Issues, Saskatoon, Saskatchewan.

Lillibridge, J., Cox, M., & Cross, W. (2002). Uncovering the secret: Giving voice to the experiences of nurses who misuse substances. *Journal of Advanced Nursing, 39,* 219–229.

Little, M. (1993). AMA's new smear campaign—fowl play. *Tennessee Nurse, 56*(4), 12–14.

Lopez, N. (1990). *The acculturation of selected Filipino nurses to nursing practice in the United States.* Unpublished doctoral dissertation, University of Pennsylvania.

Lovell, M. C. (1988). Daddy's little girl: The lethal effects of paternalism in nursing. In J. Muff (Ed.), *Women's issues in nursing: Socialization, sexism and stereotyping* (pp. 210–220). Prospect Heights, IL: Waveland Press.

Low, C. A., Bower, J. E., Kwan, L., & Seldon, J. (2008). Benefit finding in response to BRCA testing. *Annals of Behavioral Medicine, 35,* 61–69.

Lucas, M. D., Atwood, J. R., & Hagaman, R. (1993). Replication and validation of anticipated turnover model for urban registered nurses. *Nursing Research, 42,* 29–35.

MacGregor, M., & Davidson, K. (1994, April). *Gender differences in the rating of hostility.* Paper presented at the 15th meeting of the Society of Behavioral Medicine, Boston, MA.

MacIntosh, J. (2006). Tackling work place bullying. *Issues in Mental Health Nursing, 27,* 665–679.

Macnee, C. (1991). Perceived well-being of persons quitting smoking. *Nursing Research, 40,* 200–203.

Mainiero, L. A. (1986). Coping with powerlessness: The relationship of gender and job dependency to empowerment-strategy usage. *Administrative Science Quarterly, 31,* 633–653.

Malone, B. (1985, Winter). Legitimate anger: Consequences and challenges. *Nursing Administration Quarterly,* 41–45.

Manderino, M. A., & Berkey, N. (1995). Verbal abuse of staff nurses by physicians. *Image: Journal of Nursing Scholarship, 27*(3), 244.

Manion, J. (2008). Does your job make you happy? *American Journal of Nursing, 108,* Supplement to Number 1, pp. 11–12.

Mansen, T. J. (1993). Role-taking abilities of nursing education administrators and their perceived leadership effectiveness. *Journal of Professional Nursing, 9,* 347–357.

Marion, L. N., Fuller, S. G., Johnson, N. P., Michels, P. J., & Diniz, C. (1996). Drinking problems of nursing students. *Journal of Nursing Education, 35,* 196–203.

Marks, S. (1979, Summer). Culture, human energy, and self-actualization: A sociological offering to humanistic psychology. *Journal of Humanistic Psychology, 19*(3), 27–42.

Marszalek-Gaucher, E., & Elsenhans, V. (1988). Intrapreneurship: Tapping employee creativity. *Journal of Nursing Administration, 18*(12), 20–22.

Martin, C. L., & Fabes, R. A. (2001). The stability and consequences of young children's same-sex peer interactions. *Developmental Psychology, 37,* 431–446.

Martin, S. D. (2002). Striking nurses win from coast to coast. *The American Nurse, 34*(2), 8.

Maslach, C. (1982). *Burnout: The cost of caring.* Englewood Cliffs, NJ: Prentice Hall.

Maslach, C., & Leiter, M. (1999, September/October). Take this job and love it! *Psychology Today,* 50–53, 79–80.

Mason, D. J. (2001). Of mentorship and Scotch on the rocks. *American Journal of Nursing, 101*(7), 7.

Mason, D. J., Leavitt, J. K., & Chaffee, M. W. (2002). *Policy and politics in nursing and health care.* St. Louis: Saunders.

Mason, R. (1995). PACDN update: The Peer Assistance for Chemically Dependent Nurses (PACDN) Committee. *Virginia Nurses Today, 3*(3), 15–17.

McBride, A. B. (2005). Nursing and the informatics revolution. *Nursing Outlook, 53,* 183–191.

McCloskey, J. A. (1990). Two requirements for job contentment: Autonomy and social integration. *Image: Journal of Nursing Scholarship, 22,* 140–143.

McClure, M. L., Poulin, M. A., Sovie, M. D., & Wandelt, M. A. (1983). *Magnet hospitals: Attraction and retention of professional nurses.* Washington, DC: American Nurses' Association, American Academy of Nursing.

McEwen, B., & Lasley, E. N. (2003). Allostatic load: When protection gives way to damage. *Advances, 19*(1), 28–33.

McEwen, B., & Stellar, E. (1993). Stress and the individual: Mechanisms leading to disease. *Archives of Internal Medicine, 153,* 2093–2101.

McGrath, E., Keita, G., Strickland, B., & Russo, N. (1990). *Women and depression: Risk factors and treatment issues.* Washington, DC: American Psychological Association.

McElhaney, R. (1996). Conflict management in nursing. *Nursing Management, 27*(3), 49–50.

McKenna, B. G., Smith, N. A., Poole, S. J., & Coverdale, J. H. (2003). Horizontal violence: Experiences of registered nurses in their first year of practice. *Journal of Advanced Nursing, 42*(1), 90–96.

McNamee, S., & Gergen, K. (1999). *Relational responsibility.* Thousand Oaks, CA: Sage.

McNeely, E. (2005). The consequences of job stress for nurses' health: Time for a check-up. *Nursing Outlook, 53,* 291–299.

McNeese-Smith, D. K. (1997). The influence of manager behavior on nurses' job satisfaction, productivity, and commitment. *Journal of Nursing Administration, 27,* 47–55.

McWilliams, N., & Stein, J. (1987). Women's groups led by women: The management of devaluing transferences. *International Journal of Group Psychotherapy, 37,* 139–153.

Meissner, J. (1986). Nurses: Are we eating our young? *Nursing, 16*(3), 51–53.

Melamed, S., Shirom, A., Toker, S., Berliner, S., & Shapira, I. (2006). Burnout and risk of cardiovascular disease: Evidence, possible causal paths, and promising research directions. *Psychological Bulletin, 132,* 327–353.

Merleau-Ponty, M. (1962). *The phenomenology of perception.* London: Routledge & Kegan Paul.

Merjonen, P., Pulkki-Raback, L., & Keltikangas-Jarvinen, L. (2007). Anger and cardio-vascular health. In E. I. Clausen (Ed.), *Psychology of anger* (pp. 71–106). New York: Nova Science.

Migliaccio, T. A. (2002). Abused husbands: A narrative analysis. *Journal of Family Issues, 23*(1), 26–52.

Miller, G. E., Dopp, J. M., Myers, H. F., & Fahey, J. L. (1999). Psychosocial predictors of natural killer cell mobilization during marital conflict. *Health Psychology, 18,* 262–271.

Miller, J. B. (1983). The construction of anger in men and women. *Work in progress: Stone Center for Developmental Services and Studies.* Wellesley, MA: Wellesley College, Stone Center.

Mittleman, M. A., Maclure, M., Sherwood, J. B., Mulry, R. P., Tofler, G. H., Jacobs, S. C., et al. (1995). Triggering of acute myocardial infarction onset by episodes of anger. *Circulation, 92*(1), 720–725.

Moffett, B. S. (2002, July). *Caring as a mediator of burnout in nurses.* Poster presented at the American Nurses Association convention, Philadelphia, PA.

Mokdad, A. H., Ford, E. S. Bowman, B. A., Dietz, W. H., Vinicor, F., Bales, V. S., & Marks, J. S. (2003). Prevalence of obesity, diabetes, and obesity-related health risk factors. *Journal of the American Medical Association, 289,* 76–79.

Monteiro, L. (1985). Florence Nightingale on public health nursing. *American Journal of Public Health, 75,* 181–186.

Montgomery, C. L. (1991). The care-giving relationship: Paradoxical and transcendent aspects. *The Journal of Transpersonal Psychology, 13*(2), 91–104.

Moon, J. R., & Eisler, R. M. (1983). Anger control: An experimental comparison of three behavioral treatments. *Behavior Therapy, 14,* 493–505.

Moore, M. L., Parsons, L., & Zaccaro, D. (1997). *Education, attitudes and practices of nurses from three practice sites concerning domestic violence.* Paper presented at the 8th International Congress on Women's Health Issues, Saskatoon, Saskatchewan.

Morath, J. M., Casey, M., & Covert, E. (1985, Winter). The angry nurse/the angry staff. *Nursing Administration Quarterly,* 45–49.

Morris, T., Greer, S., Pettingale, K., & Watson, M. (1981). Patterns of expression of anger and their psychological correlates in women with breast cancer. *Journal of Psychosomatic Research, 25,* 111–117.

Moss, R., & Rowls, C. (1997). Staff nurse job satisfaction and management style. *Nursing Management, 28*(1), 32, 34.

Mozingo, J., Thomas, S., & Brooks, E. (1995). Factors associated with perceived competency levels of graduating seniors in a baccalaureate nursing program. *Journal of Nursing Education, 34,* 115–122.

Mrkwicka, L. (1994). Sexual harassment is no laughing matter. *International Nursing Review 41,*(4), 123–126.

Muff, J. (1988). *Women's issues in nursing: Socialization, sexism and stereotyping.* Prospect Heights, IL: Waveland Press. (Original work published 1982).

Murray, R., & Zentner, J. P. (1979). *Nursing concepts for health promotion* (2nd ed.). Englewood Cliffs, NJ: Prentice-Hall.

Mynatt, S. (1996). A model of contributing risk factors to chemical dependency in nurses. *Journal of Psychosocial Nursing and Mental Health Services, 34*(7), 13–22.

Naisbett, J., & Aburdene, P. (1990). *Megatrends 2000.* New York: William Morrow.

Namie, G. (2003). The World Bullying Institute 2003 report on abusive workplaces. Retrieved June 7, 2008, from http://www.bullyinginstitute.org

Needleman, J., Buerhaus, P., Mattke, S., Stewart, M., & Zelevinsky, K. (2002). Nurse-staffing levels and the quality of care in hospitals. *New England Journal of Medicine, 346,* 1715–1722.

Nelson, A., Fragala, G., & Menzel, N. (2003). Myths and facts about back injuries in nursing. *American Journal of Nursing, 103*(2), 32–40.

Nelson, R. (2007). U.S. hospitals need staffing makeover. *American Journal of Nursing, 107*(12), 19.

New study finds U.S. hospitals must improve workplace communication to reduce medical errors, enhance quality of care. (2005, January 26). *American Association of Critical-Care Nurses.* Retrieved June 5, 2008, from http://www.silencekills.com

Niaura, R., Todaro, J. F., Stroud, L., Spiro, A., Ward, K. D., & Weiss, S. (2002). Hostility, the metabolic syndrome, and incident coronary heart disease. *Health Psychology, 21,* 588–593.

Nightingale, F. (1992). *Notes on nursing: What it is and what it is not.* Philadelphia: J.B. Lippincott (Original work published 1859).

Nolen-Hoeksema, S. (1987). Sex differences in unipolar depression: Evidence and theory. *Psychological Bulletin, 101,* 259–282.

Nolen-Hoeksema, S. (1990). *Sex differences in depression.* Stanford, CA: Stanford University Press.

Norman, G. J., & Mills, P. J. (2004). Keeping it simple: Encouraging walking as a means to active living. *Annals of Behavioral Medicine, 28,* 149–151.

Norville, D. (2007). *Thank you power: Making the science of gratitude work for you.* Nashville, TN: Thomas Nelson.

Novaco, R. W. (1975). *Anger control: The development and evaluation of an experimental treatment.* Lexington, MA: D.C. Heath.

Novaco, R. W. (1985). Anger and its therapeutic regulation. In M. A. Chesney & R. H. Rosenman (Eds.), *Anger and hostility in cardiovascular and behavioral disorders* (pp. 203–226). Washington, DC: Hemisphere.

Novaco, R. W. (1996). Anger treatment and its special challenges. *National Center for PTSD Clinical Quarterly, 6*(3), 56, 58–60.

Nurses concerned over working conditions, decline in quality of care. (2001). Retrieved February 10, 2001, from http://www.nursingworld.org/rnrealnews

Ogus, E. D. (1990). Burnout and social support systems among ward nurses. *Issues in Mental Health Nursing, 11,* 267–281.

O'Leary, V. E. (1998). Strength in the face of adversity: Individual and social thriving. *Journal of Social Issues, 54,* 425–446.

O'Leary, V. E., & Ickovics, J. R. (1994, May). *Women's resilience: A heuristic model.* Paper presented at the American Psychological Association Conference on Psychosocial and Behavioral Factors in Women's Health, Washington, DC.

Olson, R. K., & Vance, C. N. (1993). *Mentorship in nursing: A collection of research abstracts with selected bibliographies.* Houston, TX: The University of Texas Printing Services.

O'Neill, T. (2003). Untouchables. *National Geographic, 203*(6), 2–31.

On mentorship. (2001). *American Journal of Nursing, 101*(12), 65–66.

Orbach, S. (1978). *Fat is a feminist issue.* New York: Paddington Press.

Orford, J., & Keddie, A. (1985). Gender differences in the functions and effects of moderate and excessive drinking. *British Journal of Clinical Psychology, 24,* 265–279.

Ornish, D. (1990). *Dr. Dean Ornish's program for reversing heart disease.* New York: Ballantine Books.

Palmer, A. (2003). Violent song lyrics may lead to violent behavior. *Monitor on Psychology, 34*(7), 15.

Patzer, M. (2008, Spring). NPs key to success of retail clinics. *Salute to Nurses,* 13.

Pausch, R. (2008, April 6). The lessons I'm leaving behind. *Parade,* 6–7.

Pear, R. (2008, March 29). Survey finds many patients discontent with hospital care. *The San Diego Union-Tribune,* A3.

Peden, A. R. (1996). Recovering from depression: A one-year follow-up. *Journal of Psychiatric and Mental Health Nursing, 3,* 289–295.

Pekkanen, J. (2003, September). Condition: Critical. *Reader's Digest,* 84–93.

Pelz, D. C., & Andrews, F. M. (1966). *Scientists in organization: Productive climates for research and development.* New York: Wiley.

Pennebaker, J. W. (1992). Inhibition as the linchpin of health. In H. S. Friedman (Ed.), *Hostility, coping, and health* (pp. 127–139). Washington, DC: American Psychological Association.

Pennebaker, J. W. (1997). Writing about emotional experiences as a therapeutic process. *Psychological Science, 8,* 162–166.

Perini, C., Muller, F., & Buhler, F. (1991). Suppressed aggression accelerates early development of essential hypertension. *Journal of Hypertension, 9,* 499–503.

Perls, F., Hefferline, R., & Goodman, P. (1951). *Gestalt therapy.* New York: Dell.

Pert, C. B. (2002). The wisdom of the receptors: Neuropeptides, the emotions, and bodymind. *Advances, 18*(1), 30–35.

Pew Health Professions Commission. (1993). *Health professions education for the future: Schools in service to the nation.* San Francisco: Pew Health Professions Commission.

Phillips, D. A. (2001). Methodology for social accountability: Multiple methods and feminist, poststructural, psychoanalytic discourse analysis. *Advances in Nursing Science, 23*(4), 49–66.

Pieranunzi, V. R. (1997). The lived experience of power and powerlessness in psychiatric nursing: A Heideggerian hermeneutical analysis. *Archives of Psychiatric Nursing, 11,* 155–162.

Pike, M. (2003). Who are you—Andy, Opie, or Aunt Bea? *Reflections on Nursing Leadership, 29*(2), 50–51.

Pine, R., & Tart, K. (2007). Return on investment: Benefits and challenges of a baccalaureate nurse residency program. *Nursing Economics, 25,* 13–18, 39.

Plaas, K. (2002). "Like a bunch of cattle": The patient's experience of the outpatient health care environment. In S. P. Thomas & H. R. Pollio (Eds.) *Listening to patients: A phenomenological approach to nursing research and practice* (pp. 23–251). New York: Springer.

Plas, J. M., & Hoover-Dempsey, K. V. (1988). *Working up a storm.* New York: W.W. Norton.

Podrasky, D., & Sexton, D. (1988). Nurses' reactions to difficult patients. *Image, 20,* 16–21.

Pollitt, R. A., Daniel, M., Kaufkann, J. S., Lynch, J. W., Salonen, J. T., & Kaplan, G. A. (2005). Mediation and modification of the association between hopelessness, hostility, and progression of carotid atherosclerosis. *Journal of Behavioral Medicine, 28,* 53–64.

Polster, M. (1992). *Eve's daughter: The forbidden heroism of women.* San Francisco: Jossey-Bass.

Porter-O'Grady, T. (1995). Reverse discrimination in nursing leadership: Hitting the concrete ceiling. *Nursing Administration Quarterly, 19*(2), 56–62.

Porter-O'Grady, T. (2001). Profound change: 21st century nursing. *Nursing Outlook, 49,* 182–186.

Porter-O'Grady, T. (2005). Shared governance: How to create and sustain a culture of nurse empowerment. Paper presented at the November 2005 HCPro Audioconference. Retrieved October 6, 2008, from http://hcpro.com/ppv-55059.html

Powell, L., Shaker, L., Jones, B., Vaccarino, L., Thoreson, C., & Pattillo, J. (1993). Psychosocial predictors of mortality in 83 women with premature acute myocardial infarction. *Psychosomatic Medicine, 55,* 426–433.

Powell, L., & Thoreson, C. (1987). Modifying the Type A pattern: A small group treatment approach. In J. A. Blumenthal & D. C. McKee (Eds.), *Applications in behavioral medicine and health psychology: A clinician's source book* (pp. 171–207). Sarasota, FL: Professional Resource Exchange.

Pratt, J. P., Overfield, T., & Hilton, H. G. (1994). Health behaviors of nurses and general population women. *Health Values, 18*(5), 41–46.

Prochaska, J. J., Hall, S. M., Humfleet, G., Munoz, R., Reus, V., Gorecki, J., & Hu, D. (2008). Promoting physical activity for maintaining non-smoking: A randomized controlled trial. *Annals of Behavioral Medicine, 35,* S102.

Quine, L. (1999). Workplace bullying in NHS community trust: Staff questionnaire survey. *British Medical Journal, 318,* 228–232.

Raingruber, B., & Robinson, C. (2007). The effectiveness of Tai Chi, yoga, meditation, and Reiki healing sessions in promoting health and enhancing problem solving abilities of registered nurses. *Issues in Mental Health Nursing, 28,* 1141–1155.

Ray, M. M., & Roberts, S. (2002). Lobbying policymakers: Individual and collective strategies. In D. J. Mason, J. K. Leavitt, & M. W. Chaffee (Eds.), *Policy and politics in nursing and health care* (pp. 551–561). St. Louis: Saunders.

Ray, O., & Ksir, C. (1987). *Drugs, society, and human behavior.* St. Louis: Mosby.

Rein, G., Atkinson, M., & McCraty, R. (1995). The physiological and psychological effects of compassion and anger. *Journal of Advancement in Medicine, 8*(2), 87–105.

Remen, R. N. (1996). All emotions are potentially life affirming. *Advances: The Journal of Mind-Body Health, 12*(2), 25.

Repetti, R. (1992). Social withdrawal as a short-term coping response to daily stressors. In H. S. Friedman (Ed.), *Hostility, coping and health* (pp. 151–165). Washington, DC: American Psychological Association.

Reverby, S. (1987). *Ordered to care: The dilemma of American nursing 1850–1945.* Cambridge: Cambridge University Press.

Rew, L., & Christian, B. (1993). Self-efficacy, coping, and well-being among nursing students sexually abused in childhood. *Journal of Pediatric Nursing, 8,* 392–399.

Reynolds, D. (1987). *Water bears no scars.* New York: William Morrow.

Roberts, J. D. (1986). Games nurses play: Part 2. "Pass to a Higher Authority" and "Trivial Pursuit." *American Journal of Nursing, 86,* 945–956.

Roberts, S. (1991). Nurse abuse: A taboo topic. *Canadian Nurse, 87*(3), 23–25.

Roberts, S. J. (1983). Oppressed group behavior: Implications for nursing. *Advances in Nursing Science, 5*(7), 21–30.

Roberts, S. J. (2000). Developing a positive professional identity: Liberating oneself from the oppressor within. *Advances in Nursing Science, 22*(4), 71–82.

Robbins, I., Bender, M. P., & Finnis, S. J. (1997). Sexual harassment in nursing. *Journal of Advanced Nursing, 25*(1), 163–169.

Rodgers, J. A. (1982). Women and the fear of being envied. *Nursing Outlook, 30,* 344–347.

Rogers, A., Hwang, W-T., Scott, L. D., Aiken, L. H., & Dinges, D. F. (2004). The working hours of hospital staff nurses and patient safety. *Health Affairs, 23,* 202–212.

Rosenblatt, R. (1997). Speech for a high school graduate. *Time, 149*(23), 90.

Rosenman, R. H., Brand, R. J., Jenkins, C. D., Friedman, M., Strauss, R., & Wurm, M. (1975). Coronary heart disease in the Western Collaborative Group Study: Final follow-up experience of 8 $\frac{1}{2}$ years. *Journal of the American Medical Association, 233,* 872–877.

Rosenstein, A. H. (2002). Nurse-physician relationships: Impact on nurse satisfaction and retention. *American Journal of Nursing, 102*(6), 26–34.

Rosenstein, A. H., & O'Daniel, M. (2005). Disruptive behavior and clinical outcomes; Perceptions of nurses and physicians. *American Journal of Nursing, 105*(1), 55–64.

Rosenstein, A. H., & O'Daniel, M. (2006). Impact and implications of disruptive behavior in the perioperative area. *Journal of the American College of Surgeons, 203,* 96–105.

Roth, S. (1999). The uncertain path to dialogue: A meditation. In S. McNamee & K. J. Gergen (Eds.), *Relational responsibility: Resources for sustainable dialogue* (pp. 93–97). Thousand Oaks, CA: Sage.

Rothenberg, A. (1973). The anatomy of anger. In D. Carr & E. S. Casey (Eds.), *Explorations in phenomenology* (pp. 351–366). The Hague, Netherlands: Martinus Nijhoff.

Roush, K. (2008). To the class of '08 (and '96 and '84 and '67 . . .) *American Journal of Nursing, 108,* (1, Suppl.), 9.

Rowe, M. M., & Sherlock, H. (2005). Stress and verbal abuse in nursing: Do burned out nurses eat their young? *Journal of Nursing Management, 13,* 242–248.

Rubin, L. (1996). *The transcendent child: Tales of triumph over the past.* New York: Basic Books.

Ruiz, M. J. (1988). Lack of ego differentiation. In J. Muff (Ed.), *Women's issues in nursing: Socialization, sexism and stereotyping* (pp. 307–314). Prospect Heights, IL: Waveland Press.

Russell, S., & Shirk, B. (1993). Women's anger and eating. In S. P. Thomas (Ed.), *Women and anger* (pp. 170–185). New York: Springer Publishing.

Rutter, P. (1996). *Sex, power, and boundaries.* New York: Bantam Books.

Safe staffing poll results. (2008, May 21). Retrieved June 5, 2008, from http://www.safestaffingsaveslives.org/WhatisANADoing/PollResults.aspx

Safran, J., & Greenberg, L. (1991). *Emotion, psychotherapy, and change.* New York: Guilford.

Salmon, J., Owen, N., Crawford, D., Bauman, A., & Sallis, J. F. (2003). Physical activity and sedentary behavior: A population-based study of barriers, enjoyment, and preference. *Health Psychology, 22,* 178–188.

Sanborn, M. (2006). *You don't need a title to be a leader.* New York: Doubleday.

Sandelowski, M. (1986). The problem of rigor in qualitative research. *Advances in Nursing Science, 8,* 27–37.

Sandroff, R. (1982). Hooked: The story of one RN's battle with drugs. *RN, 46*(6), 45–47.

Sanford, J. A. (1977). *Healing and wholeness.* New York: Paulist Press.

Sanford, L. T., & Donovan, M. E. (1985). *Women and self-esteem.* New York: Penguin.

Sapolsky, R. M. (1998). *Why zebras don't get ulcers.* New York: W.H. Freeman.

Sardana, R. M. (1997). *Bereavement in aging women: Psychosocial and cultural issues.* Paper presented at the 8th International Congress on Women's Health Issues, Saskatoon, Saskatchewan.

Sarna, L., Bialous, S., Wewers, M., Froelicher, E., & Danao, L. (2005). Nurses, smoking, and the workplace. *Research in Nursing and Health, 28,* 79–90.

Sartre, J-P. (1956). *Being and nothingness.* New York: Philosophical Library.

Saussy, C. (1995). *The gift of anger: A call to faithful action.* Louisville, KY: Westminster John Knox Press.

Saylor, M., & Denham, G. (1993). Women's anger and self-esteem. In S. P. Thomas (Ed.), *Women and anger* (pp. 91–111). New York: Springer Publishing.

Schaub, B., & Schaub, R. (1997). *Healing addictions: The vulnerability model of recovery.* Albany, NY: Delmar Publishers.

Schaufeli, W., Bakker, A., Hoogduin, K., Schaap, C., & Kladler, A. (2001). On the clinical validity of the Maslach Burnout Inventory and the burnout measure. *Psychology and Health, 16,* 565–582.

Scherwitz, L., & Rugulies, R. (1992). Life-style and hostility. In H. S. Friedman (Ed.), *Hostility, coping and health* (pp. 77–98). Washington, DC: American Psychological Association.

Schrader, G. (1973). Anger and inter-personal communication. In D. Carr & E. Casey (Eds.), *Explorations in phenomenology* (pp. 331–350). The Hague, Netherlands: Martinus Nijhoff.

Schraeder, C., Lamb, G., Shelton, P., & Britt, T. (1997). Community nursing organizations: A new frontier. *American Journal of Nursing, 97*(1), 63–65.

Schuckit, M. A. (1989). *Drug and alcohol abuse: A clinical guide to diagnosis and treatment* (3rd ed.) New York: Plenum.

Schultz, M. S. (2000). 1999 International Association for Health Care Security and Safety in Health Care Crime Survey. *IAHSS Newsletter, 10*(2), 1–2.

Schwartz, G., Weinberger, D., & Singer, J. (1981). Cardiovascular differentiation of happiness, sadness, anger, and fear following imagery and exercise. *Psychosomatic Medicine, 43,* 343–364.

Schwartz, J., Warren, K., & Pickering, T. (1994). Mood, location, and physical position as predictors of ambulatory blood pressure and heart rate: Application of a multi-level random effects model. *Annals of Behavioral Medicine, 16,* 210–220.

Seabrook, L. (1993). Women's anger and substance use. In S. P. Thomas (Ed.), *Women and anger* (pp. 186–208). New York: Springer Publishing.

Secunda, V. (1994, July). Victim trap. *New Woman,* 91–95.

Seldes, G. (1985). *The great thoughts.* New York: Ballantine Books.

Seligman, M. E. P. (1991). *Learned optimism.* New York: Knopf.

Seligman, M. E. P. (1998). Is depression biochemical? *American Psychological Association Monitor, 29*(9), 2.

Seligman, M. E. P., & Weiss, J. M. (1980). Coping behavior: Learned helplessness, physiological change and learned inactivity. *Behaviour Research and Therapy, 18,* 459–512.

Seppa, N. (1996). "Charlie's Angels" made a negative, lasting impression. *American Psychological Association Monitor, 26*(4), 9.

Seppa, N. (1997). Children's TV remains steeped in violence. *American Psychological Association Monitor, 28*(6), 36.

Shader, K., Broome, M. E., Broome, C. D., West, M. E., & Nash, M. (2001). Factors influencing satisfaction and anticipated turnover for nurses in an academic medical center. *Journal of Nursing Administration, 31*(4), 210–216.

Shapiro, D. (1982). Overview: Clinical and physiological comparison of meditation with other self-control strategies. *American Journal of Psychiatry, 139,* 267–273.

Shattell, M. M. (2002a). "Eventually it'll be over": The dialectic between confinement and freedom in the world of the hospitalized patient. In S. P. Thomas & H. R. Pollio (Eds.), *Listening to patients: A phenomenological approach to nursing research and practice* (pp. 214–236). New York: Springer Publishing.

Shattell, M. M. (2002b). *"Make them your friend:" A phenomenological study of patients' experience soliciting nursing care in the hospital setting.* Unpublished doctoral dissertation, University of Tennessee, Knoxville.

Shattell, M. M., Andes, M., & Thomas, S. P. (in press). How patients and nurses experience the acute care psychiatric environment. *Nursing Inquiry.*

Shea-Messler, W. C. (2007). *"Why am I still here, you ask?:" A phenomenological study of the lived experience of nurse managers.* Unpublished doctoral dissertation, University of Tennessee, Knoxville.

Shapiro, D., Schwartz, C., & Astin, J. (1996). Controlling ourselves, controlling our world: Psychology's role in understanding positive and negative consequences of seeking and gaining control. *American Psychologist, 51,* 1213–1230.

Shindul-Rothschild, J., Berry, D., & Long-Middleton, E. (1996). Where have all the nurses gone? Final results of our patient care survey. *American Journal of Nursing, 96*(11), 25–39.

Siegman, A. W. (1994). From Type A to hostility to anger: Reflections on the history of coronary-prone behavior. In A. W. Siegman & T. W. Smith (Eds.), *Anger, hostility, and the heart* (pp. 1–21). Hillsdale, NJ: Lawrence Erlbaum.

Siegman, A. W., Anderson, R. W., & Berger, T. (1990). The angry voice: Its effects on the experience of anger and cardiovascular reactivity. *Psychosomatic Medicine, 52,* 631–643.

Siegman, A. W., & Boyle, S. (1992). *The expression of anger and cardiovascular reactivity in men and women: An experimental investigation.* Paper presented at the American Psychosomatic Society, New York.

Siegman, A. W., Dembroski, T. M., & Ringel, N. (1987). Components of hostility and the severity of coronary artery disease. *Psychosomatic Medicine, 49,* 127–135.

Simmons, R. (2002). *Odd girl out: The hidden culture of aggression in girls.* New York: Harcourt.

Slaby, R., & Guerra, N. (1988). Cognitive mediators of aggression in adolescent offenders. *Developmental Psychology, 24 ,* 580–588.

Slagle, J. C. (1986). *The process of mentoring in nursing: A study of protégés' perceptions of the mentor-protégé relationship.* Unpublished doctoral dissertation, Columbia University, Teachers College.

Smith, F. (1981). Florence Nightingale: Early feminist. *American Journal of Nursing, 81,* 1021–1024.

Smith, F. (1982). *Florence Nightingale: Reputation and power.* London: Croom Helm.

Smith, M., Droppleman, P., & Thomas, S. P. (1996). Under assault: The experience of work-related anger in female registered nurses. *Nursing Forum, 31*(1), 22–33.

Smith, M. E., & Hart, G. (1994). Nurses' responses to patient anger: From disconnecting to connecting. *Journal of Advanced Nursing, 20,* 643–651.

Snyder, C. R., & Lopez, S. J. (Eds.). (2002). *The handbook of positive psychology.* New York: Oxford University Press.

Snyder, J. (2001). Can we turn our rage to poetry? *Women in the Arts, 19*(4), 14–15.

Sochalski, J. (2002). Nursing shortage redux: Turning the corner on an enduring problem. *Health Affairs, 21,* 157–164.

Spence, J. T., & Buckner, C. E. (2000). Instrumental and expressive traits, trait stereotypes, and sexist attitudes. *Psychology of Women Quarterly, 24,* 44–62.

Spencer, J. (1982). *Becoming a nurse and a cigarette smoker: The first two years.* Institute of Nursing Studies, University of Hull, Hull.

Sperberg, E. D., & Stabb, S. D. (1998). Depression in women as related to anger and mutuality in relationships. *Psychology of Women Quarterly, 22,* 223–238.

Spiegel, D., Bloom, J. R., Kraemer, H. C., & Gottheil, E. (1989, October). Effect of psychosocial treatment on survival of patients with metastatic breast cancer. *The Lancet,* 888–891.

Spiegel, D., & Cordova, M. (2001). Supportive-expressive group therapy and life extension of breast cancer patients. *Advances in Mind-Body Medicine, 17*(1), 38–39.

Spielberger, C. D. (1988). *State-Trait Anger Expression Inventory.* Orlando, FL: Psychological Assessment Resources.

Spratley, E., Johnson, A., Sochalski, J., Fritz, M., & Spencer, W. (2000). *The registered nurse population: Findings from the National Sample Survey of Registered Nurses.* Washington, DC: U.S. Department of Health and Human Services.

Staff nurse guide to work redesign. (1997). *Tennessee Nurse, 60*(2), 16, 25.

Stambor, Z. (2006). Specific environments alone can trigger smokers' cigarette cravings. *APA Monitor, 37*(3), 15.

Stanley, K. M., Martin, M. M., Nemeth, L. S., Michel, Y., & Welton, J. M. (2007). Examining lateral violence in the nursing workforce. *Issues in Mental Health Nursing, 28,* 1247–1265.

Stapley, J., & Haviland, J. (1989). Beyond depression: Gender differences in normal adolescents' emotional experiences. *Sex Roles, 20,* 295–308.

Steen, N., Firth, H., & Bond, S. (1998). Relation between work stress and job performance in nursing: A comparison of models. *Structural Equation Modeling, 5*(2), 125–142.

Stein, L. (1967). The doctor-nurse game. *Archives of General Psychiatry, 16,* 699–703

Stein, L., Watts, D., & Howell, T. (1990). The doctor-nurse game revisited. *The New England Journal of Medicine, 322,* 546–549.

Steinem, G. (1991). *Revolution from within: A book of self-esteem.* Boston: Little Brown.

Steingarten, J. (1994, August). Fancy that. *Vogue, 265,* 303.

Stevens, S. (2002). Nursing workforce retention: Challenging a bullying culture. *Health Affairs, 21,* 189–193.

Stevick, E. L. (1971). An empirical investigation of the experience of anger. In A. Giorgi, W. F. Fischer, & R. Von Eckartsberg (Eds.), *Phenomenological psychology* (Vol. 1, pp. 132–148). Pittsburgh, PA: Duquesne University Press.

Stoto, M. A. (1986). *Changes in adult smoking behavior in the United States: 1955–1983.* Discussion Paper Series, Institute for the Study of Smoking Behavior and Policy. Cambridge, MA.

Strachey, L. (1996). *Florence Nightingale.* London: Penguin Books (Original work published 1918).

Stratman, C. (1990). The experience of personal power for women. *Dissertation Abstracts International, 50,* 5896B.

Straus, M. A., & Gelles, R. (1987). The costs of family violence. *Public Health Reports, 102,* 638–641.

Street, S., Kimmel, E. B., & Kromrey, J. D. (1995). Revisiting university student gender role perceptions. *Sex Roles, 33,* 183–201.

Stringer, B. (1990). Stress factors in the hospital: A nursing perspective. In W. Charney & J. Schirmer (Eds.), *Essentials of modern hospital safety* (pp. 307–317). Chelsea, MI: Lewis.

Suarez, E. C., & Williams, R. B. (1989). Situational determinants of cardiovascular and emotional reactivity in high and low hostile men. *Psychosomatic Medicine, 51,* 404–418.

Suarez, E. C., & Williams, R. B. (1990). The relationship between dimensions of hostility and cardiovascular reactivity as a function of task characteristics. *Psychosomatic Medicine, 52,* 558–570.

Suarez, E. C., Williams, R. B., Kuhn, C. M., & Schanberg, S. M. (1990, March). *Hostility scores predict cardiovascular, neurohormonal, and testosterone responses to harassment.* Paper presented at the Society of Behavioral Medicine, Chicago.

Sullivan, E. (2002). Are we ready for the future? *Journal of Professional Nursing, 18,* 305–307.

"Survey finds consumer confidence in health care system eroding." (1997). *Capital Update, 15*(1), 5.

Take back your time. Retrieved March 5, 2008, from http://www.timeday.org

Tangney, J. P., Hill-Barlow, D., Wagner, P. E., Marschall, D. E., Borenstein, J. K., Sanftner, J., et al. (1996). Assessing individual differences in constructive versus destructive responses to anger across the lifespan. *Journal of Personality and Social Psychology, 70,* 780–796.

Tannen, D. (1994). *Talking from 9 to 5.* New York: Morrow.

Tanskanen, A., Hibbeln, J. R., Hintikka, J., Haatainen, K., Honkalampi, K., & Viinamaki, H. (2001). Fish consumption, depression, and suicidality in a general population. *Archives of General Psychiatry, 58,* 512–513.

Tavris, C. (1982). *Anger: The misunderstood emotion.* New York: Simon & Schuster.

Tavris, C. (1989). *Anger: The misunderstood emotion* (Rev. ed). New York: Simon & Schuster.

Tedeschi, R. G., Park, C. L., & Calhoun, L. G. (Eds.). (1998). *Posttraumatic growth: Positive changes in the aftermath of crisis.* Mahwah, NJ: Erlbaum.

Temoshok, L. (1985). Biopsychosocial studies on cutaneous malignant melanoma: Psychosocial factors associated with prognostic indicators, progression, psychophysiology, and tumor-host response. *Social Science and Medicine, 20,* 833–840.

Temoshok, L., & Dreher, H. (1992). *The Type C connection: The mind-body links to cancer and your health.* New York: Plume.

Temoshok, L., & Dreher, H. (1993, Spring). The Type C connection. *Noetic Sciences Review,* 21–26.

Theorell, T., & Lind, E. (1973). Systolic blood pressure, serum cholesterol, and smoking in relation to sociological factors and myocardial infarction. *Journal of Psychosomatic Research, 17,* 327–332.

The war against women. (1994, March 28). *U.S. News and World Report,* p. 44.

Thomas, C. B. (1988). Cancer and the youthful mind: A forty-year perspective. *Advances: Journal of the Institute for the Advancement of Health, 5*(2), 42–58.

Thomas, S. P. (1980). The adventures of Joey in patientland…A futuristic fantasy. *Nursing Forum, 19*(4), 350–356.

Thomas, S. P. (1982). How to conduct an assertion training course for nursing students: A step-by-step plan for instruction. *Journal of Nursing Education, 21*(3), 33–37.

Thomas, S. P. (1989). Gender differences in anger expression: Health implications. *Research in Nursing and Health, 12,* 389–398.

Thomas, S. P. (Ed.). (1993a). *Women and anger.* New York: Springer Publishing.

Thomas, S. P. (1993b). The view from Scutari: A look at contemporary nursing. *Nursing Forum, 28*(2), 19–24.

Thomas, S. P. (1995). Women's anger: Causes, manifestations, and correlates. In C. D. Spielberger & I. G. Sarason (Eds.), *Stress and emotion: Anxiety, anger, and curiosity* (Vol. 15, pp. 53–74). Washington, DC: Taylor & Francis.

Thomas, S. P. (1997a). Angry? Let's talk about it! *Applied Nursing Research, 10*(2), 80–85.

Thomas, S. P. (1997b). Women's anger: Relationship of suppression to blood pressure. *Nursing Research, 46,* 324–330.

Thomas, S. P. (1997c). Psychosocial correlates of women's self-rated physical health in middle adulthood. In M. E. Lachman & J. B. James (Eds.), *Multiple paths of midlife development* (pp. 257–291). Chicago: University of Chicago Press.

Thomas, S. P. (2000). Taking a triage approach to nurses' anger. *Tennessee Nurse, 63*(2), 17–18.

Thomas, S. P. (2001a). Teaching healthy anger management. *Perspectives in Psychiatric Care, 37,* 41–48.

Thomas, S. P. (2001b). *Healthy anger management: A manual for trainers.* Knoxville, TN: Author.

Thomas, S. P. (2002). Age differences in anger frequency, intensity, and expression. *Journal of the American Psychiatric Nurses Association, 8*(2), 44–50.

Thomas, S. P. (2003a). "None of us will ever be the same again:" Reactions of American midlife women to 9/11. *Health Care for Women International, 24,* 853–867.

Thomas, S. P. (2003b). Horizontal hostility: Nurses against themselves: How to solve this threat to retention. *American Journal of Nursing, 103*(10), 87–91.

Thomas, S. P. (2003c). Identifying and intervening with girls at risk for violence. *The Journal of School Nursing, 19,* 130–139.

Thomas, S. P. (2003d). Handling anger in the teacher-student relationship. *Nursing Education Perspectives, 24*(1), 17–24.

Thomas, S. P. (2003e). Men's anger: A phenomenological exploration of its meaning in a middle class sample of American men. *Psychology of Men and Masculinity, 4,* 163–175.

Thomas, S. P. (2005). Women's anger, aggression, and violence. *Health Care for Women International, 26,* 504–522.

Thomas, S. P. (2007). Trait anger, anger expression, and themes of anger incidents in contemporary undergraduate students. In E. I. Clausen (Ed.), *Psychology of anger* (pp. 23–69). New York: Nova Science.

Thomas, S. P., & Burk, R. (in press). Junior nursing students' experiences of vertical violence during clinical rotations. *Nursing Outlook.*

Thomas, S. P., & Donnellan, M. M. (1993). Stress, role responsibilities, social support, and anger. In S. P. Thomas (Ed.), *Women and anger* (pp. 112–128). New York: Springer Publishing.

Thomas, S. P., & Droppleman, P. (1997). Channeling nurses' anger into positive interventions. *Nursing Forum, 32*(2), 13–21.

Thomas, S. P., & Hall, J. M. (2008). Life trajectories of female child abuse survivors thriving in adulthood. *Qualitative Health Research, 18,* 149–166.

Thomas, S. P., & Pollio, H. R. (2002). *Listening to patients: A phenomenological approach to nursing research and practice.* New York: Springer Publishing.

Thomas, S. P., Shattell, M., & Martin, T. (2002). What's therapeutic about the therapeutic milieu? *Archives of Psychiatric Nursing, 16*(3), 99–107.

Thomas, S. P., Smucker, C., & Droppleman, P. (1998). It hurts most around the heart: A phenomenological exploration of women's anger. *Journal of Advanced Nursing, 28,* 311–322.

Thomas, S. P., & Williams, R. (1991). Perceived stress, trait anger, modes of anger expression, and health status of college men and women. *Nursing Research, 40,* 303–307.

Thorne, B. (1993). *Gender play: Girls and boys in school.* New Brunswick, NJ: Rutgers University Press.

Tice, D. (1990, June). *Self-regulation of mood: Some self-report data.* Paper presented at the Nags Head Conference on Self-Control of Thought and Emotion. Nags Head, NC.

Tice, D., & Baumeister, R. (1993). Controlling anger: Self-induced emotion change. In D. M. Wegner & J. W. Pennebaker (Eds.), *Handbook of mental control* (pp. 393–409). Englewood Cliffs, NJ: Prentice Hall.

Tiller, W., McCraty, R., & Atkinson, M. (1996). Cardiac coherence: A new, noninvasive measure of autonomic nervous system order. *Alternative Therapies, 2*(1), 52–65.

Tirrell, C. D. (1994). Psychoactive substance disorders among health care professionals. *Plastic Surgical Nursing, 14*(3), 169–172.

Tobin, M. L. (2007). Why choose varenicline (Chantix) for smoking cessation treatment? *Issues in Mental Health Nursing, 28,* 663–667.

Trafford, A. (1997, May 6). Seconding the motion. *The Washington Post, 13*(18), 6.

Trinkoff, A., & Storr, C. L. (1998). Substance use among nurses: Differences between specialties. *American Journal of Public Health, 88,* 581–585.

Trinkoff, A., Zhou, Q., Storr, C. L., & Soeken, K. L. (2000). Workplace access, negative proscriptions, job strain, and substance use in registered nurses. *Nursing Research, 49,* 83–90.

Trossman, S. (2003). Caring knows no gender. *American Journal of Nursing, 103*(5), 65.

Trossman, S. (2005). Who you work with matters: RN surveys reveal the importance of working relationships to job satisfaction. *The American Nurse, 37*(4), 1, 8–10.

Trossman, S. (2007). Talkin' bout my generation: Gaining awareness of differences key to easing workplace tensions. *The American Nurse, 39*(3), 1, 8.

Tsai, S., & Crockett, M. S. (1993). Effects of relaxation training, combining imagery and meditation, on the stress level of Chinese nurses working in modern hospitals in Taiwan. *Issues in Mental Health Nursing, 14,* 51–66.

Turnbull, J. (1995). Hitting back at the bullies. *Nursing Times, 91,* 24–27.

Turner, R. J., & Avison, W. R. (1989). Gender and depression: Assessing exposure and vulnerability to life events in a chronically strained population. *Journal of Nervous and Mental Disease, 177,* 443–455.

Ulrich, C., O'Donnell, P., Taylor, C., Farrar, A., Danis, M., & Grady, C. (2007). Ethical climate, ethics stress, and job satisfaction of nurses and social workers in the United States. *Social Science & Medicine, 65,* 1705–1719.

United American Nurses/American Nurses Association. (2001). *Trends in the registered nurse workforce.* Washington, DC: American Nurses Association.

Unruh, L. (2008). Nurse staffing and patient, nurse, and financial outcomes. *American Journal of Nursing, 108*(1), 62–71.

U.S. Department of Health and Human Services. (1990). *The health benefits of smoking cessation: A report of the Surgeon General.* Washington, DC: Government Printing Office.

U.S. Department of Health and Human Services (2000). *Healthy People 2010.* Washington, DC; Government Printing Office.

U.S. Department of Justice (2001, December). *Law enforcement officers most at risk for workplace violence.* Retrieved October 6, 2008, from http://www.ojp.usdoj.gov/bjs

Valentine, P. (1992). Feminism: A four-letter word? *The Canadian Nurse, 85*(12), 20–23.

Valentine, P. (2001). A gender perspective on conflict management strategies of nurses. *Journal of Nursing Scholarship, 33*(1), 69–74.

Vance, C., & Olson, R. (1998). *The mentor connection in nursing.* New York: Springer Publishing.

Vella, E. J., Kamarck, T. W., & Shiffman, S. (2008). Hostility moderates the effects of social support and intimacy on blood pressure in daily social interactions. *Health Psychology, 27* (2, Suppl.), S155–S162.

Vessey, J., & Gennaro, S. (1992). Caging the pushmi-pullu. *Nursing Research, 41,* 67.

Viorst, J. (1986). *Necessary losses.* New York: Simon & Schuster.

Vitaglione, G. D., & Barnett, M. A. (2003). Assessing a new dimension of empathy: Empathic anger as a predictor of helping and punishing desires. *Motivation and Emotion, 27,* 301–325.

Walen, S. R., DiGiuseppe, R., & Wessler, R. L. (1980). *A practitioner's guide to rational-emotive therapy.* New York: Oxford University Press.

Ward, D., & Mullender, A. (1991). Empowerment and oppression: An indissoluble pairing for contemporary social work. *Critical Social Policy, 11*(2), 21–30.

Watson, J. (1988). *Nursing: Human science and human care.* New York: National League for Nursing.

Watson, M., Pettingale, K., & Greer, S. (1984). Emotional control and autonomic arousal in breast cancer patients. *Journal of Psychosomatic Research, 28,* 467–474.

Webster, G. C., & Baylis, F. E. (2001). Moral residue. In S. R. Rubin & L. Zoloth (Eds.), *Margin of error: The ethics of mistakes in the practice of medicine* (pp. 217–230). Hagerstown, MD: University Publishing Group.

Weiner, B. (1991). Metaphors in motivation and attribution. *American Psychologist, 46,* 921–930.

Weinstein, N. D. (1984). Why it won't happen to me: Perceptions of risk factors and susceptibility. *Health Psychology, 3,* 431–457.

Welsh, D. (in press). Predictors of depressive symptoms in female medical-surgical hospital nurses. *Issues in Mental Health Nursing.*

Wethington, E. (2003). Turning points as an opportunity for psychological growth. In C. L. M. Keyes & J. Haidt (Eds.), *Flourishing* (pp. 37–53). Washington, DC: American Psychological Association.

White, V. M., English, D. R., Coates, H., Lagerlund, M., Borland, R., & Giles, G. G. (2007). Is cancer risk associated with anger control and negative affect? Findings from a prospective cohort study. *Psychosomatic Medicine, 69,* 667–674.

Whybrow, P. (1997). Making sense of mania and depression. *Psychology Today, 30*(3), 34–36, 38, 71–72.

Williams, C. L. (1995). Hidden advantages for men in nursing. *Nursing Administration Quarterly, 19*(2), 63–70.

Williams, R. B., Haney, T. L., Lee, K. L., Kong, Y., Blumenthal, J. A., & Whalen, R. (1980). Type A behavior, hostility, and coronary atherosclerosis. *Psychosomatic Medicine, 42,* 539–549.

Williams, R. B, & Williams, V. (1993). *Anger kills.* New York: Times Books.

Williams, R. B., Barefoot, J. C., Blumenthal, J. A., Helms, M. J., Luecken, L., Pieper, C. F., et al. (1997). Psychosocial correlates of job strain in a sample of working women. *Archives of General Psychiatry, 54,* 543–548.

Williams, R. L., Pettibone, T. J., & Thomas, S. P. (1991). Naturalistic application of self-change practices. *Journal of Research in Personality, 25,* 167–176.

Winerman, L. (2006, June). Psychologists testify at Senate video-game hearing. *Monitor on Psychology, 37*(6), 11.

Wing, R., Koeske, R., Epstein, L., Norwalk, M., Gooding, W., & Becker, D. (1987). Long-term effects of modest weight loss in Type II diabetic patients. *Archives of Internal Medicine, 147,* 1749–1753.

Witkin, G. (1991). *The female stress syndrome.* New York: Newmarket Press.

Wolf, N. (1993). *Fire with fire.* Toronto: Random House of Canada.

Wolpe, J. (1958). *Psychotherapy by reciprocal inhibition.* Stanford, CA: Stanford University Press.

Woodham-Smith, C. (1951). *Florence Nightingale.* New York: McGraw Hill.

Woodman, M. (1982). *Addiction to perfection: The still unravished bride.* Toronto: Inner City Books.

Worell, J. (1996). Opening doors to feminist research. *Psychology of Women Quarterly, 20,* 469–485.

Wright, N. M. J., Dixon, A. J., & Tompkins, C. N. E. (2003). Managing violence in primary care: An evidence-based approach. *British Journal of General Practice, 53,* 557–562.

Xu, Y. (2007). Strangers in strange lands: A metasynthesis of lived experiences of immigrant Asian nurses working in Western countries. *Advances in Nursing Science, 30*(3), 246–265.

Yalom, I. (2002). Religion and psychiatry. *American Journal of Psychotherapy, 56,* 301–316.

Yapko, M. D. (1997). The art of avoiding depression. *Psychology Today, 30*(3), 37, 75.

Young, B. H. (1996). From the editor. *National Center for PTSD Clinical Quarterly, 6*(3), 57.

Zazworsky, D. (2002). The nurse on a TV news team. In D. J. Mason, J. K. Leavitt, & M. W. Chaffee (Eds.), *Policy and politics in nursing and health care* (pp. 172–176). St. Louis, MO: Saunders.

Zillman, D. (1988). Mood management: Using entertainment to full advantage. In L. Donohew, H. E. Sypher, & E. T. Higgins (Eds.), *Communication, social cognition, and affect* (pp. 147–171). Hillsdale, NJ: Lawrence Erlbaum Associates.

Index